D0117697

Dear Rio Salado College Student:

The high cost of college textbooks has long been an issue for students across the nation. Rio Salado College shares this concern. In an effort to control costs for our students, Rio Salado is pleased to announce an innovative solution: the Rio Salado Textbook Savings Program that reduces your up-front costs. Rio Salado students can now purchase new customized textbooks for their courses for a savings up to 50%. The result of this savings program is that the cost of a new textbook will be much less than the cost of most used books.

Rio Salado has partnered with Pearson Custom Publishing to produce its own streamlined versions of textbooks, starting with the Spring 2008 term–and the savings will be passed on to you. During the next three years, most textbooks used by the college will be revised and published under the Textbook Saving Program. In addition to lower out-of-pocket costs, you will benefit by learning from a textbook containing exactly the material Rio Salado's faculty have determined you need to master the course.

We know this price cut occurs just when you need it the most–at the start of your class.

Best wishes for this and all future Rio courses!

Linda M. Thor

Dr. Linda M. Thor
President

MyWritingLab™ has helped students like you from all over the country.

MyWritingLab™ can help you become a better writer and help you get a better grade.

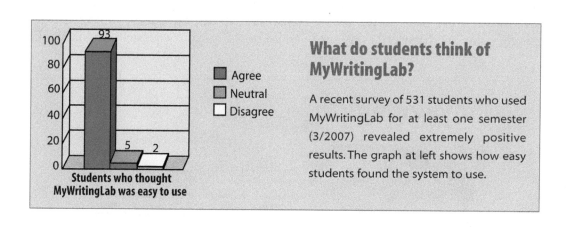

What do students think of MyWritingLab?

A recent survey of 531 students who used MyWritingLab for at least one semester (3/2007) revealed extremely positive results. The graph at left shows how easy students found the system to use.

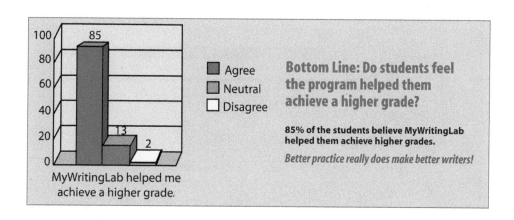

Bottom Line: Do students feel the program helped them achieve a higher grade?

85% of the students believe MyWritingLab helped them achieve higher grades.

Better practice really does make better writers!

Registering for MyWritingLab™...

It is easy to get started! Simply follow these steps to get into your MyWritingLab course.

1) **Find Your Access Code** (it is either packaged with your textbook, or you purchased it separately). You will need this access code and your course ID to join your MyWritingLab course. Your instructor has your course ID number, so make sure you have that before logging in.

2) **Click on "Students"** under "First-Time Users." Here you will be prompted to enter your access code, enter your e-mail address, and choose your own Login Name and Password. After you register, you can **click on "Returning Users"** to use your new login name and password every time you go back into your course in MyWritingLab.

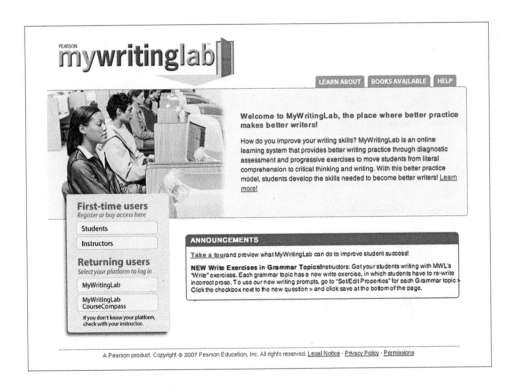

After logging in, you will see all the ways MyWritingLab can help you become a better writer.

The Homepage . . .

Here is your MyWritingLab HomePage.
You get a bird's eye view of where you are in your course every time you log in.

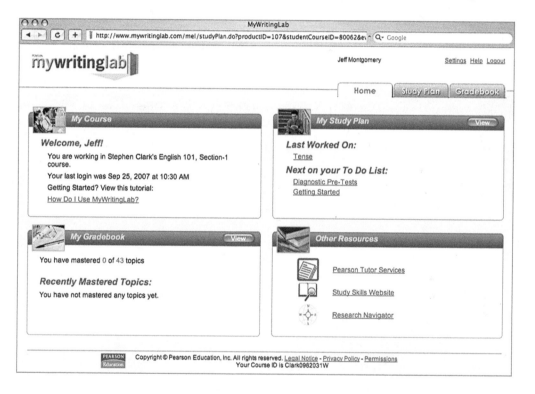

Your **Course** box shows your class details.

Your **Study Plan** box shows what you last completed and what is next on your **To Do** list.

Your **Gradebook** box shows you a snapshot of how you are doing in the class.

Your **Other Resources** box supplies you with amazing tools such as:

- **Pearson Tutor Services**—click here to see how you can get help on your papers by qualified tutors . . . before handing them in!

- **Research Navigator**—click here to see how this resembles your library with access to online journals for research paper assignments.

- **Study Skills**—extra help that includes tips and quizzes on how to improve your study skills

Now, let's start practicing to become better writers. Click on the Study Plan tab. This is where you will do all your course work.

The Study Plan ...

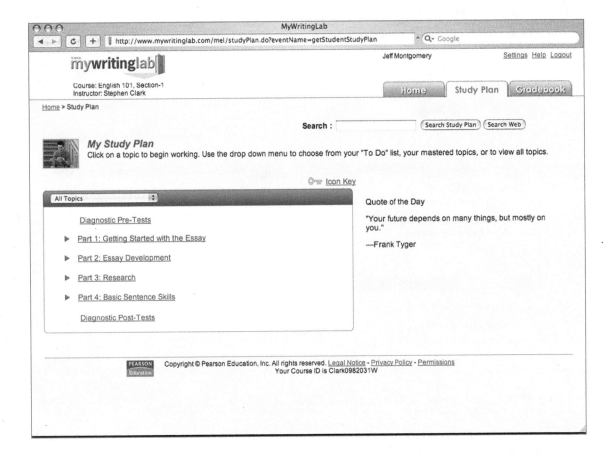

MyWritingLab provides you with a simple Study Plan of the writing skills that you need to master. You start from the top of the list and work your way down. You can start with the Diagnostic Pre-Tests.

The Diagnostic Pre-Tests . . .

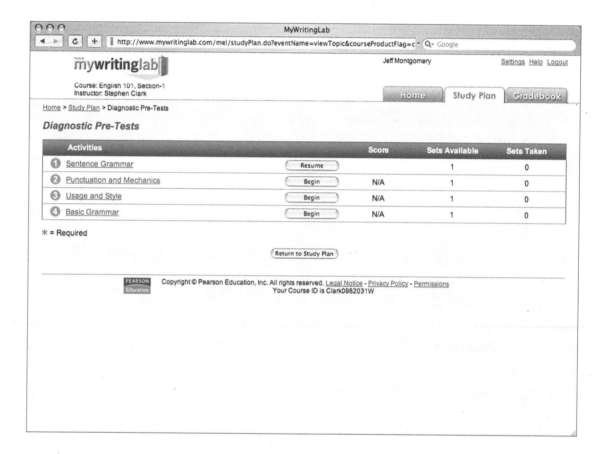

MyWritingLab's Diagnostic Pre-Tests are divided into four parts and cover all the major grammar, punctuation, and usage topics. After you complete these diagnostic tests, MyWritingLab will generate a personalized Study Plan for you, showing all the topics you have mastered and listing all the topics yet unmastered.

The Diagnostic Pre-Tests . . .

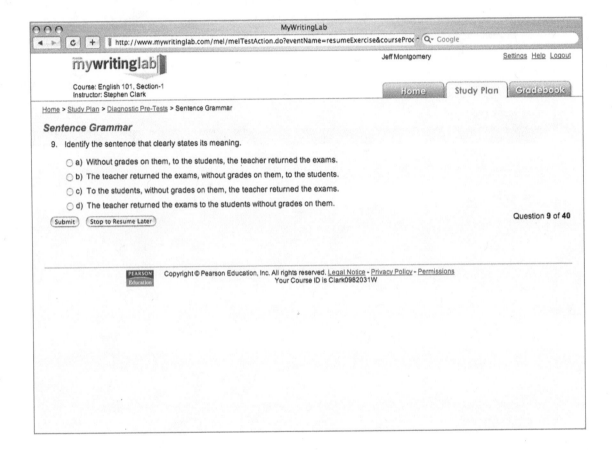

The Diagnostic Pre-Tests contain five exercises on each of the grammar, punctuation, and usage topics. You can achieve mastery of the topic in the Diagnostic Pre-Test by getting four of five or five of five correct within each topic.

After completing the Diagnostic Pre-Test, you can return to your Study Plan and enter any of the topics you have yet to master.

Watch, Recall, Apply, Write . . .

Here is an example of a MyWritinglab Activity set that you will see once you enter into a topic. Take the time to briefly read the introductory paragraph, and then watch the engaging video clip by clicking on "Watch: Tense."

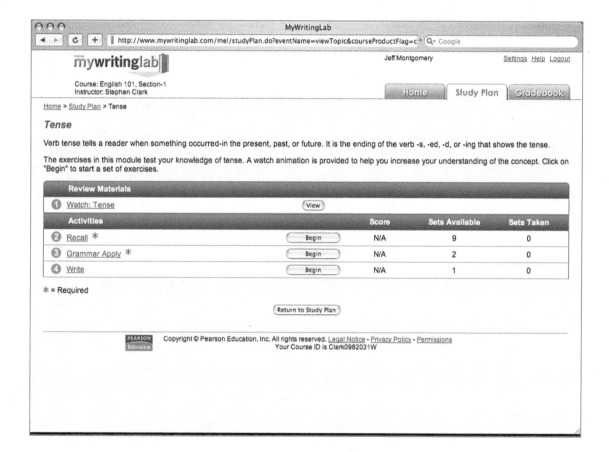

The video clip provides you with a helpful review.
Now you are ready to start the exercises. There are three types:

- Recall—activities that help you *recall* the rules of grammar

- Apply—activities that help you *apply* these rules to brief paragraphs or essays

- Write—activities that ask you to demonstrate these rules of grammar in your own writing

Watch, Recall, Apply, Write . . .

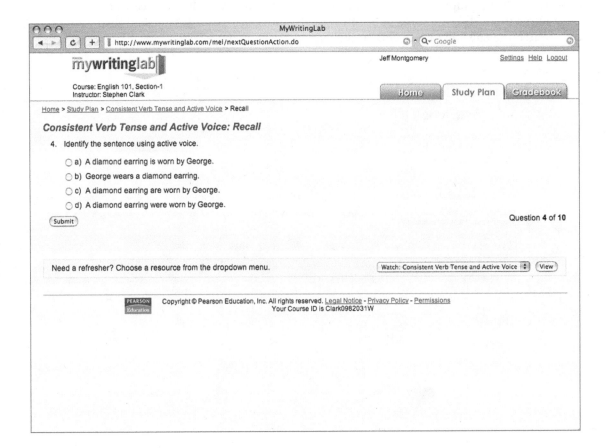

Recall questions help you recall the rules of grammar and writing when you complete multiple-choice questions, usually with four possible answers. You get feedback after answering each question, so you can learn as you go!

There are many sets available for lots of practice. As soon as you are finished with a set of activities, you will receive a score sheet with helpful feedback, including the correct answers. This score sheet will be kept in your own gradebook, so you can always go back and review.

Watch, Recall, Apply, Write . . .

Apply exercises help you *apply* writing and grammar rules to brief paragraphs or essays. Sometimes these are multiple-choice questions, and other times you will be asked to identify and correct mistakes in existing paragraphs and essays.

Your instructor may also assign **Write exercises**, which allow you to demonstrate writing and grammar rules in your own writing.

Helping Students Succeed . . .

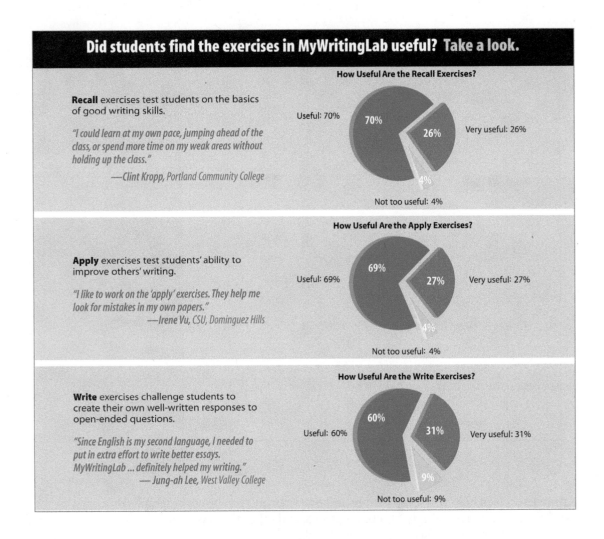

Did students find the exercises in MyWritingLab useful? Take a look.

Recall exercises test students on the basics of good writing skills.

"I could learn at my own pace, jumping ahead of the class, or spend more time on my weak areas without holding up the class."
—*Clint Kropp, Portland Community College*

How Useful Are the Recall Exercises?

Useful: 70%
70%
26%
Very useful: 26%
4%
Not too useful: 4%

Apply exercises test students' ability to improve others' writing.

"I like to work on the 'apply' exercises. They help me look for mistakes in my own papers."
—*Irene Vu, CSU, Dominguez Hills*

How Useful Are the Apply Exercises?

Useful: 69%
69%
27%
Very useful: 27%
4%
Not too useful: 4%

Write exercises challenge students to create their own well-written responses to open-ended questions.

"Since English is my second language, I needed to put in extra effort to write better essays. MyWritingLab ... definitely helped my writing."
— *Jung-ah Lee, West Valley College*

How Useful Are the Write Exercises?

Useful: 60%
60%
31%
Very useful: 31%
9%
Not too useful: 9%

Students just like you are finding MyWritingLab's Recall, Apply, and Write exercises useful in their learning.

The Gradebook ...

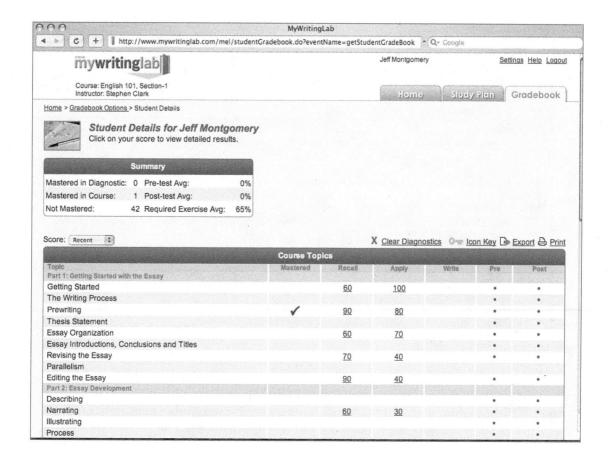

Let's look at how your own on-line gradebook will help you track your progress.

Click on the "Gradebook" tab and then the "Student Detail" report.

Here you are able to see how you are doing in each area. If you feel you need to go back and review, simply click on any score and your score sheet will appear.

You also have a Diagnostic Detail report so you can go back and review your diagnostic Pre-Test and see how much MyWritingLab has helped you improve!

Here to Help You . . .

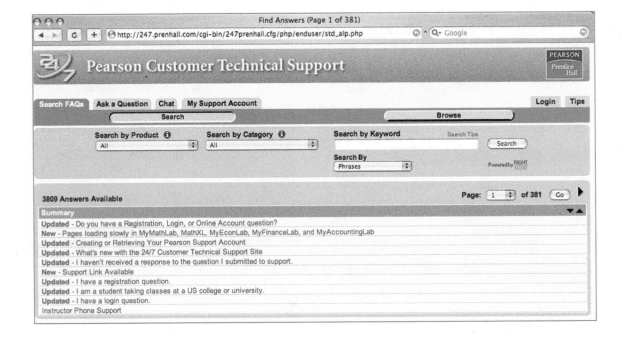

Our goal is to provide answers to your MyWritingLab questions as quickly as possible and deliver the highest level of support. By visiting **www.mywritinglab.com/help.html**, many questions can be resolved in just a few minutes. Here you will find help on the following:

- System Requirements
- How to Register for MyWritingLab
- How to Use MyWritingLab

For student support, we also invite you to contact Pearson Customer Technical Support (shown above). In addition, you can reach our Support Representatives online at **http://247.pearsoned.com**. Here you can do the following:

- Search Frequently Asked Questions about MyWritingLab
- E-mail a Question to Our Support Team
- Chat with a Support Representative

www.mywritinglab.com

The Writer's World
Sentences and Paragraphs

Taken from:

The Writer's World: Sentences and Paragraphs, Second Edition
by Lynne Gaetz and Suneeti Phadke

Learning Solutions

New York   Boston   San Francisco
London   Toronto   Sydney   Tokyo   Singapore   Madrid
Mexico City   Munich   Paris   Cape Town   Hong Kong   Montreal

Cover Art: Courtesy of EyeWire/Getty Images

Taken from:

The Writer's World: Sentences and Paragraphs, Second Edition
by Lynne Gaetz and Suneeti Phadke
Copyright © 2009 by Pearson Education, Inc.
Published by Prentice Hall
Upper Saddle River, New Jersey 07458

This special edition published in cooperation with Pearson Learning Solutions.

Pearson Learning Solutions, 501 Boylston Street, Suite 900, Boston, MA 02116
A Pearson Education Company
www.pearsoned.com

Printed in the United States of America

2008420380

KA

ISBN 10: 0-558-04978-8
ISBN 13: 978-0-558-04978-2

Contents

Inside Front Cover
Sentences Checklist
Revising and Editing Symbols

Preface   ix

 The Writing Process   2

 Exploring   3

What Is Exploring?   3
Topic   4
Audience   4
Purpose   5
Exploring Strategies   5
Journal and Portfolio Writing   10

 Developing   12

What Is Developing?   12
Narrow the Topic   14
The Topic Sentence   15
The Supporting Ideas   20
The Paragraph Plan   27
The First Draft   28

 Revising and Editing   31

What Is Revising and Editing?   31
Revise for Unity   32
Revise for Adequate Support   34
Revise for Coherence   36
Revise for Style   38
Edit for Errors   39
The Final Draft   42

Paragraph Patterns   44

What Are Paragraph Patterns?   44
A) The Illustration Paragraph   45
B) The Narrative Paragraph   50
C) The Descriptive Paragraph   55
D) The Process Paragraph   61
E) The Definition Paragraph   66
F) The Comparison and Contrast
    Paragraph   71
G) The Cause and Effect Paragraph   77
H) The Classification Paragraph   82
I) The Argument Paragraph   88

The Editing Handbook   110

SECTION I   **Some Parts of Speech**   ▪ *Section Theme* **HUMAN HISTORY AND HABITS**

Nouns, Determiners, and Prepositions   112

Nouns   113
Count Nouns and Noncount Nouns   118
Determiners   120
Prepositions   123

Pronouns   130

Pronoun-Antecedent Agreement   131
Indefinite Pronouns   133
Vague Pronouns   135
Pronoun Shifts   136
Pronoun Case   137
Problems with Possessive Pronouns   139
Relative Pronouns   143
Reflexive Pronouns (-*self*, -*selves*)   145

SECTION 2   **Problems with Verbs**   ▪ *Section Theme* **ENTERTAINMENT AND CULTURE**

Subjects and Verbs   150

Identifying Subjects   151
Identifying Prepositional Phrases   154
Identifying Verbs   156

Present and Past Tenses   162

Understanding Verb Tense   163
The Simple Present Tense   163
The Simple Past Tense   169
Avoiding Double Negatives   177

Past Participles   181

Past Participles   182
The Present Perfect Tense: *Have/Has* +
    Past Participle   186
The Past Perfect Tense: *Had* +
    Past Participle   190
The Past Participle as an Adjective   192
The Passive Voice: *Be* + Past Participle   193

Progressive Tenses   201

Understanding Progressive Tenses   202
Present Progressive   202
Past Progressive   204
Using Complete Verbs   206
Other Progressive Forms   207

Other Verb Forms   211

Modals   212
Nonstandard Forms: *gonna, gotta, wanna*   216
Conditional Forms   217
Gerunds and Infinitives   221

SECTION 3   **Verb Agreement and Consistency** ▪ *Section Theme* **BELIEFS**

 Subject-Verb Agreement 227

Basic Subject-Verb Agreement Rules   228
Verb Before the Subject   232
More Than One Subject   234
Special Subject Forms   234
Interrupting Words and Phrases   237

 Tense Consistency 243

Consistent Verb Tense   244

SECTION 4   **Effective Sentences** ▪ *Section Theme* **POLITICS**

 Compound Sentences 251

Comparing Simple and Compound
    Sentences   252
Combining Sentences Using Coordinating
    Conjunctions   252
Combining Sentences Using
    Semicolons   256
Combining Sentences Using Transitional
    Expressions   258

 Complex Sentences 264

Understanding Complex Sentences   265
Using Subordinating Conjunctions   265
Using Relative Pronouns   270
Creating Embedded Questions   273

 Sentence Variety and Exact Language 277

Achieving Sentence Variety   278
Using Specific Vocabulary   281
Avoiding Clichés   283
Slang versus Standard English   285

SECTION 5   **Common Sentence Errors** ▪ *Section Theme* **THE EARTH AND BEYOND**

 Fragments 289

Understanding Fragments   290
Phrase Fragments   290
Explanatory Fragments   291
Dependent-Clause Fragments   293

 Run-Ons 299

Understanding Run-Ons   300

 Faulty Parallel Structure 306

Identifying Parallel Structure   307
Correcting Faulty Parallel Structure   308

SECTION 6   **Modifiers** ■ *Section Theme* **RELATIONSHIPS**

 Adjectives and Adverbs   316

Adjectives   317
Adverbs   321
Comparative and Superlative Forms   325

 Mistakes with Modifiers   333

Misplaced Modifiers   334
Dangling Modifiers   338

SECTION 7   **Word Use and Spelling** ■ *Section Theme* **CREATURES LARGE AND SMALL**

 Spelling   344

Improving Your Spelling   345
Writing *ie* or *ei*   345
Adding Prefixes and Suffixes   347
Writing Two-Part Words   352
120 Commonly Misspelled Words   353

 Commonly Confused Words   359

Commonly Confused Words   360

SECTION 8   **Punctuation and Mechanics** ■ *Section Theme* **THE BUSINESS WORLD**

 Commas   370

Understanding Commas   371
Commas in a Series   371
Commas After Introductory Words
    and Phrases   372
Commas Around Interrupting Words
    and Phrases   373
Commas in Compound Sentences   375
Commas in Complex Sentences   376
Commas in Business Letters   379

 The Apostrophe   383

Understanding Apostrophes   384
Using Apostrophes in Contractions   384
Using Apostrophes to Show Ownership   387
Using Apostrophes in Expressions
    of Time   389

 Quotation Marks and Capitalization   394

Direct and Indirect Quotations   395
Quotation Marks   395
Capitalization   400
Titles   402

Reading Strategies and Selections   416

Reading Strategies and Selections   417

Reading Strategies   417
Reading Selections   421

HUMAN HISTORY, HABITS, AND RELATIONSHIPS
- "Fish Cheeks" by Amy Tan   421
- "Birth" by Maya Angelou   423
- "The Cult of Emaciation" by Ben Barry   425
- "For Marriage" by Kirsteen Macleod   429
- "Against Marriage" by Winston Murray   430

ENTERTAINMENT, CULTURE, AND BELIEFS
- "The Appalling Truth" by Dorothy Nixon   433
- "The New Addiction" by Josh Freed   436
- "Sports and Life: Lessons to Be Learned" by Jeff Kemp   439

- "What's Your Humor Style?" by Louise Dobson   441
- "The Hijab" by Naheed Mustafa   444

THE EARTH AND ITS CREATURES
- "What It Feels Like to Walk on the Moon" by Buzz Aldrin   447
- "The Zoo Life" by Yann Martel   449
- "Shark Bait" by Dave Barry   452

POLITICS AND THE BUSINESS WORLD
- "How to Handle Conflict" by P. Gregory Smith   455
- "How to Remember Names" by Roger Seip   457
- "Meet the Zippies" by Thomas L. Friedman   460
- "The Rewards of Dirty Work" by Linda L. Lindsey and Stephen Beach   462

Appendices

- Appendix 1: Grammar Glossary   467
- Appendix 2: Verb Tenses   469
- Appendix 3: Combining Ideas in Sentences   470
- Appendix 4: Punctuation and Mechanics   471
- Appendix 5: Spelling, Grammar, and Vocabulary Logs   474

Credits   479
Index   481
Inside Back Cover
Paragraph and Essay Checklists

Preface

About the Second Edition of *The Writer's World: Sentences and Paragraphs*

Thank you for making the first edition of *The Writer's World* a resounding success. We are delighted that the book has been able to help so many students across the country. The second edition of *The Writer's World* can also help students produce writing that is technically correct and rich in content. It is our goal for this preface to give you a deeper understanding of how we arranged the text and the key components you will find in this new edition of *The Writer's World: Sentences and Paragraphs*.

When we started the first edition, we set out to develop practical and pedagogically sound approaches to help students improve their writing skills. In this second edition, we have refined the approach to give students more opportunities to collaborate and more hints about grammar in the writing chapters. We have also extended the very popular visual program through Part III. We will discuss these new features, but first, for those new to the book, we will provide some background to give a more complete picture.

A Research-Based Approach

From the onset of the development process, we have comprehensively researched the needs and desires of current developmental writing instructors. We met with more than forty-five instructors from around the country, asking for their opinions and insights regarding (1) the challenges posed by the course, (2) the needs of today's ever-changing student population, and (3) the ideas and features we were proposing to provide them and you with a more effective learning and teaching tool. Prentice Hall also commissioned dozens of detailed manuscript reviews from instructors, asking them to analyze and evaluate each draft of the manuscript. These reviewers identified numerous ways in which we could refine and enhance our key features. Their invaluable feedback was incorporated throughout *The Writer's World*. The text you are seeing is truly the product of a successful partnership between the authors, the publisher, and well over one hundred developmental writing instructors.

How We Organized *The Writer's World*

The Writer's World is divided into three parts for ease of use and convenience.

Part I: The Writing Process teaches students how to formulate ideas (Exploring); how to expand, organize, and present those ideas in a piece of writing (Developing); and how to polish their writing so that they convey their message as clearly as possible (Revising and Editing). The result is that writing becomes far less daunting because students have specific steps to follow.

Chapter 4 of Part I gives students an overview of nine patterns of development. As they work through the practices and write their own paragraphs, students begin to see how using a writing pattern can help them fulfill their purpose for writing.

Part II: The Editing Handbook is a thematic grammar handbook. In each chapter, the examples correspond to a section theme, such as Human History and Habits or Entertainment and Culture. As students work through the chapters, they hone their grammar and editing skills while gaining knowledge about a variety of topics. In addition to helping retain interest in the grammar practices, the thematic material provides sparks that ignite new ideas that students can apply to their writing.

Part III: Reading Strategies and Selections offers tips, readings, and follow-up questions. Students learn how to write by observing and dissecting what they read. The readings are arranged by the themes that are found in Part II: The Editing Handbook, thereby providing more fodder for generating writing ideas.

How *The Writer's World* Meets Students' Diverse Needs

We created *The Writer's World* to meet your students' diverse needs. To accomplish this goal, we asked both the instructors in our focus groups and the reviewers at every stage not only to critique our ideas but also to offer their suggestions and recommendations for features that would enhance the learning process of their students. The result has been the integration of many elements that are not found in other textbooks, including our visual program, coverage of nonnative speaker material, and strategies for addressing the varying skill levels students bring to the course.

The Visual Program

A stimulating, full-color book, *The Writer's World* recognizes that today's world is a visual one, and it encourages students to become better communicators by responding to images. **Chapter-opening visuals in Part I** help students think about the chapters' key concepts in new ways. For example, in the Chapter 5 opener, a photograph of a skyscraper sets the stage for essay writing. Both the skyscraper and an essay need specific types of support to make them sturdy structures.

Each chapter in Part II opens with a photo to help illustrate the theme of the examples and exercises in that chapter and section.

The visuals in Part III provide students with further opportunities to write in response to images. Students get additional writing practice through different activities such as looking at photos and watching films. These visual aids inspire students and give them varied and engaging topics for writing.

Seamless Coverage for Nonnative Speakers

Instructors in our focus groups noted the growing number of nonnative/ESL speakers enrolling in the developmental writing courses. Although some of these students have special needs relating to the writing process, many of you still have a large portion of native speakers in your courses whose more traditional needs must also be satisfied. To meet the challenge of this rapidly changing dynamic, we have carefully implemented and integrated content throughout to assist these students. *The Writer's World* does not have separate ESL boxes, ESL chapters, or tacked-on ESL appendices. Instead, information that traditionally poses challenges to nonnative speakers is woven seamlessly throughout the book. In our extensive experience teaching writing to both native and nonnative speakers of English, we have learned that both groups learn best when they are not distracted by ESL labels. With the seamless approach, nonnative speakers do not feel self-conscious and segregated, and native speakers do not tune out detailed explanations that may also benefit them. Many of these traditional problem areas receive more coverage than you would find in other textbooks, arming the instructor with the material to effectively meet the needs of nonnative speakers. Moreover, the Annotated Instructor's Edition provides over seventy-five ESL Teaching Tips designed specifically to help instructors better meet the needs of their nonnative speakers.

Issue-Focused Thematic Grammar

In our survey of instructors' needs, many of you indicated that one of the primary challenges in teaching your course is finding materials that are engaging to students in a contemporary context. This is especially true in grammar instruction. **Students come to the course with varying skill levels,** and many students are simply not interested in grammar. To address this challenge, we have introduced **issue-focused thematic grammar** in *The Writer's World*.

Each section in Part II revolves around a common theme. These themes include Human History and Habits, Entertainment and Culture, Beliefs, Politics, The Earth and Beyond, Relationships, Creatures Large and Small, and The Business World. Each chapter within a section includes issues related to the theme. The thematic approach enables students to broaden their awareness of important subjects, allowing them to infuse their writing with reflection and insight. Also, we believe (and our reviewers concurred) that it makes grammar more engaging. And the more engaging grammar is, the more likely students will retain key concepts—raising their skill level in these important building blocks of writing.

We also feel that it is important not to isolate grammar from the writing process. Therefore, The Writer's Room at the end of each grammar section contains writing topics that are related to the theme of the section and that follow different writing patterns. To help students appreciate the relevance of their writing tasks, **each grammar chapter begins with a grammar snapshot**—a sample taken from an authentic piece of writing that highlights the grammar concept. There is also an editing checklist that is specific to the grammar concepts covered in that chapter. Finally, at the end of each grammar section, there is The Writers' Circle, a collaborative activity that is particularly helpful to nonnative speakers.

What Tools Can Help Students Get the Most from *The Writer's World?*

Overwhelmingly, focus group participants and reviewers asked that both a larger number and a greater diversity of exercises and activities be incorporated into the text. In response to this feedback, we have developed and tested the following items in *The Writer's World*. We are confident they will help your students become better writers.

Hints In each chapter, **Hint** boxes highlight important writing and grammar points. Hints are useful for all students, but many will be particularly helpful for nonnative speakers. For example, in Chapter 3 there is a hint about being direct and avoiding circular reasoning, and in Chapter 12 there is one about using the past conditional correctly.

The Writer's Desk Part I includes **The Writer's Desk** exercises that help students get used to practicing all stages and steps of the writing process. Students begin with prewriting and then progress to developing, organizing (using paragraph plans), drafting, and finally, revising and editing to create a final draft.

Checklists Each end-of-chapter checklist is a chapter review exercise. Questions prompt students to recall and review what they have learned in the chapter.

The Writer's Room **The Writer's Room** contains writing activities that correspond to general, college, and workplace topics. Some prompts are brief to allow students to freely form ideas while others are expanded to give students more direction.

There is literally something for every student writer in this end-of-chapter feature. Students who

respond well to visual cues will appreciate the photo writing exercises in **The Writer's Room** in Part II. Students who learn best by hearing through collaboration will appreciate the discussion and group work prompts in **The Writers' Circle** section of selected **The Writer's Rooms**. To help students see how grammar is not isolated from the writing process, there are also **The Writer's Room** activities at the end of sections 1 to 8 in Part II: The Editing Handbook.

Refinements to the Second Edition
Part I: The Writing Process

- The new student sample paragraph-in-progress used to show students the stages of the writing process in Chapters 1–3 has been changed to reflect one of the most typical purposes for writing in college—the informative purpose.

- In Chapter 1 the discussion of prewriting now distinguishes between general and focused prewriting strategies to help students sort these process purposes.

- Chapter 2 includes the new high-interest topics of fashion trends, dating, and food in The Writer's Desk in addition to the topics of technology and work.

- New photos in Chapter 3 help students understand the ideas of paragraph unity, adequate support, and coherence.

- With the addition of classification, Chapter 4 now addresses nine different paragraph patterns to help students master the methods of development. New sample paragraph plans in narrative, definition, and comparison-contrast writing have been added, and new practices in descriptive, process, and cause-and-effect writing keep the material fresh and lively.

Part II: The Editing Handbook

- Our major revisions in the Editing Handbook were to practices. Throughout the part, we carefully examined every activity to ensure that it was interesting, current, and not confusing. To that end we changed many individual items and replaced whole activities in many of the

Part II chapters. In the all-important Chapter 7 on pronouns, we changed the theme.

- In Chapter 9 on present and past tenses, we have added time lines to help nonnative speakers visualize the times expressed by the simple present and the simple past tenses.

- Some of the theme titles in Part II have been changed in response to comments that students didn't understand the names of some of the disciplines. So we have changed earlier titles to "Human History and Habits," "The Earth and Beyond," and "Creatures Large and Small."

- In the Annotated Instructor's Edition, new Teaching Tips have been added that suggest new work for pairs of students, give new suggestions for explaining points of grammar, and offer new comments about the patterns of errors your nonnative speakers may express as they write.

Part III: Reading Strategies and Selections

- Five out of the seventeen readings in Part III are new to the second edition. One is a humorous piece you and your students should enjoy reading: columnist Dave Barry's "Shark Bait." A second reading on the subject of humor asks students "What's Your Humor Style?" The pragmatic advice in a third new reading, "How to Remember Names," should benefit most of the students in the class—according to the article, eighty-three percent of the population worries about not remembering them. New readings in the broader cultural arena are on "The Cult of Emaciation," written, interestingly enough, by a fashion model agent, and "Meet the Zippies" on the young Indian people who are doing work outsourced from America, from Thomas L. Friedman's best-selling book *The World Is Flat*.

- In line with changes made to the other two books of *The Writer's World* series—*Paragraphs and Essays*, and *Essays*—the readings are now arranged in themes. The four themes relate back to the themes in the Part II sections. They are "Human History, Habits, and Relationships," "Entertainment, Culture, and Beliefs," "The Earth and Its Creatures," and "Politics and the Business World."

- New Photo and Film Writing activities have been added at the end of each theme to provide students with visual and verbal stimuli for writing.

Acknowledgments

Many people have helped us produce *The Writer's World*. First and foremost, we would like to thank our students for inspiring us and providing us with extraordinary feedback. Their words and insights pervade this book.

We also benefited greatly from the insightful comments and suggestions from over one hundred instructors across the nation, all of whom are listed in the opening pages of the Annotated Instructor's Edition. Our colleagues' feedback was invaluable and helped shape *The Writer's World* series content, focus, and organization.

We are indebted to the team of dedicated professionals at Prentice Hall who have helped make this project a reality. They have boosted our spirits and have believed in us every step of the way. Special thanks to Leslie Taggart for her magnificent job in polishing this book and to Craig Companella for trusting our instincts and enthusiastically propelling us forward. We owe a deep debt of gratitude to Yolanda de Rooy, whose encouraging words helped ignite this project. Karen Berry's attention to detail in the production process kept us motivated and on task and made *The Writer's World* a much better resource for both instructors and students. We would also like to thank Laura Gardner for her brilliant design, which helped keep the visual learner in all of us engaged.

Finally, we would like to dedicate this book to our husbands and children who supported us and who patiently put up with our long hours on the computer. Manu, Octavio, and Natalia continually encouraged us. We especially appreciate the help and sacrifices of Diego, Becky, Kiran, and Meghana.

A Note to Students

Your knowledge, ideas, and opinions are important. The ability to clearly communicate those ideas is invaluable in your personal, academic, and professional life. When your writing is error-free, readers will focus on your message, and you will be able to persuade, inform, entertain, or inspire them. *The Writer's World* includes strategies that will help you improve your written communication. Quite simply, when you become a better writer, you become a better communicator. It is our greatest wish for *The Writer's World* to make you excited about writing, communicating, and learning.

Enjoy!

Lynne Gaetz and Suneeti Phadke
thewritersworld@prenhall.com

Lynne Gaetz and family in Mexico

Call for Student Writing!

Do you want to be published in *The Writer's World*? Send your paragraphs and essays to us along with your complete contact information. If your work is selected to appear in the next edition of *The Writer's World*, you will receive an honorarium, credit for your work, and a copy of the book!

Lynne Gaetz and Suneeti Phadke
thewritersworld@prenhall.com

Suneeti Phadke and family at Monument Valley

PART I

The Writing Process

The ability to express your ideas in written form is very useful in your personal, academic, and professional life. It does not take a special talent to write well. If you are willing to practice the writing process, you will be able to produce well-written sentences, paragraphs, and essays.

The Writing Process

The writing process involves exploring, expanding, and organizing ideas and then bringing them all together in sentences and paragraphs. Before you begin working through the chapters in Part I, review the main steps in the writing process.

Exploring

Step 1: Consider your topic.

Step 2: Consider your audience.

Step 3: Consider your purpose.

Step 4: Try exploring strategies.

Developing

Step 1: Narrow your topic.

Step 2: Express your main idea.

Step 3: Develop your supporting ideas.

Step 4: Make a plan or an outline.

Step 5: Write your first draft.

Revising and Editing

Step 1: Revise for unity.

Step 2: Revise for adequate support.

Step 3: Revise for coherence.

Step 4: Revise for style.

Step 5: Edit for technical errors.

Exploring

> *The greatest mistake you can make in life is to be continually fearing you will make one.*
>
> —ELBERT HUBBARD (1856–1915)
> *American author*

CONTENTS

• What Is Exploring?
• Topic
• Audience
• Purpose
• Exploring Strategies
• Journal and Portfolio Writing

The exploring stage of the writing process is like arriving on a new shore. You fearlessly move ahead, making new discoveries.

What Is Exploring?

An explorer investigates a place to find new and interesting information. **Exploring** is also useful during the writing process. Whenever you have trouble finding a topic, you can use specific techniques to generate ideas.

There are four steps in the exploring stage of the writing process.

ESSAY LINK

When you plan an essay, you should also follow the four exploring steps.

EXPLORING

STEP 1	→	**Consider your topic.** Think about who or what you will write about.
STEP 2	→	**Consider your audience.** Determine who your intended readers will be.
STEP 3	→	**Consider your purpose.** Think about your reasons for writing.
STEP 4	→	**Try exploring strategies.** Practice using various techniques to find ideas.

Understanding Your Assignment

As soon as you are given an assignment, make sure that you understand your task. Answer the following questions about the assignment.

- How many words or pages should I write?
- What is the due date for the assignment?
- Are there any special qualities my writing should include?
- Will I write in class or at home?

After you have considered your task, think about your topic, purpose, and audience.

Topic

Your **topic** is what you are writing about. When your instructor gives you a topic for your writing, you can narrow it to suit your interests. For example, if your instructor asks you to write about relationships, you could write about marriage, divorce, children, family responsibilities, or traditions. You could focus on an aspect of the topic that you know about and find interesting.

When you think about the topic, ask yourself the following questions.

- What about the topic interests me?
- Do I have special knowledge about the topic?
- Does anything about the topic arouse my emotions?

Audience

Your **audience** is your intended reader. The reader might be your instructor, other students, your boss, your co-workers, and so on. When you write, remember to adapt your language and vocabulary for each specific audience. For example, in a formal report written for your business class, you might use specialized accounting terms, but in an e-mail to your best friend, you would probably use abbreviations or slang terms.

When you consider your audience, ask yourself the following questions.

- Who will read my assignment? Will it be my instructor, other students, or people outside my classroom?
- What do my readers probably know about the subject?
- What information will my readers expect?

 **Your Instructor as Your Audience**

For many college assignments, your audience is your instructor. When you write for him or her, use standard English. In other words, try to use correct grammar, sentence structure, and vocabulary.

Do not leave out information because you assume that your instructor knows a lot about the topic. When your instructor reads your work, he or she will expect you to reveal what you have learned or what you have understood about the topic.

Purpose

Your **purpose** is your reason for writing. Sometimes you may have more than one purpose. When you consider your purpose, ask yourself the following questions.

- Do I want to **entertain?** Is my goal to tell a story?
- Do I want to **persuade?** Is my goal to convince the reader that my point of view is the correct one?
- Do I want to **inform?** Is my goal to explain something or give information about a topic?

 **Purposes May Overlap**

Sometimes you may have more than one purpose. For example, in a paragraph about a childhood memory, your purpose could be to tell a story about your first trip to a new place. At the same time, you could inform your readers about the things to see in that area, or you could persuade readers that traveling is, or is not, worthwhile.

Exploring Strategies

After you determine your topic, audience, and purpose, try some **exploring strategies**—also known as **prewriting strategies**—to help get your ideas flowing. There are two types of prewriting strategies: general and focused. **General prewriting** will help you develop wide-ranging ideas to write about. **Focused prewriting** will help you narrow a broad topic so that the topic becomes more specific and therefore more manageable for your assignment. In this chapter, you will see examples of general prewriting.

The three most common strategies are *freewriting*, *brainstorming*, and *clustering*. It is not necessary to do all of the strategies explained in this chapter. Find the strategy that works best for you.

 **When to Use Exploring Strategies**

You can use the exploring strategies at any stage of the writing process.

- To find a topic
- To narrow a broad topic
- To generate ideas about your topic
- To generate supporting details

Freewriting

When you **freewrite,** you write without stopping for a limited period of time. You record whatever thoughts come into your mind without worrying about them. Even if you run out of ideas, you can just repeat a word or phrase, or you can write "I don't know what to say."

During freewriting, do not be concerned with your grammar or spelling. If you use a computer, let your ideas flow and do not worry about typing mistakes. Remember that the point is to generate ideas and not to create a perfect sample of writing.

College student Manuel Figuera jotted down some of his thoughts about fears. He wrote for five minutes without stopping.

> *What do I think about fears? I don't know. I'm not afraid of anything. No, that's not true. I had a lot of fears when I was a kid. I was sure a monster lived under the bed. I would check under the bed every night and when I got out of bed I'd jump a few feet so the monster couldn't grab my leg. What else? Think, think, think. . . . Probably everybody is afraid of something. My sister hates spiders and other bugs. I guess I still have some fears. I don't like to speak in public. I get nervous when I have to read out loud too. There are ways to get over fears, though. I learned some techniques about public speaking.*

PRACTICE I

Underline topics from Manuel's freewriting that could be expanded into complete paragraphs.

The Writer's Desk Freewriting

Choose one of the following topics and do some freewriting. Remember to write without stopping.

TOPICS: Food   Kindness   Work

_____

_____

_____

_____

_____

_____

_____

_____

_____

_____

Brainstorming

When you **brainstorm,** you create a list of ideas. You can include opinions, details, images, questions, or anything else that comes to mind. If you need to, you can stop and think while you are creating your list. Do not worry about grammar or spelling. Remember that the point is to generate ideas.

MADHURI'S BRAINSTORMING

College student Madhuri Desai brainstormed about the topic "families." Her audience was her instructor and other students, and her purpose was to inform.

— types of families

— reasons families are smaller

— relationship between siblings

— birth order

— mistakes parents make

— raising confident children

— problems with blended families

— the importance of family

— large versus small families

— family reunions

— family vacations

PRACTICE 2

Read Madhuri's list about families, and underline ideas that could be developed into complete paragraphs.

The Writer's Desk Brainstorming

Choose one of the following topics and brainstorm. Let your ideas flow when you create your list.

TOPICS: Traditions   College   Fashion trends

_____

_____

_____

_____

_____

_____

_____

_____

_____

Clustering

When you **cluster,** you draw a word map. To begin, write your topic in the middle of the page. Then, think of ideas that relate to the topic. Using lines or arrows, connect each idea to the central topic or to other ideas. Keep writing, circling, and connecting ideas until you have groups or "clusters" of them on your page. When you finish, you will have a visual image of your ideas.

ANTON'S CLUSTERING

College student Anton Gromyko used clustering to explore ideas about movies.

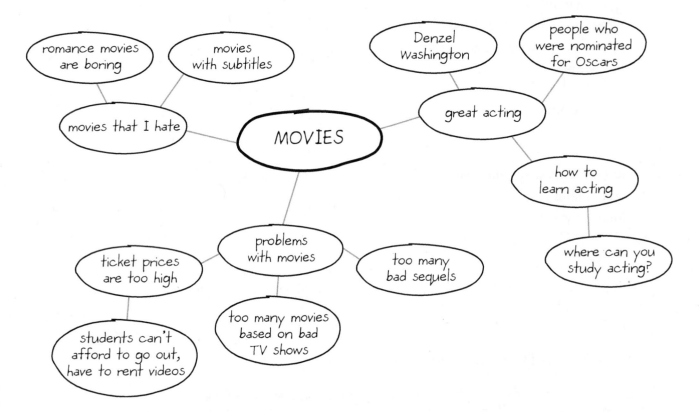

PRACTICE 3

Look at Anton's clustering. Circle one or more clusters that would make a good paragraph.

The Writer's Desk Clustering

Choose one of the following topics and try clustering on the next page. Let your ideas flow when you create your cluster.

TOPICS: Technology   Dating   Money

Hint   Questioning

Another way to generate ideas about a topic is to ask yourself a series of questions and write responses to them. The questions can help you define and narrow your topic. One common way to do this is to ask yourself *who, what, when, where, why,* and *how* questions.

Question	Possible Answers
Why do people travel?	To escape, to learn about other cultures, to enjoy good weather
How can they travel?	Flying, taking a train or bus, walking tours, hiking, sailing, cycling
What are inexpensive ways to travel?	Find last-minute deals, go backpacking, stay with friends or in youth hostels, share gas expenses

Journal and Portfolio Writing

Keeping a Journal

American educator and writer Christina Baldwin once said, "Journal writing is like a voyage to the interior." One good way to practice your writing is to keep a journal. In a journal, you record your thoughts, opinions, ideas, and impressions. Journal writing provides you with a chance to practice your writing without worrying about the audience. It also gives you a source of material when you are asked to write about a topic of your choice.

You can write about any topic that appeals to you. Here are some suggestions.

- **College:** You can describe new things you have learned, express opinions about your courses, and list ideas for assignments.
- **Your personal life:** You can describe your feelings about your career goals. You can also write about personal problems and solutions, reflect about past and future decisions, express feelings about your job, and so on.
- **Controversial issues:** You can write about your reactions to controversies in the world, in your country, in your state, in your city, in your college, or even within your own family.
- **Interesting facts:** Perhaps you have discovered new and interesting information in a course, in a newspaper, or in some other way. You can record interesting facts in your journal.

Keeping a Portfolio

A **writing portfolio** is a place where you keep samples of all of your writing. It could be in a binder or an electronic file folder. The purpose of keeping a portfolio is to have a record of your writing progress.

In your portfolio, keep all drafts of your writing assignments. When you work on new assignments, review your previous work in your portfolio. Identify your main problems, and try not to repeat the same errors.

 The Writer's Room   **Topics to Explore**

Writing Activity I

Choose one of the following topics, or choose your own topic. Then generate ideas about the topic. You may want to try the suggested exploring strategy.

General Topics

1. Try freewriting about sports. Jot down any ideas that come to mind.
2. Try brainstorming about important ceremonies. List the first ideas that come to mind.
3. Try clustering about the idea of friendship. First, write the word *friendship* in the middle of the page. Then create clusters of ideas that relate to the topic.

College or Work-Related Topics

4. Try freewriting to come up with ideas about career choices.

5. Brainstorm about an influential person. To get ideas, list anything that comes to mind when you think about this person.

6. Try clustering about stress. Write the word *stress* in the center of the page, and then create clusters of ideas about the topic.

EXPLORING CHECKLIST

When you explore a topic, ask yourself the following questions.

What is my **topic?** Consider what you will write about.

Who is my **audience?** Think about your intended reader.

What is my **purpose?** Determine your reason for writing.

Which exploring strategy will I use? You could try one of the next strategies or a combination of strategies.

Freewriting is writing without stopping for a limited period of time.
Brainstorming is making a list.
Clustering is drawing a word map.
Questioning is asking and answering questions.

How Do I Get a Better Grade?

Visit www.mywritinglab.com for audio-visual lectures and additional practice sets about prewriting strategies.
Get a better grade with MyWritingLab!

CHAPTER 2 Developing

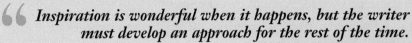

> *Inspiration is wonderful when it happens, but the writer must develop an approach for the rest of the time.*
> —LEONARD BERNSTEIN (1918–1990)
> *American composer*

CONTENTS

- What Is Developing?
- Narrow the Topic
- The Topic Sentence
- The Supporting Ideas
- The Paragraph Plan
- The First Draft

The developing stage of the writing process is like creating a sand castle. Using a variety of tools, you develop your structure.

ESSAY LINK

You can follow similar steps when you develop an essay. See Chapter 5 for more details about essay writing.

What Is Developing?

Chapter 1 explained how you can explore ideas for writing. This chapter takes you, step by step, through the development of a paragraph. There are five key steps in the developing stage.

DEVELOPING

STEP 1	→	**Narrow your topic.** Find an aspect of the topic that interests you.
STEP 2	→	**Express your main idea.** Write a topic sentence that expresses the main idea of the piece of writing.
STEP 3	→	**Develop your supporting ideas.** Generate ideas that support your topic sentence.
STEP 4	→	**Make a plan.** Organize your main and supporting ideas, and place your ideas in a plan.
STEP 5	→	**Write your first draft.** Communicate your ideas in a single written piece.

Reviewing Paragraph Structure

A **paragraph** is a group of sentences focusing on one central idea. Paragraphs can stand alone, or they can be part of a longer work such as an essay, a letter, or a report.

The **topic sentence** expresses the main point of the paragraph and shows the writer's attitude toward the subject.

The **body sentences** provide details that support the main point.

The **concluding sentence** brings the paragraph to a satisfactory close.

Topic sentence _____
      . Supporting detail
_____
_____ . Supporting detail _____
_____ . Supporting detail _____
Concluding sentence _____

VEENA'S PARAGRAPH

College student Veena Thomas wrote the following paragraph. Read her paragraph and then answer the questions.

> **As college students, we have a completely different culture than anyone else.** A few thousand students live together in what amounts to our own little city. Crowded into doubles and triples, we are brought together by our physical closeness, our similarities, and our differences. We share the bathrooms with strangers who soon become friends. We laugh together, cry together, and sleep through class together. Our dorm room becomes our refuge with its unmade beds, posters on the wall, and inflatable chairs. Money is a problem because we never have enough of it. When we get sick of cafeteria food, we subsist on 25-cent ramen noodles and boxes of oatmeal. We drink way too much coffee, and we order pizza at 1 a.m. We live on College Standard Time, which is about four hours behind everyone else. So while everyone else sleeps, we hang out with our music playing until the early hours of the morning. It's a different life, but it's our life, and we love it.

PRACTICE 1

Look at the structure of Veena's paragraph. The topic sentence (a statement of a main idea) is in bold. List Veena's supporting ideas. The first one has been done for you.

We live in our own little city of students crowded together.

_____

_____

_____

_____

_____

Paragraph Form

Your paragraphs should have the following form.

- Always indent the first word of a paragraph. Move it about 1 inch, or five spaces, from the left-hand margin.
- Leave a 1- to 1½-inch margin on each side of your paragraph.
- Begin every sentence with a capital letter, and end each sentence with the proper punctuation.
- If the last sentence of the paragraph does not go to the margin, leave the rest of the row blank.

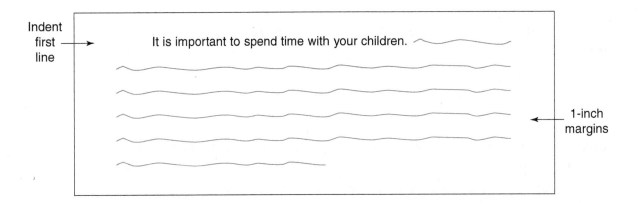

Indent first line → It is important to spend time with your children.

1-inch margins

Narrow the Topic

Sometimes you may be given a topic that is too broad for one paragraph. In those situations, you need to make your topic fit the size of the assignment. When you **narrow your topic**, you make it more specific. To narrow your topic, you can use the exploring strategies (freewriting, brainstorming, clustering, or questioning) that you learned in Chapter 1.

DONOVAN'S LIST TO NARROW THE TOPIC

College student Donovan Lynch used brainstorming to narrow his broad topic, "food."

— good restaurants

— when I ate too much junk food

— labeling genetically modified food

The Writer's Desk   Narrow the Topic

The next topics are very broad. Practice narrowing each topic.

EXAMPLE: Families: *Reasons families are small*

Mistakes parents make

Problems with blended families

1. Technology: _____

_____

_____

2. Fashion trends: _____

_____

_____

3. Dating: _____

_____

_____

4. Food: _____

_____

_____

5. Work: _____

_____

_____

The Topic Sentence

The next step in the writing process is to write a sentence that expresses the main idea. In a paragraph, the statement of the main idea is called the **topic sentence.** The topic sentence of a paragraph has several features.

- It introduces the topic.
- It states the main (or controlling) idea.
- It is the most general sentence.
- It is supported by other sentences.

The **controlling idea** is an essential part of the topic sentence because it makes a point about the topic. The controlling idea expresses the writer's opinion, attitude, or feeling. You can express different controlling ideas about the same topic. For example, the following topic sentences are about leaving the family home, but each sentence makes a different point about the topic.

narrowed topic   controlling idea
Leaving the family home is a difficult experience for some college students.

controlling idea   narrowed topic
The most exciting and important part of a youth's life is **leaving the family home**.

PRACTICE 2

Read each topic sentence. Underline the topic once and the controlling idea twice. To find the topic, ask yourself what the paragraph is about.

EXAMPLE:

<u>College students</u> <u><u>should take their studies seriously</u></u>.

1. Several interesting things happened when the probe landed on Mars.
2. Children without siblings tend to be self-reliant.
3. The bronze sculpture was truly original.
4. Become a better listener by following three simple steps.
5. There should not be a mandatory retirement age.
6. Our vacation was filled with exciting experiences.
7. Three strategies can help you speak with strangers.
8. The dorm room was an uncontrollable mess.
9. High blood pressure is caused by several factors.

Writing an Effective Topic Sentence

When you develop your topic sentence, avoid some common errors by asking yourself these four questions.

ESSAY LINK

When you write a thesis statement for an essay, ask yourself questions 1–3 to ensure that your thesis statement is complete and valid.

1. **Is my topic sentence a complete sentence?**
   Your topic sentence should always be a complete sentence that reveals a complete thought.

Incomplete:	Living alone.
	(This is a topic but *not* a topic sentence. It does not express a complete thought.)
Topic sentence:	There are many advantages to living alone.

2. **Does my topic sentence have a controlling idea?**
   Your topic sentence should make a point about your paragraph's topic. It should not announce the topic.

Announcement:	I will write about nursing.
	(This sentence announces the topic but says nothing relevant about it. Do not use expressions such as *My topic is* or *I will write about.*)
Topic sentence:	Nurses need to be in good physical and psychological health.

3. **Does my topic sentence make a valid and supportable point?**
   Your topic sentence should express a valid point that you can support with details and examples. It should not be a vaguely worded statement, and it should not be a highly questionable generalization.

Vague:	Today's students are too weak.
	(How are they weak?)

Invalid point:	Today's students have more responsibilities than those in the past.
	(Is this really true? This might be a hard assertion to prove.)
Topic sentence:	Some of the best students in this college juggle schoolwork, raise children, and hold part-time jobs.

4. **Can I support my topic sentence in a single paragraph?**
   Your topic sentence should express an idea that you can support in a paragraph. It should not be too broad or too narrow.

Too broad:	There are many good libraries.
	(It would be difficult to write only one paragraph about this topic.)
Too narrow:	The college library is located beside the student center.
	(What more is there to say?)
Topic sentence:	The college library, which is beside the student center, contains valuable resources for students.

 **Write a Clear Topic Sentence**

Your topic sentence should not express an obvious or well-known fact. Write something that will interest your readers and make them want to continue reading.

Obvious:	Work is important.
	(Everybody knows this.)
Better:	When looking for a job, remember that some things are more important than having a good salary.

PRACTICE 3

Identify why each of the following topic sentences is not effective. Then, choose the word or words from the list that best describe the problem with each topic sentence. (A topic sentence may have more than one problem.) Finally, correct the problem by revising each sentence.

Incomplete	Vague	Announces
Invalid	Broad	Narrow

EXAMPLE:

I am going to write about athletes.

Problem:	*Announces; broad*
Revised sentence:	*The salaries in professional basketball are too high.*

1. Using innocent animals to test beauty products.

   Problem: _____

   Revised statement: _____

   _____

2. Everybody watches too much television.

Problem: _____

Revised statement: _____

_____

3. In this paper, I will give my opinion about tabloid newspapers.

Problem: _____

Revised statement: _____

_____

4. Adolescents are more reckless.

Problem: _____

Revised statement: _____

_____

5. Having a part-time job.

Problem: _____

Revised statement: _____

_____

6. Money is important.

Problem: _____

Revised statement: _____

_____

Hint   **Placement of the Topic Sentence**

Because you are developing your writing skills, it is a good idea to place your topic sentence at the beginning of your paragraph. Then, follow it with supporting details. Opening your paragraph with a topic sentence helps your readers immediately identify what your paragraph is about.

PRACTICE 4

Choose the best topic sentence for each paragraph.

1.   When a person undergoes a period of high stress, he or she may experience sleep problems. Insomnia can also be caused by high alcohol consumption; although alcohol makes it easier to fall asleep, the quality of the sleep is reduced. Furthermore, irregular sleeping and waking times can provoke insomnia.

Possible topic sentences:

____ Many people in the world get insomnia.

____ Insomnia, the inability to have prolonged deep sleep, is caused by several factors.

____ Insomnia is the inability to have prolonged deep sleep.

2.   In their book *Second Chances,* Blakeslee and Wallerstein cite studies showing that boys are more likely to have external behavior problems after a marital breakup. For example, boys may become more impulsive, aggressive, and antisocial. After divorce, girls generally internalize their anger and frustration. They may become anxious and depressed.

Possible topic sentences:

____ Girls often become withdrawn after a divorce.

____ Divorce is common in North America.

____ Research suggests that male and female children react to divorce in different ways.

3.   We expect our lives to follow the pattern of such stories. We grow up believing that our true love will suddenly appear and rescue us from loneliness and boredom, just as the princes rescued Cinderella, Snow White, and Sleeping Beauty. We become convinced that we will only find happiness once we find a soul mate, and we expect this soul mate to fulfill all of our needs and to feel eternally lustful toward us. Like the heroines in those stories, we expect to live happily ever after.

Possible topic sentences:

____ Fairy tales give us unrealistic expectations about love.

____ Through stories, we learn that love never dies.

____ Love is a great thing.

The Writer's Desk Write Topic Sentences

Narrow each topic. Then, write a topic sentence that contains a controlling idea. (You could refer to your ideas in The Writer's Desk: Narrow the Topic on page 14.)

EXAMPLE: Families

Narrowed topic: *Mistakes parents make*

Topic sentence: *Good people can make some serious parenting mistakes.*

1. Technology

   Narrowed topic: _____

   Topic sentence: _____

   _____

2. Fashion trends

   Narrowed topic: _____

   Topic sentence: _____

   _____

3. Dating

   Narrowed topic: _____

   Topic sentence: _____

   _____

4. Food

   Narrowed topic: _____

   Topic sentence: _____

   _____

5. Work

   Narrowed topic: _____

   Topic sentence: _____

   _____

ESSAY LINK

In an essay, you place the thesis statement in the introduction. Then each supporting idea becomes a distinct paragraph with its own topic sentence.

The Supporting Ideas

After you have written a clear topic sentence, you can focus on **supporting details**—the facts and examples that provide the reader with interesting information about the subject matter. There are three steps you can take to determine your paragraph's supporting details.

1. Generate supporting ideas.
2. Choose the best supporting ideas.
3. Organize your ideas.

Generating Supporting Ideas

You can use an exploring strategy—freewriting, brainstorming, clustering, or questioning—to generate supporting ideas.

MADHURI'S SUPPORTING IDEAS

Madhuri Desai chose one of her narrowed topics related to "families" and wrote her topic sentence. Then she listed ideas that could support her topic sentence.

TECHNOLOGY LINK

If you write your paragraph on a computer, put your topic sentence in bold. Then you (and your instructor) can easily identify it.

TOPIC SENTENCE: **Good people can make some serious parenting mistakes.**

— too relaxed, want to be the child's friend

— don't give children enough responsibilities

— tell their child about private problems

— put work before family

— model bad behavior

— have addictions

— say nasty things during fights

— tell lies

— I don't want kids

— miss sporting events, recitals, etc.

The Writer's Desk **List Supporting Ideas**

Choose one of your topic sentences from the previous Writer's Desk, and make a list of ideas that could support it.

Topic sentence: _____

_____

Supporting ideas: _____

_____

_____

_____

_____

_____

_____

_____

Choosing the Best Ideas

A paragraph should have **unity,** which means that all of its sentences must relate directly to its topic sentence. To achieve unity, examine your prewriting carefully and then choose three or four ideas that are most compelling and that clearly support your topic sentence. You may notice that several items in your list are similar; therefore, you can group them together. Remove any ideas that do not support your topic sentence.

Madhuri's Supporting Ideas

First, Madhuri crossed out ideas that she did not want to develop. Then, she highlighted three of her most appealing ideas and labeled them A, B, and C. Finally, she regrouped other details from her list that best supported her most appealing ideas.

Topic Sentence: **Good people can make some serious parenting mistakes.**

— **too relaxed, want to be the child's friend**   *A*

— don't give children enough responsibilities

— tell their child about private problems

— put work before family   *B*

— model bad behavior   *C*

— ~~have addictions~~

— say nasty things during fights

— tell lies

— ~~I don't want kids~~

— miss sporting events, recitals, etc.

TECHNOLOGY LINK

On a computer, you can cut (ctrl X) and paste (ctrl V) similar ideas together.

 Hint   **Identifying the Best Ideas**

There are many ways to highlight your best ideas. You can circle the best supporting points and then use lines or arrows to link them with secondary ideas. You could also use highlighter pens or asterisks (*) to identify the best supporting points.

The Writer's Desk Choose the Best Ideas

For the Writer's Desk on page 21, you produced a list of ideas. Identify ideas that clearly support the topic sentence. If there are any related ideas, group them. You can cross out ideas that you do not want to develop.

ESSAY LINK

In an essay, you can also use time, space, or emphatic order to organize your ideas.

Organizing Your Ideas

The next step is to organize your ideas in a logical manner. There are three common organizational methods: time order, emphatic order, and space order. You can use **transitions**—words such as *first, then,* and *furthermore*—to guide readers from one idea to the next. You can find a more complete list of transitions on page 37 in Chapter 3, "Revising and Editing."

Time Order

When you use **time order,** you arrange the details according to the sequence in which they have occurred. Use time order to narrate a story, explain how to do something, or describe a historical event.

before   then   after that

Here are some transitional expressions you can use in time order paragraphs.

after that	first	later	next
eventually	in the beginning	meanwhile	then
finally	last	months after	while

The next paragraph uses time order.

> Throughout the history of music, financial backing has been needed to support the composition and production of musical performances. In Europe during the Middle Ages, the greatest patron of music was the church. Then, in the Renaissance, Baroque, and Classic eras, the foremost patrons were wealthy aristocrats who employed composers and performers in their courts. Later, in the nineteenth century, the main support for music gradually spread to the middle classes. Public concerts became common, and music was funded by ticket sales and by the sale of printed music for amateurs to perform at home. Finally, during the twentieth century, this reliance on wider support continued to grow. Now, the central driving force behind the production of most popular music is commercial gain. The profits are enormous.
>
> —Jeremy Yudkin, *Understanding Music*

PRACTICE 5

Use time order to organize the supporting details beneath each of the topic sentences. Number the details from 1 to 5.

1. If you win a large amount of money in a lottery, there are some things you should do to maintain your sanity.

   ____ Take a leave of absence from your job.

   ____ Keep enough money in your savings account to take a vacation.

   ____ Take a long vacation.

   ____ Collect the money and immediately deposit it in a secure bank fund.

   ____ Stay away until the publicity about your win dies down.

2. From 1897 to 1918, tragic events happened to Minik, an Inuit boy from Greenland.

   ____ The Inuit had no immunity to the diseases that were common in North America.

   ____ Through a window, museum visitors watched Minik and the other Inuit.

   ____ Minik ended up alone in America and was raised by the museum director.

   ____ Explorer Robert Peary decided to bring six Inuit, including seven-year-old Minik, to New York.

   ____ The six Inuit were put on display, like caged animals, in the American Museum of Natural History.

   ____ Minik's father was the first to die, followed by most of the others.

   ____ For the rest of his short life, Minik felt confused about his identity.

Emphatic Order

When you use **emphatic order,** you organize supporting details in a logical sequence. For example, you can arrange details from least to most important, from best to worst, from least appealing to most appealing, from general to specific, and so on. How you order the details often depends on your purpose for writing.

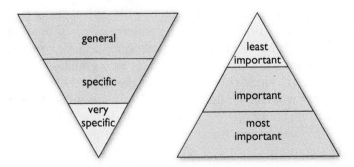

Here are some transitional expressions you can use in emphatic order paragraphs.

above all	first	moreover	particularly
clearly	furthermore	most important	principally
especially	least of all	most of all	therefore

The following paragraph uses emphatic order. The writer presents characteristics from the least to the most important.

> Psychologists have determined that people facing difficult circumstances have no single source of resilience. Rather, many factors come into play. First, those with developed social skills tend to be more resilient. For example, Oprah Winfrey, a great communicator, survived traumatic events in her childhood. Furthermore, some people have a genetic predisposition toward higher self-esteem. But one character trait, above all others, seems to help people cope, and that is the ability to maintain an optimistic attitude. According to author Martin Seligman, positive thinkers tend to believe that problems are outside themselves and not permanent, and they generally rise above failure.
>
> —Suzanne Moreau, student

 **Using Emphatic Order**

When you organize details using emphatic order, use your own values and opinions to determine what is most or least important, upsetting, remarkable, and so on. Another writer may organize the same ideas in a different way.

PRACTICE 6

Use emphatic order to organize the supporting details beneath each topic sentence. Number them in order from most important (1) to least important (5) or from least important (1) to most important (5).

1. High school students should get part-time jobs.

   ____ They will have spending money for social activities.

   ____ They will learn to be more independent and more organized.

   ____ They will learn the value of money.

   ____ They can buy more fashionable clothes.

   ____ They will no longer rely on parents for money.

2. Our new mayor has made many mistakes.

____ He made negative comments about some religious minorities.

____ He wears unflattering suits that are too large.

____ He hired his own children as advisors.

____ He made a lot of money on a land flip, and citizens believe he is corrupt.

____ He doesn't smile for photographs.

Space Order

When you use **space order,** you describe an image in the sequence in which you see it. For example, you could describe something or someone from top to bottom or bottom to top, from left to right or right to left, or from far to near or near to far.

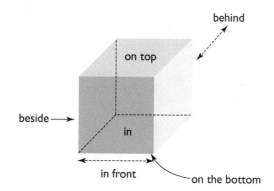

Here are some transitional expressions you can use in space order paragraphs.

above	closer in	near	next to
at the back	farther out	on the bottom	to the left
behind	in front	on the top	under

In the next paragraph, by taking the reader on a visual tour around his home, the writer describes the effects of a tornado.

> The house stopped trembling, and we knew that the tornado had passed. We jumped out of bed and did not know what we would find. We ran to the back of the house. What we found was our oldest daughter still asleep in a completely undisturbed room. We discovered our other two daughters also still asleep in another intact room. The storm did not touch the back portion of the house. Our section in the front of the home was less fortunate. The roof was in a tree. The rain was coming in and bringing globs of wet insulation with it. My wife began running around putting pots under the leaks, but I told her to forget it because the roof was gone.
>
> —Louis M. Tursi, *The Night Crawler*

PRACTICE 7

Read the next paragraph and answer the questions that follow.

> Patrick was my mate, and, as he was the first tramp I had known at all well, I want to give an account of him. He was a tallish man, aged

about thirty-five, with fair hair going grizzled and watery blue eyes. His features were good, but his cheeks had that grayish look that comes of a bread and margarine diet. He was dressed, rather better than most tramps, in a tweed jacket and a pair of old evening trousers with the braid still on them. Evidently the braid figured in his mind as a lingering scrap of respectability, and he took care to sew it on again when it came loose.

—Adapted from George Orwell, *Down and Out in London and Paris*

1. The writer uses spatial order to organize this paragraph. What main physical characteristics of the tramp does Orwell describe? List five characteristics.

    a. _____   d. _____

    b. _____   e. _____

    c. _____

2. In what order does the writer describe these characteristics? Choose the best answer.

    a. From top to bottom   b. From bottom to top

PRACTICE 8

Use spatial order to organize the supporting details beneath the topic sentence. Starting from the bottom and ending with the top, number the sentences from 1 to 5.

    Tourists and architectural students gasp in delight when they see the Casa Mila, the last completed avant-garde architectural work of Antoni Gaudí.

_____ Chimneys covered with broken ceramic tiles rise from the roof and seem to touch the sky.

_____ The sidewalk in front of the building is decorated with blue and green ceramic tiles designed in the form of starfish.

_____ The walls of the building are not straight but are in the shape of a gigantic wave.

_____ The roof, dotted with small windows, is sand-colored.

_____ Each balcony has curved black railings giving a further impression of waves on the ocean.

PRACTICE 9

Read the following topic sentences, which also appeared in Practice 2. Decide what type of order you could use to develop the paragraph details. Choose time, space, or emphatic order.

EXAMPLE:

College students should take their studies seriously.   *Emphatic*

1. Several interesting things happened when the probe landed on Mars.   _____

2. Children without siblings tend to be self-reliant.   _____

3. The bronze statue was truly original. _____

4. Become a better listener by following three simple steps. _____

5. The dorm room was an uncontrollable mess. _____

6. High blood pressure is caused by several factors. _____

The Writer's Desk Organize Your Ideas

Look at the list of ideas that you wrote for the Writer's Desk on page 21. Organize your ideas using space, time, or emphatic order by placing numbers beside the ideas.

The Paragraph Plan

A **paragraph plan**—or **outline**—is a map that shows the paragraph's main and supporting ideas. To make a plan, write your topic sentence, and then list supporting points and details in the order you wish to present them. You can use time, space, or emphatic order to organize the supporting points.

 **Hint** ▷ **Adding Specific Details**

When you prepare your paragraph plan, ask yourself whether your supporting ideas are detailed enough. If not, then you can add details to make that supporting idea stronger. For example, in Madhuri's list about mistakes parents make, one of her points was about people who put work before family. She added the following details to make that point stronger and more complete.

> **Some parents put work before family.**
> – miss sporting events, recitals, etc.
> **Added:** – don't take vacations
> – spend weekends and evenings on the cell phone or computer

MADHURI'S PARAGRAPH PLAN

After she chose her best ideas and organized them, Madhuri wrote a paragraph plan.

TOPIC SENTENCE: **Good people can make some serious parenting mistakes.**

Support 1:   Some parents are too relaxed and just want to be the child's friend.

Details: — don't give children enough responsibilities
— tell their child about private problems
— don't discipline their children

Support 2:	With the best of intentions, some parents put work before family.
Details:	— miss sporting events and recitals
	— don't take vacations
	— spend weekends and evenings on the cell phone or computer
Support 3:	Decent people can model bad behavior to their children.
Details:	— say nasty things during fights
	— tell lies
	— show that honesty isn't important

The Writer's Desk **Write a Paragraph Plan**

Look at the topic sentence and the organized list of supporting ideas that you created for the previous Writer's Desks. Now, fill in the following paragraph plan. Remember to include details for each supporting idea.

Topic sentence: _____

_____

Support 1: _____

Details: _____

_____

Support 2: _____

Details: _____

_____

Support 3: _____

Details: _____

_____

The First Draft

The next step is to write the first draft. Take information from your paragraph plan and, using complete sentences, write a paragraph. Your first draft includes your topic sentence and supporting details.

MADHURI'S FIRST DRAFT

Madhuri wrote the first draft of her paragraph about mistakes parents make. You may notice that her paragraph contains mistakes. In Chapter 3, you will see how she revises and edits her paragraph.

> **Good people can make some serious parenting mistakes.** Some parents are too relaxed and just want to be their childs friend. They do not give their children enough responsabilities. Also, no

boundaries. They talk to their children about their private problems. With the best of intentions, some people put work before family. They miss sporting events and recitals. Those types of parents also don't take no vacations because they want to focus on their careers, they spend weekends and evenings on the cell phone or computer. And decent people can model bad behavior to their children. When they say nasty things during fights, the children learn to be dirty fighters. There are also parents who lie, and they show their kids that honesty is not important.

 Writing the Concluding Sentence

Some paragraphs end with a **concluding sentence,** which brings the paragraph to a satisfactory close. If you want to write a concluding sentence for your paragraph, here are three suggestions.

- Restate the topic sentence in a new, fresh way.
- Make an interesting final observation.
- End with a prediction, suggestion, or quotation.

ESSAY LINK

Essays end with a concluding paragraph. For more information about essay conclusions, see page 105.

The Writer's Desk **Write Your First Draft**

In the previous Writer's Desk on page 28, you created a paragraph plan. Now, on a separate sheet of paper, write your first draft of that paragraph.

 The Writer's Room **Topics to Develop**

Writing Activity I

In the Writer's Room in Chapter 1, "Exploring," you used various strategies to find ideas about the following topics. Select one of the topics and write a paragraph. Remember to follow the writing process.

General Topics

1. sports
2. ceremonies
3. friendship

College or Work-Related Topics

4. career choices
5. an influential person
6. stress

Writing Activity 2

Describe your neighborhood. You could describe a person you frequently see or a place such as a park or building.

✔ **DEVELOPING CHECKLIST**

When you develop a paragraph, ask yourself the following questions.

☐ Does my **topic sentence** introduce the topic and state the controlling idea?

☐ Do I **support the topic sentence** with facts and examples?

☐ Do I **organize the details** using time, space, or emphatic order?

☐ Does my **paragraph plan** help me visualize the main and supporting ideas?

☐ Does my **first draft** use complete sentences?

How Do I Get a Better Grade?

Visit www.mywritinglab.com for audio-visual lectures and additional practice sets about developing.
Get a better grade with MyWritingLab!

Revising and Editing

> *Mistakes are the portals of discovery.*
> —JAMES JOYCE (1882–1941)
> *Irish author*

CONTENTS

- What Are Revising and Editing?
- Revise for Unity
- Revise for Adequate Support
- Revise for Coherence
- Revise for Style
- Edit for Errors
- The Final Draft

The revising and editing stages of the writing process are like adding the finishing touches to a sand castle. Small improvements can make the difference between a stable or an unstable structure.

What Are Revising and Editing?

Revising and editing are effective ways to improve your writing. When you **revise,** you modify your writing to make it more convincing and precise. You do this by looking for inadequate development and poor organization, and then you make any necessary changes. When you **edit,** you proofread your final draft. You look for errors in grammar, spelling, punctuation, and mechanics.

There are five key steps in the revising and editing stages.

REVISING AND EDITING

STEP 1	**Revise for unity.** Make sure that all parts of your work relate to the main idea.
STEP 2	**Revise for adequate support.** Ensure that you have enough details to effectively support the main idea.
STEP 3	**Revise for coherence.** Verify that your ideas flow smoothly and are logically linked.
STEP 4	**Revise for style.** Make sure that your sentences are varied and interesting.
STEP 5	**Edit for technical errors.** Proofread your work and correct errors in grammar, spelling, mechanics, and punctuation.

Revise for Unity

In a paragraph, every idea should move in the same direction just like this railroad track goes straight ahead.

ESSAY LINK

When revising an essay, ensure that each body paragraph has unity.

When a paragraph has **unity**, all of the sentences support the topic sentence. If a paragraph lacks unity, then it is difficult for the reader to understand the main point. To check for unity, verify that every sentence relates to the main idea.

ERNESTO'S PARAGRAPH WITHOUT UNITY

College student Ernesto Garcia wrote the following paragraph. As he wrote, he accidentally drifted away from his main idea. Some sentences do not relate to the topic sentence. If Ernesto removed the highlighted sentences, then his paragraph would have unity.

The writer took a detour here.

> **My father has always spent far too much time in front of the television.** When I was a child, each day my dad got home from work, took off his coat, and then went to the television to see what was on. Later, while the rest of us were eating supper in the kitchen, he would take his plate to the living room and watch the news. On weekends, he watched sports, and we would hear him yelling every time his team's players made a mistake. Growing up, we missed his conversation and company. Because of my father's influence, I became a television addict, too. After work, when my friends invited me out, I would find excuses to turn them down because I wanted to watch the latest episode of some television program. Today my father is an old man, and the television is still his constant companion.

PRACTICE I

Read paragraphs A, B, and C. For each one, underline the topic sentence. Then indicate whether the paragraph has unity. If the paragraph lacks unity, remove the sentences that do not relate to the topic sentence.

A. In this computer age, electronic voting seems like a logical way to collect and count votes. However, paperless electronic voting is both unreliable and dangerous. First, the software in voting machines may be faulty. During the 2006 midterm elections, overseers in some states noted that machines switched votes from one candidate to another because of touch-screen problems. Additionally, voting machines can be easily manipulated. In 2004, Maryland hired RABA Technologies to try to hack the state's new voting machines. Computer whizzes were able to vote more than once and change voting outcomes, and they concluded that even high-school students could hack the machines. In Holland, hackers using telephone lines were able to manipulate and delete votes. However, electronic voting has some good points. The elimination of paper ballots is good for the environment. Also, votes can be counted more quickly by machine than they can by hand. Certainly, governments should think twice about implementing electronic voting machines.

Circle the correct answer: The paragraph

a. has unity or   b. lacks unity.

B. To minimize the problems associated with divorce, parents need to maintain a stable environment for their children. For example, any fighting over finances or child visitation should not occur in front of the children. Parents should try to live near each other so that the kids have easy access to both parents. To further stabilize children's lives after a divorce, many parents now opt for the "family home." The kids don't have to change houses to visit each parent; instead, the parents take turns living in the family home. If parents just remember to put children first, then the effects of divorce on the children can be minimized.

Circle the correct letter: The paragraph

a. has unity or   b. lacks unity.

C. When people watch movies, they rarely appreciate a very important part of the filmmaking process. Foley artists make movies come alive by using simple, everyday objects to create sound effects. For example, to reproduce the sound of crickets, a foley artist can simply run a fingernail along the teeth of a comb. The sounds of a fight can be created by hitting watermelons and breaking pieces of bamboo. Twisting cellophane resembles the crackling of a fire. *The Lord of Rings* had many astounding visual effects, including computer-generated characters such as orcs. The filmmakers also used clever camera angles to make Frodo, the main hobbit, look very small. Even though technology has become more sophisticated and libraries of recorded sound effects exist, most directors still prefer the involvement of foley artists.

Circle the correct letter: The paragraph

a. has unity or   b. lacks unity.

Revise for Adequate Support

ESSAY LINK

When you revise an essay, ensure that you have adequately supported the thesis statement. Also, verify that each body paragraph has sufficient supporting details.

A bridge is built using several well-placed support columns. Like a bridge, a paragraph requires adequate support to help it stand on its own.

When you revise for **adequate support**, ensure that your paragraph contains strong and convincing supporting details. For example, Madhuri wrote a paragraph about poor parenting skills, but her sentences were too general. She added some specific examples to strengthen her paragraph.

Good people can make some serious parenting mistakes. Some

parents are too relaxed and just want to be the childs friend. They do
For instance, my cousin never had to
not give their children enough responsibilities. Also, no boundaries.
do any chores, and now he treats his mother like a servant.
They talk to their children about private problems. With the best of
Actress Lindsay Lohan, for example, has said that she was forced to be
intentions, some people put work before family. They miss sporting
her mother's confidant, and she grew to resent that role.
events and recitals. Those types of parents also don't take no vacations

because they want to focus on their careers, they spend weekends and
Indeed, my workaholic father never
evenings on the cell phone or computer. And decent people can model
watched me play baseball when I was a child.
bad behavior to their children. When they say nasty things during

fights, the children learn to be dirty fighters. There are also parents
and cheat on their taxes
who lie and they show their kids that honesty is not important.

PRACTICE 2

The following paragraph attempts to persuade, but it does not have any specific details that make strong points.

Advertising companies work hard to get our attention. Some corporations spend a fortune on music for their television commercials.

Advertisers also pay celebrities to endorse their products. Furthermore, many marketing firms work on making the consumer laugh, so some ads are very funny. Thus, many advertisements are expensive but effective.

When the preceding paragraph about advertising is expanded with specific details and examples, it becomes more convincing. Try adding details on the lines provided.

Advertising companies work hard to get our attention. Some corporations spend a fortune on music for their television commercials. For example, _____

_____

_____

Advertisers also pay celebrities to endorse their products. _____

_____

_____

Furthermore, many marketing firms work on making the consumer laugh, so some ads are very funny. _____

_____

_____

Thus, many advertisements are expensive but effective.

 **Avoiding Circular Reasoning**

Circular reasoning means that a writer restates his or her main point in various ways but does not provide supporting details. The main idea goes in circles and never progresses—kind of like a dog chasing its tail. Avoid using circular reasoning by writing a concise topic sentence and by supporting the topic sentence with facts, examples, or anecdotes.
    For example, the following paragraph has circular reasoning.

    Young people advertise for companies by wearing too many logos on their clothing. A lot of their clothing contains pictures from large corporations. These "walking billboards" are unconsciously promoting huge companies.

When a paragraph has circular reasoning, the main idea does not progress. The writer leads the reader in circles.

PRACTICE 3

The next passages do not have sufficient supporting examples. List examples for each topic.

EXAMPLE:

    My sister's apartment is a disaster zone. The kitchen is messy. So is the bathroom. There are things everywhere.

Add examples: *The front hall is filled with shoes.*

    The sink is filled with dirty dishes.

    There are wet towels on the bathroom floor.

1. Young people advertise for companies by wearing too many logos on their clothing. A lot of their clothing displays pictures from large

corporations. These "walking billboards" are unconsciously promoting huge companies.

Add examples: _____

_____

_____

2. When you prepare for a test, there are a few things that you should do. You should find out exactly what you are supposed to study. You should be ready for your test.

Add examples: _____

_____

_____

3. Since 2000, reality television has invaded our homes. There are many types of reality shows. They all include ordinary people who participate in unusual contests. Sometimes the shows take place in unusual places.

Add examples: _____

_____

_____

Revise for Coherence

Just as couplings link train cars, transitional expressions link ideas in a paragraph.

ESSAY LINK

To create coherence in an essay, you can place transitional expressions at the beginning of each body paragraph.

GRAMMAR LINK

For more practice using transitions in sentences, see Chapter 15, "Compound Sentences."

When you revise for coherence, you ensure that your reader has a smooth voyage through your paragraph. **Coherence** means that the sentences flow smoothly and are logically organized.

Transitional Expressions

Transitional expressions are linking words or phrases, and they show the reader the connections between ideas in paragraphs and essays. Here are some common transitional expressions.

Function	Transitional Word or Expression
Addition	again, also, besides, first (second, third), for one thing, furthermore, in addition, in fact, moreover, next, then
Concession of a point	certainly, indeed, no doubt, of course, to be sure
Comparison	as well, equally, likewise, similarly
Contrast	however, in contrast, instead, nevertheless, on the contrary, on the other hand
Effect or result	as a result, consequently, then, therefore, thus
Example	for example, for instance, in other words, namely, specifically, to illustrate
Emphasis	above all, clearly, in fact, in particular, indeed, least of all, most important, most of all, of course, undoubtedly
Space	above, at the back, behind, below, beside, closer in, farther out, in front, in the middle, inside, nearby, on the bottom, on the left/right, on top, outside, under
Summary or conclusion	generally, in conclusion, in other words, in short, on the whole, therefore, thus, to conclude, to summarize
Time	after that, at that time, at the moment, currently, earlier, eventually, first (second, etc.), gradually, immediately, in the future, in the past, later, meanwhile, now, one day, presently, so far, subsequently, suddenly, then, these days

 **Hint**   **Use Transitional Expressions with Complete Sentences**

When you add a transitional expression to a sentence, ensure that your sentence is complete. Your sentence must have a subject and a verb, and it must express a complete thought.

> **Incomplete:**   First, the price of movie tickets.
>
> **Complete:**   First, the price of movie tickets is <u>too high.</u>

PRACTICE 4

Add the following transitional expressions to the next paragraph. Use each transitional word once. There may be more than one correct answer for each space.

also	furthermore	undoubtedly
first	however	

When you go backpacking in a foreign country, there are a few simple things you should pack for the trip. _____, bring clothing that is easy to wash. Leave items that need ironing or dry cleaning at home. _____, make sure you pack a small medical kit. It could be difficult and expensive to find things such as aspirin and bandages if you're on a beach in Thailand.

_____, bring a comfortable money belt that you can wear under your clothing. _____, try not to overpack. After you've packed your bag, remove items so that there is a small empty space in your pack. _____, you will find and buy souvenirs during your trip.

ESSAY LINK

Revise your essays for style, ensuring that sentences are varied and that your language is exact. To learn more about sentence variety and exact language, see Chapter 17.

Revise for Style

Another important step in the revision process is to ensure that you have varied your sentences and that you have used concise wording. When you revise for sentence style, ask yourself the following questions.

- Have I used a variety of sentence patterns?
- Have I used exact language?
- Have I avoided using repetitious or vague language?

MADHURI'S REVISION

College student Madhuri Desai wrote a paragraph about parenting mistakes that good people can make. Read the revisions that she made to her paragraph. She revised for unity, support, and coherence. She also looked at style and decided to make some language more exact.

Added a transition. ➤

Good people can make some serious parenting mistakes. ~~Some~~ *First, some* parents are too relaxed and just want to be the childs friend. They do not give their children enough responsabilities. For instance, my cousin never had to do any chores, and now he treats his mother like

Added exact language. ➤

a servant. Also, no boundaries. They talk to their ~~children~~ *sons and daughters* about private problems. Actress Lindsay Lohan, for example, has said that she was forced to be her mother's confidant, and she grew to resent that role.

Added a transition. ➤

~~With~~ *Also, with* the best of intentions, some people put work before family. They miss sporting events and recitals. Those types of parents don't take no vacations because they want to focus on their careers, they spend weekends and evenings on the cell phone or computer. Indeed, my workaholic father never watched me play baseball when I was a child.

and
focus on their careers, they spend weekends and evenings on the cell
∧

phone or computer. Indeed, my workaholic father never watched me

play baseball when I was a child. Finally, decent people can model

bad behavior to their children. When they say nasty things during
,
fights the children learn to be dirty fighters. There are also parents
∧
,
who lie and cheat on their taxes and they show their impressionable
∧

youngsters that honesty is not important. Parents should really think

about the impact of their actions on their children.

TECHNOLOGY LINK

Word processors have spelling and
grammar checkers. If the program
suggests ways to correct errors,
carefully verify that the computer's
suggestions make sense before you
accept them.

The Writer's Desk Revise and Edit Your Paragraph

Choose a paragraph that you wrote for Chapter 2, or choose one that
you have written for another assignment. Carefully revise and edit
your paragraph.

Peer Feedback

After you write a paragraph or an essay, it is useful to get peer feedback. Ask
another person such as a friend, family member, or fellow student to read your
work and give you comments and suggestions on its strengths and weaknesses.

 Offer Constructive Criticism

When you peer-edit someone else's writing, try to make constructive suggestions
rather than destructive comments. Phrase your comments in a positive way. Look at
the following examples.

Instead of saying . . .	**You could say . . .**
Your examples are dull.	Perhaps you could add more details to your examples.
Your paragraph is confusing.	Your topic sentence needs a controlling idea.

When you are editing someone else's work, try using a peer feedback form as
a guideline. A sample form is on the next page.

Peer Feedback Form

Written by: _____   Feedback by: _____

Date: _____

1. Your main idea is _____

   _____

   _____

2. Your best supporting ideas are _____

   _____

   _____

   _____

3. I like _____

   _____

   _____

4. Perhaps you could change _____

   _____

   _____

   _____

5. My other comments are _____

   _____

   _____

   _____

   _____

The Final Draft

When you have finished making revisions on the first draft of your paragraph, write the final draft. Include all of the changes that you have made during the revising and editing phases. Before you hand in your final draft, proofread it one last time to ensure that you have caught any errors.

The Writer's Desk   Writing Your Final Draft

You have developed, revised, and edited your paragraph. Now write the final draft. Before you hand it to your instructor, proofread it one last time to ensure that you have found all of your errors.

 The Writer's Room   Paragraph Topics

Writing Activity 1

Choose a paragraph that you have written for this course. Revise and edit that paragraph, and then write a final draft.

Writing Activity 2

Choose one of the following topics, or choose your own topic and write a paragraph. You could try exploring strategies to generate ideas. The first sentence of your paragraph should make a point about your topic. Remember to revise and edit your paragraph before you write the final draft.

General Topics

1. an interesting dream
2. a family story
3. marriage
4. television
5. an accident

College or Work-Related Topics

6. an unusual experience at college
7. cheating
8. reasons to stay in college
9. a personality conflict at work
10. working with your spouse

✔ REVISING AND EDITING CHECKLIST

When you revise and edit a paragraph, ask yourself the following questions.

- Does my paragraph have **unity?** Ensure that every sentence relates to the main idea.

- Does my paragraph have **adequate support?** Verify that there are enough details and examples to support your main point.

- Is my paragraph **coherent?** Try to use transitional expressions to link ideas.

- Does my paragraph have good **style?** Check for varied sentence patterns and exact language.

- Does my paragraph have any errors? **Edit** for errors in grammar, punctuation, spelling, and mechanics.

- Is my **final draft** error-free?

How Do I Get a Better Grade?

Visit www.mywritinglab.com for audio-visual lectures and additional practice sets about revising and editing. *Get a better grade with MyWritingLab!*

CHAPTER 4

Paragraph Patterns

Art is the imposing of a pattern on experience.
—ALFRED NORTH WHITEHEAD (1861–1947)
Mathematician and philosopher

CONTENTS

- What Are Paragraph Patterns?
- A) The Illustration Paragraph
- B) The Narrative Paragraph
- C) The Descriptive Paragraph
- D) The Process Paragraph
- E) The Definition Paragraph
- F) The Comparison and Contrast Paragraph
- G) The Cause and Effect Paragraph
- H) The Classification Paragraph
- I) The Argument Paragraph

A fashion designer uses diverse patterns to create coats for different purposes. In this chapter, you will learn about nine writing patterns.

What Are Paragraph Patterns?

Paragraph patterns, or **modes**, are methods writers can use to develop a piece of writing. Each pattern has a specific purpose. For example, if you want to entertain your audience by telling a story about your recent adventure, you might write a narrative paragraph. If your purpose is to explain the steps needed to complete an activity, you might write a process paragraph. Sometimes, more than one pattern can fulfill your purpose. Take a moment to review nine different writing patterns.

Pattern	Use
Illustration	To illustrate or prove a point using specific examples
Narration	To narrate or tell a story about a sequence of events that happened
Description	To describe using vivid details and images that appeal to the reader's senses
Process	To inform the reader about how to do something, how something works, or how something happened

(continued)

44

Pattern	Use
Definition	To define or explain what a term or concept means by providing relevant examples
Comparison and Contrast	To present information about similarities (compare) or differences (contrast)
Cause and Effect	To explain why an event happened (the cause) or what the consequences of the event were (the effects)
Classification	To sort a topic into different categories
Argument	To argue or to take a position on an issue and offer reasons for your position

A) The Illustration Paragraph

An **illustration paragraph** uses specific examples to **illustrate** or clarify the main point. For example, if you are writing a paragraph about your most valuable possessions, you might list your grandmother's ring, your photo album, your family videos, and so on.

Illustration writing is a pattern that you frequently use in college writing because you must support your main idea with examples.

PRACTICE I

Read the paragraph and answer the questions that follow.

In recent visits to Canada, Mexico, Costa Rica, and Ecuador, I saw adolescents routinely behaving in ways American experts condemn as horrifying. **Ontario** nineteen-year-olds queued in liquor stores and drank in pubs alongside elders. Teens in **Quito, Riobamba,** and **San José** thronged to late-night discos. Unchaperoned **Ensenada** middle-schoolers strolled hand-in-hand along late-night downtown streets after emerging from unrated movies. Latin American cybercafés (often managed by teens or children) overflowed with unsupervised youths clicking unfiltered computers. Laughed a **Mountie** when I asked if Toronto had a youth curfew, "Maybe for six-year-olds." By American expert thinking, European, Canadian, and Latin American adolescents should be developmentally damaged alcoholic felons.

—Mike Males, "Freedom: For Adults Only"

Ontario: a province in Canada

Quito: the capital of Ecuador

Riobamba: a city in Ecuador

San José: a city in Costa Rica

Ensenada: a city in Mexico

Mountie: a Canadian federal police officer; the name derives from the word *Mounted* in Royal Canadian Mounted Police.

1. What is the subject? _____

2. Underline the topic sentence of this paragraph.

3. List five supporting examples.

_____

_____

_____

_____

_____

_____

4. What is the author's point of view about the treatment of teens in the United States?

_____

_____

The Writer's Desk Exploring

Think about the following questions, and write down the first ideas that come to mind. Try to write two or three ideas for each topic.

EXAMPLE: What clutter do you have in your home?

kitchen cupboard filled with junk, letters on hall table, shoes piled in closet,

basement filled with boxes

1. What are some examples of out-of-control celebrities?

_____

_____

_____

2. What are some qualities of a successful parent?

_____

_____

_____

3. What are some traits of an effective boss?

_____

_____

_____

The Topic Sentence

The topic sentence in an illustration paragraph controls the direction of the paragraph. It includes the topic and a controlling idea about the topic.

controlling idea   topic

It is very difficult to **patrol America's borders.**

The Writer's Desk **Write Topic Sentences**

Write a topic sentence for each of the following topics. Your sentence should have a controlling idea that expresses the direction of the paragraph. Remember that the goal of the paragraph is to give examples.

EXAMPLE:

Topic: Clutter in the home

Topic sentence: *Several places in my home are magnets for clutter.*

1. Topic: Out-of-control celebrities

   Topic sentence: _____

   _____

2. Topic: A successful parent

   Topic sentence: _____

   _____

3. Topic: An effective boss

   Topic sentence: _____

   _____

The Supporting Ideas

In an illustration paragraph, the examples support the topic sentence. A paragraph plan helps you organize your topic sentence and supporting details.

An Illustration Paragraph Plan

When you write an illustration paragraph plan, ensure that your examples are valid and that they relate to the topic sentence. In the following plan, the topic sentence is supported by several examples. Then, each example is supported with details.

Topic sentence: **Several places in my home are magnets for clutter.**

   Support 1:   The front closet is a mess.

     Details: — shoes piled on top of each other

              — scarves, umbrellas, hats, gloves heaped at top of closet

   Support 2:   The hallway table is never clear.

     Details: — covered with letters, newspapers, opened bills

   Support 3:   A kitchen cupboard attracts junk.

     Details: — coupons, pens, screwdriver, twist ties, and other odds and ends piled in it

Support 4: The bathroom vanity is in disarray.
Details: — comb, hair clips, razor, toothbrushes, hair products, face
cleanser all over the counter

The Writer's Desk **Develop Supporting Ideas**

Choose one of the topic sentences that you wrote for the previous
Writer's Desk, and write a detailed paragraph plan. List at least three
examples that could support the topic sentence.

Topic sentence: _____

_____

Support 1: _____

   Details: _____

_____

Support 2: _____

   Details: _____

_____

Support 3: _____

   Details: _____

_____

Support 4: _____

   Details: _____

_____

The Writer's Desk **Write an Illustration Paragraph**

You have made a list of supporting ideas for a topic. Now write an
illustration paragraph. After you finish writing, remember to revise
and edit your paragraph.

The Writer's Room

More Topics for Illustration Paragraphs

Writing Activity 1

Write an illustration paragraph about one of the following topics.

General Topics

1. mistakes
2. favorite clothing
3. inexpensive decorating solutions
4. annoying habits
5. creative hobbies

College and Work-Related Topics

6. inappropriate workplace clothing
7. qualities of a good or bad coworker
8. undesirable or difficult jobs
9. excuses for missing work
10. excuses for not finishing something

Writing Activity 2

Examine the photo. As you look at it, think about things that frustrate you or drive you crazy. Then write an illustration paragraph.

WRITING LINK

See the Writer's Rooms in the following grammar chapters for more illustration writing topics.
Chapter 8, Writer's Room topic 1 (page 161)
Chapter 12, Writer's Room topic 1 (page 225)
Chapter 20, Writer's Room topic 1 (page 315)
Chapter 22, Writer's Room topic 1 (page 342)
Chapter 25, Writer's Room topic 1 (page 382)

READING LINK

The following readings use examples to support the main idea.
"The Appalling Truth" by Dorothy Nixon (page 433)
"The Rewards of Dirty Work" by Linda L. Lindsey and Stephen Beach (page 462)

✔ ILLUSTRATION PARAGRAPH CHECKLIST

As you write your illustration paragraph, review the paragraph checklist on the inside back cover. Also, ask yourself the following questions.

☐ Does my topic sentence include a controlling idea that can be supported with examples?

☐ Do my supporting ideas contain sufficient examples that clearly support the topic sentence?

☐ Are the examples smoothly and logically connected?

B) The Narrative Paragraph

A **narrative** paragraph tells a story about what happened and generally explains events in the order in which they occurred.

There are two main types of narrative writing. When you use **first-person narration**, you describe a personal experience using *I* or *we* (first-person pronouns)—for example, "When I was a child, I played a terrible prank on my brother." When you use **third-person narration**, you describe what happened to somebody else, and you use *he*, *she*, or *they* (third-person pronouns). Most news reports use third-person narration. For example, a news article might state, "The billionaire inventor Dean Kamen has created a new type of engine. His invention, which is the size of a shoebox, works with any power source."

PRACTICE 2

Read the paragraph and answer the questions that follow.

buffarilla: an invented word that is a combination of buffalo and gorilla

When I was in seventh grade, one of the big ninth-grade girls began bullying me. She didn't shake me down for lunch money or even touch me. But she stalked me in the halls, on the playground, and in the girls' lavatory. The way that **buffarilla** rolled her eyes and worked her neck in my direction, I could feel her fingers yanking out every hair on my head—and I didn't have that much. In class, instead of paying attention, I began to envision the after-school crowd that would gather to watch me get stomped into the ground. Every day, my adversary seemed to grow bigger, meaner, and stronger. In my mind she evolved from a menacing older girl into a monster. By the time I realized that she wasn't really interested in fighting me—just intimidating me with dirty looks—I was already bruised from kicking my own butt.

—Bebe Moore Campbell, "Dancing with Fear"

1. What type of narration is this selection?

   a. First person   b. Third person

2. Underline the topic sentence.

3. What organizational method does the author use?

   a. Time order   b. Space order   c. Emphatic order

4. List what happens in the paragraph. (List only the main events.)

   _____

   _____

   _____

   _____

5. What did the author learn?

   _____

   _____

The Writer's Desk **Exploring**

Think about the following questions, and write down the first ideas that come to mind. Try to write two or three ideas for each topic.

EXAMPLE:

What are some bad purchases that you have made?

Bought black dress that is really too small

Bought a used car that was a lemon

Spent too much on a horrible haircut

1. What interesting place have you visited? What did you do in that place?

_____

_____

_____

2. Think about an accident or injury that you, or someone you know, had. What happened?

_____

_____

_____

3. Think of a moment when you felt very proud. What happened?

_____

_____

_____

The Topic Sentence

The **topic sentence** controls the direction of the paragraph and includes the topic and a controlling idea. To create a meaningful topic sentence for a narrative paragraph, you could ask yourself these questions: What did I learn? How did I change? How is the event important?

topic   controlling idea

When I visited Romania, I learned about my heritage.

The Writer's Desk **Write Topic Sentences**

Write a topic sentence for each of the following topics. Your sentence should make a point about the topic. Remember that the goal of the paragraph is to tell a story.

EXAMPLE:

> Topic: A bad purchase
>
> Topic sentence: *My problems began the moment I paid for my used car.*

1. Topic: A place I have visited

   Topic sentence: _____

   _____

2. Topic: An accident or injury

   Topic sentence: _____

   _____

3. Topic: A proud moment

   Topic sentence: _____

   _____

The Supporting Ideas

A narrative paragraph should contain details that explain what happened. To be as complete as possible, a good narrative paragraph should provide answers to most of the following questions.

- *Who* is the paragraph about?
- *What* happened?
- *When* did it happen?
- *Where* did it happen?
- *Why* did it happen?
- *How* did it happen?

WRITING LINK

For more information about organizing ideas using time, space, and emphatic order, see pages 22 to 27 of Chapter 2, "Developing."

A Narrative Paragraph Plan

When you write a narrative paragraph plan, ensure that your details are valid and that they relate to the topic sentence. Also, think about how you can organize your ideas. In the following plan, each detail explains what happened by using time order.

TOPIC SENTENCE: **My problems began the moment I paid for my used car.**

Support 1: When I paid the $500, the seller expressed relief.

Details: — actually said "Whew"

— exchanged knowing glances with his buddy

Support 2: The drive home was filled with anxiety.
   Details: — on the six-hour drive home, became concerned that the car
               wouldn't make it
              — car seemed to gain and lose power
              — twice had to stop the car because it was overheating
Support 3: I parked the car in my apartment parking space and noticed
           something dripping.
   Details: — smelled burning oil
              — black liquid dripped and stained the pavement
              — landlord, with a scowl, peered out her window at my car

The Writer's Desk Develop Supporting Ideas

Choose one of the topic sentences that you wrote for the previous Writer's Desk, and write a detailed paragraph plan. List the events in the order in which they occurred.

Topic sentence: _____

_____

Support 1:   _____

   Details: _____

_____

_____

Support 2:   _____

   Details: _____

_____

_____

Support 3:   _____

   Details: _____

_____

_____

The Writer's Desk Write a Narrative Paragraph

You have made a list of supporting ideas for a topic. Now write a narrative paragraph. After you finish writing, remember to revise and edit your paragraph.

The Writer's Room

More Topics for Narrative Paragraphs

WRITING LINK

See the Writer's Rooms in the following grammar chapters for more narrative writing topics.

Chapter 6, Writer's Room topic I (page 129)

Chapter 9, Writer's Room topics I and 2 (page 179)

Chapter 14, Writer's Room topic I (page 249)

Chapter 17, Writer's Room topic I (page 287)

Chapter 21, Writer's Room topic 2 (page 331)

READING LINK

Narrative Essays

The following readings use examples to support the main idea.

"Birth" by Maya Angelou (page 423)

"Sports and Life: Lessons to Be Learned" by Jeff Kemp (page 439)

Writing Activity 1

Write a narrative paragraph about one of the following topics.

General Topics

1. a scandal
2. a surprise
3. an anxious moment
4. a good or bad financial decision
5. something you learned from a parent or relative

College and Work-Related Topics

6. a frustrating day at college
7. a smart career decision
8. a positive college experience
9. when you were first hired
10. when you lost or quit a job

Writing Activity 2

Examine the photo. As you look at it, think about a journey you have taken. Write a narrative paragraph about a spiritual or physical journey.

NARRATIVE PARAGRAPH CHECKLIST

As you write your narrative paragraph, review the paragraph checklist on the inside back cover. Also, ask yourself the following questions.

☐ Does my topic sentence clearly express the topic of the narration, and does it make a point about that topic?

☐ Does my paragraph answer most of the following questions: who, what, when, where, why, how?

☐ Do I use transitional expressions to help clarify the order of events?

☐ Do I include details to make my narration more interesting?

C) The Descriptive Paragraph

When writing a **descriptive** paragraph, use words to create a vivid impression of a subject. Descriptive writing often contains details that appeal to the five senses: seeing, smelling, hearing, tasting, and touching. You want readers to be able to imagine that they are experiencing what you are describing. For example, you might describe a frightening experience or a stunning landscape.

PRACTICE 3

Read the paragraph and answer the questions that follow.

The last **portage** of my canoe trip was the hardest. I had been traveling through the back country of Algonquin Park for four straight days, and my shoulders were killing me. I had packed the right gear for the trip. My tent was lightweight and waterproof, the food was nutritious, and I was well hydrated. The problem was with my canoe. When choosing a canoe, I thought that I could save a dollar or two by skimping on the cost of a rental and taking an old red beater of a canoe that I had borrowed. The result of this decision was days of intense shoulder pain. To portage the canoe required that I lift it over my head and rest the cross bar on my shoulders. New canoes are designed with molded cross bars that will rest comfortably on the upper body. My canoe had a straight bar that dug into my muscles. When I mounted the canoe for the last time, it felt as though pins were being driven into my shoulders and back. The pain wore me down. My breathing was deep, and the stench of my own sweat overpowered the freshness of the northern air. My teeth were clenched together as I tried, unsuccessfully, not to think of my aching muscles. I focused on each step, my boots crunching the pine needles that covered the winding path. Occasionally, as I marched through the forest, I would try to adjust the canoe in a vain effort to lessen the pain it was inflicting. Throughout it all, I anticipated the relief that would come with the sound of the lapping water at the end of the path. I imagined the rocky edge of the lake where I could set down my burden and lay down to recover my strength for the long journey ahead. But until that gentle babbling of the water reached my ears, I could only focus on forgetting the pain.

—Stephen Laing, student

> **portage:** the act of carrying a boat and goods overland from one body of water to another

1. Underline the topic sentence.

2. The writer uses words and phrases that appeal to sight, hearing, smell, and touch. Write some words or phrases that appeal to each sentence.

Sight: _____

_____

Hearing:_____

_____

Smell:_____

_____

Touch:_____

_____

The Writer's Desk   Exploring

Think about the following questions, and write down the first ideas that come to mind. Try to write two or three ideas for each topic.

EXAMPLE: What do you remember about a difficult moment?

blackout, stuck in elevator, time I broke up with my girlfriend, when my mom

caught me smoking, when I was accused of cheating

_____

1. Where do you go when you want to relax? Think of two or three places.

   _____

   _____

   _____

2. What did you look like in the past? What fashions did you wear? What hairstyles did you have? (You might look at old photographs for inspiration.)

   _____

   _____

   _____

3. Have you ever experienced the fury of nature? What happened?

   _____

   _____

   _____

The Topic Sentence

In the **topic sentence** of a descriptive paragraph, you should convey a dominant impression about the subject. The dominant impression is the overall mood that you wish to convey. For example, the paragraph could convey an impression of tension, joy, nervousness, or anger.

topic   controlling idea

When I arrived at the secluded cabin, I felt relieved.

   **Expressing a Dominant Impression**

Sometimes, you can convey the dominant impression directly. However, you can also express it indirectly. For example, in the topic sentence "Our neighbor's yard was filled with junk," the dominant impression is *distaste*. In the body of the paragraph, you could further develop the dominant impression by including descriptions that help develop the sense of distaste. For example, you could describe the stench from a rotting pile of trash.

The Writer's Desk **Write Topic Sentences**

Write a topic sentence for each of the following topics. Your sentence should state what you are describing and express a dominant impression.

EXAMPLE:

Topic: A difficult moment

Topic sentence: *When the power went out in the elevator,*

I panicked.

1. Topic: A relaxing place

   Topic sentence: _____

   _____

2. Topic: Yourself in the past

   Topic sentence: _____

   _____

3. Topic: Nature's fury

   Topic sentence: _____

   _____

The Supporting Ideas

To create a dominant impression, think about your topic and make a list of your feelings and impressions. These details can include things that you saw, heard, smelled, tasted, or touched.

 **Hint**   **Use Interesting and Detailed Vocabulary**

In your paragraph, try to use interesting descriptive vocabulary. Avoid overused words such as *nice, bad, mean,* and *hot.* For example, instead of writing "He was mean," you might write "He was as nasty as a raging pit bull." For more information about specific and vivid language, refer to Chapter 17, Sentence Variety and Exact Language.

The Writer's Desk List Images and Impressions

Think about images, impressions, and feelings that the following topics inspire in you. Make a list under each topic.

EXAMPLE:

A difficult moment: _Stuck in_

elevator

pitch black

no sound

perspiration trickling down my back

scared and alone

stuffy air

my heart pounded

1. A relaxing place: _____

2. Yourself in the past: _____

3. Nature's fury: _____

WRITING LINK

For more information about organizing ideas using time, space, and emphatic order, see pages 22 to 27 of Chapter 2, "Developing."

A Descriptive Paragraph Plan

When you write a descriptive paragraph plan, ensure that your details are valid and that they relate to the topic sentence. You could place your details in space order, time order, or emphatic order. The order that you use depends on the topic of your paragraph. In the following plan, the details, which are in time order, appeal to the senses and develop the dominant impression.

TOPIC SENTENCE: **When the elevator jolted to a stop, I panicked.**
    Support 1:   The light in the elevator went out.
      Details: — was pitch black
    Support 2:   I was alone.
      Details: — scared
            — complete silence

Support 3:   My panic began.
  Details: — heart raced
           — pounding sounds in my ears
           — began pacing and touching the walls
Support 4:   I heard a loud banging noise.
  Details: — elevator lights came on
           — elevator began to move

The Writer's Desk **Develop Supporting Ideas**

Choose one of the topic sentences that you wrote for the Writer's Desk on page 57, and write a detailed paragraph plan. Remember to develop a dominant impression.

Topic sentence: _____

_____

Support 1: _____

  Details: _____

_____

Support 2: _____

  Details: _____

_____

Support 3: _____

  Details: _____

_____

Support 4: _____

  Details: _____

_____

The Writer's Desk **Write a Descriptive Paragraph**

You have made a list of supporting ideas for a topic. Now write a descriptive paragraph. After you finish writing, remember to revise and edit your paragraph.

WRITING LINK

See the Writer's Rooms in the following grammar chapters for more descriptive writing topics.

Chapter 11, Writer's Room topic 1 (page 209)

Chapter 19, Writer's Room topic 1 (page 304)

Chapter 21, Writer's Room topic 1 (page 331)

Chapter 23, Writer's Room topic 1 (page 357)

Chapter 25, Writer's Room topic 2 (page 382)

Chapter 26, Writer's Room topic 1 (page 392)

READING LINK

The following readings use descriptive writing.

"Fish Cheeks" by Amy Tan (page 421)

"What It Feels Like to Walk on the Moon" by Buzz Aldrin (page 447)

The Writer's Room   **Topics for Descriptive Paragraphs**

Writing Activity 1

Write a descriptive paragraph about one of the following topics.

General Topics

1. an uncomfortable room
2. a fad or fashion trend
3. a shocking experience
4. an eccentric family member
5. a messy place

College and Work-Related Topics

6. a good meeting place on campus
7. an unusual teacher from your past
8. the place where you study
9. a bad day at work
10. the style of clothing you wear to work

Writing Activity 2

Describe a celebration or ceremony that you participated in. Use words that appeal to the senses.

DESCRIPTIVE PARAGRAPH CHECKLIST

As you write your descriptive paragraph, review the paragraph checklist on the inside back cover. Also, ask yourself the following questions.

Does my topic sentence clearly show what I will describe?

Does my topic sentence make a point about the topic?

Does my paragraph have a dominant impression?

Does each body paragraph contain supporting details that may appeal to the reader's senses?

D) The Process Paragraph

A **process** is a series of steps done in chronological or emphatic order. In a **process paragraph,** you explain how to do something. For example, you might explain how to change the oil in your car, how to plan a party, or how to write a résumé. The reader should be able to follow the directions and do the process.

PRACTICE 4

Read the paragraph and answer the questions that follow.

In the biblical story "The Tower of Babel," people come together from all over the world to build a tower to Heaven but fail because they cannot communicate during the construction. Certainly, learning a new language opens the doors to the world. There are a few things you should do when you try to learn a new language. First, acquire a bilingual dictionary of your mother tongue and of the language you are learning. Be sure that the dictionary is up to date and has a good section on grammar, too. Invest in a good dictionary; you will have it for life. Also, expose yourself to the language. Watch, listen to, and read as much media as you can in the language you are learning. Practice speaking with native speakers when the opportunity presents itself. Meanwhile, be patient. Learning a new language takes time. Most importantly, you must want to learn the new language. It is through a total commitment to the process of learning a new language that you will become functional.

—Yannick Roy-Viau, student

1. Underline the topic sentence. Remember that the topic sentence may not be the first sentence in the paragraph.

2. In process paragraphs, the support is generally a series of steps. List the steps you can take to learn a new language.

_____

_____

_____

_____

3. Circle the transitional expressions that introduce each point.

4. This paragraph does not have a concluding sentence. Write a concluding sentence.

_____

_____

The Writer's Desk Exploring

Think about the following questions, and write down the first ideas that come to mind. Try to write two or three ideas for each topic.

EXAMPLE: What are some ways to find a mate?

join a club, ask your friends, be open and receptive, don't act desperate, be

yourself, use an Internet dating service

_____

1. What are some things you should do when you prepare for a move to a new place?

_____

_____

_____

2. What should you do if you want to plan a surprise party?

_____

_____

_____

3. What steps can you take to impress a date?

_____

_____

_____

The Topic Sentence

The topic sentence in a process paragraph includes the process you are describing and a controlling idea.

topic (process)   controlling idea

When you make a mosaic, there are several precautions you should take.

It is also possible to make a topic sentence that contains a map, or guide, to the details that you will present in your paragraph. To guide your readers, you can mention the main steps in your topic sentence.

topic   controlling idea

When you make a mosaic, have the proper safety equipment, tools, and workspace.

The Writer's Desk Write Topic Sentences

Write a topic sentence for each of the following topics. Your sentence should have a controlling idea that expresses the direction of the paragraph. Remember that the goal of the paragraph is to explain how to do something.

EXAMPLE:

Topic: How to find a mate

Topic sentence: *With careful preparation and screening, you can find a mate on the Internet.*

1. Topic: How to prepare for a move

   Topic sentence: _____

   _____

2. Topic: How to plan a surprise party

   Topic sentence: _____

   _____

3. Topic: How to impress a date

   Topic sentence: _____

   _____

The Supporting Ideas

When you write the supporting ideas, decide which steps your reader needs to take to complete the process. Explain each step in detail. Organize your steps chronologically. Remember to mention any necessary tools or supplies.

 **Give Steps, Not Examples**

When you explain how to do a process, describe each step. Do not simply list examples of the process.

How to Relax

List of Examples	Steps in the Process
Read a book.	Change into comfortable clothing.
Take a bath.	Do some deep breathing.
Go for a long walk.	Choose a good book.
Listen to soothing music.	Find a relaxing place to read.

A Process Paragraph Plan

When you write a process paragraph plan, decide how you will organize your plan, and ensure that you explain each step clearly. In the following paragraph plan, the writer used emphatic order to describe the process.

TOPIC SENTENCE:	**With careful preparation and screening, you can find a mate on the Internet.**
Step 1:	Prepare by finding a viable dating site.
Details:	— Ask friends about possible sites.
	— Make sure the site targets people in your area.
Step 2:	Write an interesting profile.
Details:	— Use positive terms to describe yourself, such as *dynamic* and *energetic*.
	— Get a friend or a professional to look over your profile.
Step 3:	Screen replies carefully.
Details:	— Choose your favorite responses.
	— Invite friends to help you sort potential dates.
Step 4:	Meet only in public places.
Details:	— Consider meeting in the daytime, maybe in a coffee shop.
	— Avoid alcohol (will cloud judgment).

The Writer's Desk **Develop Supporting Ideas**

Choose one of the topic sentences that you wrote for the previous Writer's Desk, and write a detailed paragraph plan.

Topic sentence: _____

_____

Support 1: _____

Details: _____

_____

Support 2: _____

Details: _____

_____

Support 3: _____

Details: _____

_____

Support 4: _____

Details: _____

_____

The Writer's Desk **Write a Process Paragraph**

You have made a list of supporting ideas for a topic. Now write a process paragraph. After you finish writing, remember to revise and edit your paragraph.

More Topics for Process Paragraphs

Writing Activity 1

Write a process paragraph about one of the following topics.

General Topics

1. how to play a specific sport
2. how to discipline a small child
3. how to find an apartment
4. how to organize your closet
5. how to listen

College and Work-Related Topics

6. how to use a particular machine
7. how to give a speech
8. how to dress for success
9. how to do an activity in your job
10. how to get fired from a job

WRITING LINK

See the Writer's Rooms in the following grammar chapters for more process writing topics.

Chapter 10, Writer's Room topic 1 (page 199)

Chapter 22, Writer's Room topic 2 (page 342)

Chapter 23, Writer's Room topic 2 (page 357)

Chapter 27, Writer's Room topic 2 (page 404)

READING LINK

The following readings contain examples of process writing.

"How to Handle Conflict" by P. Gregory Smith (page 455)

"How to Remember Names" by Roger Seit (page 457)

Writing Activity 2

Examine the photo and think about processes that you can describe. For example, you might explain how to get along with coworkers, neighbors, or family members. Other ideas include how to make friends or how to do team work.

PROCESS PARAGRAPH CHECKLIST

As you write your process paragraph, review the paragraph checklist on the inside back cover. Also, ask yourself the following questions.

Does my topic sentence make a point about the process?

Does my paragraph explain how to do something?

Do I clearly explain each step in the process?

Do I mention any supplies that my reader needs to complete the process?

Do I use transitions to connect the steps in the process?

E) The Definition Paragraph

A **definition** tells you what something means. When you write a **definition paragraph,** you give your personal definition of a term or concept. Although you can define most terms in a few sentences, you may need to offer extended definitions for words that are particularly complex. For example, you can write a paragraph or even an entire book about the term *happiness*. The way that you interpret the term is unique, and you would bring your own opinions, experiences, and impressions to your definition paragraph.

PRACTICE 5

Read the paragraph and answer the questions that follow.

The Internet has provided writers with a new method of sharing information. A blogger is a writer who expresses his or her opinions in an Internet journal. To create the word "blogger," someone likely joined the words *Web* and *logger*. Some bloggers are professional writers or journalists who want an outlet for their private opinions and feelings. Rather than striving to be objective, a blogger can rant about issues and be highly controversial or personal. Although some bloggers are well-known and have large readerships, most are just average people from all walks of life who have something to say. Thus, the blog may be aimed at a large audience or simply at family members or coworkers. Also, the content of blogs varies. Some look like personal diaries, whereas others contain insightful commentary about politics, science, and social issues. Occasionally, bloggers become famous. For example, Salam Pax is the blog name of an Iraqi interpreter. He created a vivid Web log describing his experiences before, during, and after the 2003 invasion of Iraq. He came to the attention of editors at the prestigious British newspaper, *The Guardian*, and was invited to write a bi-weekly column. The word "blogger," therefore, encompasses a variety of writers who express diverse messages.

—Pedram Sabooni, student

1. What term does the writer define? _____

2. Underline the topic sentence. Be careful; it may not be the first sentence in the paragraph.

3. List some supporting examples. _____

_____

_____

The Writer's Desk Exploring

Think about the following questions, and write down the first ideas that come to mind. Try to write two or three ideas for each topic.

EXAMPLE: What is *leet speak*?

   *Computer language; uses numbers; hackers use it*_____

1. What is a *bad hair day*? _____

_____

2. What is a *slob*? _____

_____

3. What is a *stalker*? _____

_____

The Topic Sentence

In your **topic sentence,** indicate what you are defining, and include a definition of the term. Look at the three ways to define a term.

- **Definition by synonym.** You can give a word that means the same thing as the term.

  term   +   synonyms
  Gratuitous means "unnecessary" or "uncalled for."

- **Definition by negation.** Explain what the term is not, and then explain what it is.

  term   +   what it is not   +   what it is
  Sexual harassment is not harmless banter; it is intimidating and unwanted sexual attention.

- **Definition by category.** Decide what larger group the term belongs to, and then determine the unique characteristics that set the term apart from others in that category.

  term + category   +   detail
  A blogger is a writer who expresses his or her opinions in an Internet journal.

The Writer's Desk **Write Topic Sentences**

Write a topic sentence for each of the following topics. Your sentence should have a controlling idea that expresses the direction of the paragraph. Remember that the goal of the paragraph is to define something.

EXAMPLE:

Topic: Leet speak

Topic sentence: *Leet speak is not just a passing fad; it is a unique language used by computer users.*

1. Topic: A bad hair day

   Topic sentence: _____

   _____

2. Topic: A slob

   Topic sentence: _____

   _____

3. Topic: A stalker

   Topic sentence: _____

   _____

The Supporting Ideas

A definition paragraph should include a complete definition of a term, and it should have adequate examples that support the definition. Remember to provide various types of support. Do not simply repeat the definition.

A Definition Paragraph Plan

When you write a definition paragraph plan, ensure that your details are valid and that they relate to the topic sentence.

TOPIC SENTENCE: **<u>Leet speak is not just a passing fad; it is a unique language used by computer users.</u>**

Support 1: Leet speak is not a traditional language.
 Details: —not spoken or handwritten
    —needs a keyboard

Support 2: Like all languages, leet speak reflects the culture of the user.
 Details: —created by hackers to avoid detection
    —replaces letters with numbers
    —makes communicating on the net faster

Support 3: Leet speak has pervaded cyber space.
 Details: —A Web comic, *Megatokyo*, popularized leet speak.
    —Web site communities use leet speak to express excitement.
    —Web sites have dictionaries to translate between normal script and leet speak.

The Writer's Desk   **Develop Supporting Ideas**

Choose one of the topic sentences that you wrote for the previous Writer's Desk, and write a detailed paragraph plan.

Topic sentence: _____

_____

Support 1: _____

 Details: _____

_____

Support 2: _____

 Details: _____

_____

Support 3: _____

 Details: _____

_____

The Writer's Desk **Write a Definition Paragraph**

You have made a list of supporting ideas for a topic. Now write a definition paragraph. After you finish writing, remember to revise and edit your paragraph.

WRITING LINK

See the Writer's Rooms in the following grammar chapters for more definition writing topics.

Chapter 10, Writer's Room topic 2 (page 199)

Chapter 16, Writer's Room topic 1 (page 276)

Chapter 19, Writer's Room topic 2 (page 304)

Chapter 23, Writer's Room topic 3 (page 357)

Chapter 26, Writer's Room topic 3 (page 392)

READING LINK

Definition Essays

The following readings contain examples of definition writing.

"The Hijab" by Naheed Mustafa (page 444)

"Meet the Zippies" by Thomas L. Friedman (page 460)

 The Writer's Room **Topics for Definition Paragraphs**

Writing Activity 1

Write a definition paragraph about one of the following topics.

General Topics

1. a mosh pit
2. mall rats
3. road rage
4. a mouse potato
5. a drama queen

College and Work-Related Topics

6. a golden handshake
7. hero worship
8. burnout
9. materialistic
10. an effective boss

Writing Activity 2

What is a *nest egg?* Write a paragraph explaining the term.

✔ **DEFINITION PARAGRAPH CHECKLIST**

As you write your definition paragraph, review the paragraph checklist on the inside back cover. Also, ask yourself the following questions.

☐ Does my topic sentence contain a definition by synonym, negation, or category?

☐ Do all of my supporting sentences relate to the topic sentence?

☐ Do I use concise language in my definition?

☐ Do I include enough examples to help define the term?

F) The Comparison and Contrast Paragraph

You **compare** when you want to find similarities, and you **contrast** when you want to find differences. When writing a comparison and contrast paragraph, you prove a specific point by explaining how people, places, things, or ideas are the same or different. For example, you might compare two jobs that you have had, two different ways of disciplining, or two ideas about how to stimulate the national economy.

Before you write, you must make a decision about whether you will focus on similarities, differences, or both. As you explore your topic, it is a good idea to make a list of both similarities and differences. Later, you can use some of the ideas in your paragraph plan.

PRACTICE 6

Read the next paragraph and answer the questions that follow.

There are some major differences between the supermarket and a traditional marketplace. The **cacophony** of a traditional market has given way to programmed **innocuous** music, punctuated by enthusiastically intoned commercials. A stroll through a traditional market offers an array of sensuous aromas; if you are conscious of smelling something in a supermarket, there is a problem. The life and death matter of eating, expressed in traditional markets by the sale of vegetables with stems and roots and by hanging animal carcasses, is purged from the supermarket, where food is processed somewhere else, or at least trimmed out of sight. But the most fundamental difference between a traditional market and the places through which you push your cart is that in a modern retail setting nearly all the selling is done without people. The product is totally dissociated from the personality of any particular person selling it—with the possible exception of those who appear in its advertising. The supermarket **purges** sociability because sociability slows down sales.

—Thomas Hine, "What's in a Package?"

cacophony: an unpleasant combination of sounds

innocuous: dull; inoffensive

purge: to remove or get rid of

1. Underline the topic sentence.

2. List the key features of a supermarket and a traditional market.

Supermarket	Traditional Market
_____	_____
_____	_____
_____	_____
_____	_____
_____	_____

The Writer's Desk Exploring

Think about the following questions, and write down the first ideas that come to mind. Try to write two or three ideas for each topic.

EXAMPLE: What are some key differences between you and your sibling?

Me	**My sister**
Not very fancy in my style	*Always very well dressed*
Lose my temper easily	*Very relaxed and easygoing*
Love to drive	*Doesn't have a driver's license*

1. Compare two musical eras or styles.

Type 1: _____   Type 2: _____

_____   _____

_____   _____

_____   _____

2. Compare two different jobs that you have had.

Job: _____   Job: _____

_____   _____

_____   _____

_____   _____

3. Compare what you do on two different holidays. For example, you could compare Thanksgiving and Halloween.

Holiday: _____   Holiday: _____

_____   _____

_____   _____

_____   _____

The Topic Sentence

The topic sentence in a comparison and contrast paragraph indicates whether you are making comparisons, contrasts, or both. When you write a topic sentence, indicate what you are comparing or contrasting, and express a controlling idea. The following are examples of topic sentences for comparison and contrast paragraphs.

My brother and father argue a lot, but they have very similar personalities.

Topic (what is being compared):	father and brother
Controlling idea:	similar personalities

Although women generally earn less than men, they must pay more than men do for everyday products.

Topic (what is being contrasted):	men's and women's products
Controlling idea:	women's products cost more

The Writer's Desk   Write Topic Sentences

Write a topic sentence for each of the following topics. Your sentence should have a controlling idea that expresses the direction of the paragraph.

EXAMPLE:

Topic: You and your sibling

Topic sentence: _My sister and I have radically different fashion styles._

1. Topic: Two musical eras or styles

   Topic sentence: _____

   _____

2. Topic: Two jobs

   Topic sentence: _____

   _____

3. Topic: Two holidays

   Topic sentence: _____

   _____

The Supporting Ideas

In a comparison and contrast paragraph, you can develop your supporting ideas in two different ways.

Point-by-Point Development

To develop a topic point by point, you look at similarities or differences by going back and forth from one side to the other.

Topic-by-Topic Development

To develop your ideas topic by topic, you discuss one topic in detail, and then you discuss the other topic in detail. The next plans are for a paragraph comparing two dogs.

TOPIC SENTENCE: **My two dogs are different in every way.**

Point-By-Point Comparison	Topic-By-Topic Comparison
Support 1: Appearance	Dog A: — Appearance
— Dog A	— Skills
— Dog B	— Temperament
Support 2: Skills	Dog B: — Appearance
— Dog A	— Skills
— Dog B	— Temperament
Support 3: Temperament	
— Dog A	
— Dog B	

A Comparison and Contrast Paragraph Plan

When you write a comparison and contrast paragraph plan, decide which pattern you will follow: point by point or topic by topic. Then add some details.

TOPIC SENTENCE: **My sister and I have radically different fashion styles.**

Support 1:	My sister wears expensive clothing.
Details:	— designer shirts and dresses
	— spends thousands of dollars on her shoes
Support 2:	My sister's hair is always cut and styled.
Details:	— visits a chic salon to have highlights
	— rarely has a hair out of place
Support 3:	I wear comfortable and inexpensive clothing.
Details:	— buy my clothes at discount stores
	— have comfortable but unattractive shoes
Support 4:	I like wash-and-wear hair.
Details:	— can't stand using a blow dryer
	— fluff my hair and leave it natural

The Writer's Desk Develop Supporting Ideas

Choose one of the topic sentences that you wrote for the Writer's Desk, on page 73, and write a detailed paragraph plan.

Topic sentence: _____

_____

Support 1: _____

 Details: _____

 _____

Support 2: _____

 Details: _____

 _____

Support 3: _____

 Details: _____

 _____

Support 4: _____

 Details: _____

 _____

The Writer's Desk Write a Comparison and Contrast Paragraph

You have made a list of supporting ideas for a topic. Now write a comparison and contrast paragraph. After you finish writing, remember to revise and edit your paragraph.

WRITING LINK

See the Writer's Rooms in the following grammar chapters for more comparison and contrast writing topics.

Chapter 8, Writer's Room topic 2
(page 161)

Chapter 12, Writer's Room topic 2
(page 225)

Chapter 14, Writer's Room topic 2
(page 249)

Chapter 18, Writer's Room topic 1
(page 298)

Chapter 20, Writer's Room topic 2
(page 315)

Chapter 27, Writer's Room topic 1
(page 404)

 The Writer's Room   **Topics for Comparison and Contrast Paragraphs**

Writing Activity 1

Write a comparison and contrast paragraph about one of the following topics.

General Topics

1. styles of two people in the same profession
2. two television hosts
3. two neighborhoods
4. two close friends
5. two youth subcultures

College and Work-Related Topics

6. expectations about college and the reality of college
7. a small school or college and a large school or college
8. two different coworkers
9. working alone and working in a team
10. two different bosses

READING LINK

The following readings use comparison and contrast writing.

"The New Addiction" by Josh Freed (page 436)

"The Zoo Life" by Yann Martel (page 449)

Writing Activity 2

Examine the photo, and think about things that you could compare and contrast. Some ideas might be fast food versus healthy food, street vendors versus restaurants, two restaurants, or two meals. Then write a comparison and contrast paragraph.

COMPARISON AND CONTRAST PARAGRAPH CHECKLIST

As you write your comparison and contrast paragraph, review the paragraph checklist on the inside back cover. Also, ask yourself the following questions.

Does my topic sentence explain what I am comparing or contrasting?

Does my paragraph focus on either similarities or differences?

Does my paragraph include a point-by-point or topic-by-topic pattern?

Do all of my supporting examples clearly relate to the topics that are being compared or contrasted?

G) The Cause and Effect Paragraph

Cause and effect writing explains why an event happened or what the consequences of such an event were. You often analyze the causes or effects of something. You may worry about what causes your mate to behave in a certain manner, or you may wonder about the effects of fast food on your health.

Because a paragraph is not very long, it is best to focus on either causes or effects. If you do decide to focus on both causes and effects, make sure that your topic sentence expresses your purpose to the reader.

PRACTICE 7

Read the paragraph and answer the questions that follow.

It is quite common to find university students who wait until the last minute to write a term paper or to study for an exam. However, procrastination should be avoided because it has detrimental effects on students' health and well being. First, students who procrastinate are doomed to suffer lower marks. Instead of taking the time to carefully research the subject, go over written notes, draft an outline, write a draft, and revise and edit it, students do **cursory** research and do not bother preparing an outline. The draft that results from this process is sloppy and filled with logical and grammatical errors, resulting in a poor grade. Furthermore, there are emotional **hindrances** generated by the pressured nature of rushed work. The sense of a looming deadline causes increased feelings of stress in the procrastinating student, which hinders his or her ability to concentrate. Consistent procrastinating over schoolwork combined with other everyday stresses can cause a student to break down. Finally, procrastinating students can damage their physical health. For example, many students stay up all night cramming for exams. They do not get adequate sleep, which impairs judgment and harms the body. Therefore, procrastinating can diminish a student's work, physical condition, mental condition, and academic future.

—Arthur Carlyle, student

cursory: superficial, brief

hindrances: obstacles

1. Underline the topic sentence.

2. Does the paragraph focus on causes or effects? _____

3. Who is the audience? _____

4. Circle three transitional words or phrases that lead the reader from one point to the next.

5. Using your own words, list the three causes or effects.

_____

_____

_____

The Writer's Desk Exploring

Write some possible causes and effects for the following topics. Think of two or three ideas for each topic. Then choose whether you would rather write about causes or effects.

EXAMPLE: Why do some parents spoil their children, and how does being spoiled affect the children?

Causes	**Effects**
want child to like them	*children don't appreciate material*
don't have parenting skills	*goods*
can't say no	*hurts parent–child relationship*
	children have no patience

Focus on: *Causes*

1. Why do people marry, and how does marriage affect people's lives?

Causes	**Effects**
_____	_____
_____	_____
_____	_____
_____	_____

Focus on: _____

2. What are some of the causes and effects of credit card debt?

Causes	**Effects**
_____	_____
_____	_____
_____	_____
_____	_____

Focus on: _____

3. What can cause a person to drive badly, and how can bad driving affect others?

Causes	Effects
_____	_____
_____	_____
_____	_____
_____	_____

Focus on: _____

The Topic Sentence

The topic sentence in a cause and effect paragraph must clearly demonstrate whether the focus is on causes, effects, or both.

      topic   controlling idea (causes)

I buy fast food <u>for many reasons.</u>

      topic   controlling idea (effects)

Fast food <u>has had negative effects on my health.</u>

      topic   controlling idea (causes and effects)

Fast food, <u>which I eat for many reasons,</u> <u>has had some negative effects on my health.</u>

> *Hint* **Do Not Confuse *Affect* and *Effect***
>
> *Affect* is a verb, and *effect* is a noun. *Affect* (verb) means "to influence or change," and *effect* (noun) means "the result."
>
>   verb
> Secondhand smoke can <u>affect</u> children's health.
>
>   noun
> Secondhand smoke has many negative <u>effects</u> on children's health.

The Writer's Desk **Write Topic Sentences**

Write a topic sentence for each of the following topics. Your sentence should have a controlling idea that expresses the direction of the paragraph.

EXAMPLE:

Topic: Spoiled children

Topic sentence: *Parents spoil their children for several reasons.*

1. Topic: Marriage

    Topic sentence: _____

    _____

2. Topic: Credit card debt

   Topic sentence: _____

   _____

3. Topic: Bad driving

   Topic sentence: _____

   _____

The Supporting Ideas

After you have developed an effective topic sentence, generate supporting ideas. For a cause and effect paragraph, think of examples that clearly show the causes or effects. Then arrange your examples in emphatic order. Emphatic order means that you can place your examples from the most to the least important or from the least to the most important.

A Cause and Effect Paragraph Plan

When you write a cause and effect paragraph plan, think about the order of your ideas. List details under each supporting idea.

TOPIC SENTENCE:	**Parents spoil their children for many reasons.**
Support 1:	People are not educated about good parenting skills.
Details:	— Schools do not teach how to be a good parent.
	— Some people may follow the habits of their own parents.
Support 2:	They want to be the child's friend instead of an authority figure.
Details:	— Parents won't say no.
	— Parents want to be liked.
Support 3:	They believe that children should have the best things in life.
Details:	— Parents think they are doing their children favors by buying toys, video games, and so on.
	— They feel that there is nothing wrong with instant gratification.
Support 4:	Some parents are motivated by guilt to overspend on their children.
Details:	— They spend very little time with their children.
	— Parents buy gifts, unnecessary clothing, and so on.

The Writer's Desk Develop Supporting Ideas

Choose one of the topic sentences that you wrote for the previous Writer's Desk, and write a detailed paragraph plan.

Topic sentence: _____

_____

Support 1:   _____

   Details: _____

                _____

Support 2:   _____

   Details: _____

                _____

Support 3:   _____

   Details: _____

                _____

Support 4:   _____

   Details: _____

                _____

The Writer's Desk Write a Cause and Effect Paragraph

You have made a list of supporting ideas for a topic. Now write a cause and effect paragraph. After you finish writing, remember to revise and edit your paragraph.

 The Writer's Room

Topics for Cause and Effect Paragraphs

Writing Activity 1

Write a cause and effect paragraph about one of the following topics. As you consider each topic, think about both causes and effects.

General Topics

1. losing a good friend
2. buying a car
3. having a pet
4. having plastic surgery
5. losing your temper

College and Work-Related Topics

6. participating in team sports
7. having workplace stress
8. achieving good grades
9. working with a friend, mate, or spouse
10. working nights

WRITING LINK

See the Writer's Rooms in the following grammar chapters for more cause and effect writing topics.

Chapter 6, Writer's Room topic 2 (page 129)

Chapter 7, Writer's Room topic 2 (page 148)

Chapter 13, Writer's Room topic 1 (page 241)

Chapter 15, Writer's Room topic 1 (page 262)

Chapter 22, Writer's Room topic 3 (page 342)

Chapter 24, Writer's Room topic 1 (page 368)

READING LINK

The following reading uses cause and effect writing.

"The Cult of Emaciation" by Ben Barry (page 425)

Writing Activity 2

Examine the photo. Why do people worship Hollywood actors and actresses? What are the effects of such hero worship?

CAUSE AND EFFECT PARAGRAPH CHECKLIST

As you write your cause and effect paragraph, review the paragraph checklist on the inside back cover. Also, ask yourself the following questions.

- Does my topic sentence indicate clearly that my paragraph focuses on causes, effects, or both?

- Do I have adequate supporting examples for causes and/or effects?

- Do I make logical and valid points?

- Do I use the terms *effect* and *affect* correctly?

H) The Classification Paragraph

In a **classification paragraph**, you sort a subject into more understandable categories. Each of the categories must be part of a larger group, yet they must also be distinct. For example, you might write a paragraph about different categories of housework that must be done in the kitchen, bathroom, and living room, or you could divide the topic into chores done by the children, parents, and grandparents.

To find a topic for a classification paragraph, think of something that can be sorted into different groups. Also, determine a reason for classifying the items. When you are planning your ideas for a classification paragraph, remember two points:

1. **Use a common classification principle. A classification principle** is the overall method that you use to sort the subject into categories. To find the classification principle, think about one common characteristic that unites the different categories. For example, if your subject is "relationships," your classification principle might be any of the following:
   - types of annoying dates
   - ways to meet people
   - dating alone, with another couple, or in groups
   - types of couples

2. **Sort the subject into distinct categories.** A classification paragraph should have two or more categories.

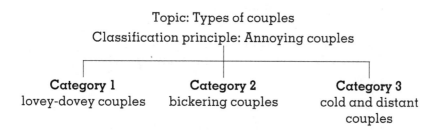

Topic: Types of couples
Classification principle: Annoying couples

Category 1 lovey-dovey couples **Category 2** bickering couples **Category 3** cold and distant couples

PRACTICE 8

Read the paragraph and answer the questions that follow.

In life, we find ourselves surrounded by many different types of friends. We have the intimate friends who are there in our day-to-day lives and who will drop everything to be with us in an emergency. These are the friends that we call after a break-up or personal tragedy, and we need a sympathetic ear. When I experience a crisis, I go to my friend Florian for help. He is a reassuring voice in my moment of suffering. The next tier of friends are our activity friends. These friends are important to us, but we only share time with them because of a common interest. We don't spend too much time together outside of that. We wouldn't call them if we needed some comfort but would rush to them if we just needed a buddy to go surfing with in the summer. My friend Anna falls into this category. During the cold months I never see her. But, once summer hits, she suddenly becomes a weekly feature in my life. We play badminton together every Friday. Come fall, we go our separate ways and rarely speak until the weather warms up. Some of our intimate friends might join us on these outings, but they are constantly involved in our lives, whereas activity friends only appear with the activities. The third tier of friends are lost friends. They are people we shared experiences with in early childhood, at school, or in a first job, but time, distance, or simply new interests conspired to separate us. If we have managed to keep in touch, it is with an infrequent e-mail or phone call. Such lost friends provide us with fond memories. These three types of friends are people who play **pivotal** roles in our lives.

pivotal: critical

—Janelle Carr, student

1. Underline the topic sentence.

2. What are the three main categories?

   _____   _____   _____

3. What is the classification principle? In other words, how are the three types of friends distinct?

   _____

4. The writer organizes her ideas using emphatic order. How does she order her friends?

   a. most distant to closest   b. closest to most distant

The Writer's Desk   Exploring

Think about the following questions, and write down the first ideas that come to mind. Try to write two or three ideas for each topic.

EXAMPLE:

What are some types of financial personalities?

cheapskates, binge spenders, sensible spenders, and squanderers

1. What are some types of pleasant smells?

   _____

   _____

2. What are some categories of eating establishments?

   _____

   _____

3. What are some different types of reality shows?

   _____

   _____

The Topic Sentence

The topic sentence in a classification paragraph clearly indicates what a writer will classify. It also includes the controlling idea, which is the classification principle that you use.

> Several types of reality shows try to manipulate the viewers.
>
> **Topic:**   reality shows
> **Classification principle:**   types that manipulate viewers

You can also mention the types of categories in your topic sentence.

> The most beautiful scenes in nature are waterfalls, pine forests, and desert landscapes.
>
> **Topic:**   scenes in nature
> **Classification principle:**   types of beautiful scenes

The Writer's Desk **Write Topic Sentences**

Write a topic sentence for each of the following topics. Your sentence should have a controlling idea that expresses the categories you will develop.

EXAMPLE:

Topic: Financial personalities

Topic Sentence: *The three types of people with irrational spending habits are cheapskates, binge spenders, and squanderers.*

1. Topic: Pleasant smells

   Topic sentence: _____

   _____

2. Topic: Eating establishments

   Topic sentence: _____

   _____

3. Topic: Reality shows

   Topic sentence: _____

   _____

The Supporting Ideas

After you have developed an effective topic sentence, generate supporting ideas. In a classification paragraph, you can list details about each of your categories.

 **Categories Should Not Overlap**

When sorting a topic into categories, make sure that the categories do not overlap. For example, you would not classify *snack foods* into sweet foods, greasy foods, and cakes because cakes are sweet foods. Each category should be distinct.

A Classification Paragraph Plan

When you write a classification plan, think of how you will organize your categories. Include different examples in each category.

TOPIC SENTENCE: **The three types of people with irrational spending habits are cheapskates, binge spenders, and squanderers.**

    Support 1: Cheapskates deprive themselves and others.

       Details: — never buy nice clothing

               — skimp on quality of food

               — never treat others

    Support 2: Binge spenders save most of the time but then overspend on crazy items.

       Details: — don't make logical choices

               — might skimp on meals but then pay a lot for a car

               — buy cheap suits but spend too much on shoes

Support 3:   The most dangerous spender is the squanderer.
Details: — might use up entire paycheck on entertainment
— can't make it to the end of the month without going broke
— constantly pays interest on loans and credit cards

Make a Classification Chart

Another way to visualize your categories and your supporting ideas is to make a detailed classification chart. Break down the main topic into several categories, and then give details about each category. A classification chart is a visual representation of your plan.

Topic sentence: The three types of people with irriational spending habits are cheapskates, binge spenders, and squanderers.

cheapstakes	binge spenders	squanderers
- deprive selves and others - never buy quality food or clothing - never treat friends or family	- skimp on food and then pay too much for a car - buy cheap suit but pay too much for shoes - illogical spending choices	- live paycheck to paycheck - buy without reflection - feed every appetite - pay a lot of interest on bank loans and credit cards

The Writer's Desk   **Develop Supporting Ideas**

Choose one of the topic sentences that you wrote for the previous Writer's Desk, and write a detailed paragraph plan. Or, if you prefer, you could make a visual classification chart on a separate sheet of paper.

Topic sentence: _____

_____

Support 1:   _____

Details: _____

_____

Support 2:   _____

Details: _____

_____

Support 3:   _____

Details: _____

_____

The Writer's Room　**Topics for Classification Paragraphs**

Writing Activity 1

Choose any of the following topics, or choose your own topic, and write a classification paragraph.

General Topics

Types of . . .

1. collectors
2. problems in a relationship
3. unhealthy foods
4. purses
5. inexpensive hobbies

College and Work-Related Topics

Types of . . .

6. uniforms
7. housing
8. workplaces
9. communicators
10. stress-coping strategies

Writing Activity 2

Examine this photo, and think about some classification topics. For example, you might discuss types of pets, types of pet owners, or types of entertainment involving animals. Then write a classification paragraph about the photo.

 CLASSIFICATION PARAGRAPH CHECKLIST

As you write your classification paragraph, review the checklist on the inside back cover. Also, ask yourself the following questions.

　Does my topic sentence explain the categories that will be discussed?

　Do I use a common classification principle to unite the various items?

　Do I offer sufficient details to explain each category?

　Do I arrange the categories in a logical manner?

　Does all of the supporting information relate to the categories that are being discussed?

　Do I include categories that do not overlap?

WRITING LINK

See the Writer's Room in the following grammar chapters for more classification writing topics.

Chapter 11, Writer's Room topic 3 (page 209)

Chapter 26, Writer's Room topic 2 (page 392)

READING LINK

Classification

The following reading uses classification writing.

"What's Your Humor Style?" by Louise Dobson (page 441)

I) The Argument Paragraph

In an **argument paragraph**, you take a position on an issue, and you try to defend your position. For example, you might argue that taxes are too high, that a restaurant is excellent, or that a certain breed of dog should be banned.

Although some people may disagree with you, try to be direct in argument writing. State your point of view clearly and unapologetically.

PRACTICE 9

Read the next paragraph and answer the questions that follow.

According to the Children's Defense Fund Action Council, about 3,300 children and teens are killed by gunfire in the United States every year, and close to 15,000 children are injured by firearms. To stem the tide of gun-related deaths and injuries, public schools should teach gun-safety courses. First, guns are **prevalent** in our society, and we cannot stop children from being fascinated with them. Even if parents have no guns in their homes, their children could come across a gun in a friend's home or on the street. Second, children who understand the danger of guns will not be so attracted to weapons. If a child is permitted to hold a gun, feel its kick, hear its deafening blast, and witness its destructiveness, he or she will realize how hazardous a gun is. Furthermore, if children know how to use guns responsibly, there will be fewer gun accidents. An uninformed child may not realize that a gun is loaded or that the safety catch is off. After taking a gun safety course, that same child would immediately recognize that a gun is ready to fire and extremely dangerous. If children are not properly educated about gun use, the numbers of accidental deaths and injuries will rise.

—Dean Cochrane, student

prevalent: widespread

1. Underline the topic sentence.

2. How does the author prove that there is a problem? _____

_____

_____

_____

3. What are the three main arguments? _____

_____

_____

_____

_____

4. What are some transitional expressions that the writer uses? _____

_____

5. How does the writer conclude his paragraph?

   a. A prediction   b. A quotation   c. A suggestion

The Writer's Desk Exploring

Think about the following questions, and write down the first ideas that come to mind. Try to write two or three ideas for each topic.

EXAMPLE: Should any dog breeds be banned?

I don't really know, maybe pit bulls. They have a bad reputation.

What else? Dobermans? Maybe the problem is with the owners.

1. Is college beneficial? Does it really change people's lives? Explain your answer.

_____

_____

_____

2. What do you think about the legal drinking age? Is it useful? Should it be raised or lowered?

_____

_____

_____

3. Is it a good idea to have a workplace romance? Why or why not?

_____

_____

_____

The Topic Sentence

The **topic sentence** in an argument paragraph mentions the subject and a debatable point of view about the subject. You can use *should, must,* or *ought to* in your topic sentence.

           controlling idea   topic (issue)

<u>Our police forces should not use</u> **racial profiling.**

Your topic sentence can further guide your readers by listing the specific arguments you will make in the paragraph.

     controlling idea   topic (issue)   argument 1

<u>Parents should not</u> **spank their children** because it is a violent act,

      argument 2   argument 3

it scares children, and it teaches children to become violent.

 **Write a Debatable Topic Sentence**

Your topic sentence should be a debatable statement. It should not be a fact or a statement of opinion.

Fact: Some breeds of dogs can be aggressive.

          (Who can argue with that point?)

Opinion: I think that pit bulls should be banned.

          (This is a statement of opinion. Nobody can deny that you want pit bulls to be banned. Do not use phrases such as *In my opinion, I think,* or *I believe* in your topic sentence.)

Argument: Pit bulls should be banned.

          (This statement is debatable.)

The Writer's Desk Write Topic Sentences

Write a topic sentence for each of the following topics. Your sentence should have a controlling idea that expresses the direction of the paragraph. Remember that the goal of the paragraph is to express your viewpoint.

EXAMPLE:

Topic: Banning a dog breed

Topic sentence: *Pit bulls should be banned for several reasons.*

1. Topic: Benefits of college

   Topic sentence: _____

   _____

2. Topic: Changing the legal drinking age

   Topic sentence: _____

   _____

3. Topic: Workplace romance

   Topic sentence: _____

   _____

The Supporting Ideas

In the body of your paragraph, give convincing supporting arguments. Try to use several types of supporting evidence such as anecdotes, facts and statistics, and answers to the opposition.

- **Anecdotes** are specific experiences or stories that support your point of view.
- **Facts** are statements that can be verified in some way. **Statistics** are a type of fact. When you use a fact, ensure that your source is reliable.
- Think about your opponents' arguments, and provide **answers to the opposition** in response to their arguments.

 **Avoid Circular Reasoning**

Circular reasoning means that a paragraph restates its main point in various ways but does not provide supporting details. Avoid it by offering separate supporting ideas and precise examples.

Circular

Film actors, who lead decadent lives, should not earn huge salaries because so many average people struggle. Many ordinary folks work long hours and have trouble making ends meet. Some actors work only a few months, earn millions, and then buy ridiculous luxury items. They lose touch with reality. Film studios should cut actors' high salaries and then disburse the remaining amount to people who really need the money.

Improved

Film actors, who often lead decadent lives, should not earn huge salaries while so many average people struggle. Many ordinary folks, **such as teachers and nurses,** work long hours and have trouble making ends meet. **Yet, actor Tom Cruise's $20-million-per-movie salary is more than the combined wages of a small city's police department.** Also, some actors lose touch with reality. **Consider the difference between John Travolta, who flies a private jet, and caregiver Luisa Moreno, who spends $18.40 a day commuting on public buses. And, in a nation with so much homelessness, actress Demi Moore owns a house that holds her doll collection.** Film studios should cut actors' high salaries and then disburse the remaining amount to people who really need the money.

An Argument Paragraph Plan

When you write an argument paragraph plan, think about how you will organize your arguments. If possible, include different types of supporting evidence: facts, statistics, anecdotes, and answers to the opposition.

TOPIC SENTENCE:	**Pit bulls should be banned from our town for several reasons.**
Support 1:	Pit bulls often attack people.
Details:	— Three children in my state have been maimed or killed by pit bulls.
	— The dogs have attacked owners.
Support 2:	Pit bulls sometimes seem to "snap."
Details:	— The dogs sometimes attack without provocation.
	— Some experts believe improper breeding has caused chemical "misfiring" in the brains of pit bulls.
Support 3:	They are difficult to control when they become aggressive.
Details:	— Their jaws clench tightly on the victim in a vise-like grip.
	— They have immensely powerful bodies.

The Writer's Desk   Develop Supporting Ideas

Choose one of the topic sentences that you wrote for the previous Writer's Desk, and write a paragraph plan. Include supporting arguments, and list a detail for each argument.

Topic sentence: _____

_____

Support 1: _____

   Details: _____

         _____

Support 2: _____

   Details: _____

         _____

Support 3: _____

   Details: _____

         _____

Support 4: _____

   Details: _____

         _____

The Writer's Desk   Write an Argument Paragraph

You have made a list of supporting ideas for a topic. Now write an argument paragraph. After you finish writing, remember to revise and edit your paragraph.

 The Writer's Room   **Topics for Argument Paragraphs**

Writing Activity 1

Write an argument paragraph about one of the following topics. Remember to narrow your topic and to follow the writing process.

General Topics

1. length of compulsory schooling
2. watching too much television
3. wearing fur coats
4. right to privacy for politicians or celebrities
5. divorce

College and Work-Related Topics

6. an unfair college rule
7. lowering college fees
8. compulsory art courses in college
9. vending machines in schools
10. compulsory voting

WRITING LINK

See the Writer's Rooms in the following grammar chapters for more argument writing topics.

Chapter 6, Writer's Room topic 3 (page 129)

Chapter 7, Writer's Room topic 1 (page 148)

Chapter 13, Writer's Room topic 2 (page 241)

Chapter 15, Writer's Room topics 2 and 3 (page 262)

Chapter 16, Writer's Room topic 2 (page 276)

Chapter 17, Writer's Room topic 2 (page 287)

Chapter 18, Writer's Room topic 2 (page 298)

Chapter 24, Writer's Room topic 2 (page 368)

Writing Activity 2

Write an argument paragraph explaining the benefits or disadvantages of day care centers.

READING LINK

The following readings use argument writing.

"For Marriage" by Kirsteen Macleod (page 429)

"Against Marriage" by Winston Murray (page 430)

✔ ARGUMENT PARAGRAPH CHECKLIST

As you write your argument paragraph, review the paragraph checklist on the inside back cover. Also, ask yourself the following questions.

Does my topic sentence clearly state my position on the issue?

Do I support my position with facts, examples, or answers to the opposition?

Do my supporting arguments provide evidence that directly supports the topic sentence?

How Do I Get a Better Grade?

Visit www.mywritinglab.com for audio-visual lectures and additional practice sets about paragraph patterns.

mywritinglab

Get a better grade with MyWritingLab!

PART II

The Editing Handbook

Why Grammar Is Important

Clear writing begins with a well-developed sentence. At the very least, a sentence needs a noun or pronoun and a verb. However, a sentence can become richer when it also includes adjectives, adverbs, conjunctions, interjections, or prepositions.

Clear writing also requires grammatically correct sentences. If your writing contains errors in grammar, you may distract readers from your message, and they may focus, instead, on your inability to communicate clearly. To improve your writing skills, it is useful to understand how the English language works. When your knowledge of grammar conventions increases, you will be better able to identify and correct errors in your writing.

In the Editing Handbook, you will learn to spot errors and you will also learn about the underlying rule that applies to each error.

SECTION 1 Some Parts of Speech THEME: Human History and Habits

CHAPTER 6 Nouns, Determiners, and Prepositions page 112
Chapter topics: primates and early humans

CHAPTER 7 Pronouns page 130
Chapter topic: issues related to food

SECTION 2 Problems with Verbs THEME: Entertainment and Culture

CHAPTER 8 Subjects and Verbs page 150
Chapter topics: music and musicians

CHAPTER 9 Present and Past Tenses page 162
Chapter topics: literature and the media

CHAPTER 10 Past Participles page 181
Chapter topics: television and film

CHAPTER 11 Progressive Tenses page 201
Chapter topics: artists and issues in the art world

CHAPTER 12 Other Verb Forms page 211
Chapter topic: cultural differences

SECTION 3 Verb Agreement and Consistency THEME: Beliefs

CHAPTER 13 Subject-Verb Agreement page 227
Chapter topics: mysteries and urban legends

CHAPTER 14 Tense Consistency page 243
Chapter topics: religious beliefs, fortune tellers, and astrology

SECTION 4 Effective Sentences THEME: Politics

CHAPTER 15 Compound Sentences page 251
Chapter topics: political history and great leaders

CHAPTER 16 Complex Sentences page 264
Chapter topic: political activists

CHAPTER 17 Sentence Variety and Exact
Language   page 277
Chapter topic: political scandals

SECTION 5 Common Sentence Errors THEME: The Earth and Beyond

CHAPTER 18 Fragments   page 289
Chapter topic: hazardous
chemical substances

CHAPTER 19 Run-Ons   page 299
Chapter topics: volcanoes
and the diamond trade

CHAPTER 20 Faulty Parallel Structure   page 306
Chapter topics: astronomy,
conspiracy theories, and space tourism

SECTION 6 Modifiers THEME: Relationships

CHAPTER 21 Adjectives and Adverbs   page 316
Chapter topic: famous couples
in history and literature

CHAPTER 22 Mistakes with Modifiers   page 333
Chapter topics: Internet dating
and workplace romances

SECTION 7 Word Use and Spelling THEME: Creatures Large and Small

CHAPTER 23 Spelling   page 344
Chapter topics: zoos and
animal conservationists

CHAPTER 24 Commonly Confused Words   page 359
Chapter topics: pet ownership
and exotic animals

SECTION 8 Punctuation and Mechanics THEME: The Business World

CHAPTER 25 Commas   page 370
Chapter topics: job searching
and unusual jobs

CHAPTER 26 The Apostrophe   page 383
Chapter topic: controversies
in the business world

CHAPTER 27 Quotation Marks and Capitalization page 394
Chapter topic: business success stories

6 Nouns, Determiners, and Prepositions

Section Theme: **HUMAN HISTORY AND HABITS**

CONTENTS

- Nouns
- Count Nouns and Noncount Nouns
- Determiners
- Prepositions

In this chapter, you will read about topics related to primates and early humans.

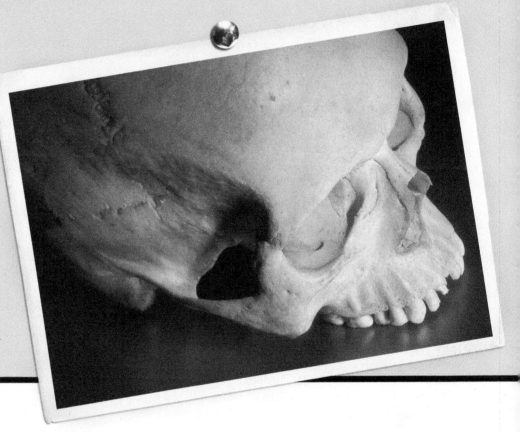

Grammar Snapshot

Looking at Nouns, Determiners, and Prepositions

In her essay "My Body Is My Own Business," Naheed Mustafa recounts her reasons for wearing the hijab. In the following excerpt, the nouns, determiners, and prepositions are underlined or printed in **bold** type.

> Young Muslim **women** are reclaiming the **hijab**, reinterpreting it in **light** of its original **purpose**—to give back to **women** ultimate **control** of their own **bodies**. The **Qur'an** teaches us that **men** and **women** are equal, that **individuals** should not be judged according to **gender**, **beauty**, **wealth**, or **privilege**.

In this chapter, you will identify and write nouns, determiners, and prepositions.

Nouns

Nouns are words that refer to people, places, or things. Nouns are divided into common nouns and proper nouns.

- **Common nouns** refer to general people, places, or things. Each begins with a lowercase letter. For example, *books, computer,* and *village* are common nouns.
- **Proper nouns** refer to particular people, places, or things. Each begins with a capital letter. For example, *Margaret Mead, the Amazon,* and *Thanksgiving* are proper nouns.

Singular and Plural Nouns

Nouns are either singular or plural. A **singular noun** refers to one of something, while a **plural noun** refers to more than one of something. Regular plural nouns end in *-s* or *-es*.

	Singular	**Plural**
People:	father	fathers
	sister	sisters
Places:	town	towns
	room	rooms
Things:	dish	dishes
	chair	chairs

 **Adding -es**

When a noun ends in *-s, -x, -ch, -sh,* or *-z*, add *-es* to form the plural.

wish–wish**es**   box–box**es**   batch–batch**es**

Irregular Plural Nouns

Irregular plural nouns do not end in *-s* or *-es*. Here are some common irregular nouns.

Singular	**Plural**	**Singular**	**Plural**
child	children	mouse	mice
foot	feet	person	people
goose	geese	tooth	teeth
man	men	woman	women

Other Plural Noun Forms

Some nouns use other rules to form the plural. It is a good idea to memorize both the rules and the exceptions.

1. For nouns ending in *f,* or *fe*, change the *f* to *v* and add *-es*.

Singular	**Plural**	**Singular**	**Plural**
life	li**ves**	self	sel**ves**
thief	thie**ves**	shelf	shel**ves**

Some exceptions: belief, beliefs; roof, roofs.

2. For nouns ending in a consonant + *y*, change the *y* to *i* and add *-es*.

Singular	Plural	Singular	Plural
baby	babies	cherry	cherries
berry	berries	lady	ladies

If a vowel comes before the final *y*, simply add *-s*.

Singular	Plural	Singular	Plural
boy	boys	key	keys

3. Some nouns remain the same in both singular and plural forms.

Singular	Plural	Singular	Plural
deer	deer	moose	moose
fish	fish	sheep	sheep

4. Some nouns are thought of as being only plural and therefore have no singular form.

Only Plural

clothes	goods	proceeds	scissors
eyeglasses	pants	savings	tweezers

5. Some nouns are **compound nouns,** or nouns with two or more words. To form the plural of compound nouns, add *-s* or *-es* to the last word of the compound noun.

Singular	Plural	Singular	Plural
graphic art	graphic arts	test tube	test tubes
human being	human beings	water pump	water pumps

If the first word in a hyphenated compound noun is a noun, add *-s* to the noun.

Singular	Plural	Singular	Plural
attorney-at-law	attorneys-at-law	passer-by	passers-by
brother-in-law	brothers-in-law	runner-up	runners-up

6. Some nouns that are borrowed from Latin keep the plural form of the original language.

Singular	Plural	Singular	Plural
alumnus	alumni	medium	media
datum	data	phenomenon	phenomena

 **Persons versus People**

There are two plural forms of *person. People* is the common plural form.

Some **people** love to visit museums. Many **people** like to see the dinosaur exhibit.

Persons is used only in a legal or official context.

The dinosaur skeleton was stolen by **persons** unknown.

PRACTICE I

Fill in each blank with either the singular or plural form of the noun. If both the
singular and the plural forms are the same, put an *X* in the space.

Singular	Plural
EXAMPLES:	
lottery	_____
_____	pants
1. child	_____
2. shelf	_____
3. _____	phenomena
4. sister-in-law	_____
5. community	_____
6. _____	media
7. _____	shorts
8. deer	_____
9. calf	_____
10. _____	goggles
11. tooth	_____
12. _____	scarves
13. _____	sunglasses
14. high school	_____
15. credit card	_____
16. _____	strawberries
17. factory	_____
18. _____	human rights
19. _____	data
20. person	_____

PRACTICE 2

Each sentence contains an incorrect plural noun form. Correct the errors.

EXAMPLE:

societies
Anthropologists study human beings and their ~~societys~~.

1. Traditionally, mens have dominated the field of anthropology.

2. However, one famous anthropologist, Margaret Mead, was a women.

3. She wanted to study the everyday lifes of people in other cultures.

4. After she completed her university studys, she went to American Samoa to study adolescent girls.

5. Then she traveled to New Guinea where she studied young childs at play.

6. She also used binocular to observe landscapes.

7. In Mead's notebook, she wrote notes and drew sketch of the people that she observed.

8. She published many books and articles that allowed American persons to understand different cultures.

9. After her death in 1978, the Library of Congress received Mead's enormous research collection and her personal diarys.

Hint   **Key Words for Singular and Plural Nouns**

• Use a singular noun after words such as *a, an, one, each, every,* and *another.*

As **a** young girl, Margaret Mead lived in Philadelphia.

Every paleontologist must examine **each** fossil very carefully.

• Use a plural noun after words such as *two, all, both, many, few, several,* and *some.*

Many anthropologists have benefited from Mead's research.

Some journalists interviewed her.

PRACTICE 3

Underline the key words that help to determine whether the noun in each sentence is singular or plural. Then, correct the errors in singular and plural nouns.

EXAMPLE:

Anthropologists have examined several case study of ancient humans.

1. Human history contains many story of famous hoaxes.

2. But historians generally agree that one hoaxes was very interesting.

3. In 1911, in Piltdown, England, some workers digging a hole found several fossil.

4. Many researcher believed that the fossils belonged to one individual and were the missing link between humans and their early ancestors.

5. One famous paleontologist spent five year researching this individual, whom researchers referred to as Piltdown man.

6. In 1925, a paleontologist, Raymond Dart, found a fossils in South Africa.

7. He called it the Taung child and believed that his discovery was another links in human evolution.

8. Few scientist believed him because his discovery did not match the information obtained from Piltdown man.

9. Technology progressed, and each new chemical testing methods proved that the Piltdown fossil was younger than paleontologists had thought.

10. By 1952, two mans named Oakley and Weiner proved that Piltdown man was a fake and was only between 520 and 720 years old.

 **Hint** **Plural Nouns Follow "*of the*" Expressions**

Use a plural noun after expressions such as *one of the, all of the, each of the,* and so on.

One of the most famous **anthropologists** in the twentieth century was Louis Leakey.

PRACTICE 4

Correct ten errors with singular and plural nouns.

EXAMPLE:

subjects
Anthropology is one of the most interesting ~~subject~~ to study.

1. Anthropology has several subfields. One of the branch is the study of primate behavior. Primates such as chimpanzees and apes exhibit behavior that has many similarity to human behavior. Two of the most famous

primatologist are Jane Goodall and Dian Fossey. Both womans did their fieldwork in Africa under the supervision of Louis Leakey. They have made important contributions to the field of primatology.

2.   Several scientists regarded Jane Goodall's research methods as unconventional. For example, she gave names to all of the chimpanzee that she studied. Dr. Goodall was also the first primatologist to observe that chimpanzees used some tool.

3.   Dian Fossey studied the mountain gorillas in East Africa. She observed several groups of gorilla family. Each groups was led by a dominant male called a silverback. The silverback protects the group from predators and leads the group to food sources.

4.   Because of Fossey's research, international interest in the lifes of mountain gorillas has grown. Unfortunately, mountain gorillas are an endangered species because of poaching. Fossey attempted to defeat poachers, but she was viciously murdered in 1985 at her camp. Most person believe that she was murdered by poachers.

Count Nouns and Noncount Nouns

In English, nouns are grouped into two types: count nouns and noncount nouns.

- **Count nouns** refer to people or things that can be counted, such as *car, book,* or *boy.* Count nouns have both a singular and a plural form.

    Louisa read **one** <u>book</u> about the life of Margaret Mead.

    Her anthropology professor wrote **five** <u>books</u> about language development.

- **Noncount nouns** refer to things that cannot be counted because they cannot be divided, such as *education* or *paint.* Noncount nouns generally have only the singular form.

    Traditional Samoan <u>clothing</u> is different from traditional Western <u>dress</u>.

    Archeologists have gathered a lot of <u>information</u> on Samoan culture.

To express a noncount noun as a count noun, you would have to refer to it in terms of *types, varieties,* or *amounts.*

    Anthropologists do many different <u>types of research</u>.

The next table shows some common noncount nouns.

Common Noncount Nouns

Categories of Objects		Food	Nature	Substances
clothing	machinery	bread	earth	chalk
equipment	mail	fish	electricity	charcoal
furniture	money	honey	fire	hair
homework	music	meat	water	ink
luggage	software	milk	wind	paint

Abstract Nouns

advice	effort	information	progress	violence
attention	evidence	knowledge	proof	
behavior	health	luck	research	

PRACTICE 5

Change each word in italics to the plural form, if necessary. If you cannot use the plural form, write an *X* in the space.

EXAMPLE:

There are many *theory* ___ies___ about the origins of human beings.

1. Africa is the home of many archeological *discovery* _____.

2. In 1974, Dr. Donald Johanson and his student, Tom Gray, were searching a *gully* _____ in Ethiopia when they noticed some *bone* _____.

3. They paid careful *attention* _____ to the area when they did their *research* _____.

4. Within two *week* _____, they had found several bone *fossil* _____ belonging to one *individual* _____.

5. They used special *equipment* _____ to date the skeleton.

6. The skeleton, which archaeologists named Lucy, was over 3 million *year* _____ old.

7. Named after the Beatles song "Lucy in the Sky with Diamonds," Lucy provided a lot of *information* _____ about hominids.

8. *Hominid* refers to all human *species* _____ that developed after humans branched out from the apes.

9. The skeleton provided *evidence* _____ that Lucy was an adult female weighing around sixty-five *pound* _____.

CHAPTER 6

10. Currently, researchers use *mold* _____ of her bones for scientific study, while the real Lucy is kept at the National Museum in Addis Ababa, Ethiopia.

Determiners

Determiners are words that identify or determine whether a noun is specific or general.

The chimpanzee named Moe used **a** twig as his tool.

You can use many words from different parts of speech as determiners.

Articles:	a, an, the
Indefinite pronouns:	any, all, both, each, either, every, few, little, many, several
Demonstrative pronouns:	this, that, these, those, such
Numbers:	one, two, three

A, An, The

Some determiners can be confusing because you can use them only in specific circumstances. *A* and *an* are general determiners, and *the* is a specific determiner.

         general   specific

I want to watch <u>a</u> new film. <u>The</u> films in that collection are fascinating.

- Use *a* and *an* before singular count nouns but not before plural or noncount nouns.

       singular count noun   noncount noun

Dr. Johanson drove <u>a</u> **jeep.** He made quick **progress** in his work.

 **A or An**

- Use *a* before words that begin with a consonant (*a* man, *a* house).

  Exception: When *u* sounds like *you*, put *a* before it (*a* uniform, *a* university).

- Use *an* before words that begin with a vowel (*an* exhibit, *an* umbrella.)

  Exception: When *h* is silent, put *an* before it (*an* hour, *an* honest man).

- Use *the* before nouns that refer to a specific person, place, or thing.

  <u>The</u> anthropologist, Dr. Johanson, found <u>the</u> skeleton of Lucy.

 **Avoid Overusing *The***

Do not use *the* before nouns that refer to certain types of things or places.

Languages:	He studies ~~the~~ Swahili.
Sports:	We played ~~the~~ football.
Most cities and countries:	Lucy was found in ~~the~~ Ethiopia.
Exceptions:	*the* United States, *the* Netherlands

PRACTICE 6

Write either *a, an,* or *the* in the space before each noun. If no determiner is necessary, write *X* in the space.

EXAMPLE:

During ___*the*___ Victorian Age, Charles Darwin wrote about
___*X*___ natural selection.

1. _____ Charles Darwin (1809–1882) was _____ English naturalist. He is famous for his theories on _____ evolution of the species. He believed that life forms have evolved over millions of years from _____ small number of sources.

2. From 1831 to 1836, Darwin sailed around _____ world on _____ *H.M.S. Beagle*. He collected _____ variety of species of _____ plants and _____ animals because he wanted to do _____ research. While on _____ voyage, Darwin gathered a lot of data about _____ natural world. Upon his return to _____ England, he developed his theory that _____ life on _____ earth has evolved over millions of years. In 1859, he published his work *The Origin of Species*. The book contained _____ information on natural selection.

3. _____ book was an immediate bestseller. However, it also caused great controversy. _____ Church of England and some scientists criticized it because it conflicted with _____ religious beliefs. But many supporters of his work referred to _____ book as _____ great milestone in _____ human knowledge.

Many, Few, Much, Little

Use *many* and *few* with count nouns.

> Many **anthropologists** have tried to find the origins of human beings, but few **experts** have found complete skeletons.

Use *much* and *little* with noncount nouns.

> Dr. Meghana Kale spent much **time** and very little **money** doing important research.

This, That, These, Those

Both *this* and *these* refer to things that are physically close to the speaker in time or place. Use *this* before singular nouns and *these* before plural nouns.

> These **days,** many articles are written about fossils. This **article** in my bag is about some new discoveries in Siberia.

Use *that* and *those* to refer to things that are physically distant from the speaker in time or place. Use *that* before singular nouns and *those* before plural nouns.

In the 1970s, anthropologists traveled to Africa. In those **years,** many anthropologists did groundbreaking fieldwork. In that **building,** there is some very old equipment for dating fossils.

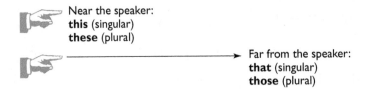

Near the speaker:
this (singular)
these (plural)

Far from the speaker:
that (singular)
those (plural)

PRACTICE 7

Underline the best determiner in each set of parentheses. If no determiner is needed, underline the *X*.

EXAMPLE:

There are not (<u>many</u>, much) gorillas in the wild.

1.   (A, The, X) hundred years ago, there were thousands of mountain gorillas in (the, X) Africa. At (this, that) time, gorilla habitats were isolated. Later, war, environmental destruction, and hunting contributed to (X, the) decline in gorilla populations.

2.   In (a, X, the) 1970s, poachers killed (much, many) gorillas and used gorilla hands as ashtrays. In (these, those) days, primatologist Dian Fossey worked hard to prevent the slaughter of the gorillas.

3.   Recently, there has been (a, the) resurgence in gorilla poaching. (Much, Many) attention has been focused on the problem. (These, Those) days, there are only about 660 mountain gorillas left in Africa. In (X, the) Rwanda, for example, very (few, little) gorillas remain.

4.   Currently, (much, many) poachers kill adult female gorillas and then sell (a, the) baby gorillas to wealthy collectors. Since (the, X) 1972, no gorillas have been taken from (a, the) wild and brought to zoos in (the, X) North America. However, there are (many, much) dealers who collect (a, the) rare animals. Recently, (a, the) Nigerian dealer asked for $1.6 million for four baby gorillas. To date, authorities have had (few, little) success in combating (a, the, X) gorilla-poaching problem.

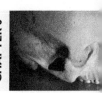

PRACTICE 8

Correct ten errors with singular nouns, plural nouns, and determiners.

EXAMPLE:

$$\text{finds}$$

One of the most exciting ~~find~~ of Stone Age Europeans is Oetzi.

1.   In 1991, hikers discovered an body in the Alps. At first, the hikers
     thought that it was the body of someone who had had a accident in the
     mountains. Using special equipments, scientists examined the body
     and realized that it was a 5,300-year-old mummy. The man, whom
     archeologists named Oetzi, was found in a valley between the Austria
     and Italy. The hikers who found Oetzi received very few money as a
     reward.

2.   Although many ancient mummy are found in Egypt and Peru, Oetzi
     is the oldest mummy in the world. He is now displayed in a museum in
     Bolzano, Italy. Oetzi is surrounded by blocks of ices to preserve his body.
     The scientists have made several discovery about him. They know that he
     died from a wound by a arrow. Oetzi was also carrying much tools,
     including a copper axe, a bow, and several arrows.

Prepositions

Prepositions are words that show concepts such as time, place, direction, and
manner. They show connections or relationships between ideas. Some common
prepositions are *about, around, at, before, behind, beside, between, for, in, of, on, to,
toward,* and *with.*

>   Anthropologists go **to** many different areas **for** their work.
>
>   **In** the spring, my brother will travel **to** Papua, New Guinea.
>
>   He will go **with** a group **of** other anthropologists.

Prepositions of Time and Place

Generally, as a description of a place or time becomes more precise, you move
from *in* to *on* to *at.*

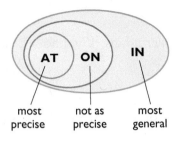

| most precise | not as precise | most general |

Preposition	Prepositions of Time	Prepositions of Place
in	in a year (in 2009) in a month (in October) in the morning, afternoon, evening in the spring, summer, fall, winter	in a city, country, etc. (in New Orleans, in China, in Central America)
on	on a day of the week (on Tuesday) on a specific date (on March 19) on a specific holiday (on Memorial Day) on my birthday on time ("punctual")	on a specific street (on Main Street) on a planet (on Venus) on certain technological devices (on TV, on the radio, on the phone, on the computer) on top
at	at a specific time of day (at 1:30) at night at breakfast, lunch, dinner	at a specific address (at 32 Cardinal Crescent) at a specific building (at the hotel)
from . . . to	from one time to another (from 10 am to 6 pm)	from one place to another (from New York to Miami)
for	for a period of time (for two hours)	for a distance (for five miles)

 **To versus At**

- Use *to* after verbs that indicate movement from one place to another.

   go to   walk to   run to   move to   return to

   Exception: Do not put *to* directly before *home*.

   I'll go ~~to~~ home with you. I won't go to his home.

- Use *at* after verbs that indicate being in one place (and not moving from one place to another).

   wait at   stay at   sit at   look at   work at

PRACTICE 9

Underline the correct prepositions in parentheses. If no preposition is needed, underline the *X*.

EXAMPLE:

(<u>In</u>, On, At) Kenya, Louis Leakey learned to speak Kikuyu.

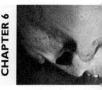

1. The famous anthropologist Louis Leakey was born (at, in) British East Africa, which is now called Kenya, (in, on) 1903.

2. He traveled (at, to) England, where he studied anthropology (at, on) Cambridge University, but he longed to go (X, at) home.

3. He returned (in, to) Africa because he believed that it was the birthplace of early humans.

4. He searched for fossils (in, on) the Olduvai Gorge (in, on) Kenya (in, for) twenty years without finding anything.

5. Eventually Leakey and his wife Mary discovered fossils (at, in) the site.

6. One day (in, on) 1959, Mary went for a walk (in, at) 6:00 (in, on) the morning and found a skull that was 1.8 million years old.

7. The couple became famous and gave interviews that were broadcast (at, in, on) the radio.

8. (From, In) approximately 1949 (in, to) 1952, Leakey also spied for the British government.

9. Leakey died of a heart attack and was buried (in, on) October 4, 1972, (at, in) Kenya.

 **For versus During**

Sometimes people confuse the prepositions *for* and *during* because both indicate that an activity happened over a period of time. However, these words are not interchangeable. Use *during* to explain when something happened. Use *for* to explain how long it took to happen.

> The tourist shop closed **for** two hours **during** the blackout.

> The environmentalists protested **for** six hours **during** the economic summit.

PRACTICE 10

Correct six errors with prepositions.

EXAMPLE:

for
My sister and I went scuba diving ~~during~~ three hours.

Many people travel at exotic destinations for their holidays. Last year, my family and I flew on a small island in the Caribbean during a week. We were there on November. Each morning we went to the beach. We did some snorkeling during two hours. We tried not to disturb the fish. After snorkeling, we returned at our hotel.

Common Prepositional Expressions

Many common expressions contain prepositions. A preposition can follow an adjective or a verb. These types of expressions usually express a particular meaning.

Example: This morning, I <u>listened **to**</u> the radio.

The next list contains some of the most common prepositional expressions.

accuse (somebody) of	dream of	prepared for
acquainted with	escape from	prevent (someone) from
add to	excited about	protect (someone) from
afraid of	familiar with	proud of
agree with	feel like	provide (someone) with
angry about	fond of	qualify for
angry with	forget about	realistic about
apologize for	forgive (someone) for	refer to
apply for	friendly with	related to
approve of	good for	rely on
argue with	grateful for	rescue from
ask for	happy about	responsible for
associate with	hear about	sad about
aware of	hope for	satisfied with
believe in	hopeful about	scared of
belong to	innocent of	search for
capable of	insist on	similar to
care about	insulted by	specialize in
care for	interested in	stop (something) from
commit to	introduce to	succeed in
comply with	jealous of	take advantage of
concerned about	keep from	take care of
confronted with	located in	thank (someone) for
consist of	long for	think about
count on	look forward to	think of
deal with	opposed to	tired of
decide on	participate in	upset about
decide to	patient with	upset with
depend on	pay attention to	willing to
disappointed about	pay for	wish for
disappointed with	pray for	worry about

CHAPTER 6

PRACTICE 11

Write the correct prepositions in the following sentences. Use the preceding list of common prepositional expressions to help you.

EXAMPLE:

Paolo belonged _____*to*_____ a travel club.

1.   More and more people are interested _____ adventure travel. They want to participate _____ white water rafting, mountain climbing, and other dangerous activities. For example, shark diving is popular in Australia, the Bahamas, and California. The divers are not afraid _____ sharks. They look forward _____ viewing marine life.

2.   Why do people like adventure tourism? Some people long _____ an adrenaline rush. Others want to associate _____ wildlife. Often, tourists are bored, and they dream _____ an escape _____ their routine lives. They get excited _____ swimming with dolphins or scaling a mountain peak because they want to challenge themselves.

3.   In Rwanda and Uganda, some agencies specialize _____ gorilla trekking. The trek consists _____ a six-hour hike to heights in excess of 7,500 feet. Tourists are not prevented _____ getting close to the wild beasts. They must be willing _____ spend over $3,000 for a one-week adventure. Cash-strapped countries in Central Africa depend _____ the foreign dollars that gorilla trekking provides.

4.   Some adventure tourists are concerned _____ the impact of their actions on the environment. However, others are not aware _____ the fragile ecosystems that they may disrupt. For example, tourists are not supposed to disturb coral reefs, but sometimes they do not pay attention _____ the rules of conservation. Perhaps adventure tourists should consider the impact of tourism on local cultures.

CHAPTER 6

FINAL REVIEW

A. Correct fourteen errors in singular and plural nouns and determiners.

evidence

EXAMPLE: Paleontologists have discovered a lot of ~~evidences~~ regarding the origin of early humans.

1.   Many scientists believe that early humans lived in the Africa in a period of times that is known as the Stone Age. According to evidences, early humans learned how to make stone tool and weapons such as axes and knifes, and they used that tools to hunt for food. However, as agricultural method improved, hunting also developed as a sports.

2.   Some persons think that hunting is barbaric. They believe that it is cruel and endangers animals such as an elephants and tigers. Certainly, there are so little wild tigers remaining that perhaps they need protection. Much hunters, on the other hand, state that responsible hunting is necessary and humane. Some animals such as wolfs are hunted if their numbers increase. One of the problem with such a debate is that there is no clear right or wrong side.

B. Correct six preposition errors.

In

EXAMPLE: ~~At~~ 2003, adventure tourism became popular.

1.   Many people travel at exotic destinations. Tourism can be both beneficial and harmful. By creating jobs, tourism helps the local economy. However, it may also have a negative impact at the culture. Often local families must migrate in order to work on a tourist resort, so they must leave their homes during many months. Furthermore, it is necessary to speak the language of the tourist in order to take advantage at the tourism industry. Therefore, indigenous people who depend of tourism may lose their languages, and they may reject traditional food, clothing, and values.

The Writer's Room

Write about one of the following topics. After you finish writing, circle any plural nouns and underline any determiners.

1. Describe an interesting vacation you have taken. Where did you go? What did you do?

2. What are some reasons people take vacations? What are the effects of taking a vacation? Write about the causes or effects of taking time off work and school.

3. Should people hunt for sport? What is your opinion?

 CHECKLIST: NOUNS, DETERMINERS, AND PREPOSITIONS

When you edit your writing, ask yourself the next set of questions.

☐ Do I use the correct singular or plural form of nouns? Check for errors with the following:

–spelling of regular plurals
–count and noncount nouns
–spelling of irregular plurals

research   *families*   *children*
According to ~~researches~~, most ~~familys~~ have two ~~childrens~~.

☐ Do I use the correct determiners? Check for errors with the following:

–*a, an, the*
–*much, many, few, little*
–*this, that, these, those*

These   *much*   *the*
~~This~~ days, there is not ~~many~~ information about ~~a~~ impact of tourism on cultures.

☐ Do I use the correct prepositions? Check for errors with the following:

–*in, on, at, to*
–*for, during*
–prepositional expressions

For   *on*
~~During~~ two months each summer, the town depends ~~of~~ tourists
at
who stay ~~to~~ the hotel.

How Do I Get a Better Grade?

Visit www.mywritinglab.com for audio-visual lectures and additional practice sets about nouns, determiners, and prepositions.

mywritinglab

Get a better grade with MyWritingLab!

Section Theme: **HUMAN HISTORY AND HABITS**

CONTENTS

- Pronoun-Antecedent Agreement
- Indefinite Pronouns
- Vague Pronouns
- Pronoun Shifts
- Pronoun Case
- Problems with Possessive Pronouns
- Relative Pronouns
- Reflexive Pronouns

In this chapter, you will read about issues related to food.

Grammar Snapshot

Looking at Pronouns

Catherine Pigott is a freelance writer. In this excerpt, Pigott shows how Western societies' attitude toward food differs from that of African societies. The pronouns are underlined.

I tried desperately, but I could not eat enough to please them. It was hard for me to explain that I come from a culture in which it is almost unseemly for a woman to eat too heartily. It's considered unattractive. It was even harder to explain that to me thin is beautiful, and in my country, we deny ourselves food in our pursuit of perfect slenderness.

Pronoun-Antecedent Agreement

Pronouns are words that replace nouns (people, places, or things), other pronouns, and phrases.

He
Max Weber was a famous sociologist. ~~Max Weber~~ wrote many books.

A pronoun must agree with its **antecedent,** which is the word to which the pronoun refers. Pronouns must agree in person and number with their antecedents.

> The <u>sociologist</u> was frustrated because **she** did not receive enough recognition for **her** work.
> (*Sociologist* is the antecedent of *she* and *her.*)

> My <u>son</u> went to work at a college in Taiwan. **He** took **his** family with **him.**
> (*Son* is the antecedent of *he, his,* and *him.*)

> <u>Farmers</u> are lobbying the government. **They** want better prices for crops.
> (*Farmers* is the antecedent of *they.*)

 **Compound Antecedents**

Compound antecedents consist of two or more nouns joined by *and* or *or.* When the nouns are joined by *and,* you must use a plural pronoun to refer to them.

> <u>Susan Brown and Alan Booth</u> published **their** book in 1997.

When the nouns are joined by *or,* you may need a singular or plural pronoun. If both nouns are singular, then use a singular pronoun. If both nouns are plural, use a plural pronoun.

> Does <u>California or Florida</u> have **its** own farming association?

> Have more <u>men or women</u> completed **their** degrees in agriculture?

PRACTICE I

The pronouns in the following sentences are in bold print. Underline each antecedent.

EXAMPLE:
Early <u>agriculture</u> began around eight thousand years ago, and **it** was a milestone in human development.

1. Early humans hunted, so **they** had to follow animal migrations to get food.

2. At some point, hunters realized that it was easier to kill an animal if **it** was contained in a small area.

3. Dr. Russell Fisch believes that agriculture started more than seven thousand years ago, but **he** says that the domestication of animals started even earlier.

4. The first domesticated animal was probably the dog, and **it** helped early humans to hunt.

5. The growth of farming helped early cities to develop because **their** populations increased quickly.

6. Around 4000 years ago, farmers first used irrigation in the Euphrates Valley, and **its** agricultural output grew enormously.

7. Ling-Mei Chang is an expert on agriculture, and **she** is researching early technology in the Nile Valley.

8. China and India also had early agricultural expansion, and **they** also grew into great early civilizations.

GRAMMAR LINK

For a list of collective nouns, see page 236 in Chapter 13.

   **Using Collective Nouns**

Collective nouns refer to a group of people or things. The group acts as a unit; therefore, it is singular. For example, *family, army, crowd, group,* and *organization* are collective nouns.

> The food <u>company</u> advertises **its** products.
>
> The <u>club</u> meets every Thursday. **It** is for overeaters.

PRACTICE 2

Underline the antecedents, and write the appropriate pronoun in each blank.

EXAMPLE:

<u>Plows</u> were invented in Mesopotamia around 5000 years ago, and
_____*they*_____ improved agricultural productivity.

1. Paintings show the ancient Greeks and Romans farming with a wooden plow, but _____ was a simple tool.

2. Ancient Chinese plows were more sophisticated because _____ were made of iron.

3. John Deere was an American blacksmith, and _____ vastly improved the design of the plow.

4. His wife believed in him, and _____ supported Deere in his business ventures.

5. American farmers experimented with Deere's new plow, and
   _____ were greatly impressed.

6. Deere sold thousands of plows when he first started to manufacture
   _____.

7. In 1855, to help his business, Deere moved to Moline, Illinois because
   _____ is near the Mississippi River.

8. In 1861, Deere incorporated his company, and _____ continues
   to manufacture agriculture equipment today.

Indefinite Pronouns

Most pronouns refer to a specific person, place, or thing. You can use **indefinite pronouns** when you talk about people or things whose identity is not known or is unimportant. The following table shows some common singular and plural indefinite pronouns.

Indefinite Pronouns

Singular:	another	each	nobody	other
	anybody	everybody	no one	somebody
	anyone	everyone	nothing	someone
	anything	everything	one	something
Plural:	both, few, many, others, several			
Either singular or plural:	all, any, some, half (and other fractions), more, most, none			

Singular Pronouns

When you use a singular indefinite antecedent, also use a singular pronoun to refer to it.

> Everybody wonders what will happen when **he or she** becomes elderly.

> No one, in **his or her** lifetime, wants to be a burden on others.

Plural Pronouns

When you use a plural indefinite antecedent, also use a plural pronoun to refer to it.

> Our town has many social problems, and several of **them** are difficult to conquer.

> Although small farmers contribute to the economy, many must sell **their** farms.

Pronouns That Can Be Singular or Plural

Some indefinite pronouns can be either singular or plural, depending on the noun to which they refer.

> Many sociologists came to the conference. <u>All</u> were experts in **their** fields.
> (*All* refers to sociologists; therefore, the pronoun is plural.)

> We read <u>all</u> of the report and agreed with **its** recommendations.
> (*All* refers to the report; therefore, the pronoun is singular.)

Hint   Using *"of the"* Expressions

The subject of a sentence appears before the words *of the*. For example, in sentences containing the expression *one of the* or *each of the*, the subject is the indefinite pronoun *one* or *each*. You must use a singular pronoun to refer to the subject.

> <u>One</u> of the books is missing **its** cover.

If the subject could be either male or female, then use *his or her* to refer to it.

> <u>Each</u> of the students has **his or her** own copy of the book.

PRACTICE 3

Underline the correct pronouns.

EXAMPLE:

Everybody is concerned about (<u>his or her</u> / their) health.

1.   These days, many think that (his or her / their) eating habits should include healthier choices. Almost everyone at some point has eaten (his or her / their) lunch at a fast food restaurant. But fast food is not only a modern American phenomenon.

2.   Every culture has (his or her / its / their) own examples of fast food. In Italy, most people eat (his or her / their) pizza slices at food stalls. In India, fast food is very popular. Few can avoid the temptation of eating (his or her / their) papri chaat or bhelpuri at food stands. In China, no one can resist buying (his or her / their) dumplings while cycling by the food vendors. Lebanon has contributed (its / their) great gift of fast food—the falafel sandwich—to North America.

3.   Fast food is popular with North Americans. McDonald's and (its /their) competitors are very successful businesses. For example, McDonald's is the largest fast food chain in the world. Presently, health care workers and (his or her / its / their) government colleagues are closely scrutinizing the

effects of fast food on North Americans. Health care workers believe that the popularity of fast food and (its / their) reliance on highly caloric ingredients is one reason for the growing obesity among young people. Each of the fast food companies has made (its / their) own response to this criticism by offering lower calorie choices such as salads. However, critics do not think the response is adequate.

Vague Pronouns

Avoid using pronouns that could refer to more than one antecedent.

Vague: Manolo introduced me to his friend and <u>his</u> sister.
(Whose sister is it: Manolo's or his friend's?)

Clearer: **Manolo** introduced me to **his** friend and his friend's sister.

Avoid using confusing pronouns like *it* and *they* that have no clear antecedent.

Vague: <u>They</u> say that farmers should receive more tax breaks.
(Who are *they?*)

Clearer: **Critics of government policy** say that farmers should receive more tax breaks.

Vague: <u>It</u> stated in the newspaper that many farmers are declaring bankruptcy.
(Who or what is *it?*)

Clearer: **The newspaper article** stated that many farmers are declaring bankruptcy.

Use *this, that,* and *which* only to refer to a specific antecedent.

Vague: The price of cattle feed was raised. <u>This</u> caused many ranchers to panic.
(What is *this?*)

Clearer: The price of cattle feed was raised. **This information** caused many ranchers to panic.

 **Avoid Repeating the Subject**

When you clearly mention a subject, do not repeat the subject in pronoun form.

Dr. MacKenzie, ~~he~~ is more than eighty years old.

His course on food science, ~~it~~ is really interesting.

CHAPTER 7

PRACTICE 4

Correct any vague pronoun or repeated subject errors.

EXAMPLE:

Doctors say
~~They say~~ that people should not eat fast food regularly.

1. It says that the rates of obesity in the general population in North America are rising.

2. John told Edmund that when he eats a super-size fast-food meal, it may contain up to 1,600 calories.

3. Dr. Feinstein he says that fast food contains high amounts of salt and fat, which cause people to overeat.

4. It stated in my book that some people eat fast-food meals every day.

5. I don't do this.

6. Many people they also don't get enough exercise.

7. This may cause people to have heart disease and diabetes.

8. They say that everybody should choose healthier food.

Pronoun Shifts

Making Pronouns Consistent in Person

Person is the writer's perspective. In some writing assignments, you may use the first person (*I, we*). For other assignments, you may use the second person (*you*) or the third person (*he, she, it, they*). Make sure that your pronouns are consistent in person. Therefore, if you begin writing from one point of view, do not shift unnecessarily to another point of view.

we
If we had studied, ~~one~~ would have passed the exam.

we
We visited every library, but ~~you~~ could not find the book.

Making Pronouns Consistent in Number

Pronouns and antecedents must agree in **number.** If the antecedent is singular, then the pronoun must be singular. If the antecedent is plural, then the pronoun must be plural.

his or her
Each nutritionist encouraged ~~their~~ clients to talk openly.

he or she
When a parent needs advice, ~~they~~ should talk to a professional.

 **Avoiding Pronoun Shifts in Paragraphs**

Sometimes it is easier to use pronouns consistently in individual sentences than in larger paragraphs or essays. When you write paragraphs and essays, always check that the pronouns agree with the antecedents in person.

In the next example, the pronouns are consistent in the first two sentences. However, they shift in person in the third sentence.

I am studying food sciences, and **I** want to be a nutritionist. In **my** program,
                                                                          I
there are so many courses that ~~you~~ cannot decide which ones to take.

PRACTICE 5

Correct the sentences that have pronoun shift errors. Write *C* beside any sentences that are correct.

EXAMPLE:

                                                              I
I have seen so many memorable documentaries that ~~you~~ don't know which one is the most interesting.

1. _____ We went to see the documentary *Supersize Me* by Martin Spurlock, and ~~you~~ were amazed by the information.

2. _____ Spurlock conducted an experiment in which ~~you~~ ate three McDonald's meals each day.

3. _____ Spurlock started his experiment because ~~one~~ heard about rising rates of obesity in America.

4. _____ As I watched the film, ~~you~~ could see the effects on Spurlock's body.

5. _____ As time went on, we saw Spurlock gaining weight, and we were shocked at how easily Spurlock's size changed.

6. _____ I read that McDonald's no longer sells supersized meals, and ~~you~~ know that Spurlock's documentary influenced the decision.

7. _____ I heard that McDonald's is very critical of the documentary, so I am going to the McDonald's website to read about it.

8. _____ My friends and I like to eat fast food, but ~~you~~ should really cut back.

Pronoun Case

Pronouns are formed according to the role they play in a sentence. A pronoun can be the subject or object of the sentence, or it can show possession. This chart shows the three main pronoun cases: subjective, objective, and possessive.

Pronoun Case

Singular	Subjective	Objective	Possessive Adjective	Possessive Pronoun
First person:	I	me	my	mine
Second person:	you	you	your	yours
Third person:	he, she, it, who, whoever	him, her, it whom, whomever	his, her, its, whose	his, hers
Plural				
First person:	we	us	our	ours
Second person:	you	you	your	yours
Third person:	they	them	their	theirs

Subjective Case

A **subject** performs an action in a sentence. When a pronoun is the subject of the sentence, use the subjective form of the pronoun. In the following sentences, *she* and *we* are the subjects.

> **She** was a chef for about twenty-five years.

> **We** listened to a lecture on food safety yesterday.

Objective Case

An **object** receives an action in a sentence. When a pronoun is the object in the sentence, use the objective form of the pronoun. In the following sentences, *him* and *us* are objects.

> My sociology class sent **him** an invitation to speak at the ceremony.

> My sister told **us** about the farmer's market.

Possessive Case

A possessive pronoun shows ownership.

- **Possessive adjectives** are always placed before the noun that they modify. In the next sentences, *his* and *her* are possessive adjectives.

> He finished **his** essay about fast food, but she did not finish **her** essay.

- **Possessive pronouns** replace the possessive adjective and noun. In the next sentence, *her* is a possessive adjective and *theirs* is a possessive pronoun.

> She finished **her** essay about fast food, but they did not finish **theirs**.

PRACTICE 6

Underline the pronouns in each sentence. Then identify the case of each pronoun. Write *S* for subjective case, *O* for objective case, and *P* for possessive case.

EXAMPLE:

P

Will Kellogg and <u>his</u> brother worked together for many years.

1. John Harvey Kellogg and his brother Will Keith Kellogg are considered to be among the first contemporary supporters of healthy lifestyles.

2. John Harvey started his career as a medical doctor, and later he opened a health spa in Battle Creek, Michigan.

3. John was a vegetarian, and he was interested in creating healthy breakfast options for his patients.

4. He asked his brother to work with him, and together they experimented with breakfast cereals.

5. They discovered wheat flake cereal by accident and served it to their patients.

6. Will tried to convince his brother to sell their cereal to grocery stores, but John told him he didn't want to.

7. John thought that selling cereal would harm his reputation as a doctor because he would be engaged in commercialism.

8. Eventually, the two brothers parted ways, and in 1906, Will started his own company, Kellogg Company.

Problems with Possessive Pronouns

When using the possessive pronouns *hers* and *theirs*, be careful that you do not add an apostrophe before the *-s*.

hers   *their*

The sociology book is ~~her's~~. The magazine is ~~their's~~.

Some possessive adjectives sound like certain contractions. Review these examples of commonly confused words.

Possessive adjective: <u>Their</u> field trip was canceled.

Contraction: <u>They're</u> going to go next week.   *(They're = they are.)*

Possessive adjective: <u>Your</u> guidance counselor will help you choose the right courses.

Contraction: <u>You're</u> going to enjoy the trip to the agricultural fair. *(You're = you are.)*

GRAMMAR LINK

See Chapter 26 for more detailed information about apostrophes.

Possessive adjective: <u>Its</u> theme is about the influence of technology on farming practices.

Contraction: <u>It's</u> a book that you should read.   (*It's* = *it is*.)

 His or Her?

To choose the correct possessive adjective, think about the possessor, *not* the object that is possessed.

- If something belongs to or is a relative of a female, use *her* + noun.

  Allison and **her** father both work as chefs.

- If something belongs to or is a relative of a male, use *his* + noun.

  John Deere wanted **his** workers to build solid plows.

PRACTICE 7

Underline the correct word in each set of parentheses.

EXAMPLE:

The tomatoes are (her/<u>hers</u>), but the corn is (my / <u>mine</u>).

1.   Wycliffe Brown has been a farmer since (his / her/ their) father retired and gave (he / him) the family farm. He and (his / her) wife, Michelle, grow organic vegetables on (they're / their / theirs) farm. Michelle also grows organic herbs on (his / her / hers) own plot of land. The herd of sheep is also (they're / their / theirs). The farm is quite successful, but (they're / their / theirs) worried about (they're / their / theirs) competitors. In the United States, more and more large corporations are involved in agricultural production.

2.   Critics say that corporate farming concentrates agriculture production, distribution, and sales into one business source. As a result, the family farm is losing (it's / its / his) competitive edge and often goes bankrupt. Furthermore, a small farmer may be forced into doing business with a corporation. Proponents of corporate farming claim that mass food production is positive because of (it's / its) cost efficiency. The corporate farm is beneficial for everybody because (it's / its) able to provide cheaper food to more people all year around.

3.   My sister and I grew up on a farm where (our / ours) parents practiced organic farming methods, and (we / us) grew up eating only organic produce. My sister and I now have completely different shopping habits. I buy (my / mine) groceries anywhere convenient, but (my / mine) sister only buys (her / hers) at an organic market. Where do (you / your) buy (you / your / you're) food?

Pronouns in Comparisons with *Than or As*

Avoid making errors in pronoun case when the pronoun follows *than* or *as*. If the pronoun is a subject, use the subjective case. If the pronoun is an object, use the objective case.

If you use the incorrect case, your sentence may have a meaning that you do not intend it to have. Look at the differences in the meanings of the next sentences.

Objective case: I like pizza as much as **him.**

   (I like pizza *as much as* I like him.)

Subjective case: I like pizza as much as **he.**

   (I like pizza *as much as* he likes pizza or I like pizza *as much as* he does.)

 **Complete the Thought**

If you are unsure which pronoun case to use, test by completing the thought.

He likes salty snacks more than **I** [like salty snacks].

He likes salty snacks more than [he likes] **me.**

Pronouns in Prepositional Phrases

A **prepositional phrase** is made up of a preposition and its object. Therefore, always use the objective case of the pronoun after a preposition.

<u>To</u> **him,** Will Kellogg was a man with great ideas.

<u>Between</u> **you** and **me,** that breakfast cereal is too sweet.

Pronouns with *And or Or*

Use the correct case when nouns and pronouns are joined by *and* or *or.* If the pronouns are the subject, use the subjective case. If the pronouns are the object, use the objective case.

He and I
~~Him and me~~ had to do a presentation on modern American culture.

            him and me
The instructor asked ~~he and I~~ to present first.

 **Finding the Correct Case**

An easy way to determine that your case is correct is to say the sentence with just one pronoun.

   The teacher asked her and (**I, me**) to do the presentation.

   Possible choices: The teacher asked **I** . . .   *or*   The teacher asked **me** . . .

   Correct answer: The teacher asked her and **me** to do the presentation.

PRACTICE 8

Correct any errors with pronoun case. Write *C* in the space if the sentence is correct.

EXAMPLE:

My friend likes this course more than ~~me~~.   *I (do)*

1. Sanjay and me are in the same economics class.   _____

2. Him and I have to write a paper on the Green Revolution, a term applied to agriculture changes in the Third World in the 1960s.   _____

3. Professor King informed our class that the term Green Revolution described the export of American farming techniques to third world nations.   _____

4. My professor told we students that the Green Revolution increased agricultural productivity in the Third World.   _____

5. Sanjay told my friend Gael and I that the Green Revolution also had negative effects.   _____

6. The United States supplied seeds to third world farmers, but this policy caused many problems.   _____

7. Prakash Gosh was a poor farmer, and wealthier farmers benefited more than him.   _____

8. Him and his wife could not afford to buy seeds because they were too expensive.   _____

9. Also, poorer farmers could not afford to buy expensive farm machinery, so them and their families suffered.   _____

10. Between you and I, I think I might change my major from agricultural economics to computer science.   _____

PRACTICE 9

Correct ten pronoun errors in the next paragraphs.

EXAMPLE:

their
Consumers should read food labels when they buy ~~they're~~ groceries.

1.   Presently, there is a lot of discussion in the media about food. Everyone wants his or hers food to taste good. But are consumers equally concerned about the nutritional quality of they're food? A recent focus group indicated that Americans would rather have one's food be tasty than nutritious. The food industry has responded to this consumer preference by adding flavors to packaged foods.

2.   The average American family eats approximately 25 percent of it's meals at restaurants. Fast food contains a lot of artificial flavors, but so does food at other types of restaurants. Macy Robards is a chef at an expensive restaurant in Chicago. Although clients eat fresh ingredients at her restaurant, their also getting a dose of artificial flavors. For example, just as a fast food chain may use artificial flavor for it's sauces and dressings, she also uses such flavoring in her's.

3.   In his book, *Fast Food Nation*, Eric Schlosser writes that approximately ten thousand new processed food products are marketed every year in the United States. Most packaged food contains added flavors and colors. Because of his book, Schlosser is a well-known personality, although some people find he a controversial figure. My friend Lindsey was more influenced by Schlosser's book than me. She and me discussed his book a lot. We are going to find out more about what we eat.

Relative Pronouns

Relative pronouns can join two short sentences. Here is a list of relative pronouns.

who	whom	which	that	whose
whoever	whomever			

- *Who* (or *whoever*) and *whom* (or *whomever*) always refer to people. *Who* is the subject of the clause, and *whom* is the object of the clause.

  The <u>chef</u> **who** specializes in Japanese cuisine is speaking today.

  The <u>restaurant critic</u> **whom** you met is my sister.

- *Which* always refers to things. *Which* clauses are set off with commas.

  Modern <u>sociology</u>, **which** has many subfields, was founded in the nineteenth century.

- *That* refers to things.

  Sociologist Robert Merton wrote the <u>book</u> **that** first included the term "self-fulfilling prophecy."

- *Whose* always shows that something belongs to or is connected with someone or something. It usually replaces the possessive pronoun *his, her,* or *their.* Do not confuse *whose* with *who's,* which means "who is."

  The food activist was selling fair-trade coffee when <u>his</u> car got towed.

  The food activist,  **whose** car got towed, was selling fair-trade coffee.

GRAMMAR LINK

Clauses with *which* are set off with commas. For more information, see Chapter 25, "Commas."

 **Who or Whom?**

If you are unsure whether to use *who* or *whom*, test yourself in the following way. Replace *who* or *whom* with another pronoun. If the replacement is a subject such as *he* or *she*, use *who*. If the replacement is an object such as *her* or *him*, use *whom*.

> I know a pastry chef **who** makes excellent croissants.
>
> (He makes excellent croissants.)
>
> The man to **whom** you gave a recipe is a restaurant critic.
>
> (You gave your recipe to him.)

PRACTICE 10

Underline the correct relative pronoun in each set of parentheses.

EXAMPLE:

Shoppers (who / which) are concerned about food sources buy organically grown produce.

1. People (who / whom) are concerned about the state of the world have a new method of expressing their views.
2. They can influence economic policy by buying food products (who / that) promote social equity.
3. Xing Feng and his wife are consumers for (who / whom) equitable trade is an important issue.
4. Therefore, they buy food (who / that) is labeled "fair trade."
5. Like the Fengs, other food activists (who / whom) believe in social causes also make political statements through consumer choices.
6. The food activism movement, (which / that) is growing rapidly, is a relatively new phenomenon.
7. In the past, consumers used to boycott products of companies (which / that) used unfair business practices.
8. Nowadays, business people, for (who / whom) profits are important, look at customer buying trends.
9. Hugo Ricci, (who / whose) company sells fair trade products, says that his business is thriving.
10. The organic food and fair trade industry, (which / that) consumers are heartily supporting, made a profit of over $30 billion last year.

PRACTICE 11

Write the correct relative pronoun from the list below in each blank. Remember that you cannot use *which* unless the clause is set off with commas.

who   whom   whose   which   that

EXAMPLE:

Consumers _____ *who* _____ strongly support environmental causes often buy organic food.

1.   Organic food has many definitions. Food _____ has been grown using little or no synthetic pesticide or fertilizer is generally labeled organic. Farmers _____ crops are labeled organic do not use genetically modified seeds.

2.   Many people _____ buy organic food think that such food is better for their health. However, this belief turns out to be controversial. Some scientists, _____ research has been published, discuss their results. Food _____ has been grown organically is not nutritionally superior to non-organically grown food.

3.   Most consumers _____ buy organic food also believe that it is better for the environment. However, not everyone agrees. Dr. Norman Borlaug is considered to be the father of the Green Revolution. In 1970, he won the Nobel Peace prize. The award, _____ is given to people for great humanitarian contributions, brought Borlaug to international prominence. He believes that organic farming produces lower crop yields, requiring more land use. Synthetic fertilizers _____ contribute to greater crop production help the environment significantly more than organic methods.

4.   Consumers for _____ health and environment are important should consider both sides of the issue. Certainly, the organic food industry, _____ is very profitable, will continue to grow in popularity in the near future.

Reflexive Pronouns (*-self, -selves*)

Use **reflexive pronouns** when you want to emphasize that the subject does an action to himself or herself.

CHAPTER 7

We ask **ourselves** many questions.

The <u>book</u> sells **itself** because it is so good.

It is not typical to use reflexive pronouns for personal care activities, such as washing or shaving. However, you can use reflexive pronouns to draw attention to a surprising or an unusual action.

My three-year-old **sister** dressed **herself.**
(The girl probably could not dress herself at a previous time.)

The next chart shows subjective pronouns and the reflexive pronouns that relate to them.

Pronouns That End with -self or -selves

Singular	Antecedent	Reflexive Pronouns
First person:	I	myself
Second person:	you	yourself
Third person:	he, she, it	himself, herself, itself
Plural		
First person:	we	ourselves
Second person:	you	yourselves
Third person:	they	themselves

Hint **Common Errors with Reflexive Pronouns**

Hisself and *theirselves* do not exist in English. These are incorrect ways to say *himself* and *themselves*.

themselves
The students went by ~~theirselves~~ to the lecture.

himself
Max Weber worked by ~~hisself~~.

PRACTICE 12

Fill in the blanks with the correct reflexive pronouns.

EXAMPLE:

I do not like to eat by _____*myself*_____.

1. Many times I wish that our dinner would get ready by _____.

2. I often cook meals by _____.

3. Sometimes my children start preparing dinner by _____.

4. My son Alex goes grocery shopping by _____.

5. My daughter plans some meals by _____.

6. When my children make a fabulous dinner, I always say, "Congratulate _____ on a job well done."

7. If my husband is late coming home from work, we eat by _____.

8. On such occasions, he humbly offers to clean the kitchen by _____.

9. Do you eat dinner with others or by _____?

FINAL REVIEW

Read the following paragraphs and correct twenty pronoun errors.

EXAMPLE:

The Slow Food movement and ~~it's~~ *its* supporters are getting publicity.

1.   In Italy, everybody loves their food. Italians they take the time to enjoy long and delicious meals. In 1986, Carlo Petrini, which was enjoying a coffee, read that McDonald's was opening an outlet in downtown Rome. To protest the growing presence of the fast-food culture, he started the Slow Food movement. This has been growing in popularity since that time.

2.   Although Petrini started the movement by hisself, he soon had many supporters. Those people, who's aim was to slow the increasingly hurried pace of daily life, developed a set of objectives. Their objectives, who are quite diverse, are published on the group's website. The organization and it's members have started a bank to preserve seed variety. The members also educate people on farming methods and lobby governments on agribusiness practices.

3.   Mr. Khalil Isoke and her wife, Farah, are members of the Slow Food movement. They took my friend Miriam and I to a cooking class. The chef, which skill was evident, was a good teacher. The other students they were all better cooks than me. But I congratulated me when my dish turned out as good as them. At the end of the class, each of the participants shared their favorite recipes with the other students. The students for who the

Slow Food philosophy is a lifestyle choice liked the cooking class very much.

4.   I am beginning to appreciate the philosophy of the Slow Food group. Sometimes I become so busy during the day that you don't have time to breathe. Between you and I, I could start to like cooking. Do you and you're friends know about the Slow Food movement?

The Writer's Room

Write about one of the following topics. After you finish writing, circle the pronouns and underline their antecedents.

1. Should fast-food companies be held responsible for some of the health problems in our society? Explain your point of view.
2. Describe your eating habits. Do you eat a lot of junk food or do you try to eat well? Are you concerned about nutrition?

✔ CHECKLIST: PRONOUNS

When you edit your writing, ask yourself the next set of questions.

Do I use the correct pronoun case? Check for errors with the following:

   –subjective, objective, and possessive case
   –comparisons with *than* or *as*
   –prepositional phrases
   –pronouns after *and* or *or*

                          me
   Between you and ~~I~~, my parents were stricter with my brother
        me
   than ~~I~~.

Do I use the correct relative pronouns? Check for errors with *who, whom,* or *whose.*

                whom
   My husband, ~~who~~ you have met, is a coffee salesman.

Do my pronouns and antecedents agree in number and person? Check for errors with indefinite pronouns and collective nouns.

The government announced ~~their~~ *its* new policy: everyone will have ~~their~~ *his or her* own identity card.

Are my pronoun references clear? Check for vague pronouns and inconsistent points of view.

Policy makers
~~They~~ say that family farms are suffering. I read the report, and ~~you~~ *I* could not believe what it said.

 The Writers' Circle

Work with a group of three to five students. Your team will compete with other teams in a short contest.

Look at the two words below. Using letter combinations from those words, brainstorm and form as many new words as possible. For example, you could create the word *car*. You can only use the letters given; you cannot add or double any letters. The team that forms the most words wins the contest.

agricultural revolution

READING LINK
Human History and Habits
To read more about issues related to human history and habits, see the next essays.
"Fish Cheeks" by Amy Tan (page 421)
"The Cult of Emaciation" by Ben Barry (page 425)

How Do I Get a Better Grade?

Visit www.mywritinglab.com for audio-visual lectures and additional practice sets about pronouns.
Get a better grade with MyWritingLab!

Subjects and Verbs

Section Theme: **ENTERTAINMENT AND CULTURE**

CONTENTS

· Identifying Subjects
· Identifying Prepositional Phrases
· Identifying Verbs

In this chapter, you will read about music and musicians.

Grammar Snapsh•t

Looking at Subjects and Verbs

Sonia Margossian teaches singing. In the next excerpt from a speech, she discusses proper breathing techniques. Notice that subjects are in bold type and the verbs are underlined. Also observe that some sentences have no visible subjects.

> Stand straight, and place your hands on your stomach, just below the ribs. Then take a long, deep breath and carry the air to the bottom of your lungs. Your **shoulders** should not move as you breathe. As **you** continue to inhale, your **chest** will inflate.

In this chapter, you will identify subjects and verbs.

Identifying Subjects

A **sentence** has a subject and verb, and it expresses a complete thought. The **subject** tells you who or what the sentence is about. The **verb** expresses an action or state. If a sentence is missing a subject or a verb, it is incomplete.

           subject   verb

Prehistoric **humans** banged on hollow logs to make music.

Singular or Plural Subjects

Subjects may be singular or plural. To determine the subject of a sentence, ask yourself who or what the sentence is about.

A **singular subject** is one person, place, or thing.

> **Mozart** learned to play piano at an early age.

> The **violin** is difficult to master.

A **plural subject** is more than one person, place, or thing.

> **People** still listen to Mozart's music.

> Some **instruments** are easy to learn.

Pronouns as Subjects

A **subject pronoun** (*he, she, it, you, we, they*) can act as the subject of a sentence.

> Greg wants that guitar, but **it** is very expensive.

> Louisa has a great voice. **She** should sing more often.

Gerunds (-*ing* Words) as Subjects

Sometimes a **gerund** (the -*ing* form of a verb, acting as a noun) is the subject of a sentence.

> **Listening** is an important skill.

> **Dancing** can improve your cardiovascular health.

 **Simple versus Complete Subject**

In a sentence, the **simple subject** is the noun or pronoun. The complete name of a person, place, or organization is a simple subject.

     he   guitar   Tupac Shakur   Sony Music Corporation

The **complete subject** is the noun, plus the words that describe the noun. In the examples, the descriptive words are underlined.

     new acoustic guitar   Michael's silver flute   the tiny microphone

                  simple subject

The expensive old **violin** is very fragile.

          complete subject

CHAPTER 8

PRACTICE I

Underline the complete subject in each sentence. (Remember to underline the subject and the words that describe the subject.) Then circle the simple subject.

EXAMPLE:

Mexico's most famous recording (artist) is Juan Gabriel.

1. His birth name was Alberto Aguilera Valadez.
2. Gabriel's family was extremely poor.
3. His hardworking mother was a housekeeper for a rich family in Juarez.
4. Twelve-year-old Gabriel started writing songs.
5. The talented young man sang in local nightclubs such as El Noa Noa.
6. El Noa Noa's name appeared in a Juan Gabriel song.
7. The young singer eventually moved to Mexico City.
8. His songs became extremely popular.
9. Gabriel's family bought a mansion in Juarez a few years ago.
10. His mother had been a housekeeper in that mansion.

Compound Subjects

Many sentences have more than one subject. These are called compound subjects. Notice that *and* is not part of the compound subject.

> **Guitars, lutes,** and **banjos** are stringed instruments.

> **Reporters** and **photographers** crowded around the singer.

PRACTICE 2

Complete each sentence by adding one or more logical subjects.

EXAMPLE:

___Beyoncé Knowles___ sings and dances.

1. In my opinion, _____ is the most interesting type of music.

2. _____ and _____ are great singers.

3. My feathered yellow _____ sings every morning.

4. _____ stopped making music a long time ago.

5. _____ and _____ recorded many number one hits.

6. The _____ is missing a string and needs to be
   tuned.

7. The _____ is my least favorite instrument.

8. _____ is important in our lives.

Special Subject Problems

Unstated Subjects (Commands)

In a sentence that expresses a command, the subject is unstated, but it is still
understood. The unstated subject is *you*. (The word *should* is implied.)

> Practice every day.

> Do not judge the musician harshly.

Here, There

Here and *there* are not subjects. In sentences that begin with *here* or *there*, the
subject follows the verb.

>   verb   subject
> There <u>are</u> five **ways** to improve your voice.

>   verb   subject
> Here <u>is</u> my **CD.**

> **Hint**   **Ask Who or What**
>
> When you are trying to determine the subject, read the sentence carefully and ask
> yourself who or what the sentence is about. Do not presume that all nouns are the
> subjects in a sentence. For example, in the next sentence, *music, dance,* and *occasions*
> are nouns, but they are not the subject.
>
> > Most **cultures** use music and dance to celebrate special occasions.

PRACTICE 3

Underline one or more simple subjects in these sentences. If the subject is unstated,
write *you.*

EXAMPLE:

You listen
~~Listen~~ to music as often as possible.

1. Every known human society has a form of music.

2. Music stimulates many parts of the brain.

3. Do not listen to extremely loud music on earphones.

4. There are various musical styles in North America.

5. Some cultures do not distinguish between musicians and ordinary people.

6. For example, music is as natural as breathing in Indonesia.

7. Some animal species use musical sounds to communicate.

8. There are many exotic birds that are unable to sing.

9. Douglas Nelson taught songs to some sparrows.

10. If possible, try to learn a musical instrument.

Identifying Prepositional Phrases

A **preposition** is a word that links nouns, pronouns, and phrases to other words in a sentence. It expresses a relationship based on movement or position.

Common Prepositions

about	before	during	of	toward
above	behind	except	off	under
across	below	for	on	until
after	beside	from	onto	up
against	between	in	out	with
along	beyond	inside	outside	within
among	by	into	over	
around	despite	like	through	
at	down	near	to	

A **phrase** is a group of words that is missing a subject, a verb, or both, and it is not a complete sentence. A **prepositional phrase** is made up of a preposition and its object (a noun or a pronoun).

Preposition	+	Object
in		the morning
among		the shadows
over		the rainbow
with		some friends

 **Hint**   **Nouns Are Not Always Subjects**

Because the object of a preposition is a noun, it may look like a subject. However, the object in a prepositional phrase is never the subject of the sentence.

subject
With her husband, **Carly** composed a hit song.

To help you identify the subject of a sentence, it is a good idea to put parentheses around prepositional phrases, cross them out, or identify them in some other way. In each of the following sentences, the subject is in bold type and the prepositional phrase is in parentheses.

(In most countries,) particular **musical styles** exist.

The **studio** (on Slater Street) is closed.

The **information** (in that magazine) is true.

PRACTICE 4

In each sentence, place parentheses around one or more prepositional phrases. Then circle the simple subject.

EXAMPLE:

(According to Kristin Leutwyler of *Scientific American,*) prehistoric (humans) listened to music.

1. In a cave in France, archeologists have found sophisticated wind instruments.

2. In the past, Neanderthals may have had a musical tradition.

3. In 1996, Slovenian archeologist Ivan Turk discovered a small bone flute.

4. Over 50,000 years ago, the sweet-sounding flute was carved from the thigh of a cave bear.

5. With four nearly perfect holes in a row, the wind instrument was quite sophisticated.

6. In a speech, Boston biologist Jelle Atema discussed the technical skills of the ancient people.

7. Early humans, with their friends and family, probably played music together.

8. In other places such as in Africa, South America, and China, scientists have found very old wind and stringed instruments.

9. Perhaps ancient people without a common language could communicate with musical sounds.

10. In the Slovenia Academy of Science, in a temperature-controlled room, visitors can examine the ancient Neanderthal flute.

PRACTICE 5

If the underlined word is the subject, write *C* (for "correct") in the space. If the underlined word is not the subject, then circle the correct subject(s).

EXAMPLES:

In the 1930s, Elvis Aaron Presley was born. _____

The musical legend was born on Jan. 8, 1935.   *C*

1. His twin brother was named <u>Jesse</u>.   _____

2. <u>Jesse</u> died at birth.   _____

3. In the <u>summer</u> of 1953, the young Southerner made his first
   <u>demo record</u>.   _____

4. <u>Elvis, Scotty Moore, and Bill Black</u> recorded "That's All Right."   _____

5. Sun Records, in <u>Memphis</u>, was a very small recording studio.   _____

6. Elvis's first number one song was called "Mystery Train."   _____

7. Elvis's manager was <u>Colonel Tom Parker</u>.   _____

8. Elvis's only non-U.S. concert was in Vancouver, Canada.   _____

9. In March, 1956, <u>"Heartbreak Hotel"</u> became the most
   popular song in <u>the United States</u>.   _____

10. In his last <u>year</u>, Elvis performed at 150 concerts.   _____

Identifying Verbs

Every sentence must contain a verb. The **verb** either expresses what the subject does or links the subject to other descriptive words.

Action Verbs

Action verbs describe the actions that the subject performs.

> The musicians <u>performed</u> in Carnegie Hall.

> The Irish dancers <u>stamped</u> their heels in time to the music.

Compound Verbs

When a subject performs more than one action, the verbs are called **compound verbs.**

> Mr. Gibson <u>makes</u>, <u>polishes</u>, and <u>sells</u> good-quality guitars.

PRACTICE 6

Fill in each space with an appropriate and interesting action verb.

EXAMPLE:

The Petersons _____*paid*_____ for their tickets and _____*entered*_____ the theater.

1. Marcella, the violinist, _____ the audience.

2. She then _____ beautifully.

3. At the end of the performance, the audience _____
   and _____ .

4. The performer _____ to her dressing room.

5. She _____ on her sofa, exhausted.

6. Somebody _____ on the door and

_____ .

Linking Verbs

Linking verbs (or state verbs) do not describe an action; instead, they describe a state of being or give information about the subject. The most common linking verb is *be* (*am, are, is, was, were*).

The harp <u>is</u> a lovely instrument.

Those sound systems <u>are</u> unreliable.

Other linking verbs link the subject with descriptive words.

     subject linking verb descriptive word
That **music** <u>sounds</u> *good.*

     subject   linking verb descriptive words
Mr. Wayland <u>seems</u> *quite eccentric.*

Here are some common linking verbs:

act	feel	seem
appear	get	smell
be (am, is, are, was, were)	look	sound
become	remain	taste

PRACTICE 7

Underline the linking verb in each sentence.

EXAMPLE:

In some cultures, musicians <u>are</u> important people in the community.

1. Among the Mandiki of Senegal, the jali is a highly specialized musician.

2. The jali acts as the official singer of the tribe.

3. His songs sound haunting and powerful.

4. The tribe's history becomes part of the jali's repertoire.

5. The music seems simple.

6. However, it is actually quite complex.

7. The jali appears confident during his performance.

8. The tribe members are ready for the jali to commemorate important events.

> **Hint** **Infinitives Are Not the Main Verb**
>
> **Infinitives** are verbs preceded by *to*, such as *to sing, to play,* and *to run*. An infinitive is never the main verb in a sentence.
>
>
>
> verb   infinitive   verb   infinitive
>
> Chuck Berry <u>wanted</u> <u>to be</u> famous. He <u>hoped</u> <u>to become</u> a music legend.
>
>

PRACTICE 8

Circle the subjects and underline the verbs in the following sentences. Some sentences have more than one verb. Write *L* beside any sentence that contains a linking verb.

EXAMPLE:

(Andrew Young) <u>changed</u> his name to Dr. Dre.

1. Andrew Young's mother raised him in a Los Angeles housing project.

2. The gangs in his environment influenced him and later affected his music.

3. Young admired basketball superstar Dr. J.

4. Later, the future music producer took the name Dr. Dre.

5. Violence was widespread in his environment.

6. Dre's brother died during a fight in the neighborhood.

7. The young musician began to work as a disc jockey at parties.

8. Dre, Ice Cube, and Easy E became the founders of West Coast hip-hop in the late 1980s.

9. Then Dre and Suge Knight decided to create Death Row Records in the early 1990s.

10. Their "gangsta rap" became the target of censorship groups.

11. *Rolling Stone* calls Dre "the most influential rapper/producer of his time."

12. Eminem and other wealthy music stars owe their careers to Dre.

Helping Verbs

Many verbs contain two or more words: a main verb and a helping verb. The **main verb** expresses what the subject does or links the subject to descriptive words. The **helping verb** combines with the main verb to indicate tense, negative structure, or question structure.

Be, Have, Do

The common helping verbs *be*, *have*, and *do* combine with the main verb to indicate a tense, negative structure, or question structure.

> HV   HV   V
>
> Some songs <u>have been</u> <u>banned</u> from radio station play lists.

Modals

A modal is another type of helping verb. It indicates ability (*can*), obligation (*must*), possibility (*may, might, could*), advice (*should*), and so on.

> HV   V
>
> Violent lyrics <u>can</u> <u>influence</u> children.

Questions

In question forms, the first helping verb usually appears before the subject.

> HV   subject   V
>
> <u>Should</u> radio **stations** <u>censor</u> song lyrics?

> HV   subject   V
>
> <u>Do</u> violent, sexist, or racist **songs** <u>influence</u> young listeners?

> **Hint**   **Interrupting Words and Phrases**
>
> Interrupting words may appear between verbs, but they are *not* part of the verb. Some interrupting words are *always, easily, ever, never, not, often, sometimes,* and *usually.*
>
> HV interrupter V
> Blues music <u>can</u> **sometimes** <u>be</u> sorrowful.

PRACTICE 9

Underline each complete verb once. Then underline each main verb twice.

EXAMPLE:
Musicians with perfect pitch <u>are</u> <u>envied</u>.

1. According to an article in *Scientific American*, very few people have achieved perfect pitch.

2. Human beings with absolute pitch will easily sing an F sharp.

3. Most people do not have this ability.

4. Only one person in ten thousand can identify a note perfectly.

5. Do people from some cultures have a superior ability to recognize tones?

6. In languages such as Vietnamese and Mandarin, people can pronounce one word in several different ways.

7. The meaning of each word may depend on the tone of the word.

8. Diana Deutch of the University of California has discussed the topic in her lectures.

9. According to Deutch, native speakers of tonal languages, even those with no musical training, can recognize and repeat notes perfectly.

10. The best way to teach children perfect pitch could be to train them with tonal words.

FINAL REVIEW

Circle each simple subject and underline each complete verb. Underline each main verb twice. If prepositional phrases confuse you, you can cross them out.

EXAMPLE:

Aaron Wherry wrote an article about music and consumerism. It is called "Say Yes to Logos."

1. Most young music consumers do not associate their favorite sounds with advertising. However, according to journalist Aaron Wherry, a lot of contemporary musicians consciously promote merchandise.

2. Lucian James is a marketing consultant in San Francisco. He has compiled a list of products. Mercedes, Lexus, and Gucci are frequently mentioned brands in the *Billboard* Top 20 list. For example, the hip-hop artist 50 Cent often mentions his Mercedes-Benz automobile in his music.

3. Hip-hop artists, according to Wherry, do not apologize for combining music and commerce. Back in 1986, Run-DMC recorded a track called "My Adidas." Then, rap mogul Russell Simmons invited Adidas executives to a Run-DMC concert. Audience members lifted up their running shoes on cue. Naturally, the running shoe company offered the rappers an endorsement deal.

4.   Some musicians have refused to promote products in their

music. They do not want to become "sellouts." Other musicians

have chosen to actively publicize products in their songs. They

do not see any problems with the practice. In the end, most

music fans do not care about the debate. They will continue to

support musicians on both sides of the issue.

 The Writer's Room

Write about one of the following topics. After you finish writing, circle your subjects and underline your verbs. Underline main verbs twice.

1. What qualities does a professional singer need? List at least five qualities.
2. Compare two different singers. How are they similar or different?

 CHECKLIST: SUBJECTS AND VERBS

To identify **subjects,** look for words that tell you who or what the sentence is about.

To identify **verbs,** look for words that express what the subject does or link the subject to descriptive words.

To identify **action verbs,** look for words that describe the action that the subject performs.

To identify **linking verbs,** look for words that describe a state of being or link the subject with descriptive words.

To identify **helping verbs,** look for words that combine with the main verb to indicate tense, negative structure, or question structure.

To identify a **prepositional phrase,** look for words that consist of a preposition and its object. The object of a prepositional phrase cannot be the subject.

                                          helping
prepositional phrase   subject verb   verb
In spite of criticism, Madonna's fame   has   endured.

How Do I Get a Better Grade?

Visit www.mywritinglab.com for audio-visual lectures and additional practice sets about subjects and verbs.
Get a better grade with MyWritingLab!

CHAPTER 9

Present and Past Tenses

Section Theme: **ENTERTAINMENT AND CULTURE**

CONTENTS

- Understanding Verb Tense
- The Simple Present Tense
- The Simple Past Tense
- Avoiding Double Negatives

In this chapter, you will read about literature and the media.

Grammar Snapshot

Looking at Present and Past Tenses

Kate Chopin, the mother of six children, began writing shortly after her husband died. In this abridged excerpt from her short story "The Storm," written in 1898, the past tense verbs are underlined.

> She went and stood at the window with a greatly disturbed look on her face. She wiped the moist frame. It was stiflingly hot. Alcée got up and joined her at the window, looking over her shoulder. The playing of the lightning was incessant. A bolt struck a tall chinaberry tree at the edge of the field. It filled all visible space with a blinding glare.

In this chapter, you will identify and write present and past tense verbs.

Understanding Verb Tense

A verb shows an action or a state of being. A **verb tense** indicates when an action occurred. For example, review the various tenses of the verb *write*.

Past time:	J. K. Rowling <u>wrote</u> parts of her first book in a coffee shop.
Present time:	She <u>writes</u> every morning.
Future:	Perhaps she <u>will write</u> a new book next year.

 **Use Standard Verb Forms**

Nonstandard English is used in everyday conversation and may differ according to the region in which you live. **Standard American English** is the common language generally used and expected in schools, businesses, and government institutions in the United States. Most of your instructors will want you to write using standard American English.

Nonstandard:	She be busy. She don't have no time to talk.
Standard:	She is busy. She doesn't have any time to talk.

The Simple Present Tense

The **simple present tense** shows that an action is a general fact or habitual activity.

Fact:	Harry Potter books <u>sell</u> in countries throughout the world.
Habitual activity:	J. K. Rowling <u>writes</u> every morning.

(past) ◄——► (future)

MONDAY MORNING	TUESDAY MORNING	WEDNESDAY MORNING
▼	▼	▼
She writes.	She writes.	She writes.

Simple present tense verbs (except *be*) have two forms.

- **Base form.** When the subject is *I*, *you*, *we*, or *they*, do not add an ending to the verb.

  They <u>read</u> magazines. We often <u>borrow</u> their magazines.

- **Third-person singular form.** When the subject is *he*, *she*, *it*, or the equivalent (*Joe*, *Anne*, *New York*), add an *-s* or *-es* ending to the verb.

  The story <u>ends</u> badly. The main character <u>leaves</u> his family.

Look at the two forms of the verb *eat*. Notice the *-s* in bold print in the third-person singular form.

Present Tense of *Eat*

	Singular	Plural
First person:	I eat	We eat
Second person:	You eat	You eat
Third person:	He eats	They eat
	She eat**s**	
	It eat**s**	

CHAPTER 9

GRAMMAR LINK

See Chapter 13 for more detailed information about subject-verb agreement.

Subject-Verb Agreement

In the present tense, the subject and verb must **agree** in number. If the subject is third-person singular (*he, she, it*), the corresponding verb must have the singular form, too.

Although plural nouns usually end in -*s*, plural verbs do not. Instead, singular verbs have the -*s* or -*es* ending. Read the following sentences and notice the errors in subject-verb agreement.

           writes   *appear*
Jan Freeman ~~write~~ for the *Boston Globe*. Her columns ~~appears~~ every Sunday.

PRACTICE 1

George Orwell, the author of *Animal Farm* and *1984*, wrote an essay called "Why I Write." The following sentences summarize his ideas. Underline the correct present tense form of each verb in parentheses.

EXAMPLE:
Authors (<u>write</u>, writes) for several reasons.

1. Every writer (want, wants) to seem clever and to be talked about, according to George Orwell.

2. Most human beings (like, likes) to be remembered.

3. Also, a beautiful or moving moment (become, becomes) immortal with writing.

4. A good writer (attempt, attempts) to show others the beauty of certain places.

5. People also (write, writes) to create a historical record of events.

6. Some writers (hope, hopes) to persuade others with their words.

7. Literary works (need, needs) to document political events.

8. George Orwell's book *Animal Farm* (show, shows) certain injustices, and it (criticize, criticizes) Soviet-style communism.

9. Some lies (need, needs) to be exposed.

10. Art (have, has) a relationship with politics.

Irregular Present Tense Verbs: *Be, Have*

Two common present tense verbs are irregular and do not follow the usual pattern for endings. Review the forms of the verbs *be* and *have*.

Present Tense of *Be* and *Have*

Singular	Be	Have
First person:	I am	I have
Second person:	You are	You have
Third person:	He is	He has
	She is	She has
	It is	It has
Plural		
First person:	We are	We have
Second person:	You are	You have
Third person:	They are	They have

> **Hint** **Using the Irregular Verb Be**
>
> Use the verb *be* to identify age, hunger, thirst, feelings, height, and temperature. Remember that the form of the verb must also agree with the subject of the sentence.
>
> **Age:** He ~~has~~ *is* forty years old.
>
> **Hunger and thirst:** He ~~has~~ *is* thirsty, and I ~~have~~ *am* hungry.
>
> **Temperature:** It ~~be~~ *is* cold outside.
>
> Do not use *be* to express agreement.
>
> I ~~am~~ agree.

PRACTICE 2

Write present tense verbs in the spaces provided. Use the correct forms of *be* and *have*.

EXAMPLE:

J. K. Rowling _____*is*_____ the world's most successful children's author.

1. Her full name _____ Joanne Katherine Rowling. She _____ from Bristol, England, and she _____ the child of middle-class parents. Currently, she _____ over forty years old.

2. Rowling's books _____ about a child named Harry Potter. The child _____ no parents. His cruel aunt and uncle _____ his guardians. They _____ their own child,

whom they spoil, but they treat Harry horribly. Harry _____ a tiny bedroom under the stairs, and he _____ extremely unhappy.

3. As the story progresses, Harry goes to a special private school. He _____ two close friends in the new school, and he _____ able to use his special powers to fight evil.

4. The *Harry Potter* novels follow a literary tradition. Many fairy tales _____ about an orphan who overcomes obstacles. Often, cruel relatives or stepparents _____ in charge of the orphan. The child _____ no option but to grow up quickly and escape from the evil surrogate family.

Question Forms: *Do* or *Does*

To create present tense questions, begin each question with *do* or *does*.

Statement	Question
He complains a lot.	**Does** he complain a lot?
They read each night.	**Do** they read each night?

In the following chart, notice when to use the third-person singular form *does*.

Question Forms Using *Do* or *Does*

	Singular	Plural
First person:	Do I work?	Do we work?
Second person:	Do you work?	Do you work?
Third person:	Does he work? Does she work? Does it work?	Do they work?

Exception: When the main verb is *be* (*is*, *am*, *are*), just move *be* before the subject to form a question.

Is the story suspenseful? **Are** they safe?

PRACTICE 3

Fill in each blank with the correct present tense form of the verb *do* or *be*. Then underline the subject in each question.

EXAMPLES:

_____*Does*_____ it have a happy ending? _____*Is*_____ it interesting?

1. _____ we have time to discuss the novel?

2. _____ you a fan of murder mysteries?

3. _____ you want to read something else?

4. _____ the main character about forty years old?

5. _____ you like the author's writing style?

6. _____ he a good storyteller?

7. _____ the characters interesting?

8. _____ you know what the critics think?

9. _____ the newspaper critic fair?

Negative Forms: *Do Not, Does Not*

To form the negative of present tense verbs, place *do* or *does* and the word *not* between the subject and the verb.

> We **do not** read her novels.   (Contraction: **don't** read)

> Simon **does not** write every day.   (Contraction: **doesn't** write)

Negative Forms of *Do* and *Does*

	Singular Forms	**Contraction**
First person:	I do not work.	don't
Second person:	You do not work.	don't
Third person:	He does not work. She does not work. It does not work.	doesn't
	Plural Forms	
First person:	You do not work.	don't
Second person:	We do not work.	don't
Third person:	They do not work.	don't

Exception: When the main verb, is *be* (*is, am, are*), just add *not*.

> The story **is not** suspenseful.   (Contraction: **isn't**)

> They **are not** happy with the ending.   (Contraction: **aren't**)

PRACTICE 4

A. Add *-s* or *-es* to each italicized verb, if necessary. Then, write the negative form and contraction in the spaces provided.

EXAMPLE:

	Negative Form	**Contraction**
Frodo *do*_**es**_ many strange things.	*does not do*	*doesn't do*
1. In *The Lord of the Rings*, a little hobbit *make*____ friends with a wizard.	_____	_____
2. He *live*____ in a small house.	_____	_____

3. His best friend, Sam, *eat*____ a lot of greasy food.

    _____ _____

4. They *leave*____ their village to go on a journey.

    _____ _____

5. Frodo *own*____ a special ring.

    _____ _____

6. They *stay*____ up late every night.

    _____ _____

7. The hobbits *meet*____ some elves.

    _____ _____

B. Write the correct form of the verb *be* in each blank. Then, write the negative form and contraction.

EXAMPLE:

	Negative Form	**Contraction**
Frodo's feet _are_ very large.	are not	aren't

8. Their journey _____ dangerous.

    _____ _____

9. The hobbits _____ brave.

    _____ _____

10. J. R. R. Tolkien's books _____ expensive.

    _____ _____

> ## Hint **Correcting Question and Negative Forms**
>
> In question and negative forms, always use the base form of the main verb even when the subject is third-person singular. Put the -s or -es ending only on the helping verb (*does*).
>
>   *have*
> Why **does** the magazine ~~has~~ so many subscribers?
>
>   *contain*
> The magazine **does** not ~~contains~~ many advertisements.

PRACTICE 5

Correct errors in present tense verb forms.

EXAMPLE:

        are
Romance novels ~~be~~ extremely popular.

1. Four Harlequin romance novels sells every second.

2. Romance novels are translated into many languages, but most of the writers be from the United States, Canada, or Britain.

3. A typical romance novel follow a formula.

4. Initially, the heroine do not like the hero, and she struggles against her growing attraction.

5. Romance novels does not have sad endings.

6. Be chick lit and romance novels the same thing?

7. In so-called "chick lit," the heroine do not always fall in love.

8. Why do Heather Graham write romance novels?

9. According to Graham, each novel express a universal human emotion.

10. Stories about exciting relationships provides readers with an escape from reality.

The Simple Past Tense

The **simple past tense** shows that an action occurred at a specific past time. In the past tense, there are regular and irregular verbs.

Regular Past Tense Verbs

Regular past tense verbs have a standard *-d* or *-ed* ending (*talked, ended, watched*). Use the same form for both singular and plural past tense verbs.

Singular subject: F. Scott Fitzerald **published** his stories in several languages.

Plural subject: Last Friday, the journalists **interviewed** us.

LAST FRIDAY   TODAY

The journalists **interviewed** us.

 Spelling of Regular Verbs

Most regular past tense verbs are formed by adding *-ed* to the base form of the verb.

   talk–talk**ed**   mention–mention**ed**

Exceptions

• When the regular verb ends in *-e*, add just *-d*.

   hope–hope**d**   bake–bake**d**

• When the regular verb ends in a consonant + *y*, change the *y* to *i* and add *-ed*.

   fry–fr**ied**   apply–appl**ied**

   Note: if the regular verb ends in a vowel + *y*, add just *-ed*.

   play–play**ed**   destroy–destroy**ed**

• When the regular verb ends in a consonant-vowel-consonant combination, double the last consonant and add *-ed*.

   stop–stop**ped**   jog–jog**ged**

GRAMMAR LINK

See Chapter 23, "Spelling," for more spelling tips.

PRACTICE 6

Write the past tense forms of the following verbs.

EXAMPLE:

watch <u>*watched*</u>

1. hope	_____	6. plan	_____
2. try	_____	7. rain	_____
3. stay	_____	8. rest	_____
4. employ	_____	9. deny	_____
5. study	_____	10. ban	_____

Hint **Past versus Passed**

Some people confuse *past* and *passed*. *Past* is a noun that means "in a previous time; before now."

She has many secrets in her <u>past</u>. Her mistakes are in the <u>past</u>.

Passed is the past tense of the verb *pass*, which has many meanings. In the first example, it means "went by"; in the second example, it means "to successfully complete."

Many days <u>passed</u>, and the nights got shorter.

She <u>passed</u> her exams.

PRACTICE 7

Write the simple past form of each verb in parentheses. Make sure that you have spelled your past tense verbs correctly.

EXAMPLE:

In 1925, two boys (wonder) <u>*wondered*</u> how to enter the comic book industry.

1. In 1933, teenagers Jerry Seigel and Joe Shuster (create) _____ a story about an evil, power-hungry man.

2. Their short story, "The Reign of Superman," (describe) _____ a bald-headed villain who (aim) _____ to take over the world.

3. Nobody (want) _____ to buy their story.

4. Seigel and Shuster (change) _____ their lead character into a noble hero with super powers.

5. Four years later, DC Comics (agree) _____ to publish the first Superman comic.

6. In 1941, Seigel and Shuster (earn) _____ $75,000 for their Superman comics.

7. The pair (battle) _____ their publisher to get a larger share of the immense profits from Superman.

8. The angry publisher then (fire) _____ Seigel and Shuster.

9. In 1948, the writers (accept) _____ a small cash settlement.

10. They (sign) _____ away their rights to any future earnings from the Superman franchise.

11. In the 1950s, both men (watch) _____ the Superman TV series, and they (receive) _____ nothing for the series.

12. In 1978, Warner Communications, the makers of the effects-laden *Superman: The Movie*, (offer) _____ to pay the penniless Superman creators a yearly pension.

CHAPTER 9

Irregular Past Tense Verbs

Irregular verbs do not end in any specific letter. Because their spellings change from the present to the past forms, these verbs can be challenging to remember.

Irregular Verbs

Base Form	Simple Past	Base Form	Simple Past	Base Form	Simple Past
be	was, were	burst	burst	eat	ate
beat	beat	buy	bought	fall	fell
become	became	catch	caught	feed	fed
begin	began	choose	chose	feel	felt
bend	bent	cling	clung	fight	fought
bet	bet	come	came	find	found
bind	bound	cost	cost	flee	fled
bite	bit	cut	cut	fly	flew
bleed	bled	deal	dealt	forget	forgot
blow	blew	dig	dug	forgive	forgave
breed	bred	do	did	freeze	froze
break	broke	draw	drew	get	got
bring	brought	drink	drank	give	gave
build	built	drive	drove	go	went

Base Form	Simple Past	Base Form	Simple Past	Base Form	Simple Past
grind	ground	read	read	spring	sprang
grow	grew	rid	rid	stand	stood
hang	hung	ride	rode	steal	stole
have	had	ring	rang	stick	stuck
hear	heard	rise	rose	sting	stung
hide	hid	run	ran	stink	stank
hit	hit	say	said	strike	struck
hold	held	see	saw	swear	swore
hurt	hurt	sell	sold	sweep	swept
keep	kept	send	sent	swim	swam
kneel	knelt	set	set	swing	swung
know	knew	shake	shook	take	took
lay	laid	shoot	shot	teach	taught
lead	led	shrink	shrank	tear	tore
leave	left	shut	shut	tell	told
lend	lent	sing	sang	think	thought
let	let	sink	sank	throw	threw
lie*	lay	sit	sat	thrust	thrust
light	lit	sleep	slept	understand	understood
lose	lost	slide	slid	upset	upset
make	made	slit	slit	wake	woke
mean	meant	speak	spoke	wear	wore
meet	met	speed	sped	weep	wept
mistake	mistook	spend	spent	win	won
pay	paid	spin	spun	wind	wound
put	put	split	split	withdraw	withdrew
quit	quit	spread	spread	write	wrote

*Lie means "to rest," for example, on a sofa or bed. When lie means "tell a false statement," it is a regular verb: lie, lied, lied.

PRACTICE 8

Write the correct past form of each verb in parentheses. Some verbs are regular, and some are irregular.

EXAMPLE:

In the 1950s, journalists at *The Confidential* (write) _____**wrote**_____ about show-business scandals.

1.   In 1833, the first American tabloid, the *New York Sun*, (hit)

_____ the streets. Boys (sell) _____ the tabloids on

street corners. Journalists (give) _____ readers stories about

political scandals, murders, and other crimes.

2.   In the 1952, a new tabloid (rise) _____ to prominence. An
Italian publisher, Generoso Pope, Jr., (buy) _____ a newspaper
called the *Enquirer*. It (be) _____ full of horse-racing tips.

3.   Pope (pay) _____ about $70,000 for the *Enquirer*. The
paper's focus (change) _____ from horse racing to bizarre and
gory stories about cannibalism and other crimes. The *Enquirer*'s staff
(make) _____ up incredible stories. Readers usually (think)
_____ that the stories were true.

The Past Form of *Be* (*Was* or *Were*)

The verb *be* has two past forms: *was* and *were*.

Past Tense of Be

	Singular	Plural
First person:	I was	We were
Second person:	You were	You were
Third person:	He was	They were
	She was	
	It was	

PRACTICE 9

Fill in each blank with *was* or *were*.

EXAMPLE:

During the early years of Hollywood, people ____*were*____ curious about celebrities.

1.   In the early 1950s, there _____ many hoax stories in the
National Enquirer. However, in the late 1950s, that situation changed. Each
journalist _____ careful to include true stories about celebrities.
The friends and employees of the famous _____ often greedy, and
they _____ ready to sell information to the tabloids.

2.   Some popular celebrities _____ on the front covers of the
tabloids each week. For example, during the 1960s, the love life of
Elizabeth Taylor _____ front-page news. Her many marriages
_____ the fodder for gossip columnists. Often, reporters
_____ disguised as bellhops or police officers. By wearing disguises,
they _____ able to get close to movie stars. For example, a
photographer _____ able to take photographs of Taylor by posing
as a waiter.

Negative Forms of Past Tense Verbs

To form the negative of past tense verbs, place *did* and the word *not* between the subject and the verb.

>The actress **did not** want to appear in tabloids.   (Contraction: **didn't**)

>We **did not** buy that newspaper.   (Contraction: **didn't**)

Exception: When the main verb is *be* (*was*, *were*), just add *not*.

>The story **was not** suspenseful.   (Contraction: **wasn't**)

>They **were not** happy with the ending.   (Contraction: **weren't**)

PRACTICE 10

Write the contracted negative forms of the underlined verbs.

EXAMPLE:

He <u>worked</u>.   ___*didn't work*___   They <u>were</u> hungry. ___*weren't*___

1. She <u>was</u> busy. _____
2. Joe <u>ate</u> a lot. _____
3. You <u>made</u> it. _____
4. We <u>spoke</u>. _____
5. I <u>lied</u>. _____

6. I <u>did</u> it.   _____
7. We <u>washed</u> up. _____
8. They <u>were</u> late. _____
9. Kay <u>went</u> out. _____
10. He <u>opened</u> it. _____

Question Forms of Past Tense Verbs

To create past tense questions, add the helping verb *did* before the subject.

>Shuster drew Superman.   **Did** Shuster draw Superman?
>They liked the story.   **Did** they like the story?

Exception: When the main verb is *be* (*was*, *were*), just move *be* before the subject to form a question.

>**Was** the story exciting?   **Were** you ready?

 **Hint**   **Use the Base Form After *Did***

In question and negative forms, remember to use the base form—not the past form—of the main verb.

>   use
>Did he ~~used~~ a computer to write his book?

PRACTICE 11

Correct the errors with question or negative forms.

EXAMPLE:

>   *did he seem*
>Why ~~he seem~~ so surprised by his success?

1. J. R. R. Tolkien don't be born in England.

2. He did not remained in South Africa.

3. When he moved to Birmingham, England?

4. Why did Tolkien wrote about hobbits?

5. His friends not believed in the value of myths.

6. Tolkien wasn't agree with his friends.

7. *The Lord of the Rings* didn't be popular at first.

8. Why the book became popular ten years after its release?

9. Why did the book sold more than 100 million copies?

10. When Amazon.com customers voted for *The Lord of the Rings* as the book

    of the millennium?

Common Errors with *Be* and *Have*

Some writers find it particularly difficult to remember how to use the irregular verbs *be* and *have*.

- Use *were*, not *was*, when the subject is plural.

    were
    The photographers ~~was~~ extremely persistent.

- Use the standard form of the verb (*is* or *was*), not *be*.

    was
    The story about the movie star ~~be~~ shocking.

- Use the past form of the verb (*had*), not the present form (*have* or *has*), when speaking about a past event.

    had
    Mike Wallace ~~has~~ to work in dangerous war zones during his early days as a reporter.

PRACTICE 12

If the underlined past tense verb is incorrectly formed or in the wrong tense, write the correct form above it. There are twenty errors.

EXAMPLE:

was
Hoax journalism <u>be</u> common in past eras.

1.   Last year, I <u>readed</u> about an alien baby in a newspaper tabloid. Of

   course, I <u>knowed</u> that the story <u>was</u> false, but I <u>haved</u> fun reading it. Hoax journalism is not new. In the nineteenth century, most respected newspapers <u>costed</u> six cents. However, "pulp fiction," <u>filled</u> with sensational stories, <u>selled</u> for one penny. The penny newspapers <u>was</u> extremely popular and profitable.

2.   Some of America's greatest writers <u>thinked</u> that pulp fiction was mediocre, but those same writers <u>craved</u> the large audiences that penny newspapers provided. Mark Twain, for example, <u>writed</u> a story about a headless killer. The killer <u>runned</u> through the streets holding his wife's scalp. Edgar Allan Poe also <u>feeled</u> curious about hoax stories. In 1844, he <u>created</u> a story about a giant balloon that could cross oceans. He <u>see</u> into the future because the first hot-air balloon <u>crossed</u> the ocean more than one hundred years later, in 1978.

3.   One of the most widespread hoaxes <u>involved</u> "moon men." In 1835, the *New York Sun* <u>printed</u> articles about the moon's furry, winged creatures. According to the newspaper, Sir John Hershel, a respected astronomer, <u>builded</u> a giant, powerful telescope. Each article <u>be</u> full of details about Hershel's observations.

4.   People <u>was</u> ready to believe the moon men stories. The articles <u>haved</u> enough facts to seem plausible. An astronomer named Hershel actually <u>existed</u>. Also, many citizens <u>be</u> worried about Halley's comet, so they often <u>looked</u> at the skies. They soon <u>realize</u> that they should not believe everything in newspapers.

5.   More recently, in 1999, newspapers and magazines <u>reported</u> dubious "facts" about the millennium bug. People <u>buyed</u> supplies and <u>digged</u> bomb shelters. They <u>was</u> scared of widespread power failures. The media <u>contributed</u> to the mass hysteria. Many people <u>were</u> amazed when nothing major happened on January 1, 2000.

Avoiding Double Negatives

A **double negative** occurs when a writer combines a negative word such as *no, nothing, nobody,* or *nowhere* with a negative adverb such as *not, never, rarely,* or *seldom.* The result is a sentence that has a double negative. Such sentences can be confusing because the negative words cancel each other.

> **Double negative:**   She <u>doesn't</u> give <u>no</u> interviews.
>
> He <u>never</u> received <u>no</u> royalties.

How to Correct Double Negatives

There are two ways to correct double negatives.

- Completely remove *one* of the negative forms.

Incorrect	**Correct**
She **doesn't** give **no** interviews.	She **doesn't** give interviews.
	She gives **no** interviews.
He **never** received **no** royalties.	He **never** received royalties.
	He received **no** royalties.

- Change *no* to *any* (*anybody, anything, anywhere*).

Incorrect	**Correct**
She **doesn't** give **no** interviews.	She doesn't give **any** interviews.
He **never** received **no** royalties.	He never received **any** royalties.

PRACTICE 13

Correct six errors with double negatives. You can correct each error in more than one way.

EXAMPLE:

Amy Tan's novel didn't have ~~no~~ negative reviews. *(any)*

Amy Tan's novel ~~didn't have~~ no negative reviews. *(had)*

1. Amy Tan's mother, Daisy, left an abusive husband in China and went to the United States. She had three daughters, but her husband did not let her take none of her daughters with her. Daisy married John Tan, and they had a daughter named Amy. Her parents did not have no other daughters, but they had two sons.

2. Amy's mother did not want her daughter to make no mistakes. She pushed Amy to enter medical school, but Amy didn't have no ambition to be a doctor. Amy rebelled and decided to study English instead.

Amy also rebelled by moving to San Francisco so that she could be near her boyfriend. There wasn't no reason for her to stay in Oakland.

3.   Amy's relationship with her mother improved in later years. In 1987, they traveled to China together to meet Mrs. Tan's long-lost daughters. Amy's first novel, *The Joy Luck Club*, was inspired by her mother's life, and it became an international best-seller. Most reviewers didn't say nothing bad about the novel.

FINAL REVIEW

Correct fifteen errors. There are present tense, past tense, and double negative errors.

EXAMPLE:

were
The books ~~was~~ offensive.

1.   The Federal Anti-Obscenity Act past in 1873. After that, citizens was not able to buy certain novels. For example, in 1915, the U.S. government did not permitted Americans to import James Joyce's classic novel *Ulysses*. Officials called the book obscene. Some activists fighted the government, and in 1930, they winned the right to publish the book in the United States. In 2000, the Modern Library choosed *Ulysses* as the best book of the twentieth century.

2.   Between 1873 and 2000, school districts and libraries in the United States banned hundreds of novels for a variety of reasons. For example, in 1939, administrators at the St. Louis Public Library stoped lending John Steinbeck's classic *The Grapes of Wrath* because they thinked that the novel's language was vulgar. In the 1960s, some people goed to other countries to buy the American classic *The Catcher in the Rye* because many states banned the novel. In the 1990s, some officials didn't want to stock no copies of Mark Twain's *Huckleberry Finn*

because they believed that the book portrayed African Americans in a negative way. Some people also disliked the portrayal of Shylock, a Jewish merchant, in Shakespeare's play *The Merchant of Venice.* They sayed that Shakespeare stereotyped certain members of society in his play.

3.   Generally, book banners wants to safeguard the values of their communities. They don't see no problem with book banning. Others believes that people should have the freedom to choose their own reading material. They feels that books give insight into the social attitudes of different eras. Book banning is an emotional issue, and people will continue to debate the subject.

The Writer's Room

Write about one of the following topics. After you finish writing, underline your verbs. Verify that you have formed your present and past tense verbs correctly.

1. Describe your major source of entertainment during your childhood. Did you read? If not, why not? What other types of things did you do?

2. Describe what happens in a story, poem, play, or article that you have read.

✔ CHECKLIST: PRESENT AND PAST TENSES

When you edit your writing, ask yourself the following questions.

Do I use the correct present tense forms? Check for errors in these cases:

–verbs following third-person singular nouns
–irregular present tense verbs
–question and negative forms

Zoey Cervantes, a young author, ~~need~~ *needs* to find a literary agent.

Do
~~Does~~ you know of anyone she could contact?

Do I use the correct past tense forms? Check for spelling errors and other mistakes with the following:

–regular past tense verbs

–irregular past tense verbs

–negative and question forms

In 1969, Maya Angelou ~~wroted~~ *wrote* her first novel. Why she ~~decided~~ *did decide* to write a novel?

Do my sentences have standard English? Check for errors in the following cases:

–use of *ain't* instead of *is not, am not,* or *are not*
–use of double negatives instead of correct negative forms

J. D. Salinger, the author of *Catcher in the Rye*, never gives ~~no~~ *any* interviews.

How Do I Get a Better Grade?

Visit www.mywritinglab.com for audio-visual lectures and additional practice sets about present and past tenses.
Get a better grade with MyWritingLab!

Section Theme: **ENTERTAINMENT AND CULTURE**

CONTENTS

- Past Participles
- The Present Perfect Tense
- The Past Perfect Tense
- The Past Participle as an Adjective
- The Passive Voice

In this chapter, you will read about topics related to television and film.

Grammar Snapshot

Looking at Past Participles

Silent film actor George Arliss wrote several autobiographies, including *Up the Years from Bloomsbury.* In this excerpt, Arliss discusses film acting. The past participles of verbs are underlined.

> I had always <u>believed</u> that, for the movies, acting must be <u>exaggerated</u>, but I saw in this one flash that restraint was the chief thing that the actor had to learn in transferring art from the stage to the screen. The art of restraint and suggestion on the screen may any time be <u>studied</u> by watching the acting of the inimitable Charlie Chaplin.

In this chapter, you will identify and write past participles.

Base Form	Simple Past	Past Participle	Base Form	Simple Past	Past Participle
make	made	made	spin	spun	spun
mean	meant	meant	split	split	split
meet	met	met	spread	spread	spread
mistake	mistook	mistaken	spring	sprang	sprung
pay	paid	paid	stand	stood	stood
put	put	put	steal	stole	stolen
quit	quit	quit	stick	stuck	stuck
read	read	read	sting	stung	stung
rid	rid	rid	stink	stank	stunk
ride	rode	ridden	strike	struck	struck
ring	rang	rung	swear	swore	sworn
rise	rose	risen	sweep	swept	swept
run	ran	run	swell	swelled	swollen
say	said	said	swim	swam	swum
see	saw	seen	swing	swung	swung
sell	sold	sold	take	took	taken
send	sent	sent	teach	taught	taught
set	set	set	tear	tore	torn
shake	shook	shaken	tell	told	told
shoot	shot	shot	think	thought	thought
show	showed	shown	throw	threw	thrown
shut	shut	shut	thrust	thrust	thrust
sing	sang	sung	understand	understood	understood
sink	sank	sunk	upset	upset	upset
sit	sat	sat	wake	woke	woken
sleep	slept	slept	wear	wore	worn
slide	slid	slid	weep	wept	wept
slit	slit	slit	win	won	won
speak	spoke	spoken	wind	wound	wound
speed	sped	sped	withdraw	withdrew	withdrawn
spend	spent	spent	write	wrote	written

PRACTICE 2

Write the simple past and the past participle of the following verbs.

Base Form	Past Tense		Past Participle

EXAMPLE:

lose   *lost*   *lost*

1. cost   _____   _____

2. choose   _____   _____

3. drive   _____   _____

4. break   _____   _____

5. ring   _____   _____

6. bring   _____   _____

7. drink   _____   _____

8. think   _____   _____

9. build   _____   _____

10. become   _____   _____

11. grow   _____   _____

12. hit   _____   _____

13. sit   _____   _____

14. go   _____   _____

15. do   _____   _____

PRACTICE 3

The irregular past participles are underlined. Correct the twelve past participle errors, and write *C* above correct verbs.

EXAMPLE:

                    learned

Many acting students have <u>learn</u> the Stanislavsky method.

1.   Most people have <u>thinked</u> about becoming famous actors. Acting seems like an easy thing to do; however, most successful actors have <u>spend</u> years developing their craft.

2.   If you want to be an actor, take some acting classes. Acting is <u>teached</u> in many colleges and private institutes. In acting classes, students are <u>given</u> the basic techniques. Acting students are often <u>telled</u> to read novels and plays as well as reference books and biographies. Most actors have <u>readed</u> many classic works.

3.   According to talent agent Myra Daly, after you have <u>took</u> your classes, you should develop your "persona." An actor is like a product; his or her persona is <u>selled.</u> Perhaps you have <u>became</u> the femme fatale, the bitter comic, the nice guy, the menacing criminal, or the girl next door. If you have <u>finded</u> a persona, it is easy for your agent to promote you. Although good actors can play many types of roles, even many well-known actors have <u>falled</u> into a "type." For example, some people say Reese Witherspoon has not <u>shaken</u> her "girl next door"

persona even though she has <u>been</u> in a variety of different roles. Some actors have <u>feeled</u> upset and frustrated when they have <u>been</u> typecast.

4. The last step is to prepare your résumé and get references from teachers and other influential people who have <u>saw</u> your work. Traditionally, good acting jobs have <u>been</u> hard to find. If you persevere, and if you believe in your abilities, you have a chance at succeeding.

The Present Perfect Tense: *Have/Has* + Past Participle

A past participle combines with *have* or *has* to form the **present perfect tense**. You can use this tense in two different circumstances.

- Use the present perfect to show that an action began in the past and continues to the present time. Some key words and expressions to look for are *since, for, ever, not yet, so far,* and *up to now.*

PAST	PRESENT PERFECT	NOW

Makeup artist Ella Chu **has lived** in Los Angeles since 1998.

- Use the present perfect to show that one or more completed actions occurred at unimportant and unspecified past times. Some key words and expressions to look for are *already, once, twice, several times,* and *many times.*

PAST (unspecified past times)   NOW
? ? ? ?

Ella Chu **has returned** to her hometown in Canada many times.

Look at the difference between the past and the present perfect tenses in the following examples.

Simple past: In August 2005, three friends <u>launched</u> the Internet site YouTube.
(This event occurred at a known past time.)

Present perfect: Since 2005, many ordinary people <u>have posted</u> homemade videos on YouTube.
(The action began in the past and continues to the present moment.)

J. Junkala <u>has made</u> more than twenty videos.
(The repeated past actions have occurred at unspecified past times.)

PRACTICE 4

Write the present perfect form of each verb in parentheses.

EXAMPLE:

Horror movies (be) _____*have*_____ _____*been*_____ around for almost a century.

1.   Since its beginning, the Internet (change) _____

_____ people's lives in various ways. Recently, with the

introduction of video-sharing Web sites, people (have)

_____ _____ the chance to flirt with fame.

In fact, since 2004, thousands of ordinary men and women (make)

_____ _____ videos for YouTube, MySpace,

or other video-sharing sites.

2.   Some of the videos (become) _____

_____ extremely popular. For example, over 25 million

people (see) _____ _____ the virtuoso guitar

playing of a young South Korean student. In the video, the young man's

face is obscured by a baseball cap, but viewers can see his fingers fly over

the strings. Since the video first appeared in February 2006, YouTube

viewers (marvel) _____ _____ over Mr.

Lim's interpretation of Johann Pachelbel's *Canon.* On many occasions,

journalists (try) _____ _____ to interview

Lim. However, Lim (say) _____ _____

repeatedly that he does not want fame.

3.   The most watched YouTube video shows a balding comic doing a series

of dance moves. Although the video is not spectacular, close to 60 million

people (watch) _____ _____ it. For over a

year, the comic (express) _____ _____

shock at the video's success.

4.   Sometimes, an online homemade video can contribute to enduring

fame. For example, British singer Lily Allen (post) _____

_____ several music videos on MySpace. Many times, she

(thank) _____ _____ MySpace for giving her

a large fan base.

5.   For the last few years, some corporations (be) _____

_____ upset with the spread of file-sharing Internet sites.

Entertainment industry officials object to unauthorized use of film clips or songs. However, they (not, stop) _____ _____ the video-sharing Websites.

Hint Time Markers

Time markers are words that indicate when an action occurred.

Simple Past Tense
To refer to an incident that occurred at a specific past time, use the following time markers.

yesterday	ago	when I was . . .	last (week, month, year . . .)
in the past	in 1925	during the 1990s	in the early days of . . .

In <u>1989</u>, Spike Lee **directed** the film *Do the Right Thing.*

Present Perfect Tense
To refer to an action that began in the past and is still continuing, use the following time markers.

since	ever, never		so far	up to now
not yet	for (a period of time up to now)	lately	recently

I **have been** a Spike Lee fan <u>since 1990</u>.

To refer to an action that occurred at an unspecified past time or past times, use the following time markers.

many	several times	repeatedly	once, twice, three times

I **have watched** *Jungle Fever* <u>once</u> and *Malcolm X* <u>twice</u>.

PRACTICE 5

Underline the correct past or present perfect tense of each verb in parentheses.

EXAMPLE:

In recent years, visual effects (became, <u>have become</u>, has become) quite sophisticated.

1. In the 1930s, special effects in movies (was, were, have been) ingenious.

2. In 1934, the movie *King Kong* (contained, has contained, have contained) sets with miniature skyscrapers and model airplanes.

3. To make the ape movie back then, *King Kong* artists (created, have created, has created) a model of the giant ape and then (moved, have moved, has moved) the model slightly every few frames of film.

4. Since 1934, audiences (appreciated, have appreciated, has appreciated) special effects.

5. Since the 1980s, computerized animation (became, have become, has become) more sophisticated.

6. In recent years, film studios (developed, have developed, has developed) new animation techniques.

7. In 1995, *Toy Story* (was, has been, have been) the first completely computer-animated film.

8. Since then, many other computer-animated films (hit, have hit, has hit) movie screens.

9. Additionally, makeup (improved, have improved, has improved) since the 1980s.

10. Recently, the use of latex (allowed, have allowed, has allowed) makeup artists to create interesting effects.

11. In the 2001 film *The Lord of the Rings*, the hobbits (wore, have worn, has worn) large latex feet.

12. Since then, many actors (wore, have worn, has worn) latex masks and suits.

PRACTICE 6

Fill in the blanks with either the simple past or the present perfect verb tense.

EXAMPLE:

I (watch) _____*have watched*_____ *General Hospital* since I was seven years old.

1. Daytime soap operas (change) _____ a lot since they began. In the 1930s, soap companies (sponsor) _____ daytime radio dramas. For example, the program *The Guiding Light* (begin) _____ in the 1930s as a radio show. Then, in the 1940s, the television network CBS (film) _____ *The Guiding Light*. It (be) _____ a popular daytime drama since then.

2. Over the years, some well-known actors (appear) _____ in soap operas. For example, Josh Duhamel (act) _____ in *All My Children* when he was younger.

3. Soap operas are popular in many nations. Since 1980, Mexican producers (sell) _____ soap operas to nations around the world. Actress Salma Hayek (have) _____ the lead role in the Mexican soap opera *Teresa* in 1989. Her career (take) _____ off since then. Since the late 1990s, Mexican soap operas (be) _____ very popular in Russia.

4.   For many years, critics (complain) _____ that the actors in soap operas are too beautiful. However, since the 1960s, British studios (bring) _____ regular-looking people to television screens. Since its debut, the long-running soap opera *Coronation Street* (star) _____ a variety of ordinary-looking actors. For more than fifty years, daytime soap operas (be) _____ an essential part of afternoon television schedules.

The Past Perfect Tense: *Had* + Past Participle

The **past perfect tense** indicates that one or more past actions happened before another past action. To form the past perfect, use *had* plus the past participle.

PAST PERFECT	PAST	NOW
▼	▼	▼

The movie **had started** when Vladimir arrived.

Notice the differences between the simple past, the present perfect, and the past perfect tenses.

Simple past: Last night I <u>rented</u> the video *No Country for Old Men*.
(The action occurred at a known past time: *last night*.)

Present perfect: I <u>have seen</u> most of Javier Bardem's movies.
(The actions have occurred at unspecified past times.)

Past perfect: When Denzel Washington appeared in *American Gangster*, he <u>had</u> already <u>acted</u> in several successful films.
(All of the actions happened in the past, but Washington had acted in good movies before he appeared in *American Gangster*.)

PRACTICE 7

Underline the correct verb tense. Choose either the simple past or the past perfect verb.

EXAMPLE:

When Charlie Chaplin left England, he (already acted, <u>had already acted</u>) in many productions.

1. Charles Spencer Chaplin was born into a London slum on April 16, 1889, and then, in 1910, he (arrived, had arrived) in America.

2. Because Chaplin (accumulated, had accumulated) a lot of acting experience in England, Mack Sennett hired him to work in Sennett comedies.

3. In 1920, Chaplin earned $10,000 per week, which was more than he (ever earned, had ever earned) in his life!

4. He (developed, had developed) his Tramp character, which was inspired by the poverty that he (experienced, had experienced).

5. When he turned twenty-six years old, he fulfilled a dream that he (had, had had) for several years.

6. Chaplin (directed, had directed) his own movies, and, in his films, he expressed sympathy for the poor.

7. FBI agents investigated Chaplin because they thought that he (joined, had joined) the Communist party.

8. At that time, Chaplin didn't have American citizenship even though he (spent, had spent) most of his professional life in the United States.

9. In 1952, the U.S. immigration authorities revoked Chaplin's re-entry permit after he (sailed, had sailed) for England.

10. Although Chaplin (made, had made) many successful American comedies, he (spent, had spent) most of the next years living in exile.

11. In 1972, Chaplin (returned, had returned) to America to accept an Academy Award for Lifetime Achievement.

12. When Chaplin passed away in 1977, his children knew that he (lived, had lived) an extremely full and rewarding life.

PRACTICE 8

Underline the correct tense of each verb in parentheses. You may choose the simple past, the present perfect, or the past perfect tense.

EXAMPLE:

For decades, parents (<u>have worried</u>, had worried) about the effects of television on children.

1.   In 1999, journalist Ellen Goodman (wrote, had written) the article "Going Thin in Fiji" about the influence of television on Fijian society. In 1994, people on the island of Fiji (appreciated, had appreciated) large women. In fact, big women (received, had received) many compliments.

2.　Then, in 1995, something (changed, has changed) on the island. That year, television (appeared, had appeared) for the first time in Fiji. Most islanders (never saw, had never seen) a TV show when the first televisions arrived.

3.　Since 1995, television (changed, has changed, had changed) the lives of people in Fiji. In recent years, young girls in Fiji (have watched, had watched) American television shows filled with thin actresses. The images (have affected, had affected) the self-esteem of Fijian women.

4.　In 1998, 75 percent of Fijian girls said that they (felt, have felt) too fat, yet most of those same girls (have never worried, had never worried) about their weight when they were younger. In that same interview, 62 percent of Fijian girls (said, had said) that they (dieted, had dieted) in the previous month. Clearly, media images influence the way people see themselves.

The Past Participle as an Adjective

A past participle can function as an adjective by modifying or describing the noun that follows it.

He sat near the **broken** window.
(*Broken* modifies *window*.)

PRACTICE 9

Write a logical past participle in each blank. Use the past participle form of the following verbs. Do not use the same verb more than once.

~~break~~	chip	fry	know	respect
bruise	dress	hide	qualify	tear

EXAMPLE:

Marla was shocked when she saw the _____*broken*_____ lock.

1.　Brad Pitt wore _____ clothing for his boxing scenes in the 1999 film *Fight Club*.

2.　Some actors had _____ faces after the fight scenes.

3.　Ed Norton, who narrated the movie, is a loved and _____ actor.

4. For some scenes, Brad Pitt removed the dental cap from his
   _____ front tooth.

5. Sometimes, tiny _____ microphones recorded the
   actors' dialogue.

6. Helena Bonham Carter played a poorly _____ woman
   named Marla Singer.

7. A _____ doctor was always on the set.

8. The caterers sometimes served _____ food.

9. The well-_____ movie won many awards.

The Passive Voice: *Be* + Past Participle

In sentences with the **passive voice,** the subject receives the action and does not perform the action. To form the passive voice, use the appropriate tense of the verb *be* + the past participle. The helping verb shows the verb tense.

passive
Acting is the art of lying well. I am **paid** to tell elaborate lies.

—Mel Gibson, actor

Look carefully at the following two sentences. Notice the differences between the active and the passive voice.

Active: Alejandro González Iñárritu **released** *Babel* in 2006.

(This sentence is active because the subject, Iñárritu, performed the action.)

Passive: The movie **was filmed** in 2005.

(This sentence is passive because the subject, the movie, did not perform the action.)

Active and Passive Voice

Verb Tenses	Active	Passive: *Be* + Past Participle
	The subject performs the action.	The subject receives the action.
Simple present:	They produce movies.	Movies are produced by them.
Present progressive:	are producing	are being produced
Simple past:	produced	were produced
Present perfect:	have produced	have been produced
Future:	will produce	will be produced
Modals:	can produce	can be produced
	could produce	could be produced
	should produce	should be produced

> *Hint*   **Avoid Overusing the Passive Voice**
>
> Generally, try to use the active voice instead of the passive voice. The active voice is more direct and friendly than the passive voice. For example, read the next two versions of the same message.
>
> **Passive voice:**   Your questions about our cable service have been received by us. You will be contacted by our sales representative.
>
> **Active voice:**   We have received your questions about our cable service. Our sales representative will contact you.

PRACTICE 10

Decide whether each underlined verb is active or passive, and write *A* (for "active") or *P* (for "passive") above each verb.

EXAMPLE:

                                  P
The story is based on a fictional event.

1.   In the early 1940s, a radio was owned by almost every American family. Then, in 1941, the first television show was broadcast. In 1942, some veteran radio performers predicted that television would never catch on. However, television has been a permanent fixture in American homes since then.

2.   It is hard for us to imagine the excitement that was felt in the 1940s. In those years, one television was watched by many people, including friends and relatives of the owners. In fact, TV watching was a social event. For example, in 1946, the first TV sports extravaganza was staged by NBC. The program featured boxing great Joe Louis. The match was seen by about 150,000 people, or about thirty viewers per television. Today, the average television is watched by only three people.

> *Hint*   **The by . . . Phrase**
>
> In many passive sentences, it is not necessary to write the *by . . .* phrase.
>
> The film was released in 2005 ~~by United Artists~~.
>
> The costumes were made in France ~~by costume designers~~.

PRACTICE 11

A. Complete the following sentences by changing each italicized verb to the passive form. Do not alter the verb tense. In some sentences, you do not have to include the *by . . .* phrase.

EXAMPLE:

Producers *make* movies all over the world.

 Movies are made all over the world (by producers).

1. Fame *attracts* many ordinary people.

   Many ordinary people _____

2. People *view* movie stars as happy, exciting people.

   Movie stars _____

3. In 2005, a producer *offered* Maria Figuera a job in a movie.

   In 2005, Maria Figuera _____

4. The director *filmed* the movie in Boston.

   The movie _____

5. Perhaps people *will recognize* Maria in the future.

   Perhaps Maria _____

B. The following sentences are in the passive voice. Change the verbs in italics to the active voice, but do not alter the verb tense.

EXAMPLE:

Some actors *are paid* too much money by the studios.

Studios *pay some actors too much money.*

6. Famous actors *have been stalked* by overzealous fans.

   Overzealous fans _____

7. A few years ago, Orlando Bloom's privacy *was invaded* by journalists.

   A few years ago, journalists _____

8. Many complaints *are made* by actors about their lack of privacy.

   Many actors _____

9. Perhaps actors *should not be chased* by paparazzi.

   Perhaps paparazzi _____

10. Tabloids *are enjoyed* by some ordinary people.

    Some ordinary people _____

> ⟨*Hint*⟩ **Using the Passive Form**
>
> In the passive voice, sometimes a form of the verb *be* is suggested but not written. The following sentence contains the passive voice.
>
> **Be is suggested:** Many movies **made** in the 1970s have become classics.
>
> **Be is written:** Many movies **that were** made in the 1970s have become classics.

PRACTICE 12

Correct fifteen errors with past participles.

EXAMPLE:

seen
I have <u>saw</u> *Pride and Prejudice* twice.

1. Comic book series such as *Batman* and *Superman* have been turn into movies. *The Fantastic Four*, publish in 1961, became a successful film with Jessica Alba. Of course, great works of literature have also influenced screenwriters.

2. Jane Austen lived from 1775 to 1817, and she published six novels. Her works were adapt by many different writers and filmmakers. For example, her novel *Pride and Prejudice* was the basis for British author Helen Fielding's novel *Brigitte Jones's Diary*. The novel was film in 2001 with Renee Zellweger. Also, Jane Austen's novel *Emma*, wrote in 1815, was update in the 1995 film *Clueless*. In the story, the main character, portray by Alicia Silverstone, is a rich Beverly Hills teenager who likes matchmaking. The story was modernize by director Amy Heckerling.

3. William Shakespeare is the most influential writer of all time. Many movies have been based on his plays. *Othello*, for example, was transform into the urban drama *O*. The movie, produce in 2001, starred Mekhi Phifer as Odin, a talented black athlete who is envy by his peers. Odin falls in love with the headmaster's daughter. Hugo, the

coach's son, is consume with jealousy, and he eventually causes Odin's downfall.

4. The rights to many best-sellers are hold by film studios. In fact, as soon as a new book is embrace by the public, producers try to determine whether the book should become a movie. Definitely, future filmmakers will be influence by great novels.

FINAL REVIEW

Correct fifteen errors with past participles or verb tense.

EXAMPLE:

For thirty years, some critics have ~~complain~~ *complained* about smoking in movies.

1. Television viewers, who are bombard with regular advertising, tune out when commercials come on. However, when the product becomes part of the television or film experience, people are often unaware of sponsor involvement. For example, back in 1982, a particular brand of candy was ate in the hit film *ET*. The exposure helped boost the candy sales by 70 percent. The candy was associate with the cute alien in the film.

2. For over fifty years, advertisers and film companies have benefit from product placement. Since the 1970s, tobacco companies have took advantage of loopholes in the laws to advertise their products. For example, in *Superman: The Movie*, release in 1978, Lois Lane smoked Marlboro cigarettes even though the original cartoon character didn't smoke, and in *Superman II*, villains threw a Marlboro truck back and forth across a New York street.

3. By 1984, audiences had saw tobacco product placements in over five hundred film productions. Health groups have consistently raise

concerns about the impact of movie smoking on teen smoking rates. Of course, many youths are teached that smoking is cool when they watch Brad Pitt or Scarlett Johanssen smoke onscreen. Emily Nixon, a twenty-six-year-old college student, admits that she had never thinked about smoking until she saw the 1994 film *Reality Bites*. "I wanted to be like the cool characters in the film, and they all smoked. The only non-smoker was the dorky guy," she now says.

4.   In 1990, tobacco companies promised Congress that they would stop promoting their products in films. The companies insist that they have not broke the rules. Some groups are skeptical, however. Stanton Glanz, a professor of medicine at the University of California, points out that although U.S. tobacco companies are binded to the agreement, their international subsidiaries can offer money in exchange for product screen time in American films.

5.   Jeffry Kluger, in an article that was wrote for *Time*, mentions that today "cigarettes are more common onscreen than at any other time since mid-century: 75 percent of all Hollywood films show tobacco use." However, some producers have make a difference. According to Kluger, when producer Lindsay Doran was helping to finance *Ferris Bueller's Day Off*, she convinced the director to make a smoke-free film. For the 2006 film *Stranger Than Fiction*, Doran was telled by the head writer that the main character needs to smoke. Doran agreed. However, the film shows Emma Thompson coughing and stubbing out her cigarette in "a palmful of spit." Thus, producers like Doran prove that smoking doesn't have to appear glamorous in films.

The Writer's Room

Write about one of the following topics. Identify all verbs, and verify that you have used and formed each verb correctly.

1. Some people spend more than four hours a day in front of the television. What steps can a television addict take to reduce his or her dependence on television?

2. Examine this photo. What are some terms that come to mind? Some ideas might be *reality television, talk show, couch potato,* or *sitcom.* Define a term or expression that relates to the photo.

CHAPTER 10

 ## CHECKLIST: PAST PARTICIPLES

When you edit your writing, ask yourself the next questions.

Do I use the correct form of past participles? Check for spelling errors in the following:

 –regular past participles
 –irregular past participles

turned *written*

Novels are often ~~turn~~ into films, and the screenplays are ~~wrote~~ by the author.

Do I use the present perfect tense correctly?

have refused

Since 2004, I ~~refused~~ to watch television.

Do I use the past perfect tense correctly?

had already seen

Ursula did not watch the movie because she ~~already saw~~ it.

Do I use the active and passive voice correctly? Check for overuse of the passive voice and errors with verb form and usage.

many people watched the documentary.

Last month, ~~the documentary was watched by many people.~~

How Do I Get a Better Grade?

Visit www.mywritinglab.com for audio-visual lectures and additional practice sets about past participles.
Get a better grade with MyWritingLab!

Progressive Tenses

CHAPTER 11

Section Theme: **ENTERTAINMENT AND CULTURE**

CONTENTS

- Understanding Progressive Tenses
- Present Progressive
- Past Progressive
- Using Complete Verbs
- Other Progressive Forms

In this chapter, you will read about well-known artists and issues in the art world.

Grammar Snapshot

Looking at Progressive Tenses

In this excerpt from one of his letters, impressionist artist Vincent Van Gogh explains his progress in drawing. Notice the underlined progressive verbs.

> Recently I <u>have been drawing</u> from the model a good deal. And I have all kinds of studies of diggers and sowers, both male and female. At present I <u>am working</u> with charcoal and black crayon, and I have also tried sepia and watercolor. Well, I cannot say that you will see progress in my drawings, but most certainly you will see a change.

In this chapter, you will identify and write progressive verb tenses.

Understanding Progressive Tenses

A **progressive tense** indicates that an action was, is, or will be in progress. Progressive verb tenses always include a form of the verb *be* and the present participle (or *-ing* form of the verb).

Past progressive:	She was <u>trying</u> to finish her painting when the phone rang.
Present progressive:	Right now, Marg <u>is visiting</u> the Louvre.
Present perfect progressive:	She <u>has been working</u> as a painter for twelve years.
Future progressive:	Tomorrow morning, at 11:00, she <u>will be working</u>.

Present Progressive

The **present progressive** shows that an action is happening now or for a temporary period of time. Use this tense with key words such as *now*, *currently*, *at this moment*, *this week*, and *this month*.

This month, Tamayo <u>is exhibiting</u> several paintings in an art gallery.

Right now, Tamayo <u>is painting</u> a portrait.

Affirmative, Question, and Negative Forms

Review the present progressive forms of the verb *work*.

Affirmative	Question Form Move *be* before the subject.	Negative Form Add *not*.
I am She is He is It is } working. We are You are They are	Am I Is she Is he Is it } working? Are we Are you Are they	I am She is He is It is } not working. We are You are They are

> ## Hint · **Spelling of Present Participles (-ing Verbs)**
>
> To form most regular present participles, add -ing to the base form of the verb.
>
>   try–try**ing**   question–question**ing**
>
> **Exceptions**
>
> • When the regular verb ends in e, remove the e and add -ing.
>
>   realize–realiz**ing**   appreciate–appreciat**ing**
>
> • When the regular verb ends in a consonant + ie, change the ie to y and add -ing.
>
>   lie–l**ying**   die–d**ying**
>
> • When the regular verb ends in a consonant-vowel-consonant combination, double the last consonant and add -ing.
>
>   stop–stop**ping**   jog–jog**ging**
>
> • When a verb of two or more syllables ends in a stressed consonant-vowel-consonant combination, double the last consonant and add -ing.
>
>   refer–refer**ring**   begin–begin**ning**
>
> Note: If the two-syllable verb ends in an unstressed syllable, add just -ing.
>
>   offer–offer**ing**   open–open**ing**

PRACTICE 1

Change each verb to the present progressive form.

EXAMPLE:

He runs. ____*is running*____

1. I paint. _____
2. We fly. _____
3. She studies. _____
4. You worry. _____
5. He writes. _____
6. I sculpt. _____
7. They fix. _____
8. I drive. _____
9. She plans. _____
10. We open. _____
11. It rains. _____
12. He shops. _____
13. It happens. _____
14. It begins. _____

Compare the Simple Present and the Present Progressive

Use the present progressive when an action is happening right now or for a temporary period of time. Use the simple present tense when the action happens habitually or when the action is a fact.

    Ellen is cleaning her brushes.   (Action is in progress.)

    Ellen cleans her brushes.   (Action is habitual or factual.)

CHAPTER II

> (Hint) **A Common Tense Error**
>
> Sometimes people overuse the progressive tense. If an action happens on a regular basis, do not use the progressive tense.
>
> *complain*
> Every week, Tamayo's students ~~are complaining~~ about the number of assignments.

PRACTICE 2

In each sentence, underline the correct verb tense. Then identify the action by writing *G* if it is a general fact or habit or *N* if it is happening now.

EXAMPLE:

This month, the Museum of Modern Art (exhibits, <u>is exhibiting</u>) the work of Jackson Pollock.   <u>N</u>

1. The Barth Gallery usually (changes, is changing) exhibits each month.   _____

2. Right now, the gallery owner (negotiates, is negotiating) with a hot young artist.   _____

3. Usually, Fandra Chang (combines, is combining) photography, silkscreening, and painting.   _____

4. These days, she (works, is working) on a large cityscape photograph.   _____

5. Currently, she (tries, is trying) to sell her photos at the gallery.   _____

6. She (develops, is developing) new art techniques each year.   _____

7. Another artist, Barri Kumar, (experiments, is experimenting) with European and Asian images these days.   _____

8. He (doesn't want, isn't wanting) to give up his art career.   _____

9. Right now, he (works, is working) on a new piece.   _____

10. Both artists (are, are being) successful.   _____

Past Progressive

The **past progressive** indicates that an action was in progress at a specific past time. It can also indicate that an action in progress was interrupted.

> Yesterday at 1 p.m., Tamayo <u>was cleaning</u> his studio.

> Tamayo <u>was cleaning</u> his studio when the fire started.

The fire started.   NOW

He **was cleaning** his studio.

Affirmative, Question, and Negative Forms

Review the past progressive forms of the verb *work*.

Affirmative		Question Form		Negative Form		
		Move *be* before the subject.		Add not.		
I was		Was I		I was		
She was		Was she		She was		
He was		Was he		He was		
It was	working.	Was it	working?	It was	not working.	
We were		Were we		We were		
You were		Were you		You were		
They were		Were they		They were		

PRACTICE 3

Fill in the blanks with the past progressive forms of the verbs in parentheses.

EXAMPLE:

Diego Rivera (work) __*was working*__ on a mural when he met his future wife, artist Frida Kahlo.

1. Diego Rivera, Mexico's most famous muralist, (draw) _____
   _____ on a wall when he discovered his passion for art.

2. At age 21, while he (visit) _____ friends in France, he
   discovered the artwork of Cézanne, Gauguin, and Matisse.

3. Later, Rivera and some friends (tour) _____ Italy
   when he developed a passion for fresco paintings.

4. In 1932, Americans (live) _____ through the Great
   Depression when Rivera visited.

5. Rivera (relax) _____ at home when Henry Ford called
   and asked Rivera to do a mural on the wall of the Detroit Institute of
   Fine Arts.

6. In Detroit, Rivera (work) _____ on his mural about
   American workers when critics first saw the image.

7. The artist and his assistants (paint) _____ the mural
   when some journalists arrived.

8. The next morning, the painter (read) _____ a Detroit
   newspaper when he saw a headline calling him a communist.

9. While Rivera (return) _____ home to Mexico on a
   train, Henry Ford's son, Edsel, defended the mural.

10. Later, Rivera said that he (try) _____ to depict the
    struggles of the working class when he created the mural.

Using Complete Verbs

In progressive forms, always include the complete form of the helping verb *be*. Also make sure that the main verb ends in *-ing*.

is

Right now, the photographer examining the scene.

taking

Adam was ~~take~~ a picture when I entered the room.

 **A Past Progressive Pitfall**

Do *not* use the past progressive to talk about past habits or about a series of past actions.

drew

Renoir ~~was drawing~~ pictures of his friends when he was younger.

PRACTICE 4

Correct eight past progressive errors.

EXAMPLE:

worked

When Vincent Van Gogh was a young man, he ~~was working~~ in many different jobs.

1.   When Van Gogh was twenty-five years old, he became a minister and worked in a poor coal-mining district in southwestern Belgium. One day, while he listening to a poor woman, he had an idea. He was deciding to stop eating. He wanted to give his food money to the poor miners. On another day, he noticed that a poor child wearing no shoes, so Van Gogh gave away his own clothing and other possessions. Eventually, he was fired. His superiors worried about Van Gogh's "excessive enthusiasm."

2.   Penniless and in despair, he isolated himself and began to draw. His brother Theo was agreeing to support Vincent financially. Soon, Van Gogh developed a passion for painting.

3.   Van Gogh settled in southern France where he wanted to start an artists' colony. He invited a fellow artist, Paul Gauguin, to come live with him. While the two men living together, they engaged in some

violent arguments. After one terrible fight, Van Gogh was cutting off the lower portion of his own ear with a razor.

4. Van Gogh voluntarily entered an asylum in Saint Remy. While he was stay in the asylum, he created beautiful, vivid pictures of wildflowers, fields, and houses. He spent twelve months in the asylum. In December 1889, in a letter to his friend Emile Bernard, Van Gogh said that his health improving a great deal. Unfortunately, six months later, Van Gogh committed suicide, and the world lost a great artist.

Other Progressive Forms

Many other tenses also have progressive forms. Review the information about the future progressive and the present perfect progressive.

Future Progressive

The future progressive indicates that an action will be in progress at a future time.

> Tomorrow morning, do not disturb Tamayo because he <u>will be working</u> in his studio.

Present Perfect Progressive

The present perfect progressive indicates that an action has been in progress, without interruption, from a past time up to the present.

> Tamayo <u>has been painting</u> for eight hours, so he is very tired.

 **Nonprogressive Verbs**

Some verbs do not take the progressive form because they indicate an ongoing state or a perception rather than a temporary action.

Perception Verbs	Preference Verbs	State Verbs	Possession
hear	care*	believe	have*
feel*	desire	know	own
look*	hate	mean	possess
smell*	like	realize	
see	love	suppose	
seem	prefer	think*	
taste*	want	understand	

*Some verbs have more than one meaning and can be used in the progressive tense. Compare the following pairs of sentences to see how these verbs are used.

Nonprogressive:
He **has** two Picassos. (Expresses ownership)
I **think** it is expensive. (Expresses an opinion)
The photo **looks** good. (Expresses an observation)

Progressive:
He **is having** a bad day.
I **am thinking** about it.
He **is looking** at the photo.

PRACTICE 5

Examine each underlined verb. Write *C* above correct verbs, and fix any verb errors. Some verbs may be incomplete or nonprogressive.

EXAMPLE:

     has

Miguel <u>been living</u> in Austin, Texas, for several years.

1. Currently, Miguel <u>working</u> in a contemporary art gallery.

2. Generally, he his job, but this morning something strange happened.

3. Sharon, an installation artist, entered and dropped paper and envelopes on the floor while Miguel the gallery.

4. Sharon <u>been working</u> as an artist for twelve years.

5. This week, she an art project called *Lost Mail.*

6. Miguel <u>is wanting</u> to understand what a work of art is.

7. He <u>is liking</u> abstract paintings, and he the value in a lot of contemporary art.

8. However, he what Sharon <u>is trying</u> to do.

9. According to Miguel, some contemporary artists to create art for each other rather than for the general public.

10. Sharon, however, <u>is believing</u> in the value of her art, and she each exhibit seriously.

FINAL REVIEW

Correct fifteen errors with progressive verbs.

EXAMPLE:

       was

Cindy Sherman living in New York in 1981 when she had her first photography show.

1.   One of America's most original photographers is Cindy Sherman. In 1980, Sherman was watch an old movie when she had an idea. She decided to take photographs of herself. In each photo, Sherman was dressing like a 1950s movie star. In 1981, her first one-woman

exhibit, *Untitled Film Stills*, was a huge success. Later that year, while she preparing for her second show, she received a call from a museum curator in the Netherlands. So, in 1982, she had her first European show at the Stedelijk Museum in Amsterdam. Sherman's original photos now appear in many museums. Presently, Sherman producing a new series of photos.

2.   It is difficult for modern artists to find an original style. Alison Stone, a California-based art student, says, "While I working on a piece, I am always aware of influences. I am try to find my own style, but it is difficult." Stone adds, "We been studying art for two years. Each one of us is attempt to do original work."

3.   Stone is also interested in photography. These days, many contemporary photographers are move out of darkrooms and renting offices. Basically, digital technology is change the way that photographers work. Recently, Stone been spending more time in her office than in her studio. When asked what she is doing these days, Stone said, "Right now, I manipulating digital images. I trying to create surreal images. This new technology is exciting, and I am loving it." Stone has lofty career goals: "I am wanting to be as famous as Cindy Sherman."

 The Writer's Room

Write about one of the following topics. Ensure that you have used and formed your verbs correctly.

1. Describe your favorite work of art. It could be a painting, a sculpture, a piece of architecture, or an illustration.

2. Choose a place on campus. You could go to the cafeteria, the lawn outside, a student center, the library, the hallway, or anywhere else on campus. Then, sit and observe what is going on around you. Use your five senses. Write a paragraph describing the things that are happening.

3. What are some categories of celebrities? Write about at least three different types of famous people.

CHECKLIST: PROGRESSIVE VERBS

When you edit your writing, ask yourself the next questions.

☐ Do I use the correct verb tenses? Check for the overuse or misuse of progressive forms.

created
Every year, Picasso ~~was creating~~ new types of paintings.

☐ Are my progressive verbs complete? Check for errors in the following:

–the verb *be*
–incomplete *-ing* forms

am posing *taking*
Right now, I ~~posing~~ beside a fountain, and Christa is ~~take~~ a picture of me.

How Do I Get a Better Grade?

Visit www.mywritinglab.com for audio-visual lectures and additional practice sets about progressive tenses.
Get a better grade with MyWritingLab!

Other Verb Forms

Section Theme: **ENTERTAINMENT AND CULTURE**

CONTENTS

- Modals
- Nonstandard Forms: *Gonna, Gotta, Wanna*
- Conditional Forms
- Gerunds and Infinitives

In this chapter, you will read about cultural differences.

Grammar Snapshot

Looking at Other Verb Forms

In this excerpt from their book *Cultural Anthropology*, Carol R. Ember and Melvin Ember discuss body types. Notice the modals in bold print.

> There is a tendency in our society to view "taller" and "more muscled" as better, which **may reflect** the bias toward males in our culture. Natural selection **may have favored** these traits in males, but different ones in females. For example, because females bear children, selection **may have favored** earlier cessation of growth, and therefore less ultimate height in females so that the nutritional needs of a fetus **would** not **compete** with the growing mother's needs.

In this chapter, you will identify and write modals, conditionals, gerunds, and infinitives.

Modals

Modals are helping verbs that express possibility, advice, and so on. Review the list of some common modals and their meanings.

Common Modal Forms

Modal	Meaning	Present Form	Past Form
can	Ability	Amir **can draw** very well.	could draw
could	Possibility	He **could sell** his work.	could have sold
may		Amir **may become** famous.	may have become
might		Amir **might become** famous.	might have become
must	Obligation Probability	We **must work** late. The buyers **must be** impatient.	had to work* must have been
should ought to	Advice	He **should see** a lawyer. He **ought to see** a lawyer.	should have seen ought to have seen
will	Future action or willingness	They **will buy** his products.	would buy
would	Desire	I **would like** to see his designs.	would have liked

*Exception: To show the past tense of *must* (meaning "obligation"), use the past tense of the regular verb *have to*.

Hint **Modal Forms Are Consistent**

Each modal has a fixed form. When the subject changes, the verb remains the same. In the example, *can* is the modal.

I **can** go.   You **can** go.   She **can** go.
We **can** go.   They **can** go.

PRACTICE 1

Read the following sentences. In the space, indicate the function of each underlined modal.

Ability   Possibility   Advice   Obligation   Desire

EXAMPLE:

People <u>ought to learn</u> about cultural differences.   *Advice*

1. You <u>could say</u> that culture is learned behavior that involves shared language, gestures, arts, attitudes, beliefs, and values.   _____

2. In the United States, people <u>may call</u> you by your first name.   _____

3. Many Americans <u>can speak</u> both English and Spanish.   _____

4. You <u>ought to remove</u> your shoes when you enter a home in India.   _____

5. In Japan, you <u>should bow</u> when you greet someone.   _____

6. In Australia, instead of saying "Good day," you <u>could say</u> "G'day."   _____

7. Many people <u>would like</u> to visit Australia.   _____

8. In Great Britain, you <u>must drive</u> on the left side of the road.   _____

9. In England, some people <u>might say</u> "I shall not" to mean "I will not."   _____

10. In Japan, you <u>should not make</u> direct eye contact with people.   _____

Present and Past Forms

For some modals, you must use a completely different word in the past tense. Review the differences between *can* and *could, will* and *would*.

Can and Could

Use *can* to indicate a present ability.

Amir **can speak** Arabic.

Use *could* to indicate a past ability.

When he was younger, he **could write** in Arabic, but he cannot do so now.

Also use *could* to show that something is possible.

With globalization, some cultures **could disappear.**

Will and Would

Use *will* to discuss a future action from the present perspective.

Michelle **will visit** Haiti next summer.

Use *would* to discuss a future action from a past perspective.

Last month, I told her that I **would go** with her.

Also use *would* to indicate a desire.

Michelle **would like** to visit her ancestral home.

> **Hint** **Negative Forms of Modals**
>
> **Negative Forms**
> When you add *not* to modals, the full form consists of two words—for example, *could not* and *should not*. However, when you add *not* to the modal *can*, it becomes one word.
>
> **cannot**   should not   could not   would not   will not
>
> **Contracted Forms**
> You can contract the negative forms of modals. Note that *will + not* becomes *won't.*
>
> can't   shouldn't   couldn't   wouldn't   won't

PRACTICE 2

Underline the correct modal forms.

EXAMPLE:

This year, the Carnival of Venice (<u>will</u>, would) occur during the last week of Lent.

1. Grazia DeCesare lives in San Diego. Her family is originally from Italy, so Grazia (can, could) speak Italian. She (can, could) also speak Spanish. Next March, she (will, would) travel to Venice to visit her aunt. Grazia loves the Carnival of Venice, which is a unique and wonderful celebration.

2. The Carnival of Venice occurs every spring. During the carnival, people wear elaborate disguises. If Grazia (can, could) afford it, she will buy a beautiful mask that she (will, would) wear during the carnival.

3. The first carnival occurred in the twelfth century. At that time, the celebration (will, would) generally begin about December 26. Citizens (will, would) wear masks made of leather, paper maché, porcelain, or plaster. They (will, would) also wear brightly colored capes and elaborate three-cornered hats. Thus, in past centuries, people (can, could) dance in the streets, drink wine, and gamble in gaming houses without being recognized. Because the carnival lasted to the end of March, citizens (will, would) spend several months wearing disguises in public.

4. During the Middle Ages, the Venetian authorities (will, would) sometimes try to stop the public debauchery, but the people of Venice loved their carnival and (can, could) not imagine giving it up. People from all over Europe (will, would) visit Venice because the city was known as an exciting place.

5. In 1797, during the reign of Napoleon, Austria took control of Venice, and the city fell into decline. For over two hundred years, citizens (can, could) not celebrate the carnival. Then, in 1979, a group

of Venetians convinced the city authorities to reintroduce a one-week carnival. Nowadays, visitors (can, could) buy masks, and they (can, could) enjoy the special atmosphere in that beautiful city. The festival (will, would) definitely be fabulous next spring.

Past of *Should, Could,* and *Would*

To form the past tense of *should, could,* and *would,* add *have* + the past participle. Review the following examples.

Before Anik and Richard went to Mexico, they **should have learned** a few words in Spanish. They **could have communicated** with the locals, and they **would have had** a better time.

> ## Hint   Use Standard Past Forms
>
> Some people say *should of* or *shoulda.* These are nonstandard forms, and you should avoid using them, especially in written communication. When you write the past forms of *should, would,* and *could,* always include *have* + the past participle.
>
>   *should have*
> Before Jeremy did business in Japan, he ~~shoulda~~ learned about Japanese business
>   *have*
> etiquette. He would ~~of~~ offended fewer people.

PRACTICE 3

Correct eight errors with modal forms.

EXAMPLE:

          should have read
In high school, I ~~shoulda read~~ Chang's novel.

1.   Jung Chang's historical novel, *Wild Swans: Three Daughters of China,* shoulda been made into a movie. Her fascinating novel describes the lives of her ancestors.

2.   Chang's grandmother, Yu-fang, was born in 1909. Yu's father would of preferred a son. When Yu-fang was a child, her toes were broken and her feet were bound tightly in cloth. She would have liked to escape such a fate, but at that time, a woman with unbound feet wouldn't of found a husband. Yu-fang's younger sister was luckier. She could have suffer the same fate, but by 1917, the practice of foot-binding had been abandoned.

3. When she was fifteen, Yu-fang became a concubine for a much older man, General Xue. She would of liked to be a first wife instead of a concubine, but she had no choice. General Xue built a large house for Yu-fang, and he stayed with her for one week. Then he left her alone for the next six years. Yu-fang would have like to spend time with her friends in the village, but she was confined to her house day and night.

4. In one generation, life in China changed drastically. Yu-fang's daughter had more freedom than women of previous generations. The daughter studied medicine, but she coulda studied something else. She married a soldier, but she coulda chosen another man for a husband.

Nonstandard Forms: *gonna, gotta, wanna*

Some people commonly say *I'm gonna, I gotta,* or *I wanna.* These are nonstandard forms, and you should not use them in written communication.

Write *going to* instead of *gonna.*

        going to
My uncle is ~~gonna~~ help me learn Hungarian.

Write *have to* instead of *gotta.*

      have to
I ~~gotta~~ learn to speak with my grandparents.

Write *want to* instead of *wanna.*

       want to
Next year, I ~~wanna~~ go to Hungary.

 **Forming the Main Verb**

When you use modals, make sure to form your main verb correctly. Use the base form of the verb that directly follows a modal.

         visit   *go*
We should ~~visited~~ France. We can ~~going~~ in March.

PRACTICE 4

Correct ten errors with nonstandard verbs and modal forms.

EXAMPLE:

  are going to learn
You ~~are gonna learn~~ about gestures.

1.   If you take a trip to a foreign country, you should studied nonverbal communication. According to experts, humans can expressing up to eighty percent of their thoughts nonverbally.

2.   One gesture can had different meanings in various countries. For example, in the United States, if you wanna indicate that you like something, you can join your thumb and forefinger into an "okay" gesture. However, you are gonna insult a waiter in France if you give the okay sign because the gesture means "zero" or "worthless." In Russia, use the okay sign only if you wanna insult someone.

3.   If you gotta go on a business trip to Brazil, do not use the thumbs up gesture because it is highly offensive. If you raise your forefinger and your pinky in Italy, you are gonna make someone very angry because the sign means that a man's wife is cheating on him. In Australia, if you wanna lose friends, make the V for "victory" sign with your palm facing towards you. It is Australia's most obscene gesture.

4.   Clearly, if you wanna get along with people from other cultures, it is a good idea to learn about their gestures.

Conditional Forms

In a **conditional sentence,** there is a condition and a result. This type of sentence usually contains the word *if* and has two parts, or clauses. The main clause depends on the condition set in the *if* clause. There are three conditional forms.

First Conditional Form: Present or Possible Future

Use the "possible future" form when the condition is true or very possible.

    If + present tense   ⟶   present or future tense

Condition (*if* clause)	**Result**
If he needs help,	he can call me.
If you visit Mexico,	you will see some amazing murals.

Second Conditional Form: Unlikely Present

Use the "unlikely present" form when the condition is not likely and probably will not happen.

If + past tense ———————➤ *would* (expresses a condition)

could (expresses a possibility)

Condition (*if* clause)	**Result**
If I knew how to speak Spanish,	I would live in Mexico for a year.
If she were taller,	she could be a runway model.

Hint **If I Were . . .**

In informal English, you occasionally hear *was* in the *if* clause. However, in academic writing, when the condition is unlikely, always use *were* in the *if* clause.

If I **were** rich, I <u>would buy</u> a new car.

If my sister **were** rich, she <u>would invest</u> in the stock market.

Third Conditional Form: Impossible Past

Use the "impossible past" form when the condition cannot happen because the event is over.

If + past perfect tense ———————➤ *would have* (+ past participle)

Condition (*if* clause)	**Result**
If you had asked me,	I would have traveled with you.
If Karl had done his homework,	he would have passed the course.

PRACTICE 5

In each case, identify the type of conditional sentence, and write *A*, *B*, or *C* in the blank.

A (possible future):   If you ask me, I will help.
B (unlikely present):   If you asked me, I would help.
C (impossible past):   If you had asked me, I would have helped.

EXAMPLE:

If I could, I would travel to Spain.   _B_

1. If Carmen Morales were younger, she would return to school. _____

2. If she had known how difficult it is to make a career in dance,
   she would have found a different profession. _____

3. If you want to learn the tango, she will teach it to you. _____

4. According to Carmen, the tango is not difficult to master if you
   practice a lot. _____

5. If she had taken better care of herself, she would not have required
   knee surgery. _____

6. Today, if she takes it easy, she can teach three dance classes a week.   _____

7. She would teach more classes if her doctor permitted it.   _____

8. Perhaps if she had not danced with passion, she would have felt unfulfilled.   _____

> **Hint**   **Avoid Mixing Conditional Forms**
>
> Avoid mixing conditional forms. If you are discussing a past event, use the third conditional form. Do not mix the second and third forms.
>
>   *had been*
> If I ~~were~~ you, I would have done the assignment.

PRACTICE 6

Fill in the blanks with the correct forms of the verbs in parentheses.

EXAMPLE:

If you (plan) _____*plan*_____ to do business abroad, you will benefit from diversity training courses.

1.   Eric Zorn went on a business trip to Japan, and, unfortunately, he made some cultural etiquette errors. While there, he made eye contact with his hosts, and he got down to business immediately. If he (take) _____ more time for small talk, his hosts would have felt more comfortable. Also, if he had avoided direct eye contact, he (appear) _____ less aggressive. Basically, if he (understand) _____ the cultural differences, he would not have insulted his hosts.

2.   Roger Axtell is an international business traveler. He has written a book called *Do's and Taboos of Humor Around the World*. If Axtell (travel, not) _____ extensively, he would have been unable to write about cultural differences.

3.   Axtell has had some interesting experiences. A few years ago, when he visited Saudi Arabia, he met with an important customer. One day, the customer grabbed his hand while they were walking. In Saudi Arabia, hand-holding is a sign of friendship

and respect. If Axtell (pull) _____ away,

he would have offended his host. If he (know) _____

_____ in advance about the hand-holding, he

(feel, not) _____ so uncomfortable.

4. Axtell says that if he (be, not) _____

_____ so busy, he would write more books about cultural

diversity.

Hint — Problems with the Past Conditional

In "impossible past" sentences, the writer expresses regret about a past event or expresses the wish that a past event had worked out differently. Avoid the following errors.

- Do not use *would have . . .* in the *if* clause. Instead, use the past perfect tense.

  had asked

  If you ~~would have asked~~ me, I would have traveled with you.

- Do not write *woulda* or *would of*. These are nonstandard forms. When you use the past forms of *should, would,* and *could,* always include *have* + the past participle.

  had done   *have*

  If you ~~would have done~~ the work, you would ~~of~~ passed the course.

PRACTICE 7

Correct ten errors with conditional forms.

EXAMPLE:

would have

If Mawlid had stayed in Somalia, his life ~~woulda~~ been different.

1. In 1994, Mawlid and Myriam Abdul moved to San Diego

   from Somalia. If he ~~would have~~ had a choice, Mawlid would

   have stayed in his native country. He misses his mother and his

   extended family.

2. Mawlid is impressed by the respectful treatment of the

   elderly in Somalia: "My grandparents were treated with love

   and attention until their deaths. If my grandparents had moved to the United States, they would of been surprised by the treatment of old people. If they would have visited a typical nursing home, they woulda been shocked."

3.   Mawlid's wife, Myriam, would not like to live in Somalia again, even if she was able to. She says, "In the United States, if I want to study or work, I can do it easily. However, if I would have stayed in Somalia, my brothers and aunts would have expected me to take care of them. When I was a child, my mother had to take care of my uncle's children because he wanted them to be educated in the city. He didn't ask my mother for permission. If she had refused to care for her nephews, family members woulda been angry with her. If she would have had a choice, she would have preferred a quieter life."

4.   Mawlid says that he will return to his native country if he amassed enough money because he misses his close-knit family. If Mawlid and Myriam wanted to resolve their differences, they will have to compromise.

Gerunds and Infinitives

Sometimes a main verb is followed by another verb. The second verb can be a gerund or an infinitive. A **gerund** is a verb with an -*ing* ending. An **infinitive** consists of *to* and the base form of the verb.

Verb + gerund: We <u>finished</u> **reading** *Wild Swans*.

Verb + infinitive: I <u>want</u> **to write** about it.

Using Gerunds

Some verbs in English are always followed by a gerund. Do not confuse gerunds with progressive verb forms. Compare a progressive verb and a gerund.

Verb: Julie is studying now.   (*Studying* is in the present progressive form. Julie is in the process of doing something.)

Gerund: Julie <u>finished</u> **studying**.   (*Studying* is a gerund that follows *finish*. After *finish*, you must use a gerund.)

CHAPTER 12

Some Common Verbs and Expressions Followed by Gerunds

acknowledge	discuss	postpone
adore	dislike	practice
appreciate	enjoy	quit
avoid	finish	recall
can't help	involve	recollect
can't stand	justify	recommend
complete	keep	regret
consider	loathe	resent
delay	mention	resist
deny	mind	risk
detest	miss	tolerate

Using Prepositions Plus Gerunds

Many verbs have the structure **verb + preposition + object.** If the object is another verb, the second verb is a gerund.

I dream <u>about</u> **traveling** to Greece.

Some Common Words Followed by Prepositions Plus Gerunds

accuse of	(be) enthusiastic about	(be) good at	prohibit from
apologize for	feel like	insist on	succeed in
discourage <u>him</u> from*	fond of	(be) interested in	think about
dream of	forbid <u>him</u> from*	look forward to	(be) tired of
(be) excited about	forgive <u>me</u> for*	prevent <u>him</u> from*	warn <u>him</u> about*

*Certain verbs must have a noun or pronoun before the preposition. Here, the pronouns are underlined.

Using Infinitives

Some verbs are followed by the infinitive (*to* + base form of verb).

Helen wants **to travel** with me.

(*To travel* is an infinitive that follows the verb *wants*.)

Some Common Verbs Followed by Infinitives

afford	decide	manage	refuse
agree	demand	mean	seem
appear	deserve	need	swear
arrange	expect	offer	threaten
ask	fail	plan	volunteer
claim	hesitate	prepare	want
complete	hope	pretend	wish
consent	learn	promise	would like

Using Gerunds or Infinitives

Some common verbs can be followed by gerunds or infinitives. Both forms have the same meaning.

begin	continue	hate	like
love	prefer	start	

LaTasha likes **to live** alone.

LaTasha likes **living** alone.

(Both sentences have exactly the same meaning.)

 **Hint**   Used to . . .

You can follow *used to* with a gerund or an infinitive, but there is a difference in meaning.

• *Used to* + infinitive expresses a past habit.

  Rowan does not smoke now, but she used to **smoke.**

• *Be used to* + gerund expresses something you are accustomed to.

  Rowan has been on her own for years, so she is used to **living** alone.

PRACTICE 8

Correct any errors in the underlined gerund and infinitive forms. If the verb is correct, write *C* above it. (Be careful. You may have to change the preposition before the gerund.)

EXAMPLE:

to have
Gustavo and Beth expect ~~having~~ a long mariage.

1. Gustavo is from Mexico City and Beth is from California. They got

   married in 2003, and they hope having a small family.

2. They rent an apartment near San Diego, but they dream to own

   a house one day.

3. Every weekend, Beth enjoys to hike in the woods, but Gustavo is not

   interested in doing outdoor activities.

4. Beth is enthusiastic about creating a large garden in their yard.

5. Gustavo does not like gardens. He <u>is used to have</u> a small cement courtyard, and he <u>does not want to spend</u> any time pulling weeds.

6. They have other differences as well. Gustavo <u>likes cooking</u> spicy food, but Beth <u>refuses eating</u> hot and spicy dishes.

7. Beth <u>avoids to be</u> in the house while Gustavo <u>practices playing</u> Mexican folk songs.

8. In spite of the differences, they <u>are learning respecting</u> each other.

9. For example, they do not share musical tastes, but it <u>does not prevent them to enjoy</u> a night out at local music clubs.

10. Although they have different backgrounds, Beth and Gustavo <u>are looking forward to have</u> a long life together.

FINAL REVIEW

Identify and correct fifteen verb errors in the next letter.

EXAMPLE:

going to
You are ~~gonna~~ enjoy reading this letter.

Dear Latisha,

1   I gotta tell you about my adventures. I enjoy to travel, and, as you know, I recently returned from a trip to England. While there, I made some mistakes. If I had understood British English, I coulda avoided some problems. I shoulda found out about British expressions and customs.

2   For example, soon after I arrived, I met a man on the airport bus. When I mentioned where I was staying, he chuckled and called my hotel a "tip." I had no idea what he meant. Although I shoulda asked him to explain himself, I didn't bother. Unfortunately, when I arrived at the hotel, I learned that the term means "a big mess." If I had understood the word beforehand, I certainly would of avoided that hotel.

3   When I arrived at my hotel, I was given the keys to a tiny room on the fourth floor. It was hard to climb the stairs everyday, but I could doing it. When I looked at the room, I noticed that the wallpaper was peeling and the bathroom was dirty. Clearly, I shoulda done more research before making the reservations.

4   The next day, when I went into a restaurant, I noticed an item on the menu called "Bubble and Squeak." I shoulda tried the item, but I did not wanna eat something unfamiliar. After I ordered, I learned that it was only cabbage and potatoes. After my meal, I asked the waiter to direct me to the ladies' room. The waiter looked suspicious. If I would have asked for the "loo," I would have been directed to the appropriate place.

5   In spite of my language blunders, I thoroughly enjoyed my stay. If I had the chance to visit England again, I will take it. In fact, I look forward going there again. I know that you are gonna visit England soon, so call me before you leave, and I promise giving you some more information.

Best regards,

Serena

 The Writer's Room

Write about one of the following topics. Ensure that you have formed any modals or conditionals correctly.

1. What can people learn when they interact with other cultures? List some things.

2. Think about someone you know who is from another culture. How are you and that person similar or different?

CHECKLIST: OTHER VERB FORMS

When you edit your writing, ask yourself these questions.

☐ Do I use the correct modal forms? Check for errors in the following:

–*will* vs. *would* and *can* vs. *could*

–past forms

       have

I should ~~of~~ packed an umbrella when I visited Ireland.

☐ Do I use the correct conditional forms? Check for errors in the following:

–possible future forms ("If I meet . . . , I will go . . .")

–unlikely present forms ("If I met . . . , I would go . . .")

–impossible past forms ("If I had met . . . , I would have gone . . .")

     had

If I ~~would have~~ more money, I would stay in good hotels.

☐ Do I use the correct gerund or infinitive form?

       traveling

I recommend ~~to travel~~ during the spring break.

The Writers' Circle

Work with a group of about three students. You need one sheet of paper for this activity.

STEP 1 Write down as much as you know about the life of a famous entertainer (such as a musician, an artist, an athlete, or an actor). Do not mention the name of the entertainer. Write at least five sentences about the person.

Example: He was born in Philadelphia, and he started rapping at age twelve. In 1990, he played a "prince" on a hit television show. Later, he had several hit movies. He is slender and thin. He has protruding ears. In 2006, he acted in a movie with his son.

STEP 2 Read your sentences aloud to another group of students. They must guess who your mystery person is. If they cannot guess, continue to give them more clues.

READING LINK

Entertainment and Culture

To read more about entertainment and culture, see the following essays:

"The Appalling Truth" by Dorothy Nixon (page 433)

"The New Addiction" by Josh Freed (page 436)

"Sports and Life: Lessons to Be Learned" by Jeff Kemp (page 439)

"What's Your Humor Style?" by Louise Dobson (page 441)

How Do I Get a Better Grade?

Visit www.mywritinglab.com for audio-visual lectures and additional practice sets about other verb forms.

Get a better grade with MyWritingLab!

Subject-Verb Agreement

Section Theme: **BELIEFS**

CONTENTS

- Basic Subject-Verb Agreement Rules
- Verb Before the Subject
- More Than One Subject
- Special Subject Forms
- Interrupting Words and Phrases

In this chapter, you will read about mysteries and urban legends.

Grammar Snapshot

Looking at Subject-Verb Agreement

David A. Locher is the author of *Collective Behavior*. In the following excerpt from his book, he describes an urban legend. The subjects are in bold print, and the verbs are underlined.

> An **urban legend** <u>gives</u> specific details about an **event** that <u>has</u> supposedly <u>occurred</u>. For example, there <u>is</u> a **legend** about a **man** who <u>wakes</u> up in a bathtub full of ice. **He** <u>finds</u> a note left by the attractive woman **he** <u>met</u> at a party or bar the night before. **She** <u>has</u> purportedly <u>stolen</u> his kidney. This **urban legend** <u>gives</u> specific **details** that <u>may change</u> every time the **story** <u>is told</u>.

In this chapter, you will practice making subjects and verbs agree.

227

Basic Subject-Verb Agreement Rules

Subject-verb agreement simply means that a subject and verb agree in number. A singular subject needs a singular verb, and a plural subject needs a plural verb.

	S V
Singular subject:	**Jay** <u>believes</u> in urban legends.
	S V
Plural subject:	The **stories** <u>have</u> strange endings.

Simple Present Tense

Writers use **simple present tense** to indicate that an action is habitual or factual. Review the rules for simple present tense agreement.

- Add *-s* or *-es* to the verb when the subject is *he, she, it,* or the equivalent (*Mike, Ella, Texas*). This is called the **third-person singular form.**

Mr. Roy <u>believes</u> in ghosts.	(one person)
The **museum** <u>displays</u> many exhibits.	(one place)
Perhaps a **giant ape** <u>roams</u> the forests of the northwestern United States.	(one thing)

- When the subject is *I, you, we, they,* or the equivalent (*the Smiths, the books, Jay and I*), do not add an ending to the verb.

    The moment **we** <u>want</u> to believe something, **we** suddenly <u>see</u> all the arguments for it and <u>become</u> blind to the arguments against it.

    —George Bernard Shaw

To see how these rules work, review the forms of the verb *run*.

GRAMMAR LINK

For more information about present tense verbs, see Chapter 9.

Present Tense of *Run*

	Singular Forms	Plural Forms
First person:	I run	We run
Second person:	You run	You run
Third person:	He runs	They run
	She runs	
	It runs	

PRACTICE I

In each sentence, underline the subject and circle the correct verb. Make sure that the verb agrees with the subject.

EXAMPLE:

Some <u>stories</u> (seem), seems) fantastic.

1. Generally, an urban legend (appear, appears) mysteriously.

2. The stories (spread, spreads) rapidly.

3. A particular legend (deal, deals) with a common fear.

4. For example, in one story a hitchhiker (vanish, vanishes).

5. Usually, the speaker (say, says), "This happened to a friend of a friend."

6. Many urban legends (focus, focuses) on insects or other creatures.

7. For example, a woman (buy, buys) a cactus, and she (take, takes) it home.

8. Suddenly, the woman (hear, hears) a humming sound, and she (call, calls) the plant store.

9. The store owner (tell, tells) the woman to put her plant outside.

10. She (put, puts) the cactus in her backyard.

11. Suddenly, the cactus (split, splits) in two and tarantulas pour out of it.

12. Many people (believe, believes) such urban legends.

Troublesome Present-Tense Verbs: *Be, Have, Do*

Some present-tense verbs are formed in special ways. Review the verbs *be*, *have*, and *do*. Be particularly careful when writing these verbs.

	Be	**Have**	**Do**
Singular Forms			
First person:	I am	I have	I do
Second person:	You are	You have	You do
Third person:	He **is**	He **has**	He **does**
	She **is**	She **has**	She **does**
	It **is**	It **has**	It **does**
Plural Forms			
First person:	We are	We have	We do
Second person:	You are	You have	You do
Third person:	They are	They have	They do

PRACTICE 2

Fill in each blank with the correct form of *be*, *have*, or *do*.

EXAMPLE:

I _____*have*_____ a book about urban legends. The stories _____*are*_____ not true.

1. Many urban legends _____ scary. I _____

    not a superstitious person, but I _____ a good friend

    who _____ very gullible. My friend, Anthony,

    _____ tax preparation for a pet store in New York

    City. The store _____ baby alligators for sale.

2.   Anthony _____ sure that some customers buy

alligators as pets. The alligators _____ from Florida.

Usually, after a few months, the alligators _____ too

big to fit into their aquariums. Customers _____ an

odd thing: they throw the alligators into the sewers. According

to Anthony, alligators _____ alive in New York City's

sewer system. I _____ not believe this urban legend.

I _____ many doubts about his story.

PRACTICE 3

In the following paragraphs, the verbs are underlined. Identify and correct ten subject-verb agreement errors. Write *C* above the correct verbs.

EXAMPLE:

        has
Mario <u>have</u> strange opinions about urban legends.

1.   Urban legends <u>is</u> not new. The "earwig" legend <u>is</u> over one

thousand years old. In the story, an earwig <u>have</u> an unusual idea.

It <u>climb</u> into the ear of a woman to lay eggs. The eggs <u>hatch</u>, and

tiny earwigs <u>eats</u> the brain of the woman. Perhaps people <u>repeat</u> this

story because they <u>is</u> afraid of insects. Personally, I <u>is</u> not afraid

of the creatures.

2.   Urban legends <u>serve</u> a purpose. They <u>is</u> about ordinary people

in frightening situations, and each legend <u>warn</u> us about a possible

danger. Sometimes, a story <u>have</u> a moral. Additionally, when

people <u>speaks</u> about a scary or traumatic event, they <u>release</u> their

collective anxiety.

Agreement in Other Tenses
Simple Past Tense

Writers use the **simple past tense** to indicate that an action was completed at a past time. In the past tense, all verbs except *be* have one form.

Regular: I worked. He worked. We worked. You worked. They worked.
Irregular: I ate.   He ate.   We ate.   You ate.   They ate.

Exception: In the past tense, the only verb requiring subject-verb agreement is the verb *be*. It has two past forms: *was* and *were*.

Was	Were
I was	You were
He was	We were
She was	They were
It was	

Past Tense of Be

Present Perfect Tense

The present perfect tense is formed with *have* or *has* before the past participle. If the subject is third-person singular, always use *has*.

She has <u>finished</u> a book about Native American legends. **I** have <u>read</u> it.

Other Tenses

When writing in most other verb tenses and in modal forms (*can, could, would, may, might . . .*), use the same form of the verb with every subject.

Future	Past Perfect	Modals
I <u>will</u> read.	I <u>had</u> finished.	I <u>can</u> go.
She <u>will</u> read.	She <u>had</u> finished.	She <u>should</u> go.
He <u>will</u> read.	He <u>had</u> finished.	He <u>might</u> go.
They <u>will</u> read.	They <u>had</u> finished.	They <u>could</u> go.

GRAMMAR LINK

For more information about using the present perfect tense, see Chapter 10.

PRACTICE 4

In each sentence, underline the subject and circle the correct verb. Make sure that the subject and verb agree.

EXAMPLE:

Some <u>mysteries</u> (have), has) been solved.

1. Benjamin Radford (have, has) written many books, including *Hoaxes, Myths, and Manias: Why We Need Critical Thinking*.

2. Most mysteries (is, are) not mysterious at all, according to Radford.

3. For example, perhaps giant apelike creatures (live, lives) in the mountainous region between British Columbia and California.

4. Radford (have, has) visited the sites where Bigfoot sightings were reported, but he (is, are) not convinced that the evidence is legitimate.

5. He (give, gives) interesting reasons for his opinion.

6. First, when a giant ape (die, dies), there should be a dead body, yet no bodies (have, has) been found.

7. Second, many people (claim, claims) that they have seen Bigfoot, but these eyewitness testimonies (is, are) likely unreliable.

8. Sometimes a large mammal may (look, looks) like a giant ape.

9. Finally, believers (refer, refers) to sightings of giant footprints, but in 2000, a man named Ray Wallace admitted that he and his son made fake footprints.

10. They (was, were) just making a joke, and they (was, were) surprised when many people believed them.

11. Many people (continue, continues) to believe in Bigfoot.

12. Radford (admit, admits) that the legend will probably continue for centuries.

Verb Before the Subject

Usually the verb comes after the subject, but in some sentences, the verb comes *before* the subject. In such cases, you must still ensure that the subject and verb agree.

Sentences Beginning with *There* or *Here*

When a sentence begins with *there* or *here*, the subject always follows the verb. *There* and *here* are not subjects.

> Here <u>is</u> a new **book** about Atlantis. There <u>are</u> many new **theories** about it.

Questions

In most questions, the helping verb, or the verb *be*, appears before the subject. In the next examples, the main verb is *be*.

> Where <u>is</u> the mysterious **island?** <u>Was</u> Plato's **story** about Atlantis fictional or factual?

In questions in which the main verb is not *be*, the subject usually agrees with the helping verb.

> Where <u>does</u> the sunken **city** rest? <u>Do</u> **scientists** <u>have</u> any answers?

PRACTICE 5

In each sentence, underline the subject and circle the correct verb.

EXAMPLE:

What (is, are) England's most well-known tourist <u>attraction</u>?

1. (Is, Are) there ancient ruins in the southern part of England?

2. What (do, does) people see when they visit Stonehenge?

3. When (do, does) the summer solstice occur?

4. Why (is, are) the giant stones arranged in a circular pattern?

5. What (do, does) the tour guide say about the stones?

6. How much (do, does) a ticket cost to visit Stonehenge?

7. (Is, Are) each stone larger than a house?

8. (Is, Are) religious groups attracted to Stonehenge?

9. (Have, has) many authors written about the mysterious ruins?

10. (Do, Does) tourists visit Stonehenge each year?

PRACTICE 6

Correct any subject-verb agreement errors. If a sentence is correct, write *C* in the blank.

EXAMPLE:

                is
There ~~are~~ a fascinating woman in my neighborhood.   _____

1. There is many stories about Anna Madeo.   _____

2. Do she see the future?   _____

3. There are five customers waiting for Anna to read their palms.   _____

4. Is her predictions often correct?   _____

5. There is some strange coincidences.   _____

6. Do that woman have a special gift?   _____

7. Do you know Anna Madeo?   _____

8. There is many possible reasons for her popularity.   _____

More Than One Subject

There are special agreement rules when there is more than one subject in a sentence.

- When two or more subjects are joined by *and*, use the plural form of the verb.
  And: **Florida, Bermuda,** and **Puerto Rico** <u>form</u> the Bermuda Triangle.
- When two or more subjects are joined by *or* or *nor,* the verb agrees with the subject that is the closest to it.

  Nor: Neither Clara Jackson nor her **children** <u>like</u> to fly in airplanes.

  Or: Either the children or **Clara** <u>is</u> claustrophobic.

PRACTICE 7

In each sentence, underline the subject and circle the correct verb. Make sure the verb agrees with the subject.

EXAMPLE:

There (is, are) an interesting <u>legend</u> about a ship that disappeared.

1. In 1872, the *Mary Celeste* (was, were) launched from New York.

2. There (was, were) ten people on the ship when it left port.

3. Later, the ship (was, were) found floating in the sea, but no survivors (was, were) on board.

4. Neither the captain nor the crew members (was, were) ever found.

5. Today, there (is, are) many versions of the story.

6. Many theories (have, has) been put forward.

7. Maybe strong winds or a giant storm (was, were) responsible for the missing crew members.

8. Perhaps either one or several crew members (was, were) violent and murderous.

9. Maybe man-eating monsters (live, lives) in the sea.

10. (Do, Does) you (know, knows) the true story?

Special Subject Forms

Some subjects are not easy to identify as singular or plural. Two common types are indefinite pronouns and collective nouns.

Indefinite Pronouns

Indefinite pronouns refer to a general person, place, or thing. Carefully review the following list of indefinite pronouns.

Indefinite Pronouns				
Singular:	another	each	nobody	other
	anybody	everybody	no one	somebody
	anyone	everyone	nothing	someone
	anything	everything	one	something
Plural:	both	many	others	
	few	several		

Singular Indefinite Pronouns

In the following sentences, the subjects are singular, so they require third-person singular verb forms.

> Almost **everyone** <u>has</u> theories about the Bermuda Triangle.

> According to Norm Tyler, **nothing** <u>proves</u> that the Bermuda Triangle is dangerous.

Plural Indefinite Pronouns

Both, few, many, others, and *several* are all plural subjects. The verb is always plural.

> The two survivors talked about their journey. **Both** <u>have</u> frequent nightmares.

> **Many** <u>were</u> still on the boat when it mysteriously disappeared.

PRACTICE 8

Underline the subject and circle the correct verb in each sentence.

EXAMPLE:

<u>Everybody</u> (has, have) an opinion on the role of religion in schools.

1. In 1859, Charles Darwin wrote *On the Origin of Species.* In Victorian England, Darwin's ideas (was, were) regarded as a threat to Christianity. Years later, the theory of evolution (was, were) still controversial.

2. In 1925, John Scopes (was, were) accused of breaking the "Butler Act" by teaching Tennessee biology students about evolution. According to the Butler Act, if anybody (teach, teaches) a theory that denies the story of divine creation,

it is unlawful. The Scopes Monkey Trial lasted for fifteen days, but nobody (was, were) prepared for defense lawyer Clarence Darrow's decision. He asked the jury to find his client guilty because he wanted to take the case to the Tennessee supreme court.

3.   Today, there (is, are) debates about the teaching of religion and science in schools. In this country, one controversial issue (is, are) school prayer. Some (think, thinks) that students should pray every day under the direction of a teacher. Others (disagree, disagrees) and (argue, argues) that parents, not schools, should teach religion and morality.

4.   If someone (say, says) that the United States is a multicultural society with a variety of religious beliefs, then someone else (reply, replies) that it was founded on a Christian theistic base and that school prayer is necessary. Certainly, everyone (has, have) an opinion about this issue.

Collective Nouns as Subjects

Collective nouns refer to a group of people or things. The group acts as a unit. Here are some common collective nouns.

army	class	crowd	group	population
association	club	family	jury	public
audience	committee	gang	mob	society
band	company	government	organization	team

Generally, each group acts as a unit, so you must use the singular form of the verb.

The **public** <u>loves</u> to hear about urban myths.

PRACTICE 9

Underline the subject of each sentence. Then, circle the correct form of the verb.

EXAMPLE:

In many communities throughout the world, <u>people</u> (believe, believes) in ghosts.

1.   Scientists and other rational thinkers (is, are) likely to question the existence of a spirit world. However, even skeptics (admit, admits) that they may not know the whole truth.

2.   In *The Power of Myth*, Joseph Campbell (state, states), "A fairy
tale is the child's myth. There (is, are) proper myths for proper
times of life. As you (grow, grows) older, you (need, needs) a
sturdier mythology." Every society (invent, invents) stories to try
to explain basic truths.

3.   In the Chinese lunar tradition, the seventh month (is, are)
"ghost month." During ghost month, a gate (separate, separates)
the spirit world from the normal world. It (open, opens), and the
spirits (enter, enters) the human world. Buddhist priests (pray,
prays) to subdue the spirits. A band (play, plays) music to
welcome the spirits, and the crowd (listen, listens) with
reverence. In China, a typical family (welcome, welcomes)
the ghosts during ghost month.

4.   Each nation (have, has) its own version of ghost stories. As
long as everyone (have, has) questions about death and the
afterlife, religious scholars will continue to examine the
spirit world.

Interrupting Words and Phrases

Words that come between the subject and the verb may confuse you. In these
cases, look for the subject and make sure that the verb agrees with the subject. To
help you see the interrupting words in the following two examples, we have put
parentheses around the words that come between the subject and verb.

> Some old **legends** (about vampires and spirits) <u>continue</u> to scare
> people.

> A **student** (in my creative writing class) <u>writes</u> updated vampire
> stories.

Hint   **Identify Interrupting Phrases**

To make it easier to find subject-verb agreement errors as you edit for subject-verb
agreement, place parentheses around any words that separate the subject and the verb
in the sentence. Then you can see whether the subjects and verbs agree.

> Many **directors**, (including the late Stanley Kubrick), <u>have made</u> horror
> films.

When interrupting phrases contain *of the*, the subject appears before the phrase.

> **One** (of the neighbors) <u>knows</u> everybody's secrets.

PRACTICE 10

Place parentheses around any words that come between each subject and verb. Then circle the correct form of the verb.

EXAMPLE:

Anne Rice, (a popular author,) write / ⟨writes⟩ about vampires.

1. One of this era's most enduring legends is / are the Dracula legend.

2. Tales about vampires was / were common in Eastern Europe and India.

3. The story about the blood-drinking human was / were especially popular after Bram Stoker wrote the novel *Dracula* in 1897.

4. Current myths about vampires emphasize / emphasizes the creature's aversion to sunlight, garlic, and the symbol of the cross.

5. Some believers in Eastern Europe surround / surrounds their homes with garlic.

6. Many Internet sites, such as Vampires.com, cater / caters to people's interest in vampires.

7. Several movies, such as one with Bela Lugosi, is / are about vampires.

8. Some legends, especially the Dracula legend, last / lasts a long time.

PRACTICE 11

Correct any subject-verb agreement errors. If the sentence is correct, write *C* in the blank.

EXAMPLE:

Many of us, in the opinion of Dr. Raoul Figuera, ~~enjoys~~ *enjoy* horror stories. _____

1. Villains and heroes in most gothic novels is very distinct. _____

2. Evil characters, including Dracula, does not have a good side. _____

3. One novel, *Dr. Jekyll and Mr. Hyde*, show us two sides of human nature. _____

4. The hero of the story has a dark side. _____

5. Sometimes Dr. Jekyll, away from the prying eyes of others, drink a powerful potion. _____

"THE FELLOW HAD A KEY"

6. His personality, usually very sweet and friendly, changes

   completely.   _____

7. The doctor, with a lack of control, become the evil Mr. Hyde.   _____

8. Both characters, however, resides within the same man.   _____

9. In the novel, Robert Louis Stevenson shows us a shocking truth.   _____

10. Both good and evil exist within us.   _____

11. A play about Dr. Jekyll and Mr. Hyde are at the regional theater.   _____

12. Tickets to Saturday's show is sold out.   _____

Interrupting Words: *Who, Which,* and *That*

If a sentence contains a clause beginning with *who, which,* or *that,* then the verb agrees with the subject preceding *who, which,* or *that.*

> There is a **man** in southern Mexico **who** <u>writes</u> about Aztec beliefs.
>
> Here are some old **books that** <u>discuss</u> unsolved mysteries.
>
> One **book, which** <u>contains</u> stories about crop circles, is very interesting.

PRACTICE 12

The next excerpt originally appeared in Chapter 13 of Bram Stoker's 1897 novel, *Dracula.* In the novel, the following story appeared in *The Westminster Gazette,* the town's local newspaper. Read the excerpt. Underline each subject and circle the correct verb form.

EXAMPLE:

A mysterious man who (wear, (wears)) a dark cloak is in our town.

1.   During the past two or three days, several cases of young
     children straying from home (have, has) occurred. In all these
     cases, the children (was, were) too young to give properly
     intelligible accounts of events. Most of the children who (have,   **intelligible:** understandable
     has) gone missing (say, says) that they (have, has) been with a
     "bloofer lady." It (have, has) always been late in the evening
     when they (have, has) been missed, and on two occasions the
     children (have, has) not been found until early the following
     morning.

2.   Some of the children, indeed all who (have, has) been missed at night, (have, has) been slightly torn or wounded in the throat. The wounds (seem, seems) such as might be made by a rat or a small dog. The animal that (inflict, inflicts) the wounds (have, has) a system or method of its own. The police officers of the division (have, has) been instructed to keep a sharp lookout for straying children, especially those who (is, are) very young.

FINAL REVIEW

Identify and correct fifteen errors in subject-verb agreement.

EXAMPLE:

are
Crop circles ~~is~~ patterns that appear in farmers' fields.

1.   Crop-circle patterns is often quite complex. Sometimes a farmer do not realize that a circle is there. It is discovered only when a plane flies over the field, and the pilot or the passengers sees it. There is different opinions about the origins of crop circles.

2.   Explanations for these circles varies greatly. There is those people who believe that aliens made them and others who think that the circles occurs naturally. For example, Colin Andrews and Pat Delgado, authors of a book about crop circles, attempts to persuade readers that crop circles transmits spiritual messages. Other researchers, such as Dr. Terrence Meaden, suggests that spiral patterns are caused by a whirlwind vortex. Neither Meaden nor his colleagues believes that the circles are caused by supernatural forces.

3.   Skeptics think that somebody create each crop circle by dragging a heavy wooden plank in a circular pattern. However,

crop-circle enthusiasts such as Colin Andrews insists that humans always break the wheat instead of bending it. Others points out that moist green wheat bends easily during the summer.

4.   Nobody know why the patterns appear in farmers' fields or why the crop-circle sightings have increased tremendously since the 1970s.

 The Writer's Room

Write about one of the following topics. When you finish writing, underline each subject, and ensure that all of your subjects and verbs agree.

1. What are the causes of urban legends? Why do people pass along such stories?

2. Many adults tell children stories about magical or mythical people, creatures, or events. For example, they might tell a tale about the tooth fairy, Santa, elves, or a stork that brings babies. Children often believe the stories. Should parents tell such yarns to children? Why or why not?

CHECKLIST: SUBJECT-VERB AGREEMENT

When you edit your writing, ask yourself these questions.

Do my subjects and verbs agree? Check for errors with the following:
—present tense verbs
—*was* and *were*

Dr. Figuera and his associates ~~was~~ *were* surprised; men ~~is~~ *are* more superstitious than women.

Do I use the correct verb form with indefinite pronouns? Check for errors with singular indefinite pronouns such as *everybody*, *nobody*, and *somebody*.

Everybody ~~know~~ *knows* about urban legends.

Do my subjects and verbs agree when there are interrupting phrases? Check for errors in these cases:
—when prepositional phrases separate the subject and verb
—when relative pronouns such as *who* or *that* separate the subject and verb

One of our cousins often ~~rent~~ *rents* horror movies. She is a girl who never ~~get~~ *gets* scared.

Do my subjects and verbs agree when the subject comes after the verb? Check for errors with the following:
—sentences containing *here* and *there*
—question forms

There ~~is~~ *are* two horror movies on television tonight.

How Do I Get a Better Grade?

Visit www.mywritinglab.com for audio-visual lectures and additional practice sets about subject-verb agreement. **Get a better grade with MyWritingLab!**

Tense Consistency

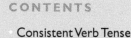

Section Theme: **BELIEFS**

CONTENTS

• Consistent Verb Tense

In this chapter, you will read about religious beliefs, fortune tellers, and astrology.

Grammar Snapsh•t

Looking at Tense Consistency

In this excerpt from David A. Locher's *Collective Behavior*, the author describes what happened during the Y2K millennium panic. The verbs are underlined.

> Intense, credible media coverage <u>plays</u> a role in spreading false beliefs in many collective delusions. This <u>was</u> certainly true for the Y2K hysteria. Mainstream media sources <u>circulated</u> false rumors of "Y2K failures" that <u>had</u> supposedly already <u>occurred</u>. It <u>was</u> constantly <u>reported</u> that sewage systems, electrical systems, financial and school records, and a variety of other systems <u>had shut</u> down completely or wildly <u>malfunctioned</u> when <u>tested</u> for Y2K compliance.

In this chapter, you will identify and correct tense inconsistencies.

Consistent Verb Tense

When you write, the verb tense you use tells the reader when the event occurred. A **tense shift** occurs when you shift from one tense to another for no logical reason. If you shift verb tenses unnecessarily, you risk confusing your audience. The next sentence begins in the past tense but then shifts to the present tense.

Tense shift: Nostradamus had a great memory and <u>becomes</u> a well-known doctor.

Consistent tense: Nostradamus had a great memory and <u>became</u> a well-known doctor.

Sometimes the time frame in a narrative really does change. In those circumstances, you would change the verb tense. The following example accurately shows two different time periods. Notice that certain key words (*In 1550*, *today*) indicate what tense the writer should use.

past
In 1550, Nostradamus <u>wrote</u> a book of prophesies. Today, some

present
researchers <u>debate</u> his ideas.

PRACTICE 1

Underline the verbs in each sentence, and then correct each tense shift. If a sentence is correct, write *C* in the blank.

EXAMPLE:

In 2005, the ABC News program *Primetime* <u>presented</u> a story about a
                                                    watched
family from Louisiana, and I ~~watch~~ the program with my brother.   _____

1. During World War II, a twenty-one-year-old Navy fighter pilot

   was flying over an island when Japanese artillery shoots at the

   plane.   _____

2. The plane went down, and the pilot, James Huston, died.   _____

3. Many years later, a child from Louisiana had vivid dreams

   about the pilot's death, and in 2005, the family tells their

   story to ABC News.   _____

4. When James Leininger was eighteen months old, he becomes

   fascinated with airplanes.   _____

5. At age two, James began to have severe nightmares, and his

   parents don't understand what was happening.   _____

6. One night, James's father, Bruce, listened as his son speaks

   about the fire in his airplane.   _____

7. Over time, James revealed details about a specific plane crash

   and was able to describe the type of plane he is flying.   _____

8. James also said that he took off from a boat called the Natoma.   _____

9. According to the Leiningers, their small child did not have

   access to any war documentaries, and at that time, they never

   discussed World War II with James.   _____

10. As James's memories became more detailed, his father decides

    to do some research.   _____

11. Bruce Leininger discovered that the details matched James

    Huston's plane crash, which occurs at Iwo Jima, in Japan.   _____

12. Today, James Huston's sister, Anna, believes that the boy is the

    reincarnation of her brother, and the Leiningers agreed with her. _____

> ## Hint   **Would and Could**
>
> When you tell a story about a past event, use *would* instead of *will*, and use *could* instead of *can*.
>
> > *would*
> > Nostradamus predicted that in the year 1999, a great terror ~~will~~ descend
> > *could*
> > from the skies, and nobody ~~can~~ stop the event.

PRACTICE 2

Correct the six tense inconsistencies in the following paragraphs.

EXAMPLE:

Fortune-tellers and psychics try to predict the future, and some psychics

  believe
genuinely ~~believed~~ that they have a special gift.

1.   A fifteenth-century British woman, Ursula Shipton, made

     many accurate predictions about the future. For example, she

     predicted that iron boats will float on water, and she also said

     that thoughts will fly around the world. She spoke of human

flight, modern ships, submarines, and wireless communications. However, one of her most famous predictions does not come true. She predicted that the world will end in 1881.

2.   In 1990, Gordon Stein wrote an article expressing his doubts about Shipton. He said that her predictions were often vague and can be interpreted in many different ways. In addition, Charles Hindley, who edited an 1862 version of Shipton's verses, admits that he added his own verses to make her prophecies seem more accurate. Perhaps readers should be skeptical when they read about ancient prophecies.

Telling a Story

When you narrate, or tell a story, you can describe events using the present, past, or future tense. The important thing is to be consistent. The next two paragraphs tell the same story using different tenses.

Past Tense

Mark Twain **went** to see a magic show. At the show, a hypnotist **made** the audience members do ridiculous things. Twain **asked** to go onstage, and he **did** not fall under the hypnotist's spell. However, he **decided** to act out everything that the hypnotist **asked.** He **realized** that the hypnotist **was** a fraud.

Present Tense

Mark Twain **goes** to see a magic show. At the show, a hypnotist **makes** the audience members do ridiculous things. Twain **asks** to go onstage, and he **does** not fall under the hypnotist's spell. However, he **decides** to act out everything that the hypnotist **asks.** He **realizes** that the hypnotist **is** a fraud.

PRACTICE 3

The following paragraph shifts between the present and the past tenses. Edit the paragraph to make the tenses consistent. You might choose to tell the story using the present or past tense.

According to Chinese astrology, one day Buddha invites all of the animals in the kingdom to the Chinese New Year's celebration. An invitation was sent to the rat, and the rat was asked to invite the cat.

However, the rat was jealous of the cat, and he did not pass along the information. On the day of the celebration, only twelve animals can attend; the first to arrive is the rat and the last to arrive is the pig. Buddha assigned each animal a year of its own, and people born in that year will have the characteristics of the animal. The next day, the cat heard about the celebration, and she sent word that she will soon arrive. Later, when the cat met Buddha, she asked to have a year named after her, but Buddha tells her that it is too late. Buddha decides that there will be no year of the cat.

FINAL REVIEW

Correct fifteen tense inconsistencies in the following paragraphs.

EXAMPLE:

want
Some people read horoscopes because they ~~wanted~~ to know about the future.

1.   The word *astrology* is an ancient Greek word that means "science of the stars." Early humans used the stars to guide them and to help them choose when to hunt, fish, and migrate. Then, as soon as people can write, they looked to the stars and write of relationships between the sky and humans.

2.   In the past, ancient Greeks, Aztecs, Babylonians, and Chinese all develop sophisticated astrological charts. For centuries, astrology's appeal has endured. There is a brief setback when, in 1594, Galileo proved that the earth was not the center of the universe. However, Sir Isaac Newton pointed out that

READING LINK

To learn more about beliefs, read the following essays:

"The Cult of Emaciation" by Ben Barry (page 425)

"The Hijab" by Naheed Mustafa (page 444)

Next, ask people why they believe a certain thing. Did they read about it? Did someone tell them about it? Keep notes about their answers. Then work with your team members, and write a paragraph about one of the following topics. Ensure that your verb tenses are consistent.

1. Choose one person you asked about his or her beliefs, and write a paragraph about that person. What does he or she believe in? Why does he or she have those beliefs? (Because you are writing about one person, take extra care to ensure that your subjects and verbs agree.)

2. Write a paragraph about the results of the survey. You could discuss any differences between males and females regarding superstitions and beliefs.

CHAPTER 14

How Do I Get a Better Grade?

mywritinglab

Visit www.mywritinglab.com for audio-visual lectures and additional practice sets about tense consistency.
Get a better grade with MyWritingLab!

Compound Sentences

Section Theme: **POLITICS**

CONTENTS

- Comparing Simple and Compound Sentences
- Combining Sentences Using Coordinating Conjunctions
- Combining Sentences Using Semicolons
- Combining Sentences Using Transitional Expressions

In this chapter, you will read about political history and great leaders.

Grammar Snapshot

Looking at Compound Sentences

Seneca Chief Red Jacket spoke to the Iroquois nation in 1805. In this excerpt, compound sentences are underlined.

> The white people had now found our country. <u>Tidings were carried back, and more came amongst us.</u> Yet we did not fear them. We took them to be friends. They called us brothers. <u>We believed them, and we gave them a large seat.</u> At length their numbers had greatly increased. <u>They wanted more land; they wanted our country.</u> <u>Our eyes were opened, and our minds became uneasy.</u>

In this chapter, you will practice identifying and writing compound sentences.

Comparing Simple and Compound Sentences

When you write, you can use sentences of varying lengths to make your writing more appealing. One of the easiest ways to create variety is to combine simple sentences to form compound sentences.

A **simple sentence** expresses a complete idea. It has one or more subjects and verbs.

One subject, one verb:	**Josh** <u>writes</u> for the campus newspaper.
Two subjects:	**Housing** and **transportation** <u>are</u> hotly discussed issues on campus.
Two verbs:	The **student president** <u>speaks</u> and <u>writes</u> about serious issues.

A **compound sentence** contains two or more simple sentences, and the two complete ideas can be joined in several ways.

	Josh is ambitious. + He hopes to win.
Add a coordinator:	Josh is ambitious, **and** he hopes to win.
Add a semicolon:	Josh is ambitious; he hopes to win.
Add a semicolon and conjunctive adverb	Josh is ambitious; **therefore,** he hopes to win.

Combining Sentences Using Coordinating Conjunctions

A **coordinating conjunction** joins two complete ideas and indicates the connection between them. When you combine two sentences with a coordinating conjunction, put a comma before the conjunction.

Complete idea	, **for** , **and** , **nor** , **but** , **or** , **yet** , **so**	complete idea.

Martin Luther King experienced injustice, **but** he was not a bitter person.

 **Recognizing Compound Sentences**

To be sure that a sentence is compound, place your finger over the coordinator, and then ask yourself whether the two clauses are complete sentences.

Simple:	Josh is ambitious and hopes to win the election.
Compound:	Josh is ambitious, and he hopes to win the election.

PRACTICE 1

Indicate whether the following sentences are simple (*S*) or compound (*C*). Underline the coordinating conjunction in each compound sentence.

EXAMPLE:

Today women can vote, <u>but</u> they did not always have that right.   *C*

1. Often, charismatic individuals gain power and influence others.   _____

2. Sometimes a particular social class controls a government.   _____

3. Democratic governments first flourished in ancient Greece, and they eventually spread around the world.   _____

4. In Athens, men could vote and run for office.   _____

5. However, women and slaves were not allowed to vote.   _____

6. In 1881, the Isle of Man became the first place in the world to give property-owning women the vote in national elections.   _____

7. Unmarried women and wealthy widows could participate in decision making, but they could not run in elections.   _____

8. For over two hundred years, American women could not vote, and they could not go to college.   _____

9. Some women made speeches and campaigned for the right to vote, and many men joined them in their fight.   _____

10. In 1920, American women won the right to express their views and vote in national elections.   _____

Meanings of Coordinating Conjunctions

Each coordinating conjunction has a specific meaning. Review the next table to see how each coordinator can be used.

Coordinating Conjunction	Function	Example
and	to join two ideas	Royal families receive public money, **and** each member gets an allowance.
but	to contrast two ideas	Spain has a monarchy, **but** the United States does not have a king or queen.
for	to indicate a reason	A monarchy is expensive to maintain, **for** it costs a lot to upkeep royal institutions.
nor	to indicate a negative idea	Americans do not have a monarchy, **nor** do they want one.
or	to offer an alternative	A king can rule, **or** he can abdicate the throne.
so	to indicate a cause and effect relationship	Some monarchies have abolished their "males only" rule, **so** some women now assume the throne.
yet	to introduce a surprising idea	Britain's Prince William is very popular, **yet** he is also quite shy.

PRACTICE 2

Read each sentence carefully and decide how the two parts of the sentence are related. Then add a comma and an appropriate coordinating conjunction.

EXAMPLE:

Is voting a right, _____*or*_____ is voting an obligation?

1. In the United States, citizens may vote during elections _____ they may stay home.

2. Americans do not have to register _____ do they have to vote.

3. Currently, about 50 percent of eligible voters exercise their right to vote _____ some people question the state of democracy in this country.

4. About twenty countries have compulsory voting _____ they oblige citizens to vote during elections.

5. Citizens must visit polling stations _____ they must show a willingness to complete the voting process.

6. Some citizens vote for a candidate _____ others spoil their ballots.

7. Brazil has compulsory voting _____ the government does not enforce the voting law.

8. Australia, on the other hand, has compulsory voting rules _____ non-voters are punished with fines or possible imprisonment.

9. Before 1924, only 47 percent of Australian citizens bothered to vote _____ elected officials worried about voter apathy.

10. Government officials passed a law making voting compulsory _____ they wanted people to exercise their democratic rights.

11. Today, Australian citizens over the age of eighteen must register to vote _____ they must turn up at the polling station during election days.

12. The voter turnout in Australia is about 95 percent _____ elected officials are pleased with the results of compulsory voting.

13. Some people support the idea of compulsory voting _____ others consider it an infringement on personal rights.

14. Will you vote during the next election _____ will you stay at home?

PRACTICE 3

Create compound sentences by adding a coordinating conjunction and another complete sentence to each simple sentence. Remember that the two ideas must be related. Try to use a variety of coordinating conjunctions.

EXAMPLE:

Many people vote *, but they do not always know about the issues.* _____

1. Barry has a car _____
   _____

2. The drinking age is twenty-one in most states _____
   _____

3. Many teenagers drink alcohol illegally _____
   _____

4. Some laws are passed to protect people _____
   _____

5. Drinking and driving is dangerous _____
   _____

6. Barry continually drives too fast _____
   _____

PRACTICE 4

In the following paragraphs, join eight pairs of sentences using coordinating conjunctions. You can keep some of the short sentences so that your paragraph has variety.

EXAMPLE:

                         , and we
We read the report. ~~We~~ did not know what to do.

1.   In 1870, for the first time, the U.S. government published

   statistics about child labor. Many people believed that work was

   good for children. Others worried about the harsh conditions faced by

   child workers. At that time, millions of children had full-time jobs in

   the United States. They were all under the age of sixteen. In

   Pennsylvania, children between the ages of eight and ten worked in

coal mines. Some of them worked as domestics. Many states permitted children to work twelve hours a day. They could also work night shifts.

2.   In the late nineteenth century, concerned people started a movement to protect child laborers in America. Leaders in this effort wanted children to get schooling. They tried to convince lawmakers to regulate child labor. For example, in Georgia, very young children worked in cotton mills. Some of them were only seven years old. The Georgia legislature refused to pass laws regulating child labor. Florence Kelley, a child advocate, worked to change the laws. She was not able to vote or be elected. She decided to organize boycotts of cotton mills. Kelley's strategies were somewhat successful. Many laws restricting child labor were passed. In 1916 and 1918, Congress passed federal child labor laws. The Supreme Court declared them unconstitutional. Finally, in 1939, the Fair Labor Standards Act was passed. It prohibited children under sixteen years of age from working in manufacturing or mining.

Combining Sentences Using Semicolons

A semicolon can join two complete sentences. The semicolon replaces a conjunction.

> Complete idea   **;**   complete idea.

> The election offices closed; many ballots were missing.

PRACTICE 5

Each sentence is missing a semicolon. Put a semicolon in the appropriate place.

EXAMPLE:

In 1945, George Orwell was discouraged ; he was very disillusioned with communism.

1. Orwell did not like state intervention in people's lives he also worried about unemployment and the exploitation of the poor.

2. According to Orwell, no book is genuinely free from political bias most of his novels had political undertones.

3. In 1945, George Orwell published a political allegory called *Animal Farm* the story traces the rise of communism in the former Soviet Union.

4. At the beginning of the story, old farmer Jones drinks too much whiskey he forgets to lock up the farm.

5. A pig called Old Major influences the animals he makes speeches about evil humans.

6. The animals feel upset with their master's incompetence they decide to revolt and take over the farm.

7. Mr. Jones and his wife flee the animals celebrate by eating a feast.

8. At first, two pigs lead the animals the animal farm runs smoothly.

9. Then the two leaders begin to fight one pig drives the other from the farm.

10. The leader becomes an evil dictator the other animals are treated badly.

Hint   **Use a Semicolon to Join Related Ideas**

Do not use a semicolon to join two unrelated sentences.

Incorrect: George Orwell wrote about political issues; he believed in voodoo.
(The second idea has no clear relationship with the first idea.)

Correct: George Orwell wrote about political issues; he criticized communism in his book *Animal Farm.*

PRACTICE 6

Create compound sentences by adding a semicolon and another complete sentence to each simple sentence. Remember that the two ideas must be related.

EXAMPLE:

Last year I returned to college *; I wanted to change careers.*

1. Some adults return to college _____
   _____

2. Many students drive cars to campus _____
   _____

3. Some students live in dorms _____
   _____

4. Students look forward to spring break _____
   _____

5. I am on the student council _____
   _____

Combining Sentences Using Transitional Expressions

A **transitional expression** can join two complete ideas and show how they are related. The next table shows some common transitional expressions.

Transitional Expressions

Addition	Alternative	Contrast	Time	Example or Emphasis	Result or Consequence
additionally	in fact	however	eventually	for example	consequently
also	instead	nevertheless	finally	for instance	hence
besides	on the contrary	nonetheless	later	namely	therefore
furthermore	on the other hand	still	meanwhile	of course	thus
in addition	otherwise		subsequently	undoubtedly	
moreover					

If the second sentence begins with a transitional expression, put a semicolon before it and a comma after it.

> Complete idea **;** **transitional expression** **,** complete idea.

> Nelson Mandela spent twenty-five years in prison; **nevertheless,** he resolved to forgive his jailors.
>
>   ; **still,**
>   ; **however,**
>   ; **nonetheless,**

PRACTICE 7

Punctuate the following sentences by adding any necessary semicolons and commas.

EXAMPLE:

Nelson Mandela was born into the royal family of the Thembu ; however , he was educated in a British missionary school.

1. Nelson Mandela went to Fort Hare University eventually he was expelled because of his political actions.

2. He returned home meanwhile his family expected him to agree to an arranged marriage.

3. His potential bride was in love with another man therefore Mandela ran away from his village and went to Soweto.

4. Mandela became a lawyer later he turned his attention to the repressive race laws of South Africa.

5. He was politically active against the apartheid system consequently he was arrested.

6. Mandela defended himself during his 1964 trial however the jury was biased.

7. He was not freed instead he was sentenced to life imprisonment.

8. Some of the prison guards were cruel nevertheless many of the guards grew to respect Mandela.

9. Mandela left prison twenty-five years later without bitterness in fact he forgave his opponents.

PRACTICE 8

Create compound sentences using the following transitional expressions. Try to use a different expression in each sentence.

consequently	furthermore	however
in fact	nevertheless	therefore

EXAMPLE:

Each vote is important*; in fact, one vote can change the outcome of* *an election.*

1. I don't care about politics _____

   _____

2. Some people make good leaders _____

   _____

3. Arthur wants to become the mayor _____

   _____

4. The mayor committed a crime _____

   _____

5. The police conducted an investigation _____

   _____

6. The police chief is outspoken _____

   _____

PRACTICE 9

Add a transitional expression to join each pair of sentences. Choose an expression from the following list, and try to use a different expression in each sentence.

consequently	for example	for instance	however
in fact	therefore	thus	

EXAMPLE:

; thus, I
I vote in every election. ~~I~~ want to know about the issues.

1. Every four years, there is a presidential election in the United

   States. Voters are bombarded with campaign advertising.

2. Sometimes the campaign advertisements attack the opponent's

   platform. Some ads attack the opponent's personal life.

3. In 1988, attack ads appeared on television. They accused presidential candidate Michael Dukakis of being soft on crime.

4. Today, many attack ads appear on Web sites. In the 2004 presidential election, a Republican Web site criticized Democratic candidate John Kerry's antiwar activities.

5. At the same time, a Democrat-supported Web site attacked George Bush. It questioned his service in the National Guard.

6. Most voters do not like attack advertising. Political parties should try to focus on issues instead of making personal attacks.

FINAL REVIEW

Read the following paragraphs. Create compound sentences by adding semicolons, conjunctive adverbs (*however, therefore,* etc.) or coordinating conjunctions (*for, and, nor, but, or, yet, so*). Try to create at least ten compound sentences.

EXAMPLE:

Political leaders have traditionally been male. ~~Many~~ *, but many* countries have elected female leaders.

1. Since 1900, there have been over forty female presidents or prime ministers. Sirimavo Bandaranaike was the world's first female prime minister. She was elected in Sri Lanka on July 20, 1960. She made Sri Lanka a republic. She nationalized private companies. Parliament expelled her in 1980.

2. Indira Gandhi was elected in 1966. She led India for nearly twenty years. Indira's last name was Gandhi. She was not related to Mahatma Gandhi. Her husband's name was Feroze Gandhi. She took his name. Some of Indira Gandhi's policies were unpopular. She made many enemies.

3.   In Pakistan, citizens also voted for a female leader. Benazir Bhutto was elected prime minister in 1988. She was the first female head of state in the Muslim world. However, a military coup by army generals forced her out of office. She was accused of corruption. She spent nearly six years in prison. Later, Bhutto campaigned for another election. Her dreams were never realized. She was assassinated on December 27, 2007.

4.   Since 2000, more females have become heads of state. There have been some surprises. In 2006, Ellen Johnson Sirleaf was sworn in as Liberia's president. In Mozambique, Loisa Diogo became prime minister. Also, in 2006 observers watched the elections in Jamaica. Maybe a male would become leader. Maybe a female would be elected. To the surprise of many, Jamaica elected Portia Simpson Miller as its first female prime minister. In her inaugural address, she vowed to fight corruption and support the poor. Many voters around the globe are asking women to lead their nations.

The Writer's Room

Write about one of the following topics. First, write at least ten simple sentences. Then, combine some of your sentences to create compound sentences. When you have finished, edit your writing and ensure that your sentences are combined correctly.

1. What are some common reasons that people give for not voting?
2. Do you think that the voting age should be raised or lowered? Explain your position.
3. Are you happy with the current administration in the White House? Why or why not?

CHECKLIST: COMPOUND SENTENCES

When you edit your writing, ask yourself these questions.

Are my compound sentences correctly punctuated? Remember to do the following:

–place a comma before a coordinating conjunction.

Students should get involved, and they should vote in elections.

–use a semicolon between two complete ideas.

A woman may run for president; she may not win.

–use a semicolon before a transitional expression and a comma after it.

The results will be close; **therefore,** it is important to cast your vote.

How Do I Get a Better Grade?

Visit www.mywritinglab.com for audio-visual lectures and additional practice sets about compound sentences.
Get a better grade with MyWritingLab!

16 CHAPTER

Complex Sentences

Section Theme: **POLITICS**

CONTENTS

• Understanding
  Complex Sentences
• Using Subordinating
  Conjunctions
• Using Relative
  Pronouns
• Combining Questions

In this chapter, you will read about political activists.

Jim Wilson/The New York Times

Grammar Snapsh•t

Looking at Complex Sentences

In this excerpt from Nelson Mandela's *The Long Road Home*, he describes his prison cell. The complex sentences are underlined.

Many mornings, a small pool of water would have formed on the cold floor overnight. When I raised this with the commanding officer, he told me our bodies would absorb the moisture. We were each issued three blankets so flimsy and worn that they were practically transparent. Our bedding consisted of a single sisal, or straw, mat. Later we were given a felt mat, and we placed the felt mat on top of the sisal one to provide some softness. At that time of year, the cells were so cold and the blankets provided so little warmth that we always slept fully dressed.

In this chapter, you will identify and write complex sentences.

Understanding Complex Sentences

A **complex sentence** contains one independent clause (complete idea) and one or more dependent clauses (incomplete ideas).

- An **independent clause** has a subject and a verb and can stand alone because it expresses one complete idea.

    Rosa Parks did not give up her seat.

- A **dependent clause** has a subject and verb, but it cannot stand alone. It "depends" on another clause to be complete.

Incomplete:	Although she was asked to move.

                          dependent clause   independent clause

    Complete: <u>Although she was asked to move</u>, <u>Rosa Parks did not give up her seat</u>.

 **Hint** **Compound-Complex Sentences**

You can combine compound and complex sentences. The next example is a **compound-complex sentence**.

                            complex

After Parks was arrested, others supported her, and they boycotted city buses.

                                    compound

Using Subordinating Conjunctions

When you add a **subordinating conjunction**—a word such as *after*, *because*, or *although*—to a clause, you make the clause dependent. *Subordinate* means "secondary," so subordinating conjunctions are words that introduce secondary ideas.

    Main idea   **subordinating conjunction**   secondary idea.

    Crowds gathered <u>**whenever** the candidate spoke</u>.

    Subordinating conjunction   secondary idea,   main idea.

    <u>**Whenever** the candidate spoke</u>, crowds gathered.

Some Subordinating Conjunctions

after	because	since	until	whereas
although	before	so that	when	wherever
as	even if	that	whenever	whether
as if	even though	though	where	while
as though	if	unless		

Subordinating conjunctions create a relationship between the clauses in a sentence. Review the next table to see how you can use subordinating conjunctions.

Subordinating Conjunction	Usage	Example
as, because, since, so that	To indicate a reason, a cause, or an effect	John F. Kennedy ran for office <u>because</u> he thought he could change things.
as long as, even if, if, provided that, so that, unless	To indicate a condition or result	A person cannot become president <u>unless</u> he or she was born in the United States.
although, even though, though, whereas	To contrast ideas	<u>Although</u> Kennedy had a bad back, he remained active.
where, wherever	To indicate a location	<u>Wherever</u> he traveled, large crowds gathered.
after, before, since, until, when, whenever, while	To show a point in time	Americans were stunned <u>when</u> President Kennedy was assassinated.

CHAPTER 16

PRACTICE I

Practice identifying dependent and independent clauses. Circle the subordinating conjunction and then underline the dependent clause in each sentence.

EXAMPLE:

Gandhi was well-respected (because) he used nonviolent action to spark political change.

1. Although such restraint is extremely rare, some political leaders refuse to use violent methods.

2. When he was still a teenager, Mahatma Gandhi developed his beliefs about nonviolence.

3. Gandhi did not believe in the use of force because "an eye for an eye leads to a world of the blind."

4. Although his political career began in South Africa, Gandhi is most known for his passive resistance movement in India.

5. When he returned to Bombay in 1915, British rulers controlled all of India.

6. After assessing the situation, Gandhi led textile workers and planters in acts of civil disobedience.

7. While he was touring India in 1919, he persuaded people across the country to stop working for one day.

8. Sometimes the country's rulers used force to stop people from going on strike even if the strikers were peaceful.

9. Gandhi complained because officials often used "a hammer to strike a fly."

10. Even though his supporters were violently attacked, Gandhi would not respond to violence with violence.

11. After twenty-eight years of peaceful noncooperation, Mahatma Gandhi's passive resistance movement was successful.

12. India became independent in 1947, although the country then split up along religious lines.

CHAPTER 16

 **Punctuating Complex Sentences**

If you use a subordinator at the beginning of a sentence, put a comma after the dependent clause. Generally, if you use a subordinator in the middle of the sentence, you do not need to use a comma.

Comma:	**Even though** she did not like the candidates, she voted in the election.
No comma:	She voted in the election **even though** she did not like the candidates.

GRAMMAR LINK

See Chapter 25 for more information about comma usage.

PRACTICE 2

The following selection is adapted from Mahatma Gandhi's autobiography, *The Story of My Experiments with Truth*. In the excerpt, Gandhi describes his first trip to England. Underline each subordinating conjunction, and add five missing commas.

EXAMPLE:

Although I did not feel at all seasick, as the days passed I became fidgety.

1. I felt shy even when I spoke to the steward. I was not used to speaking English because I had had very little practice. The other passengers were English. Whenever they were friendly and tried to speak with me I could not understand them. Even if I understood an Englishman I could not reply.

2. My friend Mazmudar had no difficulty communicating whenever he mixed with the others. While I hid in the cabin he would move about freely on deck. Because Mazmudar was a lawyer he told me about his legal experience. He advised me to take every possible opportunity to speak in English even though I might make mistakes. Although I wanted to please him nothing could make me conquer my shyness.

PRACTICE 3

Each of the sentences in this practice is missing a subordinating conjunction. Write one of the following conjunctions in each blank. Use a different conjunction each time.

~~after~~	before	until
although	even though	whenever
because	so that	when

EXAMPLE:

_____After_____ Frederick Douglass's birth in 1818, he was separated from his mother.

1. Douglass's grandmother took him to her master's plantation _____ he turned six years old. _____ Douglass understood why his grandmother gave him to the master, he always felt the pain of abandonment.

2. _____ he turned nine years old, he was sent to work as the houseboy for a Baltimore family. Sophia Auld, his mistress, taught Douglass the alphabet _____ it was illegal to instruct slaves in reading. _____ Douglass knew how to read, he could tap into the power of the written word.

3. Douglass waited _____ he turned twenty. Then he escaped from slavery by disguising himself as a sailor. He worked with the Massachusetts antislavery society _____ he could influence public opinion. _____ he could, he spoke about the abolition of slavery.

 **Putting a Subject After the Subordinator**

When you combine sentences to form complex sentences, always remember to put a subject after the subordinator.

it

The protest was unsuccessful because ‸ was not well organized.

PRACTICE 4

Add six missing subjects to this selection. Remember that a subject can be a noun or a pronoun.

EXAMPLE:

he

Arnold Schwarzenegger was born in Austria, although currently has a U.S. passport.

1.   Some people believe that acting and politics don't mix, but many famous actors have become politicians. Ronald Reagan was a well-known movie star when decided to run for office. Although had acted in 53 movies, he gave up his Hollywood career. In 1966, many observers were surprised when was elected governor of California. Then, in 1980, Reagan became the president of the United States.

2.   More recently, in 2003, Arnold Schwarzenegger became the governor of California. The former bodybuilder and *Terminator* star was a successful actor when decided to enter politics. He became governor because is a useful and important position. Perhaps actors have an advantage in politics because learn how to communicate effectively during their theatrical training.

PRACTICE 5

Combine the sentences by adding a subordinating conjunction. Write each sentence twice: once with the dependent clause at the beginning of the sentence, and once with the dependent clause at the end of the sentence. From the following list, use each conjunction once.

    after   although   ~~because~~   even though   when

EXAMPLE:

I vote. It is important.

I vote because it is important.

Because it is important, I vote.

1. I was very busy on election day. I still voted.

   _____

   _____

2. I got home. I watched the election results on television.

   _____

   _____

3. The ballots were counted. A winner was declared.

   _____

   _____

4. The losing candidate congratulated the winner. She was disappointed.

   _____

   _____

   _____

   _____

Using Relative Pronouns

A **relative pronoun** describes a noun or pronoun. You can form complex sentences by using relative pronouns to introduce dependent clauses. Review the most common relative pronouns.

who	whomever	which
whom	whose	that

Use *who* (*whom, whomever, whose*) to add information about a person.

Martin Luther King, Jr., **who** was a minister, fought for civil rights.

Use *that* to add information about a thing.

He made speeches **that** moved people.

Use *which* to add information about a thing.

In his greatest speech, **which** he wrote in 1963, he speaks about his dream for a better America.

 **Hint**   **Punctuating Sentences with Relative Pronouns**

GRAMMAR LINK

For more information about punctuating relative clauses, refer to Chapter 25, "Commas."

Which
Use commas to set off clauses that begin with *which*.

The movie, **which was very interesting**, was about the first presidential election.

That
Do not use commas to set off clauses beginning with *that*.

On the day **that we met** it was raining.

Who
When a clause begins with *who*, you may or may not need a comma. If the clause contains nonessential information, put commas. If the clause is essential to the meaning of the sentence, then it does not require commas.

Essential: The two young men **who started the riot** were arrested.

Not essential: Reporter Eli Marcos, **who once worked for the *Los Angeles Times*,** took photos of the event.

PRACTICE 6

In each of the following sentences, underline the relative clause.

EXAMPLE:
Winona LaDuke, who is a Chippewa, is director of the White Earth Land Recovery Project.

1. Winona LaDuke has done work that others have avoided. She has helped native people who live in Minnesota learn about their Ojibwe language. She has also helped women who have been abused find security and peace. Furthermore, LaDuke, who sometimes acts in movies, has worked tirelessly to retrieve Anishinabe land. In fact, nearly 1,000 acres that had been lost over the decades have been retrieved with the help of the White Earth Project.

2. In 1994, *Time* magazine, which is found on most newsstands, honored LaDuke for her work. Today, LaDuke's group, which is located in Minnesota, continues to buy back native land.

PRACTICE 7

Combine each set of sentences by using the relative pronoun in parentheses. There may be more than one way to combine some sets of sentences.

EXAMPLE:

(who) In Tiananmen Square, students were arrested. They protested against the government.

In Tiananmen Square, students who protested against the government were arrested.

1. (who) In 1989, Chinese students wanted change. They sat in a square in Beijing.

   _____

   _____

2. (who) The protesters were asking for democracy. They sang and held signs.

   _____

   _____

3. (that) Army tanks entered the square. The tanks fired on the students.

   _____

   _____

4. (who) An unknown man stood in front of the tanks. He has become a symbol of resistance to tyranny.

   _____

   _____

5. (which) The photo appeared in newspapers around the world. It had a strong emotional impact.

   _____

   _____

PRACTICE 8

Add dependent clauses to each sentence. Begin each clause with a relative pronoun (*who*, *which*, or *that*). Add any necessary commas.

EXAMPLE:

People ___*who get involved*_____ can change things in our society.

1. Washington, D. C. _____ has many attractions.

2. The students _____ rented a bus.

3. The president of the college student union _____

   _____ has done a good job.

4. The posters _____ are eye-catching.

5. This college _____ has an excellent
   student newspaper.

6. I do not vote for candidates _____.

7. My friend _____ is not interested in
   politics.

8. According to my friend, politicians are people _____
   _____.

Creating Embedded Questions

It is possible to combine a question with a statement or to combine two questions
to form a complex sentence. An **embedded question** is a question that is part of
a larger sentence.

Question:	How can she raise funds?
Embedded question:	The candidate wonders <u>how she can raise funds</u>.

In questions, there is generally a helping verb before the subject. However, when
a question is embedded in a larger sentence, either place the helping verb after the
subject or remove it. As you read the following examples, pay attention to the
word order in the embedded questions.

Combine two questions.

Separate: Do you know the answer? Why **do** they like the candidate?

(The second question includes the helping verb *do*.)

Combined: Do you know <u>why they like the candidate?</u>

(The helping verb *do* is removed from the embedded
question.)

Combine a question and a statement.

Separate: I wonder about it. How **can** we help?

(In the question, the helping verb *can* appears before the
subject.)

Combined: I wonder <u>how we can help</u>.

(In the embedded question, *can* is placed after the subject.)

 **Hint** **Use the Correct Word Order**

When editing your writing, ensure that you have formed embedded questions
properly.

I wonder why ~~do~~ people use drugs? I asked the mayor what ~~did she think~~ *she thought*
about the war on drugs.

PRACTICE 9

Identify and correct eight errors with embedded questions.

EXAMPLE:

Prohibition began.
The writer explains how ~~did Prohibition begin~~.

1.   I wonder why did the United States ban alcohol in 1920. Does anybody understand why would officials do that? According to Dr. K. Austen Kerr, many Americans were worried about social problems related to alcohol consumption. But then you have to wonder how could a government legislate morality.

2.   The Volstead Act prohibited the sale and distribution of alcohol. Do you know why was it called the Volstead Act? The author of the act was a prominent Republican named Andrew Volstead. Many citizens wondered how could the act be enforced.

3.   At first, Prohibition appeared to work, and alcohol consumption dropped. But then illegal distillers popped up, and a huge black market appeared. Do you know why were people illegally producing alcohol? They did it because it was an extremely lucrative business. Many well-known families, including the Bronfmans and the Kennedys, made fortunes during the Prohibition era. At the time, Prohibition supporters wondered why were some citizens breaking the law.

4.   Ultimately, in 1933, Prohibition was repealed. Do you know why can Prohibition never succeed? Perhaps as long as people are willing to buy intoxicating drinks or drugs, there will be others who are ready to supply those items.

FINAL REVIEW

The following paragraphs contain simple sentences. To give the paragraphs more sentence variety, form ten complex sentences by combining pairs of sentences. You will have to add some words and delete others.

EXAMPLE:

When some   *freedoms, they*
~~Some~~ people fight for our rights and ~~freedoms. They~~ risk getting jailed.

1.   Henry David Thoreau was an honest man. He did not pay poll taxes. He protested against the Mexican War. He was arrested. He subsequently wrote "On the Duty of Civil Disobedience." In his text, he stressed that some laws are immoral. It is okay to disobey such laws. There have been many other acts of civil disobedience. Such acts have changed American history. For example, there was the Boston Tea Party. Citizens threw boxes of tea into the harbor. They did not want to pay taxes to Britain.

2.   Back in 1958, Ralph Nader was studying law at Harvard University. At that time, about 5 million car accidents happened every year. Carmakers were concerned about the style, cost, and performance of automobiles. They were not concerned about safety. In 1965, Nader wrote a best-selling book. It was called *Unsafe at Any Speed.* General Motors attempted to discredit Nader. Then he sued GM for invasion of privacy. GM executives settled the case. They admitted to harassing Nader. In 1966, new safety laws were passed. Automakers had to redesign autos. They had to make them safer. Sometimes one person works hard. That person influences large corporations.

The Writer's Room

Write about one of the following topics. After you finish writing, ensure that you have formed and punctuated the complex sentences correctly.

1. Examine this photo. What are some terms that come to mind? Some ideas might be *left wing*, *right wing*, *American*, or *slogan*. Define a term or expression that relates to the photo.

2. Do you care about politics? Are you politically active? Do you vote in elections? Give your opinion about politics.

CHECKLIST: COMPLEX SENTENCES

When you edit your writing, ask yourself these questions.

Are my complex sentences complete?

> *He resigned because*
> ~~Because~~ of the scandal.

Are my complex sentences correctly punctuated?

> He resigned from office/ because of the scandal.
> The ballot box, which was full, was taken to the election office.

Do I have any embedded questions? Check for errors in these cases:
–word order
–unnecessary helping verbs

> *I will*
> I don't know which candidate ~~will I~~ vote for. I wonder which one
> ~~do~~ you like.

How Do I Get a Better Grade?

Visit www.mywritinglab.com for audio-visual lectures and additional practice sets about complex sentences.
Get a better grade with MyWritingLab!

Sentence Variety and Exact Language

Section Theme: **POLITICS**

CONTENTS

Achieving Sentence
Variety

Using Specific
Vocabulary

Avoiding Clichés

Slang versus Standard
English

*In this chapter, you will read about
political scandals.*

> **Grammar Snapshot**

Looking at Sentence Variety

On August 8, 1974, President Richard Nixon resigned because of a
political scandal. Notice the variety of sentence lengths in this excerpt
from his resignation speech.

> For more than a quarter of a century in public life, I have
> shared in the turbulent history of this evening. I have fought
> for what I believe in. I have tried, to the best of my ability, to
> discharge those duties and meet those responsibilities that
> were entrusted to me. Sometimes I have succeeded, and
> sometimes I have failed.

In this chapter, you will practice varying the length and structure of
sentences. You will also identify and correct clichés and slang.

1. _____, every nation must deal with corrupt politicians at one time or another.

2. _____, public figures risk their careers for economic gain.

3. _____, the people in many states mistrust their elected officials.

4. _____, the senator defended his conduct at his trial.

5. _____, the scandal erupted on election night.

6. _____, the congressman was sentenced to eight years in prison in 2006.

 **Punctuation Tip**

Generally, when a sentence begins with an adverb or a prepositional phrase, put a comma after the opening word or phrase.

Suddenly, he threw his papers onto the floor.

Without any warning, he got up and left the room.

PRACTICE 4

Following are some adverbs and prepositional phrases. For a variety of sentence openings, place these words and phrases at the beginnings of appropriate sentences. Do not repeat your choices. There are many possible answers.

additionally	carefully	incredibly	in people's homes
always	during his presidency	in such places	~~recklessly~~
arrogantly	in an interview	in the capital city	with flattery

EXAMPLE:

Recklessly, he

The president had expensive tastes. ~~He~~ spent the nation's wealth on enormous mansions.

1. In some nations, a cult of personality surrounds the leader. The mass media is unquestioning. Reporters constantly praise the great leader. The leaders expect extreme loyalty and do not tolerate any type of dissent.

2.   In 2007, Turkmenistan's president for life died. Saparmurat

Niyazov was very eccentric. He maintained his image as the father of

the nation. He renamed the months and days in the calendar after

himself and members of his family. He named a town, an airport,

schools, and a meteorite after himself. A photo of Niyazov was at the

top right corner of every television screen. A gold-plated statue of the

president rotated so that it would always face the sun. His photo

adorned the walls of every office building. Even brands of tea and

vodka carried his image. Niyazov once said, "I admit it, there are too

many portraits, pictures, and monuments. I don't find any pleasure in

it, but the people demand it because of their mentality."

Using Specific Vocabulary

When you revise your writing, ensure that your words are exact. Replace any
vague words with more specific ones. For example, the following words are
vague.

good	nice	interesting
bad	mean	dull

Vague: Diane Sawyer is a <u>good</u> journalist.

More precise: Diane Sawyer is a <u>respected</u>, <u>award-winning</u>
                    <u>investigative</u> journalist.

How to Create Vivid Language

When you choose the precise word, you convey your meaning exactly. To create
more vivid and detailed vocabulary, try the next strategies.

Modify Your Nouns

If the noun is vague, make it more specific by adding one or more adjectives. You
could also rename the noun with a more specific term.

Vague: the woman

Vivid: the agreeable editor   the nervous voter

Modify Your Verbs

Use more vivid, precise verbs. You could also use adverbs.

Vague: said

Vivid: commanded, spoke sharply, suggested, whispered, yelled

Include More Details

Add information to make the sentence more complete.

Vague: His decision was bad for the party.

Precise: His immoral conduct destroyed the political party's chances for reelection.

PRACTICE 5

Underline vivid, detailed words and phrases in this excerpt from British author George Orwell's *1984*.

EXAMPLE:

The hallway smelled of <u>boiled cabbage and old rag mats</u>.

CHAPTER 17

flat: British word for "apartment"

lift-shaft: British term for "elevator shaft"

At one end of the hallway, a coloured poster, too large for indoor display, depicted an enormous face more than a metre wide; it was the face of a man of about forty-five with a heavy black moustache and ruggedly handsome features.

Winston made for the stairs. The **flat** was seven flights up, and Winston, who was thirty-nine and had a varicose ulcer above his right ankle, went slowly, resting several times on the way. On each landing, opposite the **lift-shaft**, the poster with the enormous face gazed from the wall. It was one of those pictures which are so contrived that the eyes follow you about when you move. BIG BROTHER IS WATCHING YOU, the caption beneath it ran.

PRACTICE 6

In each of the following sentences, replace the words in parentheses with more precise words or add more vivid details.

EXAMPLE:

He is (bad) *fiery, opinionated, and overbearing.* _____

1. The housing crisis is (bad) _____.

2. Some students must live in (bad) _____ conditions.

3. They must wait for weeks or months to get (good) _____ _____ housing.

4. The student dorms are (in poor condition) _____

_____.

5. (Someone) _____

_____ should focus on the housing problem.

6. In our city, (many people) _____

_____ will help.

7. For example, Geo Construction has already (been helpful) _____

_____.

8. Perhaps visiting students can be housed in (different locations) _____

_____.

9. You could (do something) _____

_____.

Avoiding Clichés

Clichés are overused expressions. Because they are overused, they lose their power and become boring. Avoid using clichés in your writing.

In each example, the underlined cliché has been replaced with a more direct word.

Clichés	Direct Words
The senator was as cool as a cucumber.	relaxed
She worked like a dog.	efficiently
She liked the finer things in life.	luxuries

Some Clichés and Their Substitutions

Cliché	Possible Substitution	Cliché	Possible Substitution
a dime a dozen	common	as luck would have it	fortunately
apple of my eye	my favorite	axe to grind	a problem with
as big as a house	very big	under the weather	ill
in the blink of an eye	quickly	rude awakening	shock
bear the burden	take responsibility	slowly but surely	eventually
break the ice	start the conversation	top dog	supervisor
busy as a bee	very busy	tried and true	experienced
finer things in life	luxuries	true blue	trustworthy

PRACTICE 7

Underline each clichéd expression, and replace it with words that are more direct.

EXAMPLE:

a large and imposing man

The king was as big as a house.

1. Books about Henry VIII are a dime a dozen.

2. When Henry VIII married Catherine of Aragon, his young bride was like a deer caught in the headlights.

3. Henry VIII's second wife, Anne Boleyn, liked the finer things in life.

4. During their courtship, Henry was as busy as a bee when he tried to impress the young maiden.

5. Anne Boleyn refused to be the king's mistress; as his legitimate wife, she would be the top dog.

6. After their marriage, King Henry was kind to Anne once in a blue moon.

7. On August 26, 1533, Queen Anne gave birth to a little bundle of joy named Elizabeth.

8. Henry got bored with Anne, and, in the blink of an eye, Anne was arrested and taken to the Tower of London.

9. Finding no support, Anne was as cool as a cucumber when she accepted her fate.

10. In May 1536, Anne Boleyn, who was as pretty as a picture, was charged with treason and executed.

11. Anne's cousin, Catherine Howard, also married Henry and was also executed; in fact, very few of Henry's wives lived to ripe old ages.

12. Henry searched for another wife, but the royal women of Europe, unwilling to throw caution to the wind, were understandably reluctant to marry the British monarch.

Slang versus Standard English

Most of your instructors will want you to write using standard American English. The word *standard* does not imply "better." Standard American English is the common language generally used and expected in schools, businesses, and government institutions in the United States.

Slang is nonstandard language. It is used in informal situations to communicate common cultural knowledge. In any academic or professional context, do not use slang. Read the following examples. The first example contains slang, while the second example uses standard English.

Slang

J. Roe, the candidate, <u>hung out</u> with members of a criminal organization. He got <u>miffed</u> when a journalist published a story about him. He thought that the reporter was a <u>total jerk</u>.

Standard English

J. Roe, the candidate, <u>spent time</u> with members of a criminal organization. He got <u>angry</u> when a journalist published a story about him. He thought that the reporter was <u>unprofessional</u>.

PRACTICE 8

In the sentences that follow, the slang expressions are underlined. Substitute the slang with the best possible choice of words in standard English. You may have to rewrite part of each sentence.

EXAMPLE:

easy
During the McCarthy era, it was not <u>a cakewalk</u> to defend oneself.

1. In 1947, Republican Senator Joseph McCarthy became <u>freaked out</u> about Communists.

2. According to McCarthy, many government employees had <u>buddies</u> in the Communist party.

3. For the next eight years, <u>dudes</u> and <u>chicks</u> who worked for the government had to take loyalty oaths.

4. Also, actors, writers, directors, and other <u>bigwigs</u> had to testify before a committee headed by Senator McCarthy.

5. McCarthy even <u>took potshots at</u> esteemed comedian Lucille Ball.

6. Some Hollywood directors provided the committee with the names of people who might be <u>double crossers</u>.

7. Hollywood director Elia Kazan, for example, <u>ratted on</u> some people.

8. Playwright Arthur Miller refused to be <u>a stool pigeon</u>.

9. In 1954, the McCarthy trials were televised for the first time, and many Americans became <u>ticked off</u> with the senator.

10. Government officials then asked the unpopular senator to <u>chill out</u> and stop harassing innocent people.

FINAL REVIEW

A. Read the following paragraph. Introduce sentence variety by moving some adverbs and prepositional phrases. Also, combine some short sentences so that the paragraph has more sentence variety. Make at least five modifications to the paragraph.

EXAMPLE:

Often, politicians
~~Politicians~~ are ~~often~~ involved in political scandals.

1. Many politicians commit disagreeable or unusual acts in their private lives. Canadian Prime Minister Mackenzie King, for example, was very eccentric. He regularly spoke with spirits, including his dead mother and Leonardo Da Vinci. He even spoke to his dead dogs, all named Pat, with a crystal ball. His interest in the occult was never reported during his lifetime. France's former president also had scandalous behavior that the press ignored. Francois Mitterand publicly had a mistress. Nobody cared. He died in 1996. His wife, mistress, and illegitimate daughter were at the funeral.

B. Edit the following paragraphs. Replace ten clichés and slang expressions with direct English.

EXAMPLE:

told the media about
Somebody ~~ratted on~~ Gary Hart.

2.   Many reporters like to dig up dirt on the private lives of
politicians. In the past, however, journalists were more prudent.
John F. Kennedy, for example, had a lot of extramarital affairs,
but journalists minded their own beeswax and did not publish
information about the affairs. Today, journalists look for scandals
regarding the head honchos. Rival politicians, who are often
green with envy, help the journalists.

3.   In 1987, Gary Hart made a whopper of a mistake. In the
middle of a campaign, he dared journalists to follow him. During
a party on a boat, someone took a picture of the married
presidential candidate with a bimbo sitting on his lap. Then, a
few days later, a journalist took a picture of the same woman
leaving the dude's hotel room. Hart could not ditch the
reporters.

4.   After the scandal exploded, Hart insisted that he was a loyal
husband and would never dump his wife, but it was too late. His
career tanked. Hart took a big risk when he dared the media to
follow him.

 The Writer's Room

Write about one of the following topics. Make sure that your paragraph has
sentences of varying lengths. Also ensure that the sentences have varied opening
words.

1. Write about a political issue or scandal. You could write about an issue that
   affects your college campus, or you could write about an issue in your city,
   town, state, or country. What happened?

2. Should journalists report on the private lives of politicians? For example,
   do you think it is important to know whether an elected official has
   committed adultery or has had drug, alcohol, or other kinds of problems?
   Explain your views.

READING LINK

Politics

To read more about political issues, see the following essays:

"The Hijab" by Naheed Mustafa (page 444)

"How to Remember Names" by Roger Seip (page 457)

"Meet the Zippies" by Thomas L. Friedman (page 460)

CHAPTER 17

CHECKLIST: SENTENCE VARIETY AND EXACT LANGUAGE

When you edit your writing, ask yourself the following questions.

Are my sentences varied? Check for problems in these areas:

–too many short sentences

–long sentences that are difficult to follow

Many journalists report on the extramarital affairs of politicians

act. Their

whom they catch in the ~~act and then their~~ spouses have bad reactions, and marriages have fallen apart.

Do I use clear and specific vocabulary? Check for problems with these elements:

–vague words

–clichés

–slang

was concerned

The senator heard the news and ~~freaked~~.

The Writers' Circle

Think of ten slang terms that you commonly use. Beside each slang word, write down a standard English word that means basically the same thing. Avoid using obscene words. Then, with a team of students, write a paragraph using the standard terms. Make sure that your paragraph has a variety of sentence lengths.

EXAMPLE:

Slang	Standard English
homie	*good friend from the neighborhood*

How Do I Get a Better Grade?

Visit www.mywritinglab.com for audio-visual lectures and additional practice sets about sentence variety and exact language.

Get a better grade with MyWritingLab!

Fragments

Section Theme: **THE EARTH AND BEYOND**

CONTENTS

• Understanding Fragments
• Phrase Fragments
• Explanatory Fragments
• Dependent-Clause Fragments

In the next chapters, you will read about the world of chemistry and hazardous substances.

Grammar Snapshot

Looking at Fragments

Student writer Amin Baty Konde wrote a paragraph about working with chemicals. The underlined errors are called fragments.

> <u>Working with hazardous chemicals.</u> It can have far-reaching consequences on a person's life. I have personal experience because for three years I worked for a pesticide company. I sprayed large expanses of lawn with commercial pesticides each day. I was not always careful about wearing a protective mask or gloves. After two years, I began to develop red rashes on my arms. <u>Then, asthma.</u> Although I cannot be certain that exposure to chemicals caused my problems, the timing of my illness has convinced me that it is possible.

In this chapter, you will identify and correct sentence fragments.

Understanding Fragments

A **sentence** must have a subject and verb, and it must express a complete thought. A **fragment** is an incomplete sentence. Either it lacks a subject or a verb, or it fails to express a complete idea. You may see fragments in newspaper headlines and advertisements ("Three-month trial offer"). However, in college writing, it is unacceptable to write fragments.

> **Sentence:**   Exposure to radium is very serious.
>
> **Fragment:**   Causes various illnesses.

The following sections explain common types of fragments.

Phrase Fragments

Phrase fragments are missing a subject or a verb. In the examples, the fragment is underlined.

> **No subject:**   My father did a dangerous job. <u>Worked with hazardous chemicals.</u>
>
> **No verb:**   <u>First, sulfuric acid.</u> It is very dangerous.

How to Correct Phrase Fragments

To correct phrase fragments, add the missing subject or verb, or join the fragment to another sentence. Here are ways to correct the two previous examples of phrase fragments.

> **Add a word(s):**   My father did a dangerous job. **He** worked with hazardous chemicals.
>
> **Join sentences:**   First, sulfuric acid is very dangerous.

 **Incomplete Verbs**

If a sentence has an incomplete verb, it is a phrase fragment. The following example contains a subject and part of a verb. However, the helping verb is missing; therefore, the sentence is not complete.

> **Fragment:**   Many of the experiments with radium done by Marie Curie.

To make this sentence complete, you must add the helping verb.

> **Sentence:**   Many of the experiments with radium <u>were</u> done by Marie Curie.

PRACTICE I

Underline and correct five phrase fragments.

EXAMPLE:

First, Marie Curie. ~~She~~ was a great scientist.

Marie Curie discovered radium. In 1898. After her discovery, there was a radium craze. Across the United States. Companies added radium to different products. In some factories, the workers used paint with radium in it. To paint the faces of clocks and wristwatches. Sometimes they licked their paintbrushes to make the ends pointed. Very dangerous, indeed. The factory owners knew the radium-laced paint was not safe. They were more concerned with protecting their business interests than with protecting the health of their workers. Unfortunately.

Explanatory Fragments

An **explanatory fragment** provides an explanation about a previous sentence and is missing a subject, a complete verb, or both. Such fragments are often written as an afterthought. Explanatory fragments begin with one of the following words.

as well as	especially	for example	including	particularly
also	except	for instance	like	such as

In these two examples, the fragment is underlined.

We did many new experiments. <u>For example, with mercury.</u>

Some new chemical compounds are useful. <u>Particularly in the production of fabrics.</u>

How to Correct Explanatory Fragments

To correct explanatory fragments, add the missing subject or verb, or join the explanation or example to the previous sentence. Here are ways to correct the two previous examples of explanatory fragments.

Add words: We did many new experiments. For example, **we learned** about mercury.

Join sentences: Some new chemical compounds are useful, particularly in the production of fabrics.

PRACTICE 2

Underline and correct five explanatory fragments.

EXAMPLE:

                                                                    , especially
The media reports high levels of blue algae. ~~Especially~~ in nearby lakes.

In the 1970s, many new models of household appliances were marketed. For instance washing machines. Cleaning products also changed. Especially laundry detergent. Phosphates were added to washing detergent to make laundry very clean. However, phosphates had a negative effect on the environment. Particularly on water systems. When they reached lakes and rivers, phosphates harmed the water system. Harmful bacteria started growing in the water. Like blue algae. Blue algae causes a lot of problems. Such as reducing oxygen in lakes and rivers.

CHAPTER 18

PRACTICE 3

Underline and correct five phrase and explanatory fragments.

EXAMPLE:

                                            across
Water pollution made headlines. ~~Across~~ the nation.

Phosphates are found in the soil, in food, and in chemical fertilizer. Legislators became concerned about phosphate pollution. Due to public pressure. In 1972, the United States and Canada signed a treaty limiting the amount of phosphates in various products. For example, laundry detergent. The law was successful because it reduced the amount of phosphates entering lakes and rivers. By fifty percent. Presently, however, there is a recurrence of blue algae. In some areas of the country. Experts blame the current outbreak on common products. Like dishwashing detergent and fertilizers.

Dependent-Clause Fragments

A **dependent clause** has a subject and verb, but it cannot stand alone. It "depends" on another clause to be a complete sentence. Dependent clauses may begin with subordinating conjunctions or relative pronouns. This chart contains some of the most common words that introduce dependent clauses.

Common Subordinating Conjunctions				Relative Pronouns
after	before	though	whenever	that
although	even though	unless	where	which
as	so that	until	whereas	who(m)
because	that	what	whether	whose

In each example, the fragment is underlined.

Marie Curie had a successful professional life. <u>Although her personal life was plagued with scandal.</u>

<u>Marie Curie, who won the Nobel Prize for chemistry.</u> She was born in Poland.

How to Correct Dependent-Clause Fragments

To correct dependent-clause fragments, join the fragment to a complete sentence, remove words, or add the necessary words to make it a complete idea. Here are ways to correct the two previous examples of dependent-clause fragments.

Join sentences: Marie Curie had a successful professional life, although her personal life was plagued with scandal.

Join sentences and remove words: Marie Curie, who won the Nobel Prize for chemistry, was born in Poland.

Another way to correct dependent-clause fragments is to delete the subordinating conjunction or relative pronoun that makes the sentence incomplete.

Delete *although*:   Her personal life was filled with scandal.

Delete comma and *who*:   Marie Curie won the Nobel Prize for chemistry.

PRACTICE 4

Underline and correct five dependent-clause fragments.

EXAMPLE:

asbestos because

The ancient Greeks liked working with ~~asbestos. Because~~ they could weave the fibers into beautiful tablecloths.

Asbestos is a common mineral. That has been used in many

household products for approximately 4,000 years. Since the Industrial

Revolution, asbestos has been used in cement, wall board, putty, paints, hair dryers, vinyl floor tiles, and so on. However, in the 1980s, legislators implemented regulations limiting the use of asbestos. Because of potential health risks to the public. If people breathe in asbestos fibers, they may contract illnesses such as cancer. Some people may not know that they are exposed to asbestos. Unless they have the material in their homes tested. Homeowners and contractors should be extremely careful. Whenever they are doing home renovations. Older homes may have been built with materials containing asbestos. When removing insulation, replacing vinyl asbestos floor tiles, or sanding plaster that contains asbestos, they should be careful. They should wear masks and goggles. So that they are protected.

PRACTICE 5

Write *C* next to correct sentences and *F* next to fragments.

EXAMPLE:

There are many poisonous chemicals. __*C*__ In our environment. __*F*__

1.   Sometimes people do not know that they have been exposed to hazardous chemicals. _____ In their homes. _____ Many household-cleaning products contain toxic chemicals. _____ Some people may have adverse reactions to these products. _____ For example, hives. _____

2.   Furthermore, sometimes there are dangerous chemicals in the land around residential neighborhoods. _____ In the 1970s, people who lived in the Love Canal region of Niagara Falls, New York, did not know a very important fact. _____ That their homes had been built on a toxic dump. _____ Parents in Love Canal worried. _____ When their children got sick. _____ Eventually, the parents found out the cause. _____ The

school. _____ It was built on a site where an old factory had

dumped poisonous chemicals. _____

3.   Moreover, in our professions. _____ Many of us are exposed

to hazardous materials. _____ For instance, scientists in laboratories.

_____ They work with dangerous chemicals every day. _____ Also

in nuclear power plants. _____ There are sometimes spills or leaks

that can poison workers. _____ For example, Karen Silkwood

worked at the Kerr-McGee plutonium plant laboratory. _____

Polishing plutonium pellets. _____ She discovered that she had

radiation poisoning. _____ Because there were inadequate safety

measures at the plant. _____

4.   On a positive note. _____ Today's labor laws require that

employers tell employees about the possible effects of working with

hazardous materials. _____ There are also strict safety regulations

in workplaces. _____ That have hazardous products. _____

Therefore, governments and industries are doing something about

the problem. _____

PRACTICE 6

The next paragraphs contain various types of fragments. Underline and correct ten
fragment errors.

EXAMPLE:

reduced by

Environmental waste can be greatly ~~reduced. By~~ recycling and using
biodegradable products.

1.   Nowadays, the public has become very aware of environmental

pollution. Because of education, urban regulations, and media attention.

Many citizens recycle household items. Such as plastic containers,

newspapers, and tin cans. People also try to use biodegradable products.

However, this term is often misunderstood and misused.

2.   The term *biodegradable* means that a product has the ability to break down into raw materials. A product can be decomposed. By biological organisms. Such products break up into soil. Or water. A flower is a good example of a biodegradable product. First, it grows and matures. Then, falls to the ground. Finally, it decomposes and fertilizes the soil.

3.   There is a difference between products that are biodegradable and recyclable. Many common products are biodegradable. For instance, soap and oil. However, crude oil spills are an environmental hazard. Because the oil spill is usually large, and there are not enough microorganisms to break the oil down. Ecologists worry about the 1989 Exxon Valdez oil spill. Because toxins from the spill continue to affect wildlife in the region. The term *recyclable* refers to items that can be turned into other products. For example, glass bottles. They can be melted into new glass bottles.

4.   Concerned citizens recycle and use biodegradable products. So that environmental damage is minimized. For instance, if a glass bottle is not recycled and reused, it will take approximately one million years to biodegrade. As science advances, people will develop improved ways to cut waste.

FINAL REVIEW

Identify and correct fifteen fragment errors.

EXAMPLE:

Each year, the Nobel Prize is awarded to people. ~~Who~~ *who* are exceptional.

1.   Most people have heard of the Nobel Prize. However, they may not know a lot about the founder. Of that prize. Alfred

Nobel is most famous for his invention of dynamite. He started the Nobel Prize. For the world's greatest scientific and literary advances.

2.   Nobel was born on October 21, 1833. In Stockholm, Sweden. He died in 1896. In Italy. He developed an interest in chemistry. At an early age. While he was visiting Paris in 1847, he met Ascanio Sobrero. Who had developed nitroglycerine. Nitroglycerine was a liquid. That was highly explosive. Nobel realized that if the substance could be controlled, then it would be valuable for industrial use. For example, in mining.

3.   Nobel experimented with many methods. To control and transport the nitroglycerine safely. At last, he was successful. He mixed nitroglycerine with silica and made a paste that could be safely transported. He also invented a detonator. And named his new discovery dynamite.

4.   Nobel also invented other products. Such as synthetic rubber and artificial silk. In addition to his interest in science, he loved all types of literature. Including poetry. In his will, he bequeathed $9 million to a foundation. That would give prizes in physics, chemistry, medicine, literature, and peace. A prize in economics was added. In 1969.

5.   Curiously, Nobel did not create a prize for mathematics. For many years, there was a rumor stating that Nobel did not give a prize in mathematics because his wife had run off with a famous mathematician. However, there is no historical evidence. That can back up this rumor.

The Writer's Room

Write about one of the following topics. After you finish writing, underline the sentences. Make sure you do not have any sentence fragments.

1. Have modern scientific discoveries made our lives easier? Compare contemporary life with life in a previous era.

2. In your opinion, what is the world's greatest invention? Explain why that invention is so important.

CHECKLIST: SENTENCE FRAGMENTS

When you edit your writing, ask yourself the next questions.

☐ Are my sentences complete? Check for different types of fragments.
  –phrase fragments
  –explanatory fragments
  –dependent clause fragments

                                           He also
First, Joseph Priestly. ~~He~~ discovered eight gases. ~~Also~~ drank soda
  , which
water. ~~Which~~ he invented in 1772.

How Do I Get a Better Grade?

mywritinglab Visit www.mywritinglab.com for audio-visual lectures and additional practice sets about fragments.
Get a better grade with MyWritingLab!

Section Theme: **THE EARTH AND BEYOND**

CONTENTS

• Understanding
Run-Ons

In this chapter, you will read about geology and learn about volcanoes and the diamond trade.

Grammar Snapshot

Looking at Run-Ons

College student Marnie Harris wrote a definition paragraph about volcanoes. The error in bold print is called a run-on sentence.

> A volcano is a fissure in the earth's crust that allows hot magma to rise up. There are many active volcanoes in the world. One of the most famous is Mount Etna, located in Sicily, Italy. The first recorded eruption was in 475 B.C., and since then it has erupted about 250 times. **The last time it erupted was in 1979 it displaced many people who lived around the mountain.** People should be aware of the destructive force of volcanoes.

In this chapter, you will identify and correct run-on sentences.

Understanding Run-Ons

Sometimes two or more complete sentences are joined together without correct connecting words or punctuation. In other words, a **run-on sentence** "runs on" without stopping. There are two types of run-on sentences.

- A **fused sentence** is a run-on sentence that has no punctuation to mark the break between ideas.

Fused sentence:	Geologists learn about the origins of the earth they study rocks.
Correct sentence:	Geologists learn about the origins of the earth through their study of rocks.

- A **comma splice** is a run-on sentence that uses a comma to connect two complete ideas. In other words, the comma "splices" or "splits" the sentence.

Comma splice:	Mount St. Helens is an active volcano, it violently erupted on May 18, 1980.
Correct sentence:	Mount St. Helens is an active volcano. It violently erupted on May 18, 1980.

 **Identifying Run-Ons**

To identify run-on sentences in your writing, look for sentences that are too long. Such sentences may either lack punctuation or have incorrect comma placement.

CHAPTER 19

PRACTICE I

Write *C* beside correct sentences and *RO* beside run-ons.

EXAMPLE:

A volcano is a fissure in the earth's crust, it allows lava to come out.   *RO*

1. The earth is composed of the core, the mantle, and the crust.   _____

2. Geologists developed a new theory in the 1960s it is called plate tectonics.   _____

3. The earth's crust is made of hard material, it is formed into several "plates."   _____

4. As the plates move over the mantle, they go toward or away from each other.   _____

5. The plates move slowly the movement causes molten rock to seep out.   _____

6. The molten rock oozes up through gaps in the earth's surface.   _____

7. The molten rock is called lava, it is extremely hot and dangerous.   _____

8. The lava can move quickly down the volcano's side, burning everything in its path.   _____

How to Correct Run-Ons

You can correct run-on sentences in a variety of ways.

Run-On: Some volcanoes erupt violently others erupt very slowly.

1. **Make two separate sentences by adding end punctuation, such as a period.**

    Some volcanoes erupt violently. **Others** erupt very slowly.

2. **Add a subordinator** (*after, although, as, because, before, since, when, while*).

    Some volcanoes erupt violently, **while** others erupt very slowly.

3. **Add a coordinator** (*for, and, nor, but, or, yet, so*).

    Some volcanoes erupt violently, **but** others erupt very slowly.

4. **Add a semicolon.**

    Some volcanoes erupt violently; others erupt very slowly.

PRACTICE 2

A. Correct each run-on by writing two complete sentences.

EXAMPLE:

. *Some*

There are about 500 active volcanoes ~~some~~ have caused massive destruction.

1. Mount St. Helens erupted for nine hours it covered 230 square miles of forest with ash.

2. Over fifty people died ~~many~~ animals and fish also died.

B. Correct the run-ons by joining the two sentences with a semicolon.

EXAMPLE:

; *they*

Geologists monitor volcanic activity~~, they~~ share their information.

3. Mount Vesuvius is a famous volcano, it buried Pompeii in A.D. 79.

4. Vesuvius is located near Naples, Italy, over 2 million people live near it.

C. Correct the run-ons by joining the two sentences with a coordinator (*for, and, nor, but, or, yet, so*).

EXAMPLE:

, *and he*

In 1748, a farmer tried to dig in his vineyard ~~he~~ discovered some ruins.

5. Pliny the Younger saw the volcano erupt he wrote an account of the event.

6. Pompeii was first discovered by laborers digging a well nobody thought the discovery was significant.

D. Correct the run-ons by joining the two sentences with a subordinator such as *after, although,* or *when.*

EXAMPLE:

In A.D. 63, many houses fell to the ground,$\overset{\textit{when}}{\diagup}$ Vesuvius rumbled loudly.

7. Archeologists excavated the site they found loaves of bread from the time of the eruption.

8. The bread was almost 2,000 years old, it was still intact.

PRACTICE 3

Correct eight run-on errors using a variety of correction methods.

EXAMPLE:

~~The~~ Hope Diamond had a reputation of bad ~~luck many~~ people refused to buy it.

Because the   *luck, many*

1.   Throughout history, diamonds have intrigued kings, queens, and commoners. Diamonds were first discovered in India around 800 B.C. they were found in riverbeds. The Indians valued them for their beauty, they also thought that diamonds would protect them from evil. India was the world's main source of diamonds until the nineteenth century. Since then, discoveries of diamond deposits have been made in Brazil, South Africa, Siberia, and Canada.

2.   The world's largest diamond is called the Star of Africa. In 1905, Frederick Wells, the superintendent of the Premier Mine in South Africa, discovered it. He saw something shining on the mine wall, it was a crystal. Tests showed that the crystal was a diamond, and it weighed about 1⅓ pounds. In 1907, the

Transvaal government of South Africa gave the stone to King Edward VII it was a gift to mark his sixty-sixth birthday. This diamond remains a part of the British crown jewels.

3.   De Beers has been in the diamond business since diamonds were first discovered in South Africa. The company was started by Cecil Rhodes in 1888 it is the largest diamond firm in the world. In the 1940s, in response to competition, De Beers wanted to increase its sales of diamonds, the corporation launched a successful marketing campaign by promoting diamonds as engagement rings. The company endorsed the diamond as a symbol of love and marriage, the sales of diamond rings increased. De Beers also had another marketing strategy. The slogan "A diamond is forever" was used to reduce the secondhand diamond market. The idea behind the catchphrase was to discourage people from buying used diamonds. Both campaigns were extremely successful, they influenced the shopping habits of consumers in many different cultures. Now the diamond ring represents the idea of love and marriage around the world, and De Beers' profits have swelled.

FINAL REVIEW

Correct ten run-on sentence errors. Use a variety of correction methods.

1.   Diamonds have been a symbol of love and glamour they have also become a symbol of violence and exploitation. In many countries, diamonds are linked to severe human rights abuses. In those countries, diamonds are used to perpetuate wars, they are also used to finance the activities of terrorist groups.

2.   Sierra Leone had a ten-year civil war, it ended in 2001. The cause of the conflict was greed. Sierra Leone has many diamond deposits,

antigovernment groups waged military warfare to gain control of the diamonds. Rebel groups in Angola and Liberia have also financed wars, they used money obtained from the diamond trade to do so.

3.   Terrorist groups also benefit from the illegal diamond trade they use diamonds to buy arms and pay informants. *Washington Post* reporter Douglas Farah brought attention to this problem he spoke at a congressional hearing in 2003. Diamonds are small, they are easy to move from one country to another. Therefore, officials find them harder to trace than other contraband items.

4.   Trade in diamonds has come under international scrutiny, to decrease the illicit trade, many countries have agreed to abide by the Kimberley Process. This agreement requires that all international diamonds have a certificate of origin such regulations will curb violence created by the illegal diamond trade.

 The Writer's Room

Write about one of the following topics. After you finish writing, ensure that you do not have any run-on sentences.

1. Describe your jewelry. What is your favorite type of jewelry? If you do not like to wear jewelry, explain why not.

2. Examine this photo and think of a term that you could define. Some ideas might be *bling bling*, *costume jewelry*, or *ostentatious*. Write a definition paragraph about any topic related to the photo.

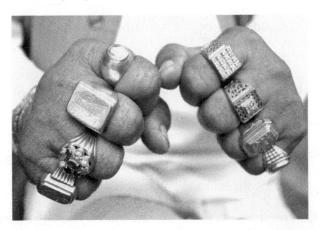

CHECKLIST: RUN-ONS

When you edit your writing, ask yourself the next questions.

Are my sentences joined together without punctuation or with incorrect punctuation? Check for fused sentences and comma splices.

Mauna Loa is the world's largest ~~volcano it~~ is located in Hawaii.

Kilauea is the world's most active ~~volcano, it~~ has been erupting continuously since 1983.

How Do I Get a Better Grade?

mywritinglab

Visit www.mywritinglab.com for audio-visual lectures and additional practice sets about run-ons.

Get a better grade with MyWritingLab!

CHAPTER 19

Faulty Parallel Structure

CHAPTER 20

Section Theme: **THE EARTH AND BEYOND**

CONTENTS

- Identifying Parallel Structure
- Correcting Faulty Parallel Structure

In this chapter, you will read about astronomy and learn about discoveries, conspiracy theories, and space tourism.

Grammar Snapshot

Looking at Parallel Structure

President John F. Kennedy's 1962 speech at Rice University was about the U.S. space program. Review the underlined ideas to see how they are parallel.

> There is no strife, no prejudice, and no national conflict in outer space as yet. Its hazards are hostile to us all. Its conquest deserves the best of all mankind, and its opportunity for peaceful cooperation may never come again.

In this chapter, you will identify and correct faulty parallel structure.

Identifying Parallel Structure

Parallel structure occurs when pairs or groups of items in a sentence are balanced. By using parallel grammatical structure for words, phrases, or clauses, you will make your sentences clearer and your writing smoother.

In the following sentences, the underlined phrases contain repetitions of grammatical structure, but not repetitions of ideas. Each sentence has parallel structure.

> The <u>United States</u>, <u>Russia</u>, and <u>Japan</u> have spent funds on the space station.
> (The nouns are parallel.)
>
> The astronomer went <u>through the doors</u>, <u>up the stairs</u>, and <u>into the observatory</u>.
> (The prepositional phrases are parallel.)
>
> She <u>observes</u>, <u>records</u>, and <u>predicts</u> planet cycles.
> (The present tenses are parallel.)
>
> I am <u>awed</u>, <u>excited</u>, and <u>terrified</u> at the prospect of space flight.
> (The adjectives are parallel.)
>
> Copernicus was a scientist <u>who took risks</u>, <u>who made acute observations</u>, and <u>who developed new theories</u>.
> (The "who" clauses are parallel.)

CHAPTER 20

PRACTICE I

All of the following sentences contain parallel structures. Underline the parallel items.

EXAMPLE:

The space race was a <u>hazardous</u>, <u>exciting</u>, and <u>innovative</u> adventure.

1. In 1957, the space race began when Soviet scientists developed, built, and launched the space satellite *Sputnik*.

2. Soviet engineers, scientists, and politicians worked together.

3. American government officials felt shock, anxiety, and then determination.

4. The officials wanted to build their own satellite, to launch it quickly, and to surpass the Soviet achievements.

5. With an injection of funds, with some planning, and with the support of many scientists, the United States launched a satellite called *Explorer* in 1958.

6. The National Aeronautics and Space Administration (NASA) began operations on October 1, at noon, in Florida.

7. U.S. scientists who used available resources, who took risks, and who believed in their vision were able to create an automated moon probe.

8. President John F. Kennedy said that humans choose to go to the moon and do other difficult things "not because they are easy, but because they are hard."

Correcting Faulty Parallel Structure

Faulty parallel structure occurs when you present equivalent ideas with different grammatical structures. The result is a sentence with ideas that are not balanced. To avoid imbalances, use parallel structure.

A Series of Words or Phrases

Use parallel structure when words or phrases are joined in a series.

Not parallel:	I like to read articles, watch documentaries, and listening to seminars.
Parallel:	I like <u>to read</u> articles, <u>to watch</u> documentaries, and <u>to listen</u> to seminars. (The infinitives are parallel.)
Not parallel:	The expanding universe, black holes, and scientists studying matter are all problems relating to the study of cosmology.
Parallel:	<u>The expanding universe</u>, <u>black holes</u>, and <u>matter</u> are all problems relating to the study of cosmology. (The nouns are parallel.)

Paired Clauses

Use parallel structure when independent clauses are joined by *and, but,* or *or.*

Not parallel:	The space station is costing a lot of money, but it provides essential data.
Parallel:	The space station <u>costs</u> a lot of money, but it <u>provides</u> essential data. (The present tense verbs are parallel.)
Not parallel:	Copernicus observed the stars carefully, and he recorded his findings with accuracy.
Parallel:	Copernicus observed the stars <u>carefully</u>, and he recorded his findings <u>accurately</u>. (The adverbs are parallel.)

 **Correcting Faulty Parallel Structure**

When you identify faulty parallel structure, correct it by looking carefully at repeated grammatical units and then rewriting the unit that is not parallel.

$$\text{\textit{sends}}$$
The satellite collects data, stores it, and ~~is sending~~ images.

PRACTICE 2

Correct the faulty parallel structure in each sentence.

EXAMPLE:

Today, amateur astronomers are looking for satellites, watching the

$$\textit{observing}$$
constellations, and ~~to observe~~ shooting stars.

1. Scientists are doing research on the expanding universe, on the Big Bang theory, and black and white holes.

2. To observe the universe, astrophysicists not only use powerful telescopes, but they are also relying on modern satellite images.

3. In ancient times, the Babylonians, the Greeks, and people from Egypt observed and predicted the position of planets and stars.

4. Copernicus worked quietly and at a slow pace on his observations.

5. When Copernicus announced that the sun was the center of the universe, the public reacted angrily, passionately, and with force.

6. Galileo Galilei invented the telescope to look at the night sky and recording his observations.

7. Galileo discussed his theories, experiments, and what he observed.

8. Large telescopes and cameras that are powerful have helped scientists observe poorly lit celestial bodies.

9. Early photographers attempted to take pictures of the moon, the stars, and photograph solar eclipses.

10. The general public can learn about the universe by going to planetariums, to observatories, and science museums.

Comparisons

Use parallel structure in comparisons containing *than* or *as*.

Not parallel:	I wanted a better explanation rather than to remain confused.
Parallel:	I wanted <u>to receive</u> a better explanation rather than <u>to remain</u> confused. (The infinitive forms are parallel.)
Not parallel:	His raw intelligence was as important as working hard.
Parallel:	<u>His raw intelligence</u> was as important as <u>his hard work.</u> (The nouns are parallel.)

Two-Part Constructions

Use parallel structure when comparing or contrasting ideas using these constructions: *either . . . or, not . . . but, both . . . and,* or *neither . . . nor.*

Not parallel:	My experience was both exciting and a challenge.
Parallel:	My experience was both <u>exciting</u> and <u>challenging</u>. (The adjectives are parallel.)
Not parallel:	She decided either to publish her research or burning it.
Parallel:	She decided either <u>to publish</u> her research or <u>to burn</u> it. (The infinitives are parallel.)

PRACTICE 3

Correct any errors in parallel construction. If the sentence is correct, write *C* in the blank.

EXAMPLE:

Our solar system not only includes the sun and planets but also

   consists

is consisting of more than sixty moons, millions of asteroids, and

billions of comets.   ____

1. Not only do scientists divide the solar system into the inner part

   and outer part, but they are listing the celestial bodies in each. ____

2. Mercury, Venus, Earth, and the planet Mars are found in

   the inner solar system. ____

3. Jupiter, Saturn, Uranus, Neptune, and Pluto are in the outer

   solar system. ____

4. Scientists now say that Pluto is a dwarf planet, not a planet
   that is regular. _____

5. The earth is revolving around the sun as well as to spin on
   its axis. _____

6. When a planet completes one journey around the sun, its path
   is called an orbit. _____

7. Earth's orbit lasts 365 days while the orbit of Mercury lasts
   88 Earth days. _____

8. Earth takes twenty-four hours to complete its spin while Jupiter
   takes only ten Earth hours finishing its spin. _____

9. The stars look smaller than the sun because they are farther
   away from us. _____

10. Astronomers have realized that some of those stars are both
    larger and more bright than our sun. _____

PRACTICE 4

A. Fill in the blanks with parallel and logical words, phrases, or clauses.

EXAMPLE:

We studied _____*after class*_____ and _____*on weekends*_____.

1. At college, I am studying both _____ and

   _____.

2. To get to the college library, you must go _____,

   _____, and _____.

3. My friend is _____, _____,

   and _____.

4. As a child, I _____, _____,

   and _____.

5. My instructor complained that _____, and

   _____.

B. Compose three sentences that contain parallel structure. Try to use a variety of constructions. For example, you might use parallel nouns in one sentence and parallel verbs in another.

6. _____

_____

7. _____

_____

8. _____

_____

PRACTICE 5

Correct eight errors in parallel construction.

EXAMPLE:

Many people still believe that the history books ~~lie~~ *are lying*, that the encyclopedias are lying, and that NASA engineers and astronauts are lying when they claim that human beings landed on the moon.

1. According to conspiracy theorists, the U.S. government, the space agencies, and engineers with aeronautical degrees had two very good reasons to fake the moon landing. First, the government wanted to divert attention from the Vietnam War and instilling pride in the American people. Second, the space and research agencies wanted to keep the flow of money into their institutions.

Astronaut Edwin Aldrin, Jr. (1969)

2. There are many theories about how the U.S. government engineered the space travel reports. One theory states that the

military forces flew the rockets to the South Pole instead of to the

moon. They carefully picked up the command module, and they

sent the module to the South Pacific with speed. Those scientists who

knew about the conspiracy were coerced, threatened, and

others bribed them.

3.　　Some skeptics who are American, French, Japanese, and

those who live in Germany post Internet messages about their

theories. They believe that the U.S. government forced film

director Stanley Kubrick to direct the moon-landing film and

distributing it. Skeptics offer photos of the flag on the moon as

evidence. They say that there is no wind on the moon; therefore,

the flag could not wave.

4.　　NASA officials deny any part in a conspiracy. They say that

a pole held the flag out in the moon-landing photos. The flag

was not waving in the wind. Furthermore, the twelve astronauts

who have walked on the moon are serious, professional, and

act with honesty.

5.　　Many people wonder why believers of conspiracy theories promote

such ideas. Perhaps they do it because they believe it, because they

want to be famous, or for money. The only thing that is certain is that

there will always be believers in conspiracy theories.

FINAL REVIEW

Correct twelve errors in parallel construction.

EXAMPLE:

challenging

Space travel is exciting and ~~a challenge~~.

1.　　Space travel has changed a lot over four decades. In the past,

only highly trained astronauts went to outer space, but today

tourists who are rich can do it. For example, in April 2001, California millionaire Dennis Tito was the 415th person in orbit. Tito paid the Russian Space Agency about $30 million for a seat on a Russian flight and traveling to the International Space Station. He was clearly a man who had a plan, who worked hard, and made his dream come true. Since that time, space tourism has become extremely popular. Hundreds of people have booked tickets with the Russian Space Agency. Such tourists think that space travel will be thrilling, thought-provoking, and a challenge.

2.   Some analysts, people who are politicians, and scientists are strongly opposed to space tourism. They argue that space travel is expensive and has dangers. According to a member of Congress, it is unfair to expect taxpayers to contribute to space research, to have no say in how the funds are spent, and watch rich citizens take flights to space. Representative Ralph Hall argues that space travel should be reserved for trained astronauts, research scientists, and engineers who are skilled. Additionally, space travel is still very dangerous, so it is premature to spend time and wasting money on space tourism.

3.   However, former astronaut Buzz Aldrin believes that ordinary people should have the chance to orbit the earth. Perhaps space travel is both dangerous and not easy. However, fulfilling a lifelong desire is more important than to worry about the dangers of space flight. Tony Webb, organizer of a space lottery, believes in space tourism. He thinks it should be available for everyone, not just for people with money and famous people.

The Writer's Room

READING LINK
The Earth and Beyond
To read more about space travel, see the following essay:
"What It Feels Like to Walk on the Moon" by Buzz Aldrin (page 447)

Write about one of the following topics. After you finish writing, make sure that you have no faulty parallel structure.

1. Explain why you would or would not travel to outer space.

2. How are space explorers comparable to other types of explorers? Compare space explorers with other explorers.

CHECKLIST: PARALLEL STRUCTURE

When you edit your writing, ask yourself the next questions.

Are my grammatical structures balanced? Check for errors in these cases:

–when words or phrases are joined in a series

–when independent clauses are joined by *and, but,* or *or*

–in comparisons or contrasts

                                        the harshest weather
Mars has the largest volcano, the deepest valley, and ~~its weather is very harsh~~ of any planet in our solar system.

CHAPTER 20

 The Writers' Circle

Form a team with two other students. Imagine that your team has won first-class seats on a space cruise. Each one of you can bring only five small items on the flight. Work together to create a paragraph explaining what items you would bring. You can share the items, so consider what items would be most useful for all of you.

When you finish writing, verify that your paragraph contains no fragments or run-ons. Also, make sure that your sentences have parallel structure.

How Do I Get a Better Grade?

Visit www.mywritinglab.com for audio-visual lectures and additional practice sets about faulty parallel structure.
Get a better grade with MyWritingLab!

21 Adjectives and Adverbs

CHAPTER

Section Theme: **RELATIONSHIPS**

CONTENTS

- Adjectives
- Adverbs
- Comparative and
  Superlative Forms

In this chapter, you will read about famous couples in history and in literature, such as Charles Lindberg and Ann Morrow and Romeo and Juliet. You will also read about relationship issues.

Grammar Snapshot

Looking at Adjectives and Adverbs

Comedian Bill Cosby describes a high school romance. Review the underlined adjectives and adverbs.

> During my <u>last</u> year of high school, I fell in love <u>so hard</u> with a girl that it made my love for Sarah McKinney seem like a <u>stupid</u> infatuation with a teacher. Charlene Gibson was the <u>real</u> thing, and she would be Mrs. Charlene Cosby, serving me hot dogs, watching me drive to the hoop, and giving me the <u>full-court</u> press for the rest of my life.

In this chapter, you will identify and use adjectives and adverbs.

Adjectives

Adjectives describe nouns (people, places, or things) and pronouns (words that replace nouns). In other words, adjectives add more information and detail to the words they are modifying. They add information explaining how many, what kind, or which one. They also describe how things look, smell, feel, taste, and sound.

> The **handsome** <u>Romeo</u> loved the **beautiful** <u>Juliet</u>.
>
> My English class studied **two** of Shakespeare's <u>plays</u>.
>
> William Shakespeare wrote the **fabulous** <u>play</u> called *Romeo and Juliet*.
>
> Romeo and Juliet are the **main** <u>characters</u> in the play. <u>They</u> are **impulsive** and **creative.**

PRACTICE I

Underline all of the adjectives and adverbs in these sentences.

EXAMPLE:

Marilyn Monroe was a <u>gorgeous</u> and <u>troubled</u> woman.

1. The stunning blond woman, Marilyn Monroe, transformed herself from plain actress to American sex icon.

2. Americans adored her striking face, sexy body, and charming personality.

3. The aggressive paparazzi loved her public romances, and photographed her with famous actors and powerful politicians.

4. The media portrayed her as a tragic dumb blond, and as a sad, lonely, and insecure woman.

5. The unhappy and vulnerable celebrity had five volatile marriages.

Placement of Adjectives

You can place adjectives either before a noun or after a linking verb such as *be, look, appear,* or *become.*

> **Before the noun:**   The **young** <u>Frida Kahlo</u> fell in love with a much older painter.
>
> **After a linking verb:**   Their <u>relationship</u> was **passionate** and **volatile.**

> (Hint) **Problems with Adjective Placement**
>
> In some languages, adjectives can appear directly after nouns. However, in English, never place an adjective directly after the noun that it is describing.
>
>   *very elegant lady.*
> Martha Dandridge Washington was a ~~lady very elegant.~~
>
>   *forty and a half years.*
> She was married to George Washington for ~~forty years and half.~~

PRACTICE 2

Some of the following sentences have errors in adjective placement. Underline and correct each error. If a sentence is correct, write *C* in the blank.

EXAMPLE:

                         magnificent palace.
The young lovers lived in a ~~palace magnificent.~~ _____

1. Cleopatra, the last queen of Egypt, and Marc Antony, the man

   she loved, planned to conquer the powerful city of Rome. _____

2. After the fierce battle, Marc Antony heard a rumor false that

   the vivacious Cleopatra was dead. _____

3. The handsome and shrewd general, Marc Antony, became

   depressed and killed himself. _____

4. Cleopatra heard the horrible news about Marc Antony, and she

   committed suicide by allowing a snake poisonous to bite her. _____

5. With the death of Cleopatra, the rule of the pharaohs ended,

   and Egypt became a province Roman. _____

Order of Adjectives

When using two or more adjectives together, place them in this order: number, quality, size, age, color, origin, and type. The following chart indicates the order of adjectives.

Determiner (number, etc.)	Quality	Size or Shape	Age	Color	Origin	Type	Noun
We bought two	beautiful		old	red		Persian	rugs.
Santa Fe is a	lovely	large			New Mexico	desert	town.

 **Punctuating Adjectives**

Place commas between adjectives of equal weight. In other words, if two adjectives describe a quality, place a comma between them.

    Comma: Shah Jahan presented the <u>lovely, rare</u> sculpture to the princess.

Do not place commas between adjectives of unequal weight. For example, if one adjective describes a quality and another describes a place of origin or color, do not put a comma between them.

    No comma: Shah Jahan presented the <u>rare Greek</u> sculpture to the princess.

PRACTICE 3

Complete these sentences by writing the adjectives in parentheses in the correct order.

EXAMPLE:

The (young / handsome) ___*handsome young*___ Shah Jahan became the Mughal emperor of seventeenth-century India.

1. A (Indian / 15-year-old / shy) _____ princess

   named Mumtaz married Shah Jahan in 1612 and became his favorite wife.

   They shared a (long / passionate) _____ love that

   lasted until she died in 1629.

2. Shah Jahan constructed the (white / beautiful) _____

   Taj Mahal as a symbol of their love. Around (skilled / 20,000)

   _____ workers and (Indian / gray / 1,000)

   _____ elephants took nearly twenty years to

   complete the Taj Mahal.

3. The mausoleum is made of (white / smooth)

   _____ marble and sits on a sandstone

   platform. The interior contains (intricate / Islamic)

   _____ designs made of semiprecious

   stones. Shah Jahan planned to build a (marble / black / stunning)

   _____ mausoleum for himself, but the

   project was never started. When he died, he was buried beside

   his (beloved / young) _____ queen in the Taj Mahal.

Problems with Adjectives

You can recognize many adjectives by their endings. Be particularly careful when you use the following adjective forms.

Adjectives Ending in *-ful* or *-less*

Some adjectives end in *-ful* or *-less*. Remember that *-ful* ends in one *l* and *-less* ends in two *s*'s.

> Diego Rivera, a **skillful** artist, created many **beautiful** paintings and murals. His work appeared **effortless** because he was so prolific.

Adjectives Ending in *-ed* and *-ing*

Some adjectives look like verbs because they end in *-ing* or *-ed*.

- When the adjective ends in *-ed*, it describes someone's expression or feeling.

   The **pleased** and **well-regarded** artist presented his mural to the public.

- When the adjective ends in *-ing*, it describes the quality of the person or thing.

   His **exciting, surprising** images are displayed on public buildings in Mexico

Hint **Keep Adjectives in the Singular Form**

When a noun describes another noun, always make it singular, even if the noun following it is plural.

year
Juliet was a thirteen-~~years~~-old girl when she met Romeo.

dollar
We bought several ten-~~dollars~~ tickets to see the play *Romeo and Juliet*.

CHAPTER 21

PRACTICE 4

Correct nine adjective errors in the paragraphs. The adjectives may have the wrong form, or they may be misspelled.

EXAMPLE:

interesting
Frida Kahlo was one of the world's most ~~interested~~ painters.

1.   Frida Kahlo was born in 1907 and was raised in an upper-class Mexican neighborhood. From an early age, she enjoyed wearing flamboyant, shocked clothing. She would appear in men's suits or long dresses, and she often wore beautifull flowers in her hair.

2.   In high school, the restles young girl first met the great Mexican artist Diego Rivera when he painted a wonderfull mural

for her school. At the age of twenty, Frida met Diego again when she showed him some of her colorfull paintings. Diego encouraged Frida and told her that her self-portraits were very originals.

3.   Even though Diego was much older than Frida, they fell in love and married in 1929. Their stormy relationship included many affairs. Diego was a skilfull womanizer and, after several years of marriage, he pursued Frida's younger sister, Cristina. Perhaps to retaliate, Frida also had extramarital relationships. She had a surprised romance with the Communist leader Leon Trotsky when he was a guest at her home.

4.   The scandalous, passionate relationship between Frida Kahlo and Diego Rivera remains one of Mexico's most publicizing love stories.

Adverbs

Adverbs add information to adjectives, verbs, or other adverbs. They give more specific information about how, when, where, and to what extent an action or event occurred.

Robin Hood **often** robbed from the rich and gave to the poor.

Robin Hood learned archery **easily.**

Robin Hood fell in love with Maid Marian **quite quickly.**

Robin Hood and his merry men were **tremendously** intelligent.

Adverb Forms

Adverbs often end in *-ly*. In fact, you can change many adjectives into adverbs by adding *-ly* endings.

Adjective: honest   **Adverb:** honestly

- If you add *-ly* to a word that ends in *l*, then your new word will have a double *l*.

  joyful + -ly

  Eros watched **joyfully** as Psyche walked toward him.

- If you add *-ly* to a word that ends in *e*, keep the *e*. Exceptions to this rule are *true–truly* and *due–duly*.

  passionate + -ly

  In Greek mythology, Eros, the god of love, fell **passionately** in love with Psyche.

> ## Hint — Some Adverbs and Adjectives Have the Same Form
>
> Some adverbs look exactly like adjectives. The only way to distinguish them is to see what they are modifying or describing.
>
> | **Examples:** | early | far | high | often | right |
> |---|---|---|---|---|---|
> | | fast | hard | late | past | soon |
>
> **Adjective:** In the **early** morning, Eros pierced the heart of a mortal.
>
> **Adverb:** Psyche arrived **early** at the wedding.

PRACTICE 5

Change each adjective into an adverb. Make sure that you spell the adverb correctly.

EXAMPLE:

pure   *purely*

1. beautiful _____   6. extreme _____

2. often _____   7. delightful _____

3. virtual _____   8. heavy _____

4. soon _____   9. wonderful _____

5. real _____   10. entire _____

Placement of Frequency Adverbs

Frequency adverbs are words that indicate how often someone performs an action or when an event occurs. They are words such as *always, often, sometimes, usually,* and *ever.*

- Place frequency adverbs before regular present and past tense verbs.

  Zeus **usually** lived on Mount Olympus.

- Place frequency adverbs after the verb *be.*

  The bridegroom is **usually** very dependable.

- Place frequency adverbs after helping verbs.

  Michael has **never** been married before.

PRACTICE 6

Correct six errors with word order or adjective and adverb forms.

EXAMPLE:

often contain

Newspapers and magazines ~~contain often~~ articles about the love affairs of the rich and famous.

1.   One of the most famous love stories of the twentieth century was the romance between John Lennon and Yoko Ono. In 1967, John met Yoko in a gallery where she was exhibiting her artwork. John climbed up a ladder and careful examined a tiny painting. On the painting was the word *yes*, and John liked the fact that the message was positive.

2.   When John and Yoko married, the press followed often them, and they usually were chased by photographers. The couple also had a truely difficult time because Beatles fans did not accept Yoko. In 1973, the couple broke up, but John eventualy realized that he wanted to be in New York with the love of his life. Unfortunately, when John was forty years old, he was killed by a deranged gunman. John's fans never have forgiven the killer.

Problems with Adverbs

Sometimes people use an adjective instead of an adverb after a verb. Ensure that you always modify your verbs using an adverb.

really quietly

Aphrodite waited ~~real quiet~~ for the celebrations to begin.

PRACTICE 7

Each sentence has one error with adverb or adjective forms or placement. Correct the errors.

EXAMPLE:

sincerely

Some people ~~sincerelly~~ believe in arranged marriages.

1. Arranged marriages are ~~commonly~~ in many parts of the world.

2. Parents find often a mate for their son or daughter based on criteria such as level of education, job prospects, and family background.

3. Advocates of arranged marriages believe real strongly that love can come later in the relationship.

4. Love marriages happen regular in many countries.

5. In love marriages, people sometimes fall in love quick.

6. In some Western societies, common-law unions have gradualy become popular.

7. The Netherlands officialy recognizes common-law unions.

8. In your opinion, should common-law couples have the same legally rights as married couples?

Good and *Well, Bad* and *Badly*

Good is an adjective, and *well* is an adverb.

Adjective: The pastry chef made a **good** wedding cake.

Adverb: The pastry chef cooks **well.**

Exception: Use *well* to describe a person's health.

Adverb: I do not feel **well**.

Bad is an adjective, and *badly* is an adverb.

Adjective: I am a **bad** singer.

Adverb: I sang **badly** at the wedding.

CHAPTER 21

PRACTICE 8

Underline the correct adjectives or adverbs.

EXAMPLE:

Generally, couples who communicate (good, <u>well</u>) have successful relationships.

1. Varied wedding traditions exist in the world. In Fiji, it is considered a (good, well) practice to give a whale tooth symbolizing wealth to the bride's father.

2. At Greek weddings, guests throw dishes on the floor for (good, well) luck.

3. In North American Christian weddings, it is (bad, badly) luck for the groom to see the bride's dress before the wedding. There is usually a big wedding feast, and sometimes the food is cooked (bad, badly).

4. At traditional Jewish weddings, an Israeli dance called the hora is performed. Some people dance (good, well) while others dance (bad, badly).

5. Many people consider a community center to be a (good, well) place to hold a wedding reception.

Comparative and Superlative Forms

Use the **comparative form** to compare two items.

Adjectives: Romeo is <u>younger</u> than Mercutio.

Juliet is <u>more romantic</u> than her nurse.

Adverbs: Shakespeare wrote <u>more quickly</u> than most other playwrights.

Romeo debated the issue <u>more convincingly</u> than Juliet.

Use the **superlative form** to compare three or more items.

Adjectives: Juliet was one of the <u>youngest</u> characters in Shakespeare's plays.

Shakespeare was the <u>most creative</u> playwright of his era.

Adverbs: Benvolio reacted the <u>most swiftly</u> of all of Romeo's cousins.

Romeo spoke the <u>most convincingly</u> of all of Juliet's suitors.

CHAPTER 21

How to Write Comparative and Superlative Forms

You can write comparative and superlative forms by remembering a few simple guidelines.

Using -er and -est Endings

Add -*er* and -*est* endings to one-syllable adjectives and adverbs.

	Comparative	**Superlative**
short	shorter than	the shortest
fast	faster than	the fastest
quick	quicker than	the quickest

Double the last letter when the adjective ends in one vowel + one consonant.

	Comparative	**Superlative**
hot	hotter than	the hottest

Using *More* and *The Most*

Generally add *more* and *the most* to adjectives and adverbs of two or more syllables.

	Comparative	**Superlative**
modern	more modern than	the most modern
clearly	more clearly than	the most clearly
worried	more worried than	the most worried

When a two-syllable adjective ends in *y*, change the *y* to *i* before you add the *-er* or *-est*.

	Comparative	**Superlative**
happy	happier than	the happiest

Using Irregular Comparative and Superlative Forms

Some adjectives and adverbs have unique comparative and superlative forms. Study this list to remember how to form some of the most common ones.

	Comparative	**Superlative**
good, well	better than	the best
bad, badly	worse than	the worst
some, much, many	more than	the most
little (a small amount)	less than	the least
far	farther, further	the farthest, the furthest

 **Farther versus Further**

- *Farther* indicates a physical distance.

    The wedding reception was **farther** from my home than it was from my fiancé's home.

- *Further* means "additional."

    I need **further** information before I can make a decision.

PRACTICE 9

Write the comparative and superlative forms of each adjective and adverb.

	Comparative	**Superlative**
EXAMPLE:		
famous	*more famous*	*most famous*
1. easy	_____	_____
2. easily	_____	_____
3. good	_____	_____

	Comparative	**Superlative**
4. bad	_____	_____
5. happy	_____	_____
6. quickly	_____	_____
7. careful	_____	_____
8. fast	_____	_____
9. thin	_____	_____
10. lazy	_____	_____
11. red	_____	_____
12. decent	_____	_____

PRACTICE 10

Underline the correct comparative or superlative form of each adjective or adverb.

EXAMPLE:

In my opinion, William Shakespeare's tragedy *Romeo and Juliet* is his
(better / <u>best</u>) play.

1. William Shakespeare is considered to be the (greater / greatest) playwright
   in English literature.

2. During the Renaissance, Shakespeare was (better / best) known than his
   contemporaries.

3. Queen Elizabeth I regarded him as the (more / most) talented author in
   her kingdom.

4. His (better / best)-known play is *Romeo and Juliet*.

5. In the play, the main character, Romeo, likes Juliet (more / most) than
   other girls.

6. Romeo wants (farther / further) information about Juliet, so he interrogates
   his cousin.

7. One of the (worse / worst) days of Romeo's life occurs when he realizes that
   his family is feuding with Juliet's family.

8. The (bigger / biggest) mistake Romeo makes is when he believes that Juliet
   has died.

9. *Romeo and Juliet* is a (sadder / saddest) play than some of Shakespeare's other tragedies.

10. Critics claim that Shakespeare's plays have been the (more / most) studied literary works in English literature.

PRACTICE II

Fill in each blank with either the comparative or superlative form of the adjective in parentheses.

EXAMPLE:

Many people find love stories to be the (interesting) _most interesting_ form of literature.

1.   Some of the (great) _____ works of fiction are based on some of the (passionate) _____ relationships. Many of Shakespeare's plays were based on relationships, including *Antony and Cleopatra* and *Romeo and Juliet*. Shakespeare also wrote romantic sonnets. I think that love poetry is (good) _____ than love stories. I like to read horror stories the (little) _____ of all types of literature.

2.   Henry Wadsworth Longfellow wrote a poem in 1858 called *The Courtship of Miles Standish.* This poem was about one of the (early) _____ romances that took place in the American colonies.

3.   Miles Standish was an upstanding leader who fell in love with Priscilla Mullins, the (beautiful) _____ maiden in the colonies. Oddly, although he was one of the (respected) _____ men in the colony, he was also one of the (timid) _____. Because of his acute shyness, Standish could not bring himself to express his love for Priscilla. His friend John Alden, who was (outgoing) _____ than he, decided to tell Priscilla about Standish's feelings. Unfortunately, Priscilla fell in love with Alden, who was the (charming) _____ man she had ever met. The love triangle resolved itself, and Alden eventually married Priscilla with Miles Standish's blessing.

CHAPTER 21

Problems with Comparative and Superlative Forms

In the comparative form, never use *more* and *-er* to modify the same word. In the superlative form, never use *most* and *-est* to modify the same word.

>   *better*
> His date with Jan was ~~more better~~ than his date with Catherine.

>   *best*
> It was the ~~most best~~ date of his life.

 **Using "the" in the Comparative Form**

Although you would usually use *the* in superlative forms, you can use it in some two-part comparatives. In these expressions, the second part is the result of the first part.

>   action   result
> The more you work at a relationship, the better it will be.

PRACTICE 12

Correct twelve adjective and adverb errors.

EXAMPLE:

>   *most*
> One of the ~~more~~ famous relationships in the twentieth century was between Charles Lindbergh and Anne Morrow.

1.   Charles Lindberg was an all-American hero because, in 1927, he was the first person to fly safe across the Atlantic Ocean. Charles originaly pursued Anne Morrow's sister. However, when he saw the more younger Anne, he fell in love with her. She was real beautiful. They lived happy for a while. She wrote a memoir of their relationship that led to more greater celebrity status for the pair. The more Anne wrote, the happiest she became.

2.   In some respects, the couple had a perfect relationship. Anne worked tireless beside her husband, helping him navigate during his flights. In an era when most women did not work outside the home, Anne was more happier pursuing her writing and flying careers than being a housewife.

3.   However, the relationship between Charles and Anne was not perfect. They both had affairs, and at one point, Anne fell in love

with one of the most best writers of the era, Antoine de Saint-Exupéry. Charles and Anne also lived through the more tragic event of their lives. In 1932, their first child was kidnapped and murdered. About four years later, Bruno Richard Hauptmann was executed for the crime.

4.   The more Charles and Anne suffered, the strongest their relationship became. They went on to have more children, and they were together until the death of Charles in 1974.

FINAL REVIEW

Correct fifteen adjective or adverb errors.

EXAMPLE:

Reporters write ~~surprised~~ *surprising* articles about same-sex marriage.

1.   One of the more controversial issues in contemporary American politics is same-sex marriage. Same-sex marriage refers to a legally union between people of the same sex. People have strong-held opinions about this topic.

2.   In the United States, individual states have jurisdiction over marriage. Therefore, the states have conflicted laws on gay marriage. Massachusetts recognizes gay marriage. Vermont, Connecticut, and New Hampshire acknowledge civil unions between couples of the same sex. Other states bar same-sex marriage, arguing that it is worst than other crimes.

3.   The more this issue remains unsolved, the most divisive it becomes. Jim and Paul have been together for five years. Paul writes good and runs a magazine for the gay community. They both work tireless to lobby their state government to change laws about marriage. They argue that same-sex marriage is a civil right. Therefore, as citizens, gay couples should have the same rights as

heterosexual couples. The worse mistake a democratic government can make is to discriminate against a minority group. On the other hand, Edward and Christabel are opposed to same-sex marriages. They have been married for ten years and have a seven-years-old daughter. They believe marriage is based on natural law, and procreation can only happen naturally between a man and a woman. Families are the most greatest cornerstones of civilization.

4.   Religious groups also have opinions about this issue. They state that same-sex marriage will change the concept of traditional marriage real quickly. Some conservative Christians believe that same-sex marriage contradicts biblical laws. Other religious groups support same-sex marriage because they believe that two consenting adults should have the right to form a loving and committed union.

5.   Differents groups voice various opinions. This issue will eventualy be resolved, but in the meantime, the interested debate continues.

 The Writer's Room

Write about one of the following topics. After you finish writing, underline any adjectives and adverbs. Decide whether your paragraph has enough descriptive words and phrases.

1. Describe your ideal partner. What characteristics should he or she have?
2. Narrate what happened on a funny, boring, or romantic date that you have had.

CHECKLIST: ADJECTIVES AND ADVERBS

When you edit your writing, ask yourself the following questions.

Do I use adjectives correctly? Check for errors in these cases:

–placement of adjectives
–order of adjectives
–spelling

                     countless
Throughout history, ~~countles~~ people have enjoyed having
wonderful romances
~~romances wonderfull~~.

Do I use adverbs correctly? Check for errors in these cases:

–spelling of adverbs that end in *-ly*
–placement of frequency adverbs

             often
Many marriages take place ~~often~~ in places of worship.

Do I use the correct adverb form? Check for errors in these cases:

–use of adjectives instead of adverbs to modify verbs
–use of *good, well* and *bad, badly*

                                                well
The Romantic poet Elizabeth Barrett Browning wrote ~~good~~ when
she was a child.

                                             quickly
She and her husband, Robert Browning, eloped rather ~~quick~~ to
escape her father.

Do I use the correct comparative and superlative forms? Check for
errors in these cases:

–*more* and *-er* comparisons
–*the most* and *-est* comparisons

                       better
The more you write, the ~~more better~~ writer you become.

CHAPTER 21

How Do I Get a Better Grade?

Visit www.mywritinglab.com for audio-visual lectures
and additional practice sets about adjectives and adverbs.
Get a better grade with MyWritingLab!

Mistakes with Modifiers

Section Theme: **RELATIONSHIPS**

CONTENTS

- Misplaced Modifiers
- Dangling Modifiers

In this chapter, you will read about relationship issues such as Internet dating and workplace romances.

Grammar Snapshot

Looking at Modifiers

In an essay titled "Marriage Is an Outdated Institution," college student Winston Murray writes about the decline of marriage. In the following excerpt, some of the modifiers are underlined.

> Weddings are expensive and extravagant affairs <u>that indebt families for years to come</u>. Parents of the bride and groom <u>often</u> take out second mortgages to give their children the ideal wedding. <u>After paying for the wedding dress</u>, they must pay for the reception hall, flowers, music, catering, and limousines to have a one-night party.

In this chapter, you will identify and correct misplaced and dangling modifiers.

Misplaced Modifiers

A **modifier** is a word, phrase, or clause that describes or modifies nouns or verbs in a sentence. To use a modifier correctly, place it next to the word(s) that you want to modify.

modifier   modified noun
Holding her hand, **Charles** proposed.

A **misplaced modifier** is a word, phrase, or clause that is not placed next to the word that it modifies. When a modifier is too far from the word that it is describing, the meaning of the sentence can become confusing or unintentionally funny.

Confusing: I saw the Golden Gate Bridge riding my bike.

(How could a bridge ride a bike?)

Clear: **Riding my bike,** I saw the Golden Gate Bridge.

Confusing: Boring and silly, Amanda closed the fashion magazine.

(What is boring and silly? Amanda or the magazine?)

Clear: Amanda closed the **boring and silly** fashion magazine.

Commonly Misplaced Modifiers

Some writers have trouble placing certain types of modifiers close to the words they modify. As you read the sample sentences for each type, notice how they change meaning depending on where a writer places the modifiers. In the examples, the modifiers are underlined.

Prepositional Phrase Modifiers

A prepositional phrase is made of a preposition and its object.

Confusing: Sheila talked to the man in the bar <u>with dirty hands.</u>

(Can a bar have dirty hands?)

Clear: When Sheila was in the bar, she talked to the man <u>with dirty hands.</u>

PRACTICE I

In each sentence, underline the prepositional phrase modifier. Then draw an arrow from the modifier to the word that it modifies.

EXAMPLE:

<u>With anticipation,</u> Arianne contacted the dating service.

1. Arianne found Cupid Dating Service in a phone book.

2. On the table, a glossy pamphlet contained information.

3. Arianne, in a red dress, entered the dating service office.

4. With a kind expression, the interviewer asked Arianne personal

    questions.

5. Arianne, with direct eye contact, discussed her preferences.

Present Participle Modifiers

A present participle modifier is a phrase that begins with an *-ing* verb.

Confusing:	The young man proposed to his girlfriend <u>holding a diamond ring</u>.
	(Who is holding the diamond ring?)
Clear:	While <u>holding a diamond ring</u>, the young man proposed to his girlfriend.

PRACTICE 2

In each sentence, underline the present participle modifier. Then draw an arrow from the modifier to the word that it modifies.

EXAMPLE:

<u>Swallowing nervously</u>, Arianne explained her dating history.

1. Hoping to find a soul mate, Arianne described what she wanted.

2. Matching people with similar tastes, Cupid Dating Service is very successful.

3. Some customers using the service express satisfaction.

4. Feeling disappointed, customer Stephen Rooney has never met a suitable

    companion.

5. However, the owner of Cupid Dating, citing statistics, says that most

    clients are very satisfied.

Past Participle Modifiers

A past participle modifier is a phrase that begins with a past participle (*walked, gone, known,* and so on).

Confusing:	<u>Covered with dust</u>, my girlfriend wiped the windshield of her new car.
	(What was covered with dust? The girlfriend or the car?)
Clear:	My girlfriend wiped the windshield of the car that was <u>covered with dust</u>.

PRACTICE 3

In each sentence, underline the past participle modifier. Then draw an arrow from the modifier to the word that it modifies.

EXAMPLE:

Shocked, Arianne met her first blind date.

1. Covered in paint, Stephen sat at Arianne's table.

2. Torn between staying and leaving, Arianne smiled at Stephen.

3. Bored with life, Stephen talked for hours.

4. Trapped in a horrible date, Arianne longed to escape.

5. Stephen, surprised by her actions, watched Arianne stand up and leave.

Other Dependent-Clause Modifiers

Other dependent-clause modifiers can begin with a subordinator or a relative pronoun such as *who, whom, which,* or *that.*

> **Confusing:**   I presented Jeremy to my mother who is my boyfriend.
> (How could "my mother" be "my boyfriend?")
>
> **Clear:**   I presented Jeremy, who is my boyfriend, to my mother.

PRACTICE 4

In each sentence, underline the relative clause modifier. Then draw an arrow from the modifier to the word that it modifies.

EXAMPLE:

Arianne complained about the date that had gone horribly wrong.

1. She discussed the date with her friend, Maggie, who was sympathetic.

2. Maggie knew about a place that had many single people.

3. The women went to a club where they met a new friend, Mel.

4. Maggie told Mel, who was also single, about her dating problems.

5. But Mel, whom Maggie really liked, asked Arianne out on a date instead.

PRACTICE 5

Read each pair of sentences on the next page. Circle the letter of the correct sentence. Then, in the incorrect sentence, underline the misplaced modifier.

EXAMPLE:

    a. We read about the love lives of celebrities <u>with curiosity</u>.

    (b.) With curiosity, we read about the love lives of celebrities.

1. a. In the past, increasing their sales, tabloid newspapers focused on scandalous stories about celebrities.

    b. In the past, tabloid newspapers focused on scandalous stories about celebrities increasing their sales.

2. a. Today, many journalists publish stories about celebrities on the front page.

    b. Today, many journalists publish stories on the front page about celebrities.

3. a. Followed by paparazzi, celebrities such as Jude Law have no privacy.

    b. Celebrities such as Jude Law have no privacy followed by paparazzi.

4. a. In 2003, Kobe Bryant spoke to a female reporter with his wife.

    b. In 2003, with his wife, Kobe Bryant spoke to a female reporter.

5. a. I read an article saying that some celebrities are angry in the newspaper.

    b. I read an article in the newspaper saying that some celebrities are angry.

6. a. Celebrities should not complain about the curiosity of the public appearing on thousands of movie screens daily.

    b. Appearing on thousands of movie screens daily, celebrities should not complain about the curiosity of the public.

CHAPTER 22

 **Correcting Misplaced Modifiers**

To correct misplaced modifiers, do the following:

1. Identify the modifier.
    Ricardo and Alicia saw the beach <u>driving past Miami</u>.

2. Identify the word or words that are being modified.
    Ricardo and Alicia

3. Move the modifier next to the word(s) that are being modified.
    Driving past Miami, **Ricardo and Alicia** saw the beach.

PRACTICE 6

Correct the misplaced modifiers in the following sentences.

EXAMPLE
Sitting in my car,
I listened to the radio ~~sitting in my car~~.

1. The law professor spoke on the radio about marriage laws from Indiana.

2. Mixed-race couples were prohibited from marrying by legislators lacking their basic human rights.

3. Mixed-race couples felt angry who were prohibited from marrying legally.

4. In 1967, allowing interracial couples to marry, a decision was made by the U.S. Supreme Court.

5. The professor explained why these laws were morally wrong last week.

6. My sister married a man of another race who is my twin.

7. The wedding was in a beautiful garden photographed by a professional.

8. My parents welcomed the groom with champagne who supported my sister's choice.

CHAPTER 22

Dangling Modifiers

A **dangling modifier** opens a sentence but does not modify any words in the sentence. It "dangles," or hangs loosely, because it is not connected to any other part of the sentence. To avoid having a dangling modifier, make sure the modifier and the first noun that follows it have a logical connection.

Confusing: Phoning the company, a limousine was booked in advance.
(Can a limousine book itself?)

Clear: Phoning the company, **the groom** booked the limousine in advance.

Confusing: Walking down the aisle, many flower petals were on the ground.
(Can flowers walk down an aisle?)

Clear: Walking down the aisle, **the bride** noticed that many flower petals were on the ground.

PRACTICE 7

Read each pair of sentences. Circle the letter of each correct sentence, and underline the dangling modifiers.

EXAMPLE:

    a. On July 29, 1981, <u>in a beautiful white gown</u>, the royal wedding

       occurred.

    (b.) On July 29, 1981, in a beautiful white gown, Diana married Charles.

1. a. Falling in love with a prince, Diana Spencer was envied by many people.

    b. Falling in love with a prince, many people envied the royal couple.

2. a. Chased by members of the press, a high level of stress was experienced.

    b. Chased by members of the press, Diana experienced a high level of stress.

3. a. By ignoring his wife, the relationship was doomed.

    b. By ignoring his wife, Charles doomed the relationship.

4. a. Unhappy with the situation, Diana became increasingly depressed and

      lonely.

    b. Unhappy with the situation, there was an increasing sense of loneliness

      and depression.

5. a. By cheating, the marriage vows were broken.

    b. By cheating, Charles broke his marriage vows.

6. a. To get revenge, there were many extramarital affairs.

    b. To get revenge, Diana entered into many extramarital affairs.

7. a. Unhappy with their relationship, the couple separated.

    b. Unhappy with their relationship, a separation occurred.

8. a. To understand why the wedding took place, we must examine the rules

      regarding royal marriages.

    b. To understand why the wedding took place, rules regarding royal

      marriages must be examined.

CHAPTER 22

> ⟨**Hint**⟩   **Correcting Dangling Modifiers**
>
> To correct dangling modifiers, follow these steps.
>
> 1. Identify the modifier.
>   <u>Walking down the aisle</u>, many flower petals were on the ground.
>
> 2. Decide who or what should be modified.
>   the bride
>
> 3. Add the missing subject (and in some cases, also add or remove words) so that the sentence makes sense.
>   Walking down the aisle, **the bride noticed that** many flower petals were on the ground.

PRACTICE 8

Correct the dangling modifiers in the following sentences. Begin by underlining each dangling modifier. Then rewrite the sentence. You may have to add or remove words to give the sentence a logical meaning.

EXAMPLE:

<u>Always having to remain beautiful,</u> bodies are changed.

<u>Always having to remain beautiful, movie stars change their bodies.</u>

1. Reading through old magazines, ideas about beauty have changed over time.

   _____

   _____

2. In the past, seeing curvy movie stars, dieting was not very common.

   _____

   _____

3. Today, making their clients thinner, the bodies of famous people are altered.

   _____

   _____

4. Watching Jessica Alba, her natural beauty is envied.

   _____

   _____

5. While looking in the mirror, her puppy sat on her lap.

   _____

   _____

6. Reading about Whitney Houston her problems were serious.

_____

_____

PRACTICE 9

Underline each dangling or misplaced modifier, and correct the mistakes. Remember that you may have to add or remove words to give some sentences a logical meaning. If a sentence does not have modifier errors, simply write _C_ to indicate it is correct.

EXAMPLE.

     whom I like
I met a man at my workplace ~~whom I like~~.   _____

1. Some personnel department employees are debating the

   subject of workplace relationships in their meetings. _____

2. Two employees can have a lot of problems with their

   superiors who fall in love. _____

3. Some people believe that companies should develop

   policies prohibiting workplace romances. _____

4. Debating sexual harassment, discussions have been

   heated. _____

5. Couples can develop antagonistic feelings who work

   together. _____

6. Perhaps employers have no right to forbid relationships

   between employees. _____

7. Policies can cause problems in people's lives that prohibit

   workplace romances. _____

8. Many couples have successfully worked together. _____

9. Workplace romance in the future is a topic that will be

   debated. _____

FINAL REVIEW

Correct ten errors with dangling or misplaced modifiers.

EXAMPLE:

she scandalized the public.

Divorcing her husband, ~~the public was scandalized.~~

1. In the 1920s, Prince Edward was an eligible bachelor. One day, the prince met a married American woman named Wallis Simpson who was going to be king. Feeling very guilty, the relationship developed into love. Wallis sometimes stayed in a hotel near the palace wearing a wig.

2. On January 30, 1936, people were pleased when King George V died with the news that Edward would be the next king. Soon after, Wallis got a divorce who was in love with the king. As the king, Edward VIII ruled England for 325 days. Edward gave interviews to the press who wanted to abdicate the throne. Edward had decided that his love for Wallis was more important than his role as the British monarch.

3. Wallis ran off with Edward in high heels. Not caring about the monarchy, the marriage lasted for many years. Wallis Simpson appeared to love Edward in magazine interviews. Chasing after the couple, there were many articles written by prominent journalists.

 The Writer's Room

Write about one of the following topics. Take care to avoid writing misplaced or dangling modifiers.

1. How are romance movies unrealistic? List examples of some movies or scenes that are not realistic.
2. What is the best way to break up with somebody? Give some steps that a person can take.
3. What causes people to search for love on the Internet? Explain why people visit online dating sites.

CHAPTER 22

READING LINK
Relationships
To read more about relationships, see the following essays:
"Birth" by Maya Angelou (page 423)
"For Marriage" by Kirsteen Macleod (page 429)
"Against Marriage" by Winston Murray (page 430)

CHECKLIST: MODIFIERS

When you edit your writing, ask yourself the following questions.

☐ Are my modifiers in the correct position? Check for errors with the following:

–prepositional phrase modifiers

–present participle modifiers

–past participle modifiers

–*who, whom, which,* or *that* modifiers

> *Eating ice cream, the*
> ~~The~~ young couple looked at the sportswear ~~eating ice cream~~.

☐ Do my modifiers modify something in the sentence? Check for dangling modifiers.

> *my girlfriend created*
> Reading love poetry, a romantic atmosphere ~~was created~~.

The Writers' Circle

Work with a group of students on the following activity.

STEP 1 Choose one of the following topics. Brainstorm and come up with adjectives, adverbs, and phrases that describe each item in the pair.
a. A good date and a bad date
b. A great relationship and an unhappy relationship
c. A good romance movie and a bad romance movie

EXAMPLE: A good friend and a bad friend.

> *A good friend: smart, makes me laugh, good talker*

> *A bad friend: ignores my calls, insults me, rude*

STEP 2 For each item in the pair, rank the qualities from most important to least important.

STEP 3 As a team, write a paragraph about your topic. Compare the good with the bad.

STEP 4 When you finish writing, edit your paragraph. Ensure that you have written all adjectives and adverbs correctly Also, ensure that you have no dangling or misplaced modifiers.

CHAPTER 22

How Do I Get a Better Grade?

Visit www.mywritinglab.com for audio-visual lectures and additional practice sets about mistakes with modifiers.
Get a better grade with MyWritingLab!

23 Spelling

Section Theme: **CREATURES LARGE AND SMALL**

CONTENTS

- Improving Your Spelling
- Writing *ie* or *ei*
- Adding Prefixes and Suffixes
- Writing Two-Part Words
- 120 Commonly Misspelled Words

In this chapter, you will read about zoos and the conservation of endangered species.

Grammar Snapshot

Looking at Spelling

In this excerpt from the novel *The Life of Pi*, writer Yann Martel discusses the characteristics of zoos. The underlined words are sometimes difficult to spell.

> A house is a compressed territory where our basic needs can be fulfilled close by and safely. Such an enclosure is subjectively neither better nor worse for an animal than its condition in the wild; so long as it fulfills the animal's needs, a territory, natural or constructed, simply *is*, without judgment, a given, like the spots on a leopard.

In this chapter, you will identify and correct misspelled words.

Improving Your Spelling

It is important to spell correctly. Spelling mistakes can detract from good ideas in your work. You can become a better speller if you always proofread your written work and if you check a dictionary for the meaning and spelling of words about which you are unsure.

Hint   Reminders About Vowels and Consonants

When you review spelling rules, it is important to know the difference between a vowel and a consonant. The vowels are *a, e, i, o, u,* and sometimes *y*. The consonants are all of the other letters of the alphabet.

The letter *y* may be either a consonant or a vowel, depending on its pronunciation. In the word *happy,* the *y* is a vowel because it is pronounced as an *ee* sound. In the word *youth,* the *y* has a consonant sound.

PRACTICE I

Answer the following questions.

1. Write three words that begin with three consonants.

   EXAMPLE: strong   _____   _____   _____

2. Write three words that begin with *y* and contain at least two vowels.

   EXAMPLE: yellow   _____   _____   _____

3. Write three words that have double vowels.

   EXAMPLE: moon   _____   _____   _____

4. Write three words that end with three consonants.

   EXAMPLE: birth   _____   _____   _____

Writing *ie* or *ei*

Words that contain *ie* or *ei* can be tricky. Remember to write *i* before *e* except after *c* or when *ei* is pronounced *ay*, as in *neighbor* and *weigh*.

i **before** *e:*	chief	patient	priest
ei **after** *c:*	conceit	perceive	deceive
ei **pronounced as** *ay:*	weigh	neighbor	freight
Exceptions:	efficient	either	neither
	science	foreigner	seize
	society	height	their
	species	leisure	weird

PRACTICE 2

Underline the correct spelling of each word.

EXAMPLE:

<u>ceiling</u>, cieling

1. conceive	concieve	7. efficient	efficeint
2. field	feild	8. weird	wierd
3. receipt	reciept	9. deciet	deceit
4. hieght	height	10. acheive	achieve
5. vien	vein	11. weight	wieght
6. science	sceince	12. decieve	deceive

PRACTICE 3

Correct the spelling error with *ie* or *ei* in each sentence. If the sentence is correct, write *C* in the blank.

EXAMPLE:

Efficient

~~Efficeint~~ management of natural habitats is necessary for the preservation of many animals.   _____

CHAPTER 23

1. The giant panda is one of the most endangered speceis in the

   world.   _____

2. The giant panda is revered in Chinese soceity, but there

   are fewer than two thousand of these animals left in the wild.   _____

3. The pandas inhabit the Yangtze River basin, an area that

   has been heavily populated since anceint times.   _____

4. A loss of habitat and poaching are the cheif reasons that

   the population of the giant pandas is diminishing.   _____

5. Environmentalists believe that humans must save the pandas.   _____

6. Pateintly conserving the natural biodiversity of the area

   will help the pandas.   _____

7. For example, well-conceived tourism management will

    help the economy of the area.   _____

8. In the last ten years, the Chinese government has acheived

    significant success in creating panda nature reserves.   _____

9. In addition, most foriegn zoos have a partnership with China

    to help conserve the giant panda.   _____

10. For example, if an American zoo wants to receive a panda,

    it must develop a research project to help pandas in the wild.   _____

Adding Prefixes and Suffixes

A **prefix** is added to the beginning of a word, and it changes the word's meaning.

    <u>re</u>organize   <u>pre</u>mature   <u>un</u>fair   <u>mis</u>understand

A **suffix** is added to the ending of a word, and it changes the word's tense or meaning.

    amuse<u>ment</u>   sure<u>ly</u>   offer<u>ing</u>   watch<u>ed</u>

When you add a prefix to a word, keep the last letter of the prefix and the first letter of the main word.

    u**n** + **n**erve = u**nn**erve   di**s** + **s**imilar = di**ss**imilar

When you add the suffix -*ly* to a word that ends in *l*, keep the *l* of the root word. The new word will have two *l*'s.

    beautifu**l** + **l**y = beautifu**ll**y   rea**l** + **l**y = rea**ll**y

Hint   **Words Ending in -*ful***

Although the word *full* ends in two *l*'s, when -*full* is added to another word as a suffix, it ends in one *l*.

wonderful   **peaceful**

Notice the unusual spelling when *full* and *fill* are combined: *fulfill*.

CHAPTER 23

PRACTICE 4

Underline the correct spelling of each word.

EXAMPLE:

<u>awful</u>, awfull

1.	unecessary	unnecessary	8. universaly	universally
2.	dissolve	disolve	9. fullfilled	fulfilled
3.	personally	personaly	10. usually	usualy
4.	irational	irrational	11. disrespectfull	disrespectful
5.	immature	imature	12. joyfuly	joyfully
6.	mispell	misspell	13. useful	usefull
7.	plentiful	plentifull	14. ilogical	illogical

Adding -s or -es Suffixes

Generally, add -s to nouns and to present tense verbs that are third-person singular. However, add -es to words in the following situations.

- When a word ends in s, sh, ss, ch, or x, add -es.
    Noun: porch–porch**es**   **Verb:**   mix–mix**es**
- When a word ends in the consonant y, change the y to i and add -es.
    Noun: lady–lad**ies**   **Verb:**   carry–carr**ies**
- Generally, when a word ends in o, add -es.
    Noun: tomato–tomato**es**   **Verb:**   go–go**es**
    Exceptions: piano–piano**s**, radio–radio**s**
- When a word ends in f or fe, change the f to a v and add -es.
    Nouns: calf–cal**ves**   wife–wi**ves**
    Exceptions: roof–roof**s**, belief–belief**s**

PRACTICE 5

Add an -s or -es ending to each word.

EXAMPLE:

reach   *reaches* _____

1. piano _____	7. volcano _____
2. watch _____	8. spy _____
3. fax _____	9. kiss _____
4. leaf _____	10. baby _____
5. marry _____	11. belief _____
6. box _____	12. vanish _____

Adding Suffixes to Words Ending in -e

When you add a suffix to a word ending in *e*, make sure that you follow the next rules.

▪ If the suffix begins with a vowel, drop the *e* on the main word. Some common suffixes beginning with vowels are *-ed*, *-er*, *-est*, *-ing*, *-able*, *-ent*, and *-ist*.

    creat**e**–creating   mov**e**–movable

Exceptions: For some words that end in the letters *ge*, keep the *e* and add the suffix.

    courag**e**–courageous   chang**e**–changeable

▪ If the suffix begins with a consonant, keep the *e*. Some common suffixes beginning with consonants are *-ly*, *-ment*, *-less*, and *-ful*.

    definit**e**–definitely   improv**e**–improvement

Exceptions: Some words lose the final *e* when you add a suffix that begins with a consonant.

    argu**e**–argument   tru**e**–truly   judg**e**–judgment

PRACTICE 6

Rewrite each word by adding the suggested ending.

EXAMPLE:

    use + ed   *used*

1. advertise + ment _____
2. convince + ing _____
3. complete + ly _____
4. give + ing _____
5. true + er _____
6. cure + able _____
7. produce + er _____
8. judge + ment _____
9. believe + ing _____
10. move + ing _____
11. use + able _____
12. late + er _____

PRACTICE 7

Correct the spelling mistakes in the underlined words.

EXAMPLE:

                     truly
The story of the gray wolf in Yellowstone is <u>truely</u> amazing.

1.   Before the arrival of Europeans, gray <u>wolfs</u> were found in all parts

of North America. By the 1920s, these animals had been almost

<u>completly</u> destroyed in the United States. Early settlers <u>unecessarily</u>

shot large numbers of the animals. Biologists from the Fisheries and Wildlife Department decided to try <u>reintroduceing</u> the gray wolf into the wild in Yellowstone National Park. In 1995, fifteen animals were transferred from Alberta, Canada, to Yellowstone.

2.   The wolf reintroduction program has <u>definitly</u> been a success. The animals have multiplied and the secondary effects have <u>actualy</u> been very positive. For example, the elk population has been reduced. As a result, trees around the banks of lakes are <u>thriveing</u>. The numbers of <u>foxs</u> have increased in the area because they eat the carcasses of the elks.

3.   Today, there are many wolf packs in the park, and it is <u>ilegal</u> to hunt them. Each wolf pack <u>flourishs</u> in Yellowstone National Park.

Adding Suffixes by Doubling the Final Consonant

Sometimes when you add a suffix to a word, you must double the final consonant. Remember these tips when spelling words of one or more syllables.

One-Syllable Words

- Double the final consonant of one-syllable words ending in a consonant-vowel-consonant pattern.

    stop–sto**pp**ing   drag–dra**gg**ed

Exception: If the word ends in *w* or *x*, do not double the last letter.

    snow–snowing   fix–fixed

- Do not double the final consonant if the word ends in a vowel and two consonants or if it ends with two vowels and a consonant.

    look–looking   list–listed

Words of Two or More Syllables

- Double the final consonant of words ending in a stressed consonant-vowel-consonant pattern.

    confer–confe**rr**ing   omit–omi**tt**ed

- If the word ends in a syllable that is not stressed, then do not double the last letter of the word.

    open–opening   focus–focused

PRACTICE 8

Rewrite each word with the suggested ending.

<table>
<tr><td colspan="2" align="center">**Add -ed**</td><td colspan="2" align="center">**Add -ing**</td></tr>
<tr><td colspan="2">**EXAMPLE:**</td><td colspan="2">**EXAMPLE:**</td></tr>
<tr><td>park</td><td>_parked_</td><td>open</td><td>_opening_</td></tr>
<tr><td>1. answer</td><td>_____</td><td>6. happen</td><td>_____</td></tr>
<tr><td>2. clean</td><td>_____</td><td>7. run</td><td>_____</td></tr>
<tr><td>3. prod</td><td>_____</td><td>8. drag</td><td>_____</td></tr>
<tr><td>4. mention</td><td>_____</td><td>9. refer</td><td>_____</td></tr>
<tr><td>5. prefer</td><td>_____</td><td>10. question</td><td>_____</td></tr>
</table>

Adding Suffixes to Words Ending in -y

When you add a suffix to a word ending in *y*, follow the next rules.

- If a word has a consonant before the final *y*, change the *y* to an *i* before adding the suffix.

  heav**y**–heav**i**ly   angr**y**–angr**i**ly   eas**y**–eas**i**ly

- If a word has a vowel before the final *y*, if it is a proper name, or if the suffix is *-ing*, do not change the *y* to an *i*.

  pla**y**–pla**y**ed   fr**y**–fr**y**ing   Binch**y**–Binch**y**s

  Exceptions: Some words do not follow the previous rule.

  da**y**–daily   la**y**–laid   sa**y**–said   pa**y**–paid

PRACTICE 9

Rewrite each word by adding the suggested ending.

EXAMPLES:

   say + ing =   _saying_

<table>
<tr><td>1. justify + able</td><td>_____</td><td>6. lively + hood</td><td>_____</td></tr>
<tr><td>2. fly + ing</td><td>_____</td><td>7. day + ly</td><td>_____</td></tr>
<tr><td>3. enjoy + ed</td><td>_____</td><td>8. mercy + less</td><td>_____</td></tr>
<tr><td>4. Kowalsky + s</td><td>_____</td><td>9. duty + ful</td><td>_____</td></tr>
<tr><td>5. beauty + ful</td><td>_____</td><td>10. pretty + est</td><td>_____</td></tr>
</table>

PRACTICE 10

Correct eight spelling mistakes in the next selection.

EXAMPLE:

Some environmentalists ~~mentionned~~ *mentioned* that sharks are an endangered species.

1.   Since ancient times, sharks have had a bad reputation. Many
people display their negative opinion of sharks by refering to them
as man-eating predators. The movie *Jaws* emphasized the menacing
nature of sharks. It draged their image down to an all-time low.
In the past, nobody questionned shark hunters. But sharks must
be protected from extinction because they help keep the marine
environment in balance.

2.   Sharks are being overfished dayly. Millions of sharks are killed
each year by commercial fishers who depend on shark products for
their livelyhood. The mercyless overfishing of sharks has led to
dramatic consequences for the environment and the economy.
Sharks eat other predators like stingrays. Smaller predators eat
seafood such as shrimps and scallops, and that is begining to hurt the
commercial fishing industry. Therefore, ecologists have focussed their
efforts on saving the shark population.

CHAPTER 23

Writing Two-Part Words

The following indefinite pronouns sound as if they should be two separate words,
but each is a single word.

Words with *any*:	anything, anyone, anybody, anywhere
Words with *some*:	something, someone, somebody, somewhere
Words with *every*:	everything, everyone, everybody, everywhere

   **Writing *Another* and *A lot***

- *Another* is always one word.

    Another gorilla has escaped from the zoo.

- *A lot* is always two words.

    A lot of people are looking for the animal.

PRACTICE 11

Correct ten spelling errors in the next paragraph.

EXAMPLE:

Everyone
~~Every one~~ should be concerned about the destruction of the Amazon rain forest.

1.   One of the most amazeing and crucial ecosystems on the planet is the Amazon River basin. It is an immense area and contains 20 percent of the world's fresh water. This region includes the rain forest. It houses unnusual species of plants and animals that are not found any where else in the world. For example, alot of giant river otters swim in the Amazon. An other unique species is the emerald tree boa.

2.   Naturaly, it is disheartening to hear that the Amazon jungle is being completly destroyed through logging, mineral extraction, and livestock grazing. It is in every one's interest to protect the fragile Amazon basin. Our planet depends on this ecosystem, and it is ilogical not to develop policies that will protect it. Stoping the destruction of the rain forest is crucial.

120 Commonly Misspelled Words

The next list contains some of the most commonly misspelled words in English. Learn how to spell these words. You might try different strategies, such as writing down the word a few times or using flash cards to help you to memorize the spelling of each word.

absence	argument	cemetery	desperate
absorption	athlete	clientele	developed
accommodate	bargain	committee	dilemma
acquaintance	beginning	comparison	disappoint
address	behavior	competent	embarrass
aggressive	believable	conscience	encouragement
already	business	conscientious	environment
aluminum	calendar	convenient	especially
analyze	campaign	curriculum	exaggerate
appointment	careful	definite	exercise
approximate	ceiling	definitely	extraordinarily

familiar	mathematics	prejudice	technique
February	medicine	privilege	thorough
finally	millennium	probably	tomato
foreign	mischievous	professor	tomatoes
government	mortgage	psychology	tomorrow
grammar	necessary	questionnaire	truly
harassment	ninety	receive	Tuesday
height	noticeable	recommend	until
immediately	occasion	reference	usually
independent	occurrence	responsible	vacuum
jewelry	opposite	rhythm	Wednesday
judgment	outrageous	schedule	weird
laboratory	parallel	scientific	woman
ledge	performance	separate	women
legendary	perseverance	sincerely	wreckage
leisure	personality	spaghetti	writer
license	physically	strength	writing
loneliness	possess	success	written
maintenance	precious	surprise	zealous

 **Hint**   **Using a Spelling Checker**

Most word processing programs have spelling and grammar tools that will alert you about some common errors. They will also suggest ways to correct them. Be careful, however, because these tools are not 100 percent accurate. For example, a spelling checker cannot differentiate between *your* and *you're*.

PRACTICE 12

Underline the correctly spelled words in parentheses.

EXAMPLE:

Many interest groups (campaine, <u>campaign</u>) to raise public awareness.

1.   Ever since the (legendary / ledgendary) French actress Brigitte

Bardot photographed herself with a baby harp seal in 1977, the

Canadian seal hunt has been (aggresively / aggressively) debated.

The sight of celebrities on ice floes protecting baby seals from being

bludgeoned to death has become a (familar / familiar) scene. It

has raised public sympathy for the seals. Yet there are two

(oposite / opposite) views in this debate.

2.   Animal rights activists claim that the seal hunt is cruel to

animals and must be stopped (immediately / imediately). Such

groups (believe / beleive) that the manner in which baby seals are killed is inhumane. Furthermore, animal welfare groups think that the seal hunt is (unnecesary / unnecessary) for the economy. People who rely on the (business / buisness) can make their money elsewhere. For instance, activists are (encourageing / encouraging) the Canadian (goverment / government) to develop the northern region for ecotourism. Animal rights groups are also pressuring (foriegn / foreign) countries to ban seal product imports.

3. According to the pro-sealing movement, animal welfare activists have greatly (exaggerated / exagerrated) the claim that sealing is inhumane. Moreover, sealers argue that the seal hunt provides an income in a region of Canada where jobs are scarce. In addition, sealers also point out that it is (convenient / convienient) to accuse hunters of cruelty to animals simply because baby harp seals are cute.

4. Clearly, the seal hunt arouses different points of view. Each group will continue to influence the other's (jugement / judgment) about the seal hunt, and the seal hunt issue will remain a (dilemma / dillema).

Hint   **Becoming a Better Speller**

These are some useful strategies to improve your spelling.

- In your spelling log, which could be in a journal, binder, or computer file, keep a record of words that you commonly misspell. (See Appendix 5 for more on spelling logs.)
- Use memory cards or flash cards to help you memorize difficult words.
- Write down the spelling of difficult words at least ten times to help you remember how to spell them.
- Always check a dictionary to verify the spelling of difficult words.

FINAL REVIEW

Correct twenty spelling errors in the following selection.

EXAMPLE:

their

Historically, zoos have displayed ~~thier~~ collections of wild animals for public entertainment and profit.

1. Since the begining of civilization, human beings have always enjoyed viewing animals. Originaly, wild animals were captured

and displayed for the pleasure of the upper classes. By the early
twentieth century, zoos were openned to the general public.
Today, the role of zoos is a hotly debated subject in our soceity.

2.   Supporters of zoos argue that in the past two decades, zoos have
tried to acheive different goals and objectives. They claim that
zoos in the Western world have spent millions of dollars on
upgrading facilities by creating truely naturalistic enviroments
for the animals. Furthermore, supporters state that the role of
zoos has become neccesary and educational. Zoos bring to the
public's attention the threat of the extinction of many species,
and zoo breeding programs have helped bring about a noticable
increase in the population of alot of threatened species.

3.   Zoo opponents from countrys around the world beleive that zoos
are imoral prisons for wild animals, and they say that a zoo's only
function is to entertain the public and run a profitable buisness.
According to various animal rights groups, displaying animals in small
cages is cruel, unatural, and unethical. Furthermore, zoo opponents
have questionned the validity of breeding statistics released by zoos.
Animal Aid, an animal rights group in the United Kingdom, argues
that only 2 percent of endangered animals are bred in zoos.

4.   Conservationist Gerald Durrell, who started the Jersey Zoological
Park, has stated that a zoo is successfull if it can contribute to the
conservation of forests and feilds. However, others think that zoos
should be banned. Certainly, everyone should consider whether zoos
are helpfull or harmfull.

The Writer's Room

Write about one of the following topics. After you finish writing, circle any words that you may have misspelled.

1. If you could live in a natural environment, what type of environment would you prefer: a forest, a seashore, a mountain, a desert, a lakefront, or a prairie? Explain your answer.

2. Do you do anything to help conserve the environment? For example, do you recycle or take public transit? What are some steps that you and others can take to help the environment?

3. Examine this photo. What are some terms that come to mind? Some ideas might be *zoo*, *captivity*, or *conservation*. Define a term or expression that relates to this photo.

CHECKLIST: SPELLING RULES

When you edit your writing, ask yourself the next questions.

Do I have any spelling errors? Check for errors in words that contain these elements:

–an *ie* or *ei* combination

–prefixes

–suffixes

(continued)

GRAMMAR LINK

Keep a list of words that you commonly misspell. See Appendix 5 for more about spelling logs.

species   *disappearing*

Many ~~speices~~ of animals and plants are ~~dissappearing~~ from our planet.

☐ Do I repeat spelling errors that I have made in previous assignments? (Each time you write, check previous assignments for errors or consult your spelling log.)

How Do I Get a Better Grade?

Visit www.mywritinglab.com for audio-visual lectures and additional practice sets about spelling.
Get a better grade with MyWritingLab!

CHAPTER 23

Commonly Confused Words

Section Theme: **CREATURES LARGE AND SMALL**

CONTENTS

• Commonly Confused Words

In this chapter, you will read about pet ownership and exotic animals.

Grammar Snapshot

Looking at Commonly Confused Words

In his book *Animal Wonderland*, Frank W. Lane examines experiments with animals. In this excerpt, commonly confused words are underlined.

> A feeding apparatus was installed in a cage whereby a pellet of food fell <u>through</u> a slot when a lever was pressed. Lever and slot <u>were</u> side by side. Three rats were placed one at a time in the cage, and soon each learned <u>to</u> use the lever. <u>Then</u> Mowrer put the lever on the side of the cage opposite the food slot, thus making it necessary for a rat to run from one end of the cage to the other for every <u>piece</u> of food. Again the rats learned, separately, how to obtain <u>their</u> food.

In this chapter, you will identify and use words that sound the same but have different spellings and meanings.

Commonly Confused Words

Some English words can sound the same but are spelled differently and have different meanings. For example, two commonly confused words are *for*, which is a preposition that means "in exchange," and *four*, which is the number. Dictionaries will give you the exact meaning of unfamiliar words.

Here is a list of some commonly confused words.

Commonly Confused Words

	Meaning	**Examples**
accept	to receive; to admit	Presently, the public <u>accepts</u> the need for wildlife preservation.
except	excluding; other than	Everyone in my family <u>except</u> my sister wants a pet.
affect	to influence	Pollution <u>affects</u> our environment in many ways.
effect	the result of something	Deforestation has bad <u>effects</u> on global climate.
been	past participle of the verb *be*	Joy Adamson has <u>been</u> a role model for conservationists.
being	present progressive form (the *-ing* form) of the verb *be*.	She was <u>being</u> very nice when she agreed to give a speech.
by	next to; on; before	Gerald Durell sat <u>by</u> the rocks to film the iguana. He hoped to finish filming <u>by</u> next year.
buy	to purchase	Many people <u>buy</u> exotic animals for pets.
complement	to add to; to complete	The book will <u>complement</u> the library's zoology collection.
compliment	to say something nice about someone or something	Ann Struthers receives many <u>compliments</u> for her book on snakes.

PRACTICE I

Underline the appropriate word in each set of parentheses.

EXAMPLE:

Owners of exotic pets must (<u>accept</u>, except) responsibility for the behavior of these creatures.

1.   Many people (buy, by) exotic animals for pets. Stop (buy, by) some pet stores, and you will see monkeys, snakes, and wild cats. For example, a capuchin monkey is (been, being) displayed at our local pet shop. The monkey has (being, been) on display for three weeks. Evan, a good friend of mine, wants to buy the monkey to (complement, compliment) his menagerie of exotic pets. Everyone,

(accept, except) me, supports Evan's plan. I don't think that Evan would make a good monkey owner.

2.   Capuchin monkeys are tiny and appealing creatures, but they are difficult to care (for, four). Owners must (accept, except) a change in lifestyle because the monkeys require a great deal of attention. For instance, it is difficult to take vacations because the monkeys cannot be left alone. Also, capuchins bond with their owners and are badly (affected, effected) (buy, by) change. They can suffer negative (effects, affects) if the original owner decides to sell the animal.

3.   Certainly, people (compliment, complement) monkeys because the creatures are so cute and human-like. However, monkeys are expensive to house and feed. Those wanting to own monkeys must (accept, except) that they are making a serious long-term commitment.

Commonly Confused Words

	Meaning	Examples
conscience	a personal sense of right or wrong	Poachers have no conscience.
conscious	to be aware; to be awake	The poacher was conscious of his crime.
considered	thought about; kept in mind; judged	Dian Fossey was considered a leader in her field. She never considered leaving Africa.
considerate	thoughtful; understanding; selfless	She was very considerate and patient with the gorillas.
everyday	ordinary; common	Poaching is an everyday occurrence.
every day	during a single day; each day	Government officials search every day for poachers.
find	to locate	Biologists are trying to find the nesting grounds of parrots.
fine	of good quality; a penalty of money for a crime	A robin prepares a fine nest. Poachers must pay a fine when caught.
fun	an experience of amusement	In the past, many people had fun shooting passenger pigeons.
funny	comical; odd	Ostriches look very funny.
its	possessive case of the pronoun *it*	The baby elephant was separated from its herd.
it's	contraction for *it is*	It's known that elephants are very intelligent.

(continued)

	Meaning	Examples
knew	past tense of *know*	We <u>knew</u> that the lioness had three cubs.
new	recent; unused	We used a <u>new</u> camera to film the cubs.
know	to have knowledge of	Photographers <u>know</u> that the public loves pictures of animals.
no	a negative	I have <u>no</u> photos of Bengal tigers.

PRACTICE 2

Underline the appropriate word in each set of parentheses.

EXAMPLE:

Did you (no, <u>know</u>) that snakes cannot hear?

1. Snakes are (considered, considerate) dangerous creatures. Herpetologists, or people who study reptiles, (know, no) that not all snakes are dangerous. However, they are (conscience, conscious) that people, in general, fear snakes. (Its, It's) believed that there are around 2,700 species of snakes in the world today.

2. In the fashion industry, (new, knew) trends are an (everyday, every day) occurrence. Because many trends involve snakeskins, snakes are killed (everyday, every day). Poachers (fine, find) and kill snakes for money. These criminals have (know, no) (conscience, conscious) about their actions. They may receive a (find, fine) if they are caught.

3. I never (new, knew) that people could buy poisonous snakes, but my friend bought one two weeks ago. It ejects venom through (its, it's) fangs. Sometimes it makes (fun, funny) noises. I'm not too crazy about the creature, but my friend has a lot of (fun, funny) with his pet. He is a (considered, considerate) and gentle pet owner.

Commonly Confused Words

	Meaning	Examples
lose	to misplace or forfeit something	If we <u>lose</u> a species to extinction, we will <u>lose</u> a part of our heritage.
loose	too big or too baggy; not fixed	They wear <u>loose</u> clothing at work.
loss	a decrease in an amount; a serious blow	The <u>loss</u> of forests is a serious problem.

	Meaning	**Examples**
past	previous time	In the past, people shot big game for fun.
passed	accepted or sanctioned; past tense of *to pass*	Recently, governments have passed laws forbidding the killing of endangered species.
peace	calm; to stop violence	I feel a sense of peace in the wilderness.
piece	a part of something else	I found a piece of deer antler in the woods.
personal	private	My professor showed us her personal collection of snake photographs.
personnel	employees; staff	The World Wildlife Fund hires a lot of personnel.
principal	main; director of a school	The principal researcher on snakes is Dr. Alain Leduc.
principle	rule or standard	I am studying the principles of ethical research techniques.

PRACTICE 3

Commonly confused words are underlined. Correct six word errors. If the word is correct, write *C* above it.

EXAMPLE:

piece

Sometimes, a snake can regrow its tail if a peace of it breaks off.

1.   India has many species of snakes, and laws have been past

to protect them. One of the best-known snakes in India is the

cobra. It has been worshipped in the past and continues to play

a principle role in the Hindu religion today.

2.   Nagpanchami is a religious festival to honor the cobra. It

is based on Hindu religious principles in which nature plays

an important role. On festival day, many people make a personnel

offering of milk to the cobra. Snake charmers wearing loose

clothing bring snakes into villages and cities. Everyone prays

for piece, and it is customary to eat pieces of sweets during

the holiday.

3.   Snakes are vital to the Indian economy. Without snakes, Indian

farmers would loose a large part of their crops to rodents. The

farmers would not be able to withstand such a lost.

Commonly Confused Words

	Meaning	Example
quiet	silent	It was <u>quiet</u> in the woods.
quite	very	The herd was moving <u>quite</u> fast.
quit	stop	The zoo director <u>quit</u> after receiving a bad report.
sit	to seat oneself	I will <u>sit</u> on this rock to watch the birds.
set	to put or place down	He <u>set</u> his book about birds on the grass.
taught	past tense of *to teach*	Dr. Zavitz <u>taught</u> a class on sharks.
thought	past tense *to think*	His students <u>thought</u> that he was a good teacher.
than	word used in comparisons	Whales are larger <u>than</u> dolphins.
then	at a particular time; after a specific time	The grizzly entered the river, and <u>then</u> it caught some salmon.
that	word used to introduce a clause	Some people do not realize <u>that</u> grizzlies are extremely dangerous.
their	possessive form of *they*	Anita and Ram went to see <u>their</u> favorite documentary on bird migration.
there	a place; something exists	<u>There</u> are many birds in the park. The students went <u>there</u> by bus.
they're	contraction of *they are*	<u>They're</u> both very interested in falcons.

CHAPTER 24

PRACTICE 4

Underline the appropriate word in each set of parentheses.

EXAMPLE:

(<u>There</u>, Their) are many types of exotic birds.

1.   One hundred years ago, parrots were (quiet, quite) common in
tropical countries. Today, (there, their, they're) are about 350 different
types of parrots, each with a distinct size and appearance. With (there,
their, they're) beautiful colors, parrots have become one of the most
sought-after exotic animals.

2.   Some people think (than, then, that) parrots are easy to maintain.
In fact, parrots are more difficult to care for (than, then, that) many
other bird species. For one thing, some types of parrots love to

vocalize, so (there, their, they're) not ideal for owners who want peace and (quite, quiet). Parrots are social creatures (than, then, that) mate for life, and they become very attached to (there, their) owners. They do not like to (sit, set) in one place for long periods of time. Instead, (there, their, they're) happiest when being caressed or permitted to fly around a room. When owners ignore parrots, the birds can develop (quiet, quite) strange behavior. Sara Jorba, for example, rescued a parrot (than, then, that) had become self-destructive. The bird, which had often (being, been) left alone, would pull out (its, it's) own feathers. With a lot of patience, Jorba managed to rehabilitate the bird.

3.   In the (past, passed), people (taught, thought) that parrots simply mimicked human sounds. In fact, recent research has shown (than, then, that) parrots are capable of complex thinking. Irene Pepperberg began studying African gray parrots thirty years ago. (Than, Then, That), after many experiments, she published articles about them. She (taught, thought) a parrot named Alex to recognize about one hundred objects. Alex could differentiate between colors, and he could even count. Pepperberg loves her job and would never (quite, quiet, quit). Nowadays, thanks to her research, gray parrots are (considered, considerate) the most intelligent bird species.

CHAPTER 24

Commonly Confused Words

	Meaning	Examples
through	in one side and out the other; finished	The monkeys climbed through the trees. Although they were still active, we were through for the day.
threw	past tense of *throw*	The monkeys threw fruit down from the tree.
thorough	complete	The biologist did a thorough investigation of monkey behavior.
to	indicates direction or movement; part of an infinitive	I want to go to Africa.
too	*very* or *also*	Kenya is too hot in the summer. It is hot in Somalia, too.
two	the number after one	Africa and the Amazon are two places that intrigue me.

(continued)

	Meaning	**Examples**
write	to draw symbols that represent words	I <u>write</u> about conservation issues for the newspaper.
right	correct; the opposite of *left*	Is this the <u>right</u> way to go to the village? The <u>right</u> turn signal of the jeep does not work.
where	question word indicating location	<u>Where</u> did the zoo keep the gorillas?
were	past tense of *be*	The gorillas <u>were</u> in the enclosure.
we're	contraction of *we are*	<u>We're</u> going to see a film about gorillas.
who's	contraction of *who is*	Makiko, <u>who's</u> a friend of mine, is doing research on lemurs.
whose	pronoun showing ownership	Animals <u>whose</u> habitat is disappearing need to be protected.
you're	contraction of *you are*	<u>You're</u> going on the field trip, aren't you?
your	possessive adjective	<u>Your</u> sister went to the pet store.

PRACTICE 5

In the next sentences, write one of the words in parentheses in each blank.

EXAMPLE:

(We're, Were) ____We're____ going to watch a presentation about primates.

1.   (we're, were, where) _____ learning a lot about chimpanzee

intelligence. In Illinois, research scientists work with Bonono chimps.

Ten years ago, the animals _____ put into a room _____

there were several computers. The chimps _____ able to use

the machines to talk to humans.

2.   (to, two, too) In a 1960 experiment, _____ scientists wanted

_____ communicate with chimps. Allen and Beatrice Gardner

knew that chimps would not be able _____ speak because their

vocal cords are _____ high and _____ short. They

decided _____ teach a chimp American Sign Language.

3.   (threw, through, thorough) We sat outside a lab and watched spider

monkeys _____ a window. The zoologist _____ some food

behind a door. The monkeys smelled the food and did a _____

search of their cage. Then one monkey noticed the door and reached

_____ it to pick up the food. When the experiment was

_____, the zoologist rewarded the monkeys with more food.

4.   (right, write) We plan to _____ an article about the monkey experiment. At the _____ time, we will present our paper to our instructor.

5.   (who's, whose) A zoologist _____ profession involves close contact with various species studies animal habitats. A friend of ours, _____ an excellent zoologist, will receive government funding.

6.   (your, you're) _____ welcome to come with us to a presentation. You can bring _____ friend with you. If _____ late, the presentation will start without you.

FINAL REVIEW

Correct fifteen errors in word choice.

EXAMPLE:

through
The parrot escaped ~~thorough~~ the window.

1.   Recently, more and more pet owners have tried to purchase exotic animals. In many shops, people can by a variety of rats, snakes, and lizards. Ownership of exotic animals has become a passionately debated subject.

2.   Some people believe that it is wrong to keep exotic animals as pets. They argue than exotic animals need to be kept in there natural environment. If they're caged, they will suffer. Furthermore, exotic animals have diseases that can be transmitted to humans. For example, scientists believe that Gambian pouch rats where responsible for the monkeypox virus. Additionally, exotic animals are often released into the wild when they're owners become tired of them. For example, Thomas Sawland, whose a fisherman, found the Chinese snakehead fish thriving in some lakes and killing native fish species. Unfortunately, many owners of exotic pets do not really no

CHAPTER 24

how to take care of their animals because they have never been thought. For example, 90 percent of pet snakes die within the first year of captivity because they have been mistreated.

3.   Owners of exotic pets state that its perfectly reasonable to keep such animals. Proponents say that accept for the occasional case, most exotic pet owners are very responsible and have strong principals. Owners with a strong conscious would never neglect their pets. Moreover, the sale of exotic pets is a huge and profitable business, and many business owners would loose their income if the sale of exotic pets were prohibited. Also, everyday some people abuse dogs and cats, but few people pressure the government to ban the ownership of such pets.

4.   Lawmakers are hoping to past laws that limit the exotic animal market. Some people will support the legislation, and others will oppose it.

 The Writer's Room

Write about one of the following topics. After you finish writing, proofread your paragraph for spelling or word-choice errors.

1. What are some reasons that people own pets? How can pet ownership affect a person's life? Write about the causes or effects of pet ownership.

2. Would you ever own an exotic pet such as a snake, an alligator, or a tiger? Should people have the right to own exotic pets?

 CHECKLIST: COMMONLY CONFUSED WORDS

When you edit your writing, ask yourself whether you have used the correct words. Check for errors with commonly confused words.

My friend Patricia, ~~whose~~ *who's* a veterinarian, believes ~~than~~ *that* pet owners should take courses on how to take care of ~~they're~~ *their* pets.

The Writers' Circle

This activity is similar to the spelling bees we participated in as children. As a team, you will try to spell words from the list of commonly misspelled words on pages 353–354 in Chapter 23.

1. In a team of five students, appoint a leader to write answers and then spell words out loud.

2. Listen carefully to the word your instructor or another student asks your team to spell.

3. Consult with your team members, and, when you come to an agreement, ask the team leader to spell it aloud.

4. If your team spells the word correctly, you get a point. If your team spells the word incorrectly, you lose your turn, and the next team has a chance to spell it. The team with the most points wins.

READING LINK

Creatures Large and Small

To read more about zoology, see the following essay:

"The Zoo Life" by Yann Martel (page 449)

"Shark Bait" by Dave Barry (page 452)

How Do I Get a Better Grade?

Visit www.mywritinglab.com for audio-visual lectures and additional practice sets about commonly confused words. *Get a better grade with MyWritingLab!*

CHAPTER 24

25 Commas

Section Theme: **THE BUSINESS WORLD**

CONTENTS

- Understanding Commas
- Commas in a Series
- Commas After Introductory Words and Phrases
- Commas Around Interrupting Words and Phrases
- Commas in Compound Sentences
- Commas in Complex Sentences
- Commas in Business Letters

In this chapter, you will read about business-related topics, including job searching and unusual jobs.

Grammar Snapshot

Looking at Commas

Jeff Kemp is a former NFL quarterback. In his article "Sports and Life: Lessons to Be Learned," Kemp narrates his experiences as a professional athlete. Notice the use of commas in this excerpt from his article.

In 1988, I was playing for the Seattle Seahawks against my old team, the 49ers, when I learned firsthand that there are two competing value systems. I wasn't bitter that my old team had traded me, but I wanted to beat them all the same. Quarterback Dave Krieg had been injured, and I was to start.

In this chapter, you will learn how to use commas correctly.

Understanding Commas

A **comma (,)** is a punctuation mark that helps keep distinct ideas separate. Commas are especially important in series, after introductory words and phrases, around interrupting words and phrases, and in compound and complex sentences.

Some jobs, especially those in the service industry, pay minimum wage.

Commas in a Series

Use a comma to separate items in a series of three or more items. Remember to put a comma before the final *and* or *or:*

| item 1 | , | item 2 | , | and
or | item 3 |

Series of nouns: The conference will be in <u>Dallas,</u> <u>Houston,</u> <u>Galveston,</u> or <u>Austin</u>.

Series of verbs: During the conference, guests will <u>eat,</u> <u>drink,</u> and <u>network</u>.

Series of phrases: She <u>dressed well,</u> <u>kept her head up,</u> and <u>maintained eye contact</u>.

 **Punctuating a Series**

In a series of three or more items, do not place a comma after the last item in the series (unless the series is part of an interrupting phrase).

His mother, father, and sister were at the ceremony.

Do not use commas to separate items if each item is joined by *and* or *or.*

The audience clapped <u>and</u> cheered <u>and</u> stood up after the speech.

PRACTICE I

Each sentence contains a series of items. Add the missing commas.

EXAMPLE:

John L. Holland, a psychology professor from Johns Hopkins University, has taught students, done research, and published books.

1. According to John L. Holland, the six basic types of jobs include realistic jobs conventional jobs investigative jobs artistic jobs social jobs and leadership jobs.

2. When trying to choose a career, you should try a variety of jobs work in different places and volunteer for various tasks.

3. Realistic jobs involve working with tools large machines or other types of equipment.

4. People who work with tools or machines are usually strong competitive and physically healthy.

5. Bank tellers secretaries office managers and accountants have conventional jobs.

6. People who describe themselves as outgoing cooperative helpful and responsible have social jobs.

7. Eric Townsend wants to be a teacher nurse or social worker.

8. Investigative workers often do market surveys develop military strategies or tackle economic problems.

9. Adela Sanchez is energetic self-confident and ambitious.

10. Sanchez hopes to get a leadership job in sales politics or business.

Commas After Introductory Words and Phrases

Place a comma after an **introductory word**. The word could be an interjection such as *yes* or *no*, an adverb such as *usually*, or a transitional word such as *therefore*.

> Introductory word(s)   ,   sentence   .

Yes, I will help you finish the project.

Honestly, you should reconsider your promise.

However, the job includes a lot of overtime.

Introductory phrases of two or more words should be set off with a comma. The phrase could be a transitional expression such as *of course* or a prepositional phrase such as *in the morning*.

As a matter of fact, the manager explained the new policy.

In the middle of the meeting, Nancy decided to leave.

After his speech, the employees asked questions.

PRACTICE 2

Underline the introductory word or phrase in each sentence. Add fifteen missing commas.

EXAMPLE:

Honestly, interviews can be very stressful.

1.   Before a job interview you should do certain tasks. After contacting the company take some time to prepare for the interview. First of all do some research about the company. As soon as possible you could go on the Internet and find out about the company's performance. Certainly you can impress the hiring committee if you appear knowledgeable about the business.

2.   Undoubtedly talking to new people adds to the stress of a job interview. Nonetheless you can do well if you are confident. In fact try to make direct eye contact with the interviewer. After a difficult question take the time you need to think about it. Of course it is important to answer questions honestly. However try to find a positive spin. For example the interviewer may ask why you left a previous job. At that moment do not criticize your former boss or complain about your former job. Instead simply say that you needed new challenges. Clearly it is important to be positive.

Commas Around Interrupting Words and Phrases

Interrupting words or phrases appear in the middle of sentences. Such interrupters are often asides that break the sentence's flow but do not really affect the meaning.

> Noun   ,   interrupting word(s)   ,   rest of sentence.

My co-worker, <u>for example,</u> has never taken a sick day.
Kyle, <u>frankly,</u> should never drink during business lunches.
The company, <u>in the middle of an economic boom,</u> went bankrupt!

> **Hint**   **Using Commas with Appositives**
>
> An appositive comes before or after a noun or pronoun and adds further information about the noun or pronoun. The appositive can appear at the beginning, in the middle, or at the end of the sentence. Set off appositives with commas.
>
> *beginning*
> <u>An ambitious man,</u> Donald has done well in real estate.
>
> *middle*
> Cancun, <u>a coastal city,</u> depends on tourism.
>
> *end*
> The hotel is next to Alicia's, <u>a local restaurant.</u>

PRACTICE 3

Underline any interrupting phrases, and ensure that the necessary commas are there. If the sentence needs commas, add them. If the sentence is correct, write *C* in the blank.

EXAMPLE:

Some young entrepreneurs, <u>for instance</u>, are very successful. _____

1. Bill Gates, a successful businessman started out as a young entrepreneur. _____

2. Young entrepreneurs, showing ingenuity continue to develop interesting products. _____

3. Mark Zuckerberg, for example was a young college student when he and his friends developed Facebook. _____

4. Facebook a social Internet site, was first aimed at Harvard undergraduates in 2004. _____

5. Since then, millions of people have become members of Facebook. _____

6. Evan Williams another young entrepreneur, created one of the first Web applications for blogs. _____

7. Google bought Williams's Web site, Blogger.com in 2003. _____

8. YouTube one of the fastest growing Web sites, was launched in 2006. _____

9. Three young friends, former PayPal employees created this popular site. _____

10. Risk takers, with insight and skill are finding creative ways to profit from the Internet. _____

PRACTICE 4

Add ten missing commas to the following passages.

EXAMPLE:

Life coaches, funeral directors, and square dance callers are people who have out-of-the-ordinary careers.

1.   Many people have interesting, fulfilling and unique jobs. Newton Proust is a freelance greeting card writer. He writes verses for birthday cards graduation cards, and sympathy cards. He feels that the sentiments expressed in a greeting card bring people together. To express accurate

CHAPTER 25

emotions Mr. Proust studies the latest cultural trends. In fact he constantly reads magazines, comic strips and pulp fiction to acquire knowledge of what people are thinking and feeling.

2.   Angelica Pedersen a master coffee taster, travels to coffee-producing regions around the world. She works for Blue Coffee a small business. However the company is a supplier to some of the biggest coffee retailers in North America. Ms. Pedersen, an experienced professional must develop the perfect blend of coffee for her clients. She smells and tastes about three hundred cups of coffee per day. Clearly she loves her job and would not consider doing anything else.

Commas in Compound Sentences

A **compound sentence** contains two or more complete sentences joined by a coordinating conjunction (*for, and, nor, but, or, yet, so*).

> Sentence   , and   sentence.

The job is interesting, **and** the pay is decent.

The job requires fluency in Spanish, **so** maybe I will be hired.

Michael works as a bank teller, **but** he is looking for a better position.

Hint   **Commas and Coordinators**

You do not always have to put a comma before coordinating conjunctions such as *and, but,* or *or.* To ensure that a sentence is truly compound, cover the conjunction with your finger and read the two parts of the sentence.

• If each part of the sentence contains a complete idea, then you need to add a comma.

>   **Comma:**   Anna does marketing surveys, and she sells products.

• If one part is incomplete, then no comma is necessary.

>   **No comma:**   Anna does marketing surveys and sells products.

PRACTICE 5

Add six missing commas to the following letter.

EXAMPLE:

I am honest, and I am hardworking.

Dear Mr. Yamasaki,

I am looking for work and I saw an ad in the <u>Boston Globe</u> stating that your clinic needs a nurse. I am a nursing student and have just completed my studies. I am interested in the job so I have enclosed a résumé highlighting my skills in this field.

Your advertised position mentions shift work but this would not be a problem for me. I am able to work the day or night shift. I also know that nursing requires both physical strength and emotional stability and I have both of those qualities.

I am available for an interview at any time so please do not hesitate to contact me. Thank you for your consideration and I look forward to hearing from you.

Yours truly,

Jamilla Shabbaz

Jamilla Shabbaz

Commas in Complex Sentences

A **complex sentence** contains one or more dependent clauses (or incomplete ideas). When a **subordinating conjunction**—a word such as *because*, *although*, or *unless*—is added to a clause, it makes the clause dependent.

dependent clause   independent clause

When <u>opportunity knocks</u>, you should embrace it.

Use a Comma After a Dependent Clause

If a sentence begins with a dependent clause, place a comma after the clause. Remember that a dependent clause has a subject and a verb, but it cannot stand alone. When the subordinating conjunction comes in the middle of the sentence, it is not necessary to use a comma.

Dependent clause   **,**   main clause.

Comma: Because she loves helping people, she is studying nursing.

Main clause   **dependent clause.**

No comma: She is studying nursing <u>because she loves helping people</u>.

PRACTICE 6

Edit the following sentences by adding or deleting commas. If a sentence is correct, write *C* in the blank.

EXAMPLE:

Before she went to the interview, Ellen removed her eyebrow ring.   _____

1. Because first impressions count, it is important to dress well for an interview. _____

2. Before you leave the house review your wardrobe. _____

3. Although your current boss may accept casual clothing, your future boss may object. _____

4. Monica Zacharias wants to work as a restaurant manager, because she is ambitious. _____

5. Although she loves her tattoos she will cover them with clothing during the interview. _____

6. After she gets the job Zacharias will dress to show her personality. _____

7. When Clayton Townsend wore a T-shirt and baggy pants to the interview he was not hired. _____

8. Because Townsend wanted to be hired, he should have tried to make a better impression. _____

9. After she left her job as a personnel director Amy Rowen started an employment consulting business. _____

10. According to Rowen, unless job applicants want to work in an artistic milieu they should wear conservative clothing to interviews. _____

Use Commas with Nonrestrictive Clauses

Clauses beginning with *who*, *that*, and *which* can be restrictive or nonrestrictive. A **restrictive clause** contains essential information about the subject. Do not place commas around restrictive clauses.

No commas: The woman <u>who invented the windshield wiper</u> never became wealthy.

(The clause is essential to understand the sentence.)

A **nonrestrictive clause** gives nonessential information. In such sentences, the clause gives additional information about the noun, but it does not restrict or define the noun. Place commas around nonrestrictive clauses.

Commas: The restaurant, <u>which is on Labelle Boulevard,</u> has excellent seafood.

(The clause contains extra information. If you removed it, the sentence would still have a clear meaning.)

Hint: Using *Which, That,* and *Who*

which
Use commas to set off clauses that begin with *which*.

> Apple Computer, **which** started in 1976, was co-founded by Steve Wozniak and Steve Jobs.

that
Do not use commas to set off clauses that begin with *that*.

> One product **that** changed the world was the personal computer.

who
When a clause begins with *who*, you may or may not need a comma. If the clause contains nonessential information, put commas around it. If the clause is essential to the meaning of the sentence, then it does not require commas.

> **Essential:** The man **who** employs me uses Apple computers.
>
> **Not essential:** Steve Jobs, **who** has four children, is a billionaire.

PRACTICE 7

Each sentence contains a clause beginning with *who*, *which*, or *that*. Underline the clause, and then set it off with commas, if necessary.

EXAMPLE:

People <u>who do not want mainstream jobs</u> can work in various fields.

1. Jobs that are unusual can provide people with entertaining stories.

2. Lyle Baker who lived in Vancouver worked for the police department.

3. The department which had several police dogs trained the animals to find criminals.

4. Lyle who was a student acted as prey for the police dogs.

5. A piece of clothing that Lyle had worn would be shown to the dogs.

6. The job which required quick reflexes involved hiding from the animals.

7. Lyle who was young and agile would hide in the nearby woods.

8. Lyle's protective gear which included a plastic bat and a padded leather armpiece usually kept him safe.

9. One experience that left a scar on his leg occurred during the training.

10. A dog that found Lyle tried to pull him out of a tree.

11. Today, the scar which appears on Lyle's ankle is a souvenir from his summer job.

12. People who have scars usually have interesting stories to tell.

CHAPTER 25

Commas in Business Letters

When you write or type formal correspondence, ensure that you use commas correctly in all parts of the letter.

Addresses

In the address at the top of a business letter, put a comma between these elements.

- The street and apartment number
- The city and state or country

Do not put a comma before the zip code.

> Anita Buchinsky
>
> XYZ Company
>
> 11 Maple Lane, Suite 450
>   ^
> Brownfield, Texas 79316
>   ^

If you include an address inside a complete sentence, use commas to separate the street address from the city as well as the city from the state or country. If you include only the street address, do not put a comma after it.

Commas: The building at 1600 Pennsylvania Avenue,

Washington, D.C., is called the White House.
          ^   ^

No comma: The building at 1600 Pennsylvania Avenue is called

the White House.

Dates

In the date at the top of the letter, put a comma between the full date and the year. If you write just the month and the year, then no comma is necessary.

> January 28, 2008   January 2008
>   ^

If you include a date inside a complete sentence, separate the elements of the date with commas.

> We flew to Dallas on Friday, March 14, 2008.
>   ^   ^

 **Writing Numbers**

In business letters, do not write ordinals, which are numbers such as *first* (1st), *second* (2nd), *third* (3rd), and *fourth* (4th). Instead, write just the number *1, 2, 3, 4,* and so on.

> May 13, 2004   September 25, 1954

Salutations

Salutations are formal letter greetings. The form "To Whom It May Concern" is no longer used regularly. The best way to address someone is to use the recipient's name followed by a comma.

Dear Ms. Cheng,	Dear Mrs. Kulkarni,	Dear Sir or Madam,
Dear Miss Kim,	Dear Mr. Copely,	Dear Claims Department,

Complimentary Closings

Capitalize the first word of a complimentary closing, and place a comma after the closing. Here are some formal complimentary closings.

Respectfully,	Sincerely,	Yours truly,
Respectfully yours,	Yours sincerely,	Many thanks,

PRACTICE 8

Add eight missing commas to the following business letter.

Amanda Sitlali
33 Green Avenue
Las Vegas NV 89101

September 4 2008

Elwood River Rafting
1771 Center Street
Redwood Falls MN 56283

Dear Mr. Elwood

On Tuesday August 2 2008, I went on a river rafting expedition with your company. When I returned home, I realized that I had lost a bracelet. It may have dropped inside the raft. The bracelet is made of gold, and it has great sentimental value.

If you have found it, please contact my parents. They live at 34 Reed Avenue Redwood Falls. Their phone number is 309-555-3933.

Yours truly

Amanda Sitlali

Amanda Sitlali

FINAL REVIEW

Edit the following essay by adding or removing commas. There are seventeen missing commas and three unnecessary commas.

EXAMPLE:

Some workers, especially those in sales' travel on a regular basis.

1.   On March 11, 2008 when I went to the airport for a winter vacation I saw several passengers in business suits with laptop computers. The passenger who was sitting beside me typed on his laptop during most of the flight. After we had spoken for a few minutes this man, Antonio Morales, told me about his travel fatigue. Morales who has a job at Anderson Plastics, spends over 180 days a year on the road. On the day we met, he had to fly to Los Angeles drive to San Diego and return to Los Angeles within twenty-four hours. Many people think that workplace travel is glamorous, because business travelers visit exotic places. Those who travel on a regular basis, however can have physical and psychological problems.

2.   Alina Tugend, a writer for the *New York Times* has written about the stressed business traveler. According to Tugend business travel is not as exciting as it appears. Frequent travel which is defined as six or more business trips each year can cause eating, sleeping and breathing disorders. It can also cause serious heart problems, that require hospitalization. Executive Ted Burke, for example had a stroke that may have been linked to his long hours spent on airplanes.

3.   The World Bank, which conducted a study in 1997 looked at health-care claim forms that were filed by workers. According to the study, male workers who traveled extensively filed 80 percent more forms than their colleagues, who did not travel. My travel companion, for example suffers from stress-related ailments.

4.   Businesses should reconsider the travel schedules of employees. Perhaps frequent travelers should be given days off to recuperate after trips and they should also be given fewer responsibilities after returning to work. If corporate culture does not change, good employees will leave their jobs. For example, although he loves working in sales Morales is looking for a new job that requires less travel.

The Writer's Room

Write about one of the following topics. After you finish writing, make sure that you have used commas correctly.

1. Would you like to have a job that includes a lot of travel? List some reasons for your answer.

2. Have you, or has someone you know, ever had an interesting or unusual job? Describe the job.

CHECKLIST: COMMAS

When you edit your writing, ask yourself the following questions.

Do I use commas correctly in series of items?
The store sells bikes, inline skates, and skateboards.

Do I use commas correctly after introductory words or phrases?
In fact, many sportswear companies hire athletes to promote their products.

Do I use commas correctly around interrupting words and phrases?
The campaign, in my opinion, is extremely creative.

Do I use commas correctly in compound sentences?
The advertisement is unusual, and it is quite shocking.

Do I use commas correctly in complex sentences?
When the commercial airs, the company will track viewer responses.
The company, which was founded in 1998, is very successful.

How Do I Get a Better Grade?

mywritinglab Visit www.mywritinglab.com for audio-visual lectures and additional practice sets about commas.
Get a better grade with MyWritingLab!

The Apostrophe

Section Theme: **THE BUSINESS WORLD**

CONTENTS

- Understanding Apostrophes
- Using Apostrophes in Contractions
- Using Apostrophes to Show Ownership
- Using Apostrophes in Expressions of Time

In this chapter, you will read about controversies in the business world.

Grammar Snapshot

Looking at Apostrophes

This excerpt is taken from the article "How to Handle Conflict" by P. Gregory Smith. Review the underlined words.

> "I <u>don't</u> mind doing my fair share of the dirty jobs around here," Ramon continued, "but I feel like <u>I'm</u> getting a lot more mop time than anyone else." By using a statement that began with "I," Ramon was able to state his feelings honestly, without accusing Mr. Jefferson. "I" statements usually <u>can't</u> be considered false or cause an argument because <u>they're</u> a simple statement of feelings.

In this chapter, you will learn to use apostrophes correctly.

Understanding Apostrophes

An **apostrophe** (') is a punctuation mark. It shows that two words have been contracted into one word, or it shows ownership.

Richard's business is new, but **it's** growing.

Using Apostrophes in Contractions

A **contraction** is two words joined into one. When you contract two words, the apostrophe generally indicates the location of the omitted letter(s).

is + not = isn't   I + am = I'm

 **Formal Writing**

Do not use contractions when you write a formal academic paper. For example, in a literary analysis, you would not use contractions.

Common Contractions

There are two types of common contractions. You can join a verb with *not*; you can also join a subject and a verb.

Verb + *not*

When a verb joins with *not*, the apostrophe replaces the letter *o* in *not*.

Common Contractions	
is + not = isn't	has + not = hasn't
are + not = aren't	have + not = haven't
could + not = couldn't	must not = mustn't
do + not = don't	should + not = shouldn't
does + not = doesn't	would + not = wouldn't

Exception: can + not = can't, will + not = won't

PRACTICE I

Write contractions for the underlined words in the next sentences.

EXAMPLE:

don't

Many American companies <u>do not</u> think twice about outsourcing to other countries.

1. If you plan to get information about a credit card, chances are great that

   you <u>will not</u> speak to an American customer service representative.

2. It <u>is not</u> unusual to speak with a person from another part of the world.

3. You <u>would not</u> even know that he or she <u>is not</u> an American.

4. He or she <u>does not</u> have an accent when speaking English.

5. Also, you <u>should not</u> be surprised that the person at the call center knows everything about American culture.

6. Companies outsource because they <u>do not</u> have to pay high salaries in other nations.

Subject + Verb

When you join a subject and a verb, you must remove one or more letters to form the contraction.

Contractions with *be*
I + am = I'm
he + is = he's
it + is = it's
she + is = she's
they + are = they're
we + are = we're
you + are = you're
who + is = who's

Contractions with *will*
I + will = I'll
he + will = he'll
it + will = it'll
she + will = she'll
they + will = they'll
we + will = we'll
you + will = you'll
who + will = who'll

Contractions with *have*
I + have = I've
he + has = he's
it + has = it's
she + has = she's
they + have = they've
we + have = we've
you + have = you've
who + has = who's

Contractions with *had* or *would*
I + had *or* would = I'd
he + had *or* would = he'd
it + had *or* would = it'd
she + had *or* would = she'd
they + had *or* would = they'd
we + had *or* would = we'd
you + had *or* would = you'd
who + had *or* would = who'd

Exception: Do not contract a subject with the past tense of *be*. For example, do not contract *he + was* or *they + were*.

she was
When you asked her about the product, ~~she's~~ not helpful.

They were
The sales staff were in a meeting. ~~They're~~ discussing new products.

Hint **Contractions with Proper Nouns**

You can contract a proper noun with the verb *be* or *have*.

Shania is   *Deiter has*

Shania's late for work. **Deiter's** been waiting for her since 9 a.m.

PRACTICE 2

Add the missing apostrophes to the underlined words in this selection.

EXAMPLE:

who's

Daniel Pink is a journalist <u>whos</u> written articles for *Wired* magazine.

1. In "The New Face of the Silicon Age," Daniel Pink describes Americans who are losing their jobs because of outsourcing. He mentions Aparna Jairam, a computer programmer <u>whos</u> thirty-three years old. <u>Shes</u> worked in various jobs in the software industry. Currently, <u>shes</u> working for Hexaware Technologies in Mumbai, India. Compared to U.S. programmers, she <u>doesnt</u> earn a high salary. However, <u>shes</u> happy with her job, and <u>shed</u> like to keep it.

2. According to Pink, many Americans are worried that people like Jairam are stealing their jobs. For example, Scott Kirwin, a Delaware programmer, says that <u>hes</u> angry about the situation. In 2007, he lost his job when his employer outsourced the work of his entire department. <u>Hes</u> been trying to get members of Congress to do something about outsourcing.

3. Executives know that <u>theyre</u> cutting costs by outsourcing. Highly qualified Indian or Chinese workers can do the same jobs as Americans for a fraction of the cost. For U.S. companies, <u>its</u> about the bottom line, or profit maximization. On the other hand, massive changes in the agricultural and manufacturing sectors have occurred before, and the workplace has adjusted with jobs opening up in entirely new sectors. Perhaps <u>its</u> difficult right now, but the job situation may improve in the future.

CHAPTER 26

 **Contractions with Two Meanings**

Sometimes one contraction can have two different meanings.

I'd = I had *or* I would   **he's** = he is *or* he has

When you read, you can usually figure out the meaning of the contraction by looking at the words in context.

     He is   *He has*
He's starting up a new company. **He's** had three successful businesses.

PRACTICE 3

Look at each underlined contraction, and then write out the complete word.

EXAMPLE:

He'd like to hire more people.   *He would*_____

1. Hanif's a chocolatier.   _____

2. He's been working at his present job for three years.   _____

3. His company's been providing chocolate fountains to catering services.   _____

4. He'd like to expand the business.   _____

5. When we met last year, I was impressed because I'd never seen such a hardworking person before.   _____

Using Apostrophes to Show Ownership

Possession means that someone or something owns something else. Nouns and indefinite pronouns such as *anyone* and *everyone* use an apostrophe to show ownership.

    the office of the businessman = the businessman's office

Singular Nouns: To show possession of singular nouns, add -'s to the end of the singular noun.

    Sheila's mother works as a dispatcher.

    Everyone's computer was upgraded.

Even if the noun ends in *s*, you must still add -'s.

    Dennis's dad helped him find a job.

    My **boss's** assistant arranges her schedule.

Plural Nouns: To show possession when a plural noun ends in *s*, add just an apostrophe.

Many **employees'** savings are in pension plans.

Taxi drivers' licenses are regulated.

Add -*'s* to irregular plural nouns to indicate ownership.

That **men's** magazine is very successful.

The **children's** toy department is on the main floor.

Compound Nouns: When two people have joint ownership, add the apostrophe to the second name only.

joint ownership

Mason and **Muhammad's** restaurant is successful.

(They share ownership of a restaurant.)

When two people have separate ownership, add apostrophes to both names.

separate ownership

Mason's and **Muhammad's** cars are parked in the garage.

(They each own a car.)

PRACTICE 4

Write the possessive forms using apostrophes.

EXAMPLE:

the office of Nicolas   *Nicolas's office*

1. the bank account of James   _____
2. the committee of the ladies   _____
3. the company of Matt and Harrison   _____
4. the promotion of the manager   _____
5. the desks of Marcia and Lewis   _____
6. the building of the company   _____
7. the club of the women   _____
8. the accounting book of Dolores   _____
9. the work force of China   _____
10. the lawyers of the Smiths   _____

PRACTICE 5

Correct nine errors in possessive forms.

EXAMPLE:

company's

The ~~companys~~ profits are very high this year.

CHAPTER 26

1. Nike has become synonymous with Americas corporate success. Nikes' beginnings are very interesting. The business started from the back of Phil Knights car in the early 1960s. In 1963, Knight went to Japan. By chance, he met with Japanese businessmen who manufactured running shoes. At the businessmens' meeting, Knight asked to import Japanese running shoes to America.

2. Back in the United States, Knight taught an accounting class at Portland State University. In the departments hallway, he saw several design student's work. He commissioned student Carolyn Davidson to come up with a design. Davidsons swoosh symbol became Nikes logo. At the time, she was paid only $35 for her design. However, several years later, Knight presented her with an envelope containing some of the companys stock. Davidson says that she has been adequately compensated for her design.

Using Apostrophes in Expressions of Time

If an expression of time (year, week, month, or day) appears to possess something, you can add an apostrophe plus -*s*.

> My mother won a **month's** supply of groceries.

> Eve Sinclair gave **three weeks'** notice before she left her job.

When you write out a year in numerals, you can use an apostrophe to replace the missing numbers.

> The graduates of the class of **'04** often networked with each other.

However, if you are writing the numeral of a decade or century, do not put an apostrophe before the final *s*.

> In the **1800s,** many farmers took factory jobs in nearby towns.

> Many investors lost money in the **1990s.**

 **Common Apostrophe Errors**

- Do not use apostrophes before the final *s* of a verb.

  wants
  Zaid ~~want's~~ to start a new business.

- Do not confuse contractions with possessive pronouns that have a similar sound. For example, the contraction *you're* sounds like the pronoun *your*. Remember that possessive pronouns never have apostrophes.

  Its
  The corner store is new. ~~It's~~ owner is very nice.

  theirs
  That is our account. It is not ~~their's~~.

PRACTICE 6

Correct the apostrophe mistakes in each sentence.

EXAMPLE:

your
I saw ~~you're~~ friend at the meeting.

1. Its well known that many clothing manufacturers receive criticism for poor working conditions of employees in Third World countries.

2. Theres documented evidence that these workers are usually underpaid.

3. For example, Nikes directors have admitted that there was a problem in Indonesia in the late 1990's.

4. In 2001, Nike realized that its' Indonesian plant managers were abusing workers.

5. Kathie Lee Giffords clothing line for Wal-Mart was manufactured in Honduras.

6. In 1995, reports revealed that the plants employees were working under terrible conditions.

7. Gifford publicly acknowledged that working condition's had to be improved.

8. Mitsumi work's as a buyer for an internationally known clothing company.

9. Her companys official policy is to buy clothing from manufacturers who

   pay fair wages.

10. As a consumer, I!! always try to be well informed about the things that I buy.

FINAL REVIEW

Correct fifteen apostrophe errors. Apostrophes may be used incorrectly, or there
may be errors with possessive nouns.

EXAMPLE:

    don't   *shouldn't*
If you ~~dont~~ like the product, you ~~should'nt~~ buy it.

1. The worlds largest company is Wal-Mart. Its larger than
    Exxon, Microsoft, or General Electric. In the 1990's, Wal-Mart's
    expansion into Mexico, Canada, and many other nations
    occurred. Mexico City and Toronto's stores have been
    extremely successful.

2. Wal-Mart's company policy is to supply it's customers with
    the cheapest prices possible. Customers are happy because theyre
    getting good deals. However, some Wal-Mart suppliers are'nt as
    thrilled.

3. In an article for *Fast Company* magazine, Charles Fishman
    examines Wal-Marts pricing policies. According to Fishman,
    suppliers for Wal-Mart are pressured to reduce prices. When
    prices are too low, it force's them out of business. For example,
    Fishman mentions the Loveable Company, which used to supply
    lingerie to Wal-Mart. Executives at Wal-Mart asked the
    company to lower its prices. Loveable refused. Within three
    year's, Loveable went out of business.

4. On the other hand, some suppliers say that theres a positive
    outcome when they supply to Wal-Mart. Most companies

manufacturing practices must become very efficient in order to supply Wal-Mart with low-cost products. Also, many suppliers want to do business with Wal-Mart because they can get huge boosts in their sales.

5. Consumer's also benefit from pricing policies at Wal-Mart. Families' with low incomes can afford to shop there for quality products. Many consumers budgets are helped by the low cost of goods at Wal-Mart.

The Writer's Room

Write about one of the following topics. After you finish writing, underline any words with apostrophes, and verify that you have correctly used the apostrophes.

1. Do you enjoy shopping, or do you consider it to be a tedious chore? Describe your shopping personality.

2. Think about at least three types of jobs. Divide your topic into categories and find a classification principle. For example, you could write about jobs that are high stress, medium stress, and low stress.

3. Define a term or expression that relates to the photo. Examples are *plugged in*, *drone*, or *workaholic*.

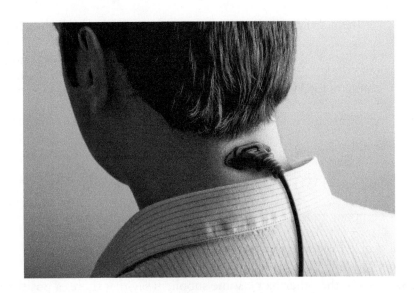

CHECKLIST: APOSTROPHES

When you edit your writing, ask yourself the next questions.

Do I use the apostrophe correctly in contractions? Check for errors in these cases:

- —contractions of verbs + *not*
- —contractions with subjects and verbs

　　shouldn't　　　　　　*Weston's*
You ~~should'nt~~ be surprised that ~~Westons'~~ going to be a consultant in China.

Do I use the apostrophe correctly to show possession? Check for errors in these possessives:

- —singular nouns (*the student's*)
- —plural nouns (*the students'*)
- —irregular plural nouns (*the women's*)
- —compound nouns (*Joe's and Mike's motorcycles*)

Chris's
~~Chris'~~ company gave him the use of a car.

Do I place apostrophes where they do not belong? Check for errors in these cases:

- —possessive pronouns
- —spelling of third-person singular present tense verbs

　looks　　　　　　　　　*its*
It ~~look's~~ like my company is moving ~~it's~~ headquarters to Tokyo.

How Do I Get a Better Grade?

Visit www.mywritinglab.com for audio-visual lectures and additional practice sets about the apostrophe.
Get a better grade with MyWritingLab!

CHAPTER 26

Quotation Marks and Capitalization

Section Theme: **THE BUSINESS WORLD**

CONTENT

- Direct and Indirect Quotations
- Quotation Marks
- Capitalization
- Titles

In this chapter, you will read about business success stories.

Grammar Snapshot

Looking at Quotation Marks

This excerpt is taken from Ben Carson's autobiography, *Gifted Hands*. The quotation marks and associated capital letters are underlined.

> One of the counselors at our high school, Alma Whittley, knew my predicament and was very understanding. One day I poured out my story, and she listened with obvious concern. "I've got a few connections with the Ford Motor Company," she said. While I sat next to her desk, she phoned their world headquarters. I particularly remember her saying, "Look, we have this young fellow here named Ben Carson. He's very bright and already has a scholarship to go to Yale in September. Right now the boy needs a job to save money for this fall." She paused to listen, and I heard her add, "You have to give him a job."

In this chapter, you will learn how to use direct quotations correctly. You will also learn about capitalization and punctuation of titles.

Direct and Indirect Quotations

A **direct quotation** reproduces the exact words of a speaker or writer. An **indirect quotation,** however, simply summarizes someone's words. Indirect quotations often begin with *that.*

Direct quotation: Mrs. Delaware said, "I'm moving to a new office."

Indirect quotation: Mrs. Delaware said **that** she was moving to a new office.

The next sections discuss proper capitalization and punctuation of direct quotations.

Quotation Marks

Use **quotation marks** (" ") to set off the exact words of a speaker or writer. If the quotation is a complete sentence, there are some standard ways that it should be punctuated.

- Capitalize the first word of the quotation.
- Place quotation marks around the complete quotation.
- Place the end punctuation inside the closing quotation marks.

Generally, attach the name of the speaker or writer to the quotation in some way.

. . . said,   **"Complete sentence."**

Mrs. Delaware said, "You are hired."

Using Quotation Marks with an Introductory Phrase

When the quotation is introduced by a phrase, place a comma after the introductory phrase.

. . . says,   "_____."

Miguel Lanthier says, "You should feel passionate about your work."

PRACTICE I

Place quotation marks around the direct quotations in the following sentences. Add capitals and other punctuation where necessary.

EXAMPLE:

Beverly Sills stated , "You ~~you~~ may be disappointed if you fail, but you are doomed if you don't try."

1. According to businessman J. C. Penney   every business is built on friendship.

2. Mahatma Gandhi once said   you must be the change you wish to see in the world.

3. Booker T. Washington, a political pundit, stated   success is to be measured not so much by the position that one has reached in life as by the obstacles one has overcome.

4. Senator Dianne Feinstein said   toughness doesn't have to come in a pinstripe suit.

5. General Norman Schwarzkopf declared   when placed in command, take charge.

Using Quotation Marks with an Interrupting Phrase

When the quotation is interrupted, do the following:

- Place a comma after the first part of the quotation.
- Place a comma after the interrupting phrase.

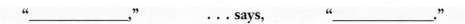

"To cultivate kindness," said essayist Samuel Johnson, "is a valuable part of business life."

PRACTICE 2

Place quotation marks around the direct quotations in the following sentences. Add capital letters and other punctuation marks where necessary.

EXAMPLE:

One chance, said Jessie Owens, is all you need.

1. Hard work without talent is a shame said entrepreneur Robert Half but talent without hard work is a tragedy.

2. I like Mr. Gorbachev remarked former British Prime Minister Margaret Thatcher so we can do business together.

3. Whether you think you can said famous automaker Henry Ford or whether you think you can't, you're right!

4. When you're riding declared jockey Bill Shoemaker only the race in which you're riding is important.

CHAPTER 27

5. Singleness of purpose is one of the chief essentials for success in life said

   millionaire John D. Rockefeller no matter what may be one's aim.

Using Quotation Marks with an End Phrase

When you place a phrase at the end of a quotation, end the quotation with a comma instead of a period.

> "_____,"   **says** . . . .

"There's no business like show business," said Irving Berlin.

If your quotation ends with another punctuation mark, put it inside the ending quotation mark.

> "_____?"   **says** . . . .

"Don't do that!" he yelled.

"Why did you hire her?" she asked.

PRACTICE 3

Place quotation marks around the direct quotations in the following sentences. Add capital letters and other punctuation marks where necessary.

EXAMPLE:

"
You're never beaten until you admit it," said General George S. Patton.

1. To succeed in business or to reach the top, an individual must know all it is

   possible to know about that business stated businessman John Paul Getty.

2. The first one gets the oyster and the second one gets the shell! said steel

   magnate Andrew Carnegie.

3. We fall forward to succeed declared Mary Kay Ash, the founder of Mary

   Kay Cosmetics.

4. Power is the ability to do good things for others said philanthropist

   Brooke Astor.

5. What I do best is share my enthusiasm stated Bill Gates, the founder of

   Microsoft.

Using Quotation Marks with an Introductory Sentence

You can introduce a quotation with a complete sentence. Place a colon (:) after the introductory sentence.

> **He explains his views: "_____."**

Writer William Feather explains his views on parenthood: "Setting a good example for children takes all the fun out of middle age." ^

PRACTICE 4

Place quotation marks around the direct quotations in the following sentences. Add capital letters and other punctuation marks where necessary.

EXAMPLE:

The philosopher Friedrich Nietzsche explained perseverance ~~what~~ : "What doesn't kill us makes us stronger. "

1. Entrepreneur P. D. Armour expressed his views anybody can cut prices, but it takes a brain to produce a better article.

2. Malcolm Forbes, a magazine publisher, discusses how to succeed try hard enough.

3. Spanish writer Miguel Cervantes referred to his success to be prepared is half the victory.

4. We discussed the words of Norman Vincent Peale it's always too soon to quit.

5. Philanthropist Thomas Dewar discusses human minds they only function when open.

6. Ayn Rand, a philosopher and writer, ponders success the ladder of success is best climbed by stepping on the rungs of opportunity.

PRACTICE 5

Place quotation marks around the direct quotations in bold print. Add capital letters and punctuation marks to the direct quotations.

EXAMPLE:

My supervisor Lisa said , "Learn ~~learn~~ **from the words of Henry Ford.** "

1. Henry Ford often said **an idealist is a person who helps other people to prosper.** Ford's innovations changed the American way of life. Before his Model T, only two out of ten Americans lived in a city. By World War II, that number had changed significantly.

2. Ford was born in 1863, on a farm near Dearborn, Michigan. Since his childhood, Ford experimented with mechanical objects. He was determined to manufacture cars. **You can't build a reputation on what you are going to do** he once stated. In 1903, he became the vice president of the Ford Motor Company and started to build cars.

3. Ford was a risk taker. His contemporaries thought that his company would be successful if he built expensive cars for the rich, but he was against that idea. **There is one rule for the industrialist** Ford often said **and that is make the best quality of goods possible, at the lowest cost possible, and pay the highest wages possible.**

4. In 1908, he introduced the Model T, which was affordable for a large number of people. Some customers asked for the car in other colors, to which Ford said **people can have the Model T in any color so long as it's black.** To meet the growing demand for the car, Ford introduced the assembly line in 1913. Ford explained **nothing is particularly hard if you divide it into small jobs.** The assembly line made car production quick and efficient. By 1913, the Ford Motor Company had become the largest car manufacturing company in the world. Ford summed up his life philosophy **you can do anything if you have enthusiasm.**

Capitalization

Remember to always capitalize the following:

- The pronoun *I*
- The first word of every sentence

    My coworkers and **I** share an office.

There are many other instances in which you must use capital letters. Always capitalize the following:

- **Days of the week, months, and holidays**

    Wednesday   January 1   New Year's Eve

Do not capitalize the seasons: summer, fall, winter, spring.

- **Titles of specific institutions, departments, companies, and schools**

    IBM   U.S. **D**epartment   Pinewood
                 of **D**efense   Elementary **S**chool

Do not capitalize general references.

    the company   the department   the school

- **Names of specific places, such as buildings, streets, parks, cities, states, and bodies of water**

    Dale **S**treet   Times **S**quare   Los Angeles, California
    Central **P**ark   Mississippi   Lake Erie

Do not capitalize general references.

    the street   the state   the lake

- **Names of specific languages, nationalities, tribes, races, and religions**

    Portuguese   Navaho   Buddhist   an **I**talian restaurant

- **Titles of specific individuals**

    General Eisenhower   President Kennedy   Dr. Marcos
    Professor **W**ong   Prime Minister Blair   Mrs. Eleanor Roosevelt

If you are referring to the profession in general, or if the title follows the name, do not use capital letters.

    a senator   my professor   the doctors

- **Titles of specific courses and programs**

    Mathematics 201   Civil Engineering 100   Beginner's Spanish

If you refer to a course but do not mention the course title, then it is not necessary to use capitals.

    He is in economics.   I study hard for my civil engineering class.

- **The major words in titles of literary or artistic works**

  The Lord of the Rings   *The Bourne Identity*   *War and Peace*

- **Names of historical events, eras, and movements**

  the **K**orean **W**ar   **I**mpressionism   the **I**ndustrial **R**evolution

 **Capitalizing Computer Terms**

Always capitalize the following computer terms.

Internet   World Wide Web

Capitalize software titles as you would any other published work.

Netscape   Microsoft Office

PRACTICE 6

Add any necessary capital letters to the following sentences.

EXAMPLE:

I often forget to call my father on ~~f~~ather's ~~d~~ay.
(F above "father's"; D above "day")

1. Samuel Gompers founded the American federation of Labor.

2. He believed that Labor day was created to recognize the achievements of the american worker.

3. It is generally believed that Matthew McGuire, from paterson, new jersey, proposed a workers' holiday.

4. McGuire was the secretary of the Central Labor union in New york.

5. The first Labor Day holiday was actually on tuesday, september 5, 1882.

6. Eventually, in 1884, the first monday of September was proposed as the holiday.

7. On february 21, 1887, oregon became the first state to legislate Labor Day as a legal holiday.

8. I work for a company called golden flowers, which is a flower wholesaler.

9. Each year, my company has a picnic and golf tournament near lake ambrosia to celebrate Labor Day.

10. The president of our company, ms. Kahn, gives a speech.

11. We raise money for the United way.

12. Our annual Labor Day event is reported in our daily newspaper, *The Phoenix mail.*

Titles

Punctuating Titles

Place the title of a short work in quotation marks. Underline (or italicize, if you are using a computer) the title of a longer document.

Short Works		Long Works	
Short story:	"The Bear"	**Novel:**	The Da Vinci Code
Chapter:	"Abbreviations"	**Book:**	MLA Handbook for Writers of Research Papers
Newspaper article:	"Missing in Action"	**Newspaper:**	New York Times
Magazine article:	"History's Fools"	**Magazine:**	Newsweek
Web article:	"Music Artists Lose Out"	**Web site:**	Blackbeat.com
Essay:	"Neighborhoods of the Globe"	**Textbook:**	Essentials of Sociology
TV episode:	"Shrunk"	**TV series:**	Lost
Song:	"Naughty Girl"	**CD:**	Dangerously in Love
Poem:	"The List of Famous Hats"	**Collection:**	Reckoner

Capitalizing Titles

When you write a title, capitalize the first letter of the first word and all the major words. Do not capitalize the letters *.com* in a Web address.

This Side of Paradise   Monster.com   "Lucy in the Sky with Diamonds"

Also, do not capitalize the following words, except as the first or last word in a title.

Articles:	a, an, the
Coordinators:	but, and, or, nor, for, so, yet
Short prepositions:	of, to, in, off, out, up, by

PRACTICE 7

Add ten capital letters to the next paragraph. Also, add quotation marks or underlining to six titles.

EXAMPLE:

Ayn Rand's book <u>A</u>nthem begins with strong words: "It was a sin to write this."

Ayn Rand, a writer and philosopher, was born in 1905 in st. petersburg, Russia. Her most famous novel, The fountainhead, was published in 1943. Her next novel was Atlas shrugged. Rand proposed that self-interest should guide people, and her views have been widely debated. Michael Shermer criticized Rand in a magazine called skeptics. He compares her followers to sheep in the article The Unlikeliest cult in history. Rand also has numerous supporters, and her philosophy, objectivism, has been analyzed by many distinguished thinkers. Peter St. Andre, for example, wrote the essay Why I Am a libertarian, which appeared in the magazine full context. Rand's books continue to sell millions of copies, and her supporters have created numerous Web sites to promote her work and philosophy.

FINAL REVIEW

A. Add three missing capital letters, and properly punctuate the two quotations in bold point.

EXAMPLE:

                                  W
Graham Lopez was born in Seattle, ~~w~~ashington.

The labor movement has an interesting history in the united states. There are many proponents and opponents of unionization. Graham Lopez is a member of the United Auto workers Union. He believes that unions help workers get better pay and social and health benefits. Neela Subramanyam works for a small car parts company. There is no union at her company. **None of the workers want one** she says **because they believe that unions create disharmony between managers and workers.** Subramanyam also believes that unions support mediocrity. **It is hard to remove union members who do not do their jobs** she argues.

B. Add seven missing capital letters, and properly punctuate three titles.

EXAMPLE:

There was an article about unions in the magazine called ~~f~~ortune 500.

        I read about the history of the union movement in a book called Working Detroit: The Making of a union town. The United auto Workers Union started in 1935, in Detroit, michigan. One of the most famous union strikes was at the Ford motor company. Henry Ford was against unionization. In the magazine The Industry standard, Kevin Baker wrote an article called Ford's Paradox. Baker discussed how Ford increased car sales by raising the wages of his workers. However, Baker also stated that Ford was so powerful that he could cut workers' wages at a whim. Nowadays, a president could not make such a decision alone.

The Writer's Room

Write about one of the following topics. After you finish writing, circle any words that you have capitalized or directly quoted.

1. Have you, or has anyone you know, ever worked in a unionized workplace? Compare or contrast a unionized and a nonunionized workplace.
2. What are some things that you should do to get your dream job? List at least five steps that you should take.

CHECKLIST: QUOTATION MARKS AND CAPITALIZATION

When you edit your writing, ask yourself the next questions.

Are there any direct quotations in my writing? Check for errors with these elements:

–punctuation before or after quotations

–capital letters

–placement of quotation marks

READING LINK

The Business World

To read more about the business world, see the next essays:

"How to Handle Conflict" by P. Gregory Smith (page 455)

"Meet the Zippies" by Thomas L. Friedman (page 460)

"The Rewards of Dirty Work" by Linda L. Lindsey and Stephen Beach (page 462)

"   ,"
You're fired said Donald Trump to his latest apprentice.

Do my sentences have all the necessary capital letters?

             I   War
About two years ago, ~~i~~ saw a movie about World ~~war~~ II.

Are the titles of artistic works properly punctuated?

                                        Saving Private
Steven Spielberg directed the award-winning movie ~~Saving private~~
Ryan
~~ryan.~~

The Writers' Circle

Work with a partner. Take turns reading a dialogue from an essay at the back of this book. Write down everything that your partner says. When you are both finished, exchange papers, compare them with the original essays, and mark any misspelled words or incorrectly placed punctuation or quotations marks. Here are some suggested readings.

"Birth" (page 423), paragraphs 3 to 8 (stop at the word _condemnation_)

"The Appalling Truth" (page 433), paragraphs 3 to 9 (stop at the words _Mr. Ed._)

In a dialogue, begin a new paragraph every time the speaker changes.

How Do I Get a Better Grade?

mywritinglab   Visit www.mywritinglab.com for audio-visual lectures and additional practice sets about quotation marks and capitalization.
Get a better grade with MyWritingLab!

CHAPTER 27

Reading Strategies and Selections

In Chapter 29, you will learn strategies that can help you improve your reading skills. Then, you will read a number of thought-provoking essays that present a wide range of viewpoints about topics related to human history and habits, entertainment and culture, beliefs, politics, relationships, the earth and its creatures, and the business world. The predominant writing pattern of each essay is shown in parentheses.

HUMAN HISTORY, HABITS, AND RELATIONSHIPS
- Reading 1: "Fish Cheeks" by Amy Tan, page 421   (Description)
- Reading 2: "Birth" by Maya Angelou, page 423   (Narration)
- Reading 3: "The Cult of Emaciation" by Ben Barry, page 425   (Cause and Effect)
- Reading 4: "For Marriage" Kirsteen Macleod, page 429   (Argument)
- Reading 5: "Against Marriage" by Winston Murray, page 430   (Argument)

ENTERTAINMENT, CULTURE, AND BELIEFS
- Reading 6: "The Appalling Truth" by Dorothy Nixon, page 433   (Illustration)
- Reading 7: "The New Addiction" by Josh Freed, page 436   (Comparison and Contrast)
- Reading 8: "Sports and Life: Lessons to Be Learned" by Jeff Kemp, page 439   (Narration)
- Reading 9: "What's Your Humor Style?" by Louise Dobson, page 441   (Classification)
- Reading 10: "The Hijab" by Naheed Mustafa, page 444   (Definition)

THE EARTH AND ITS CREATURES
- Reading 11: "What It Feels Like to Walk on the Moon" by Buzz Aldrin, page 447   (Description)
- Reading 12: "The Zoo Life" by Yann Martel, page 449   (Comparison and Contrast)
- Reading 13: "Shark Bait" by Dave Barry, page 452   (Narration)

POLITICS AND THE BUSINESS WORLD
- Reading 14: "How to Handle Conflict" by P. Gregory Smith, page 455   (Process)
- Reading 15: "How to Remember Names" by Roger Seip, page 457   (Process)
- Reading 16: "Meet the Zippies" by Thomas L. Friedman, page 460   (Definition)
- Reading 17: "The Rewards of Dirty Work" by Linda L. Lindsey and Stephen Beach, page 462   (Illustration)

CHAPTER 29

CONTENTS

- Reading Strategies
- Reading Selections

Aspiring sculptors study historical and contemporary works to learn about composition, technique, and material. In the same way, by reading different types of writing, you can observe how other writers develop their essays.

Reading Strategies

Reading helps you develop your writing skills. Each time you read, you accomplish these goals.

- Expand your vocabulary.
- Learn how other writers develop topics.
- Learn to recognize and use different writing patterns.
- Find ideas for your own paragraphs and essays.

The strategies discussed in this chapter can help you become a more successful reader and writer.

Previewing

When you **preview** a passage, you quickly look at key points. You can get a general sense of a passage's topic and main ideas by checking visual clues.

- Read the title and the main headings.
- Look at the first and last sentence of the introduction.
- Look at the first sentence of each paragraph.

- Look at the concluding sentences in the essay.
- Review any photos, graphs, or charts, and read the captions that accompany them.

Previewing helps you prepare for the next step, which is reading the essay.

Taking Notes

To help you remember and quickly find the important points in a text, you can highlight key ideas and make annotations. An **annotation** is a comment, question, or reaction that you write in the margin of a passage.

Highlighting and Making Annotations

Each time you read a passage, do the following:

- Look at the introductory and concluding paragraphs, and underline sentences that sum up the main idea.
- Using your own words, write the main idea in the margin.
- Underline or highlight supporting ideas. You might even want to number the arguments or ideas. This will allow you to understand the essay's development.
- Circle words that you do not understand.
- Write questions in the margin if you do not understand the author's meaning.
- Write notes beside passages that are interesting or that relate to your own experiences.
- Jot down possible writing topics.

If you are reading a library book, or if you have borrowed a book from somebody else, use sticky notes to make annotations. Do not write in the book!

A Highlighted and Annotated Passage

Is this true? ➤

How could racism be a cause of death? ➤

Main point is that police harassment causes stress for minorities. ➤

Who is Norman Podhoretz? ➤

What is vantage? ➤

1   Black Americans live shorter lives than whites and are more likely to suffer stress-related maladies like high blood pressure, which contributes to stroke and heart attack. The medical profession has yet to list "racism" as a cause of death. But some social scientists now see tension related to discrimination as a health hazard on par with smoking and a high-fat diet. Among the day-to-day acts of discrimination that shadow African-Americans, none are more stressful or dangerous than those committed by police, some of whom treat black people as criminals until proved otherwise.

2   The situation is largely invisible to whites, many of whom see the complaints as a function of what the writer Norman Podhoretz once described as "paranoid touchiness" among black people. Not all whites hold the Podhoretz view, of course, and the current police scandals in New York City and New Jersey are broadening the vantage point on this problem. When these sagas are over, millions of white people who thought black people paranoid will have substantial insight into a nightmarish reality that whites barely glimpse but that black people live through day after day.

—Brent Staples, "When the Paranoids Turn Out to Be Right"

Understanding Unfamiliar Words

When you read, you will sometimes come across an unfamiliar word. You can try to guess the word's meaning, or you can circle it and look it up later.

Use Context Clues

Context clues are hints in the text that help define a word. To find a word's meaning, try the next steps.

1. **Determine the word's function.** For example, is it a noun, a verb, or an adjective? Sometimes you can understand a word if you know how it functions in the sentence.

2. **Look at surrounding words.** Try to find a relation between the difficult word and the words that surround it. Maybe there is a **synonym** (a word that means the same thing) or an **antonym** (a word that means the opposite). Maybe other words in the sentence help define the word.

3. **Look at surrounding sentences.** Look at the sentences, paragraphs, and punctuation surrounding the word. If you use logic, you may understand what the word means.

PRACTICE I

Can you define the word *heed?* _____ Yes _____ No

Can you define *yearn?* _____ Yes _____ No

If you do not understand the meaning of those two words, then read the words in context in the next example. You will notice that it is much easier to guess their meanings in context.

> Travel makes it impossible to pay no **heed** to the suffering of others, simply because they are far away. It erases distance, and makes you a more sensitive citizen of the world, **yearning** for peace everywhere.
>
> —Arthur Frommer, "How Travel Changed My Life"

Now write your own definitions of the words.

1. heed: _____

2. yearn: _____

 **Cognates**

Cognates, also known as word twins, are English words that may look and sound like words in another language. For example, the English word *graduation* is similar to the Spanish word *graduacion*, but it is spelled differently.

If English is not your first language, and you see an English word that looks similar to a word in your language, check how the word is being used in context. It may, or may not, mean the same thing in English that it means in your language.

For example, in English, *deception* means "to deliberately mislead someone." In Spanish, *decepcion* means "disappointment." If you are not sure of a word's meaning, consult a dictionary.

Use a Dictionary

If you are unable to understand the meaning of an unfamiliar word by using context clues, then you should look up the word in a dictionary. Review the following tips for proper dictionary usage.

- Look at the preface and notes in your dictionary. The preface contains explanations about the various symbols and abbreviations. Find out what your dictionary has to offer.
- Some words have many definitions. When you are looking up a word, *do not stop after you read the first meaning!* Keep reading, and look for the meaning that best fits the context of your sentence.
- If the difficult word has a prefix such as *un-* or *mis-*, you may have to look up the root word.

For example, the word *sensible* has the following definitions.

Word-Break Divisions
Your dictionary may use heavy black dots to indicate places for dividing words.

Stress Symbol (') and Pronunciation
Some dictionaries provide the phonetic pronunciation of words. The stress symbol (') lets you know which syllable is stressed.

Parts of Speech
This means that *sensible* is an adjective. If you don't understand the "parts of speech" symbol, look in the front or the back of your dictionary for a list of symbols and their meanings.

sen•si•ble /(sen'sə-bəl)/ *adj* 1. reasonable. 2. aware; cognizant. 3. perceptible through the senses. 4. capable of sensation.

From *The New American Webster Handy College Dictionary,*
New York: Signet, 2000

Writing About the Reading

After you finish reading a text, you may have to answer questions about it or write about it. There are several steps you can take to help you better understand a reading passage.

- **Summarize** the reading. When you summarize, you use your own words to write a condensed version of the reading. You leave out all information except for the main points.
- **Outline** the reading. An outline is a visual plan of the reading. First, write the main idea of the essay, and then write the most important idea from each paragraph. Under each idea, you can include a detail or an example.

Respond to the Reading

Before you make a written response to the reading, ask yourself the next questions.

- What is the writer's main point?
- What is the writer's purpose: to entertain, to persuade, or to inform?

- Who is the intended reader? Is the writer directing the message at someone like me?
- What is my opinion of the reading?
- What aspects of the topic can I relate to?

Reading Selections

Theme: **Human History, Habits, and Relationships**

READING I

Fish Cheeks
Amy Tan

> Amy Tan, the author of the best-selling novel *The Joy Luck Club*, wrote this essay for an issue of *Seventeen* magazine. Using vivid detail, Tan describes a family dinner. As you read, notice how the author uses mainly description but also elements of narration and illustration.

1   I fell in love with the minister's son the winter I turned fourteen. He was not Chinese but as white as Mary in the manger. For Christmas, I prayed for this blond-haired boy, Robert, and a slim new American nose.

2   When I found out that my parents had invited the minister's family over for Christmas Eve dinner, I cried. What would Robert think of our shabby Chinese Christmas? What would he think of our noisy Chinese relatives who lacked proper American manners? What terrible disappointment would he feel upon seeing not a roasted turkey and sweet potatoes but Chinese food?

3   On Christmas Eve, I saw that my mother had outdone herself in creating a strange menu. She was pulling black veins out of the backs of fleshy prawns. The kitchen was littered with appalling mounds of raw food: a slimy rock cod with bulging eyes that pleaded not to be thrown into a pan of hot oil; tofu, which looked like stacked wedges of rubbery white sponges; a bowl soaking dried fungus back to life; and a plate of squid, their backs crisscrossed with knife markings so they resembled bicycle tires.

4   And then they arrived—the minister's family and all my relatives in a clamor of doorbells and rumpled Christmas packages. Robert grunted hello, and I pretended he was not worthy of existence.

5   Dinner threw me deeper into despair. My relatives licked the ends of their chopsticks and reached across the table, dipping them into the dozen or so plates of food. Robert and his family waited patiently for platters to be passed to them. My relatives murmured with pleasure when my mother brought out the whole steamed fish. Robert grimaced. Then my father poked his chopsticks just below the fish eye and plucked out the soft meat. "Amy, your favorite," he said, offering me the tender fish cheek. I wanted to disappear.

6   At the end of the meal, my father leaned back and belched loudly, thanking my mother for her fine cooking. "It's a polite Chinese custom to show you are satisfied," explained my father to our astonished guests. Robert was looking down at his plate with a reddened face. The minister managed

to muster up a quiet burp. I was stunned into silence for the rest of the night.

7 After everyone had gone, my mother said to me, "You want to be the same as American girls on the outside." She handed me an early gift. It was a miniskirt in beige tweed. "But inside you must always be Chinese. You must be proud you are different. Your only shame is to have shame."

8 And even though I didn't agree with her then, I knew that she understood how much I had suffered during the evening's dinner. It wasn't until many years later—long after I had gotten over my crush on Robert—that I was able to fully appreciate her lesson and the true purpose behind our particular menu. For Christmas Eve that year, she had chosen all my favorite foods.

Vocabulary and Comprehension

1. What is the meaning of *muster* in paragraph 6?
   a. To summon up or create
   b. To gather
   c. A yellow sauce

2. What three reasons does Tan give for her embarrassment when Robert comes for dinner? Use your own words.

   _____

   _____

   _____

3. What lesson was the author's mother trying to teach her?

   _____

   _____

4. On the surface, Tan's purpose is to entertain, but what is her deeper purpose?

   _____

   _____

5. Tan uses descriptive imagery. Imagery includes active verbs, adjectives, and other words that appeal to the senses (sight, smell, touch, sound, taste). Highlight at least five examples of imagery.

Grammar Link

6. Underline six adjectives in paragraph 3. Then circle the nouns that the adjectives modify. Discuss how the adjectives make the writing more vivid.

7. Identify six irregular past tense verbs not including the verb *be*. Write the present- and past-tense forms of each verb on the lines provided.

   _____   _____

   _____   _____

   _____   _____

DISCUSSION AND WRITING

8. Think about a time when you felt different from others. Explain what happened. Try to use some descriptive vocabulary.
9. What are the possible causes for a person to give up his or her own cultural traditions (language, dress, food, ceremonies, etc.)? What are the effects when people lose their cultural distinctiveness? Discuss the causes or effects of losing cultural traditions.

READING 2

Birth

Maya Angelou

Maya Angelou is an award-winning author. In this selection from her best-known autobiographical work, *I Know Why the Caged Bird Sings*, Angelou writes about the birth of her son. As you read, notice how the author uses mainly narration but also elements of description and cause and effect writing.

1   Two days after V-Day, I stood with the San Francisco Summer School class at Mission High School and received my diploma. That evening, in the bosom of the now-dear family home, I uncoiled my fearful secret, and in a brave gesture left a note on Daddy Clidell's bed. It read, "Dear Parents, I am sorry to bring this disgrace upon the family, but I am pregnant. Marguerite."

2   The confusion that ensued when I explained to my stepfather that I expected to deliver the baby in three weeks, more or less, was **reminiscent** of a **Molière** comedy. Daddy Clidell told Mother that I was "three weeks gone." Mother, regarding me as a woman for the first time, said indignantly, "She's more than any three weeks." They both accepted the fact that I was further along than they had first been told but found it nearly impossible to believe that I had carried a baby, eight months and one week, without their being any the wiser.

> **reminiscent:** similar to
>
> **Molière:** a French playwright (1622–1673)

3   Mother asked, "Who is the boy?" I told her. She recalled him, faintly.

4   "Do you want to marry him?"

5   "No."

6   "Does he want to marry you?" The father had stopped speaking to me during my fourth month.

7   "No."

8   "Well, that's that. No use ruining three lives." There was no **overt** or subtle **condemnation.**

> **overt:** evident, open
>
> **condemnation:** criticism; disapproval

9   Daddy Clidell assured me that I had nothing to worry about. He sent one of his waitresses to I. Magnin's to buy maternity dresses for me. For the next two weeks, I whirled around the city going to doctors, taking vitamin shots and pills, buying clothes for the baby, and except for the rare moments alone, enjoying the **imminent** blessed event.

> **imminent:** forthcoming, soon to arrive

10 After a short labor, and without too much pain (I decided that the pain of delivery was overrated), my son was born. Just as gratefulness was confused in my mind with love, so possession became mixed up with motherhood. I had a baby. He was beautiful and mine. No one had bought him for me. No one had helped me endure the sickly gray months. I had had help in the child's conception, but no one could deny that I had had an **immaculate** pregnancy.

> **immaculate:** untainted by other people's knowledge and actions (in the biblical sense of Immaculate Conception)

11   I was afraid to touch him. Home from the hospital, I sat for hours by his bassinet and absorbed his mysterious perfection. His extremities were so dainty they appeared unfinished. Mother handled him easily with the casual confidence of a baby nurse, but I dreaded being forced to change his diapers. Wasn't I famous for awkwardness? Suppose I let him slip, or put my fingers on that throbbing pulse on the top of his head?

12   Mother came to my bed one night bringing my three-week-old baby. She pulled the cover back and told me to get up and hold him while she put rubber sheets on my bed. She explained that he was going to sleep with me.

13   I begged in vain. I was sure to roll over and crush out his life or break those fragile bones. She wouldn't hear of it, and within minutes the pretty golden baby was lying on his back in the center of my bed, laughing at me.

14   I lay on the edge of the bed, stiff with fear, and vowed not to sleep all night long. But the eat-sleep routine I had begun in the hospital, and kept up under Mother's dictatorial command, got the better of me. I dropped off.

15   My shoulder was shaken gently. Mother whispered, "Maya, wake up. But don't move."

16   I knew immediately that the awakening had to do with the baby. I tensed. "I'm awake."

17   She turned the light on and said, "Look at the baby." My fears were so powerful I couldn't move to look at the center of the bed. She said again, "Look at the baby." I didn't hear sadness in her voice, and that helped me to break the bonds of terror. The baby was no longer in the center of the bed. At first I thought he had moved. But after closer investigation, I found that I was lying on my stomach with my arm bent at a right angle. Under the tent of blanket, which was poled by my elbow and forearm, the baby slept touching my side.

18   Mother whispered, "See, you don't have to think about doing the right thing. If you're for the right thing, then you do it without thinking."

19   She turned out the light, and I patted my son's body lightly and went back to sleep.

VOCABULARY AND COMPREHENSION

1.   In paragraph 10, Angelou says, "I had had help in the child's conception, but no one could deny that I had had an immaculate pregnancy." Why does she call her pregnancy *immaculate?*

_____

_____

_____

2.   How does Angelou's family react to the pregnancy?

_____

3.   In paragraph 11, the author says that she was afraid to touch her own baby. Why did she feel this way?

_____

4.   Were her fears well-founded? Why or why not?

_____

_____

5. What does the reading suggest about becoming a parent?

_____

_____

Grammar Link

6. The author uses quotations in her narration. How do the quotations enhance the story?

_____

_____

7. Angelou uses the following vivid verbs. Look at the verbs in the paragraphs. Then write two or three synonyms next to each verb.

whirled (paragraph 9) _____

handled (paragraph 11) _____

dreaded (paragraph 11) _____

begged (paragraph 13) _____

Discussion and Writing

8. In paragraph 18, the author's mother says, "See, you don't have to think about doing the right thing." Do you agree that people instinctively know how to become parents? Explain your answer.

9. The author acted impulsively when she was an adolescent. Write about an impulsive act that you did when you were an adolescent. What happened, and what were the consequences? Try to use some descriptive language in your writing.

READING 3

The Cult of Emaciation

Ben Barry

> Ben Barry is CEO of Ben Barry Agency, a model consultancy in Toronto. A graduate of Cambridge University, Barry is the author of _Fashioning Reality_. As you read this cause and effect essay, notice how the author also uses narration and description.

1   On this final day of L'Oreal Fashion Week, Canada's top models are strutting their stuff in Toronto. For some, this will have been their first chance to walk the runway. Others will be veterans of the global catwalk circuit. But they will all have one thing in common: extreme, some would say freakish, thinness.

2   Models are the stars of every fashion week. Sure, designers create the outfits, but the models bring those clothes to life. Their faces and bodies saturate our televisions, newspapers, and computer screens. Models are the ones with glamour on tap, the kind of glamour we all supposedly want to taste.

3   For the past nine years, since I was fifteen years old, I have attended countless fashion shows. I was initially an up-and-coming modeling agent sneaking into the shows through back doors. I eventually became established, and I was officially invited to sit among the fashion elite. "Ben, you're so lucky," my friends bemoan, "going to fashion shows and meeting the models. It must all be so glamorous." They plead to be invited just to one show. Just to meet one model. Just to be glamorous, too. That sad truth is that I have always found fashion modeling to be a tragic and demeaning experience.

4   In the days before a fashion week begins, models rush to meet with designers for castings. The designers flip through models' portfolios, ask them to walk the length of the room, have them try on articles of clothing, and of course, take their pictures. The models are in and out without saying anything more than "yes" and "thank you." When asked what these designers remember about the models, they respond, "her size." Physical attributes constitute the only job requirement.

5   Things start going wrong for many models right away. At one casting, "Ashley," nineteen years old, size zero, 5'10", is asked to try on a pair of trousers. After a couple of minutes of struggling to close the top button, the designer marches over. "Your hips are too big, you need to make them smaller," he says in front of all the other models before shooing her out the door. Ashley leaves, humiliated and confused, wondering how she is supposed to alter the size of her hips.

6   The girls who do get booked for shows aren't allowed to leave their body stress behind them. Backstage is where things get really frightening. At London Fashion Week in 2007, I took it all in. One model, "Jennifer," was trying to close a zipper on her designer jacket. The designer stood before her, shaking his head. "You've gotten fat," he said to the eighteen-year-old, size zero model. "I'll need to let this jacket out. It will ruin the cut. They're not made for big girls like you." Jennifer turned red. She managed to hold back her tears as the designer made his adjustments, and everyone stopped to gawk.

7   On another occasion, I witnessed an equally thin model get even worse treatment when she couldn't fit into her size zero dress. The designer pointed to another model and proclaimed, "She'll wear the dress instead. Your stomach has gotten too big. Dismissed!" The girl tried to hide between the racks of clothing while she peeled off the tiny dress. She was later escorted out as everyone stared.

8   The situation is worse for mature models; we are talking about anyone older than twenty. Most begin their careers at a time when their body shape is still pre-pubescent. They get older, they develop curves, and bye-bye sample sizes. I met Rena, twenty-two years old, size two, backstage at London Fashion Week. She told me that this had to be her last season. "I can't handle it any more. Every time I do a show now, I get so anxious. There are so many teenage girls. I'm on Slim-Fast, but there's no way I can compete any longer." I offered her an apple. "No, thanks," she replied. "My agent said fruit causes bloating." I assured her that there is no fat in fruit, but she didn't care.

9   Megan, sixteen years old, put it this way: "No matter how skinny you are, you always think you can be skinnier, and there are other girls that are going to be skinnier than you." If the very women representing the beauty ideal feel excluded from it, how can anyone feel included?

10   Agents are always there to make sure a model's weight remains first and foremost in her mind. Rebecca, eighteen years old, dropped by her agency before a casting to surprise her hard-working booker with a latte. Her kindness was repaid by her being unexpectedly weighed and measured in front of everyone who happened to be there.

11   Constant public humiliation—whether at the casting, the fashion show, or the agency—is the norm in the so-called glamorous life of a model. Everyone in the fashion world, from the agents to the designers to the make-up artists, feels he or she has a God-given right to comment on a model's appearance. And everyone is prepared to tell painfully thin models that they need to be thinner. Such comments would amount to harassment in any other profession.

12   It is no wonder that many models develop eating disorders. No one values their thoughts, personalities, or feelings. Everyone values them for their bodies alone. In time, models internalize the dangerous idea that they are worth what they look like. I have met many models who had a passion for politics or writing or basketball when they first started. Two or three years later, any other interests are squelched to make way for a deep and abiding obsession with weight and appearance. The sad irony is the qualities that make supermodels—the ones who rise to the very top of the industry exude energy, attitude, and character with every strut and pose—are progressively stripped away by the casting process when it comes to most girls.

13   Fashion industry insiders claim that they are not to blame for any deaths by malnutrition. Those are isolated incidents. The ways models are treated and valued supposedly has nothing to do with the tragedies. I beg to differ. Just You Tube any episode of *Top Model* and watch how girls are transformed in front of your eyes from multi-faceted, confident young women to weight-obsessed, insecure wrecks. The heartrending incidents are the result of working within an industry that objectifies women, which, in turn, teaches them to objectify themselves.

14   This must sound very hypocritical coming from a modeling agent. But I do things differently. My models span all ages, sizes, colors, and abilities. They are accepted, promoted, and hired based on their natural physical attributes. I don't represent any models full-time. They go to school, work as doctors and sales clerks, and run their own businesses. Modeling is something they do on the side for a few days every month— a performance to which they bring their varied experiences to bear.

15   I don't expect our entire "glamorous" modeling industry to follow my example overnight. What can we do to protect the wellbeing of models in the short term? L'Oreal Fashion Week needs to follow the lead of event organizers in Madrid and Milan by mandating medical tests for each model to ensure they are of healthy weight. Let them feel like they can get away with eating an apple now and then.

16   In the long run, we should go all the way and make true body diversity the fashion: models of all ages, sizes, colors, and abilities. Body diversity on the catwalks might be attainable. The March, 2007, issue of *Vogue*, arguably the most powerful fashion player in the world, featured size 12/14 Jennifer Hudson on its cover. If *Vogue* can do it, L'Oreal Fashion Week can give it a shot.

17   Any major fashion house choosing such a strategy would receive international attention. For those worried about the bottom line, diversity

would allow consumers to relate to the models, relate to the brand, and demonstrate that positive relationship through spending power. Most significantly, women reading magazines and watching fashion television who say, "I could never look like that," will be free to rediscover themselves. Then, and only then, will modeling truly be a glamorous life.

VOCABULARY AND COMPREHENSION

1. Using context clues, define *bemoan* as it is used in paragraph 3.

    _____

2. Underline the thesis statement of the essay. Remember that it may not be in the first paragraph of the text.

3. How does the writer support his point that modeling is demeaning?

    _____

    _____

4. How does life in the modeling industry affect the models?

    _____

    _____

    _____

5. What is the main problem that Ben Barry identifies in the fashion industry?

    _____

    _____

6. What solution does Barry suggest to help solve the problem?

    _____

    _____

GRAMMAR LINK

7. In the first sentence of paragraph 3, the author writes *have attended*, using the present perfect form of the verb. Why does he use the present perfect instead of the simple past (*attended*)?

    _____

    _____

8a. In paragraph 3, the writer uses sentence fragments, which are incomplete sentences. Correct the fragments.

    _____

    _____

8b. Why does he use sentence fragments in paragraph 3?

    _____

    _____

9. In the second sentence in paragraph 4, why does the word *models'* have an apostrophe after the final *s* rather than before the final *s*?

    _____

    _____

DISCUSSION AND WRITING

10.   How does the entertainment industry reinforce unrealistic or negative body images? Give examples to support your point.
11.   Barry suggests that the modeling industry has contributed to the rise in eating disorders. What other factors cause people to develop eating disorders?
12.   What can the fashion industry and the media do to provide viewers with more positive body images? Give examples to support your point.

Readings 4 and 5: Two Views About Marriage

The next two essays provide opposing viewpoints about the institution of marriage. Read both essays, and then answer the questions that follow.

READING 4

For Marriage
Kirsteen Macleod

> British medical student Kirsteen Macleod is a member of the Cambridge debating team. She wrote this argument essay as part of a debating competition in which she had to defend the institution of marriage.

1   Marriage is arguably losing its appeal, claim many social scientists and tabloid journalists. With one out of every three marriages ending in divorce, the institution of marriage as a religious and legal bond may be considered outdated in today's society. Cohabitation is no longer unacceptable; indeed, it is commonplace among the youth of today, and illegitimacy no longer carries a social stigma. However, the marital bond helps maintain a stable family environment.

2   Just because some marriages may fail, it does not mean that we should give up on an ideal. Marriage statistics show that one out of three marriages is a remarriage; therefore, such statistics actually suggest that people continue to have faith in marriage as an institution. We are frequently disillusioned by the criminal justice system when it fails, but we support the principles it upholds in society. The same can be said for marriage.

3   Furthermore, marriage is still important because it presents a rational view of what a loving and committed relationship is. Passionate love is **transient,** so it is important to have a foundation that holds couples together. True love includes friendship, support, trust, and commitment, and it is more lasting than feelings of passionate love.

transient: temporary; of short duration

4   Legally, marriage represents a solid and protected base for both parties, whereas cohabitation does not. Marital laws provide financial protection for a surviving spouse after the death of the partner. In addition, if a couple does decide to separate, each partner gets a fair share of the marital property and access to the children. Most importantly, spouses may decide to work harder at the relationship because they are bound together by a legal as well as an emotional contract.

5   Marriage as an institution still retains its validity. It provides families with stability, especially regarding the children's welfare. Spouses are more protected financially when they are legally married than when they simply live together. Because marriage is a socially recognized symbol of love and commitment, we should continue to support it.

READING 5

Against Marriage
Winston Murray

College student Winston Murray attacks the institution of marriage in the next argument essay.

1   My friends Donna and Doug want a fairy-tale wedding. They believe that marriage will provide them with a lifelong partner. They hope to live happily ever after in their dream home with their two children and their dog. However, it is not necessary to get married to have a committed, long-term relationship.

2   A marriage certificate does not guarantee that a relationship will be happy and long lasting. One out of three marriages ends up in divorce, and married partners often take each other for granted and feel trapped. Cohabiting partners, on the other hand, choose to be together. Indeed, many cohabiting couples have stronger and longer-lasting relationships than married couples. If one partner does not hold up his or her end of the relationship, the other partner can simply leave. Thus, cohabiting partners often treat each other better than married partners do. Ultimately, if people want to be together, they do not need a piece of paper to unite them. If they want to split up, the formal bond of matrimony simply creates a longer and more painful separation process.

3   Couples do not need marriage to provide children with a stable home environment. Actors Goldie Hawn and Kurt Russell have had a common-law relationship for over twenty years. Together, they have raised Goldie's two children, Kate and Oliver, and they have had one child together. They claim that they are as devoted to each other and to their children as any married couple would be.

4   Moreover, there are laws that protect couples who live together. If a separated couple has children, for example, both partners are legally responsible for the financial support of the children. Also, many jurisdictions have laws protecting the property rights of common-law spouses. In fact, fifteen states recognize common-law relationships and accord them the same rights and obligations as legal marriages.

5   Finally, weddings are expensive and extravagant affairs that indebt families for years to come. Parents of the bride and groom often take out second mortgages to give their children the ideal wedding. After paying for the wedding dress, they must pay for the reception hall, flowers, music, catering, and limousines to have a one-night party. Common-law couples are under no obligation to have an expensive ceremony. They can, if they choose, celebrate their partnership, but they do not have societal pressure to put on an elaborate affair.

6   Marriage is an old-fashioned institution that no longer needs to be protected or supported. It is extremely expensive to have a wedding, and it is also costly to get a divorce. Common-law relationships are now socially acceptable and popular. Therefore, if you plan to have a long-term relationship, consider having a common-law partnership.

VOCABULARY AND COMPREHENSION

1. What introduction style does Macleod use in Reading 4?
   a. Anecdote   c. Historical
   b. General   d. Contrasting position
2. What introduction style does Murray use in Reading 5?
   a. Anecdote   c. Historical
   b. General   d. Contrasting position
3. Underline the thesis statement in each essay.
4. Write two different terms that mean the same thing as "living together without marriage."

   _____

5. In Reading 4, paragraph 1, the author says that "illegitimacy no longer carries a social stigma." What does the author mean? Rewrite the sentence using your own words.

   _____

   _____

6. Make two columns, and list the main arguments in each essay.

   "For Marriage"   **"Against Marriage"**

   _____   _____
   _____   _____
   _____   _____
   _____   _____
   _____   _____
   _____   _____
   _____   _____
   _____   _____
   _____   _____

7. In your opinion, which essay argues more convincingly? Why?

   _____

   _____

   _____

8. At one point, both authors use the same point to justify one of their arguments. Which point is it? How does each author interpret the information?

   _____

   _____

   _____

   _____

   _____

GRAMMAR LINK

9. Underline at least five transitional words or expressions in Reading 5.
    Look for words that appear at the beginning of sentences. For example,
    in paragraph 1, *However* is a transitional expression.
    a. How are the transitional expressions punctuated?

    _____

    b. What purpose do transitional expressions serve?

    _____

DISCUSSION AND WRITING

10. Add one more argument to each side of the marriage debate.
11. Argue for or against large, extravagant weddings. Support your point of view
     with many examples.
12. Describe your first infatuation. Give a detailed description of the person that
     you had a crush on.

The Writer's Room   **Images of Human History, Habits, and Relationships**

Writing Activity 1: Photo Writing

1. Would you prefer to have a large or small family? Give your reasons.
2. Compare and contrast a large family and a small family.
3. Why do most people decide to have small families? List some reasons and
    give examples to support your points.

Writing Activity 2: Film Writing

1. The movie *Atonement* depicts a family in 1930s England. Compare and contrast two items in the film. For example, you could compare two characters, two settings, or two periods of history (pre-war and post-war), or youth versus old age. You could also compare the family in *Atonement* to a family in a film of your choice.

2. *Gone Baby Gone* examines the aftermath of a child's kidnapping. Write an argument paragraph based on an issue that is presented in the film.

3. *Little Miss Sunshine* follows the journey of a family. Using examples from the film, define "family."

Theme: **Entertainment, Culture, and Beliefs**

READING 6

The Appalling Truth
Dorothy Nixon

> Dorothy Nixon, a freelance writer, has written for *Salon.com*, *Chatelaine*, and *Today's Parent* magazine. In the next reading, she discusses the issue of television addiction. As you read this illustration essay, notice how the writer also uses elements of narration, description, and comparison and contrast.

1   Technology changes us. With the invention of the clock, we have lost the ability to live in the present. The telephone has made us slaves, in the **Pavlovian** sense, to a ringing bell. With the advent of television, we all moved indoors, leaving the streets empty and clear for the criminal element, and we left our minds open and susceptible to the mash served up on the screens.

2   As a mother and very serious media watcher, I am as troubled as anyone about the violent and sexist content on television. But were television wall-to-wall PBS type programming, without commercials, I would be just as concerned. I just don't like what it is doing to my family. It has become some kind of **oracle**—never mind **McLuhan**'s "electronic fireplace"—it commands all of our attention, and we don't listen to each other: husband to wife, parents to kids, or kids to parents. It is with this in mind that I suggest to my husband that we ban the tube from the house, on an experimental basis, for, say, about a year.

3   "No way!" he says.

4   "Why not?" I ask.

Pavlovian: refers to Russian behavior psychologist Ivan Pavlov

oracle: a prophet who gives advice and answers questions

McLuhan: Marshall McLuhan, an academic and media commentator who developed theories about the influences of the electronic media on popular culture

5   "Because it would be hypocritical," he deftly answers. "We both work in the TV industry."

6   "You work in TV. I don't," I counter.

7   "Well, you like to criticize TV for the local paper. How can you criticize something you don't watch?"

8   "Good point. I just don't like what that thing is doing to our family," I continue. "It's noisy. It jangles the nerves. It's like a drug. It's addictive. With satellite TV, we watch anything, even those stupid reality shows and retro shows like *Mr. Ed*. That show is about a talking horse, for heaven's sake. It was my favorite show when I was 8! We used to read thoughtful books like *1984*; now we watch *24*. Besides, the stupid contraption keeps us from doing what human beings are really supposed to be doing."

foraging: searching

9   "What's that? **Foraging** for nuts and berries?" My husband, the TV junkie, sees nothing wrong with the boob tube: "I grew up on TV, and I'm no psycho."

10   If my husband had his way, there would be a TV in every room. And they would all be tuned into *24*, twenty-four hours a day. And, I must admit, there are times when I have felt that the only interests we have in common are the *Sopranos* or *CSI*. In the early months of my first pregnancy, we would cuddle together on the couch like two spoons, and I would fall asleep, head cradled in his lap, eyes on the tube. Togetherness.

11   But now we are like two channel-zapping zombies. "You know, *they* say that spending time together in front of the television does nothing to enhance a relationship," I tell my now bleary-eyed husband, trying to make him feel guilty. It's a war of **attrition**, and it is working, sort of.

attrition: gradual wearing away of resistance

12   "OK. Two weeks," my husband relents. "We'll try no TV for two weeks. That's all. But *you* tell the kids." We have two boys, Andrew and Mark, seven and four. They kick up a huge fuss when I tell them that our tiny bungalow has been unilaterally declared a TV free zone. Now it is their turn to try to make me feel guilty. They hang their pathetic little heads in genuine mourning as they watch their dad reluctantly disconnect the enormous tangle of wires enabling the miracle of modern home theater in our suburban castle. And am I feeling guilty? No way! I stand tall and victorious in our living room, the protector of my children.

13   That evening, we read our children books, sing them songs, and tuck them in for the night. I go to bed with that Margaret Drabble I have been using as a giant paperweight for the past year, and my husband snuggles up with Stephen King.

14   Two days pass. The kids have finally stopped complaining about their terrible loss. In fact, they do not appear to care at all, anymore. They have found other more interesting things to do. I, on the other hand, am suffering from a mean case of withdrawal.

15   "It's *The Office* night, and it's the *only* show I like. Do you think maybe you can bring the TV up for just this show?" I ask my husband, who happens to be down in his workroom drilling a hole into a six foot piece of plywood for no apparent reason. "We'll keep the sound really low" (because kids can hear hypocrisy even in their sleep).

16   "Why don't you read, Ms. Literature Freak? You haven't exactly been burning up the library shelves," my husband sneers, rather condescendingly, as he stops to wipe some sawdust from his nosehairs.

17   "Well, that's because I only read the best, and my brain's too fried at the end of the day to read the best," I answer, convincing even myself. (That has been my pat excuse for my intellectual lethargy since becoming a mother.)

18   My husband rolls his eyes and puts down the drill. There is no further argument from him. He happily carries the TV upstairs and reconnects the wires in no time. We sit back and laugh at the antics of Michael, Dwight, Jim, and Pam. The problem is, we do the same for *Lost* a few days later. And for *The Wire*, each night my husband clambering up the basement stairs with a twenty-inch Sony stuck to his face, and then stumbling down again thirty-something minutes later, trailing his wires behind him.

19   Then there is the true test. Indeed, it is a real dilemma for us. A brand new episode of *Desperate Housewives* is airing, and the kids are still awake. What can we do? There is clearly no sleazy hypocritical way around this.

20   "I can always get a tape and watch it at work," my husband, the news editor, smiles, taunting me once again. "You, on the other hand, will have to do without."

21   It is a real dilemma. The hottest show on TV features four fortyish suburban women at various stages of freak out. Have I died and gone to heaven? My friends tell me the show is better than marriage therapy because their husbands love to watch it too.

22   So here are **Stepford wife** Bree, timid Susan, wacked out Lynette, and sexy Gabrielle who are forcing me to face a very real truth. It is not my kids. I am the real TV addict in my family.

Stepford wife: submissive, domestic, married woman (from the Ira Levin novel *The Stepford Wives*)

VOCABULARY AND COMPREHENSION

1.   Television "has become some kind of oracle" (paragraph 2). What does Nixon mean?

_____

_____

_____

2.   Compare the author's attitude toward television with that of her children.

_____

_____

_____

_____

_____

_____

3.   What does Nixon learn about herself?

_____

_____

4. What is the significance of the title?

   _____

   _____

5. The author gives many examples to illustrate how hypocritical she is. List some of those examples.

   _____

   _____

   _____

   _____

GRAMMAR LINK

6. Choose five present tense verbs from the essay. Choose verbs that have irregular past forms. Then write the past and past participle of each verb.

   _____

   _____

7. Underline all of the television show titles in the essay. Write a rule explaining how to write the titles of television shows.

   _____

   _____

DISCUSSION AND WRITING

8. Originally, the television was intended to provide us with a pleasurable leisure-time activity. However, the author complains that television is addictive. Do you agree that someone can be seriously addicted to television? Explain your answer by giving specific examples.
9. What harmful or harmless products or activities can be addictive? List them.
10. Why do people become addicted to things? What are they looking for, or what are they trying to escape? Describe how the pursuit of pleasure can become a full-blown addiction.

READING 7
The New Addiction
Josh Freed

Josh Freed is an award-winning columnist for the *Montreal Gazette*. Freed has published many books, including *Fear of Frying and Other Fax of Life*. In the next comparison and contrast essay, Freed makes an interesting comparison. As you read, notice how the author also uses definition writing.

scourge: affliction; serious problem

1 Is the cell phone the cigarette of our times? That is what I have been asking myself lately as the **scourge** of smokers slowly disappears from city life, and a scourge of cell-phone users takes their place. Everywhere I look, people hold cell phones up to their mouths instead of cigarettes, and non-users react as intolerantly as nonsmokers ever did. How does the cell phone resemble the cigarette? Let me count the ways.

2   It is an oral habit. For many users, the cell phone is an obvious substitute for smoking. It is a nervous habit that gives them something to do with their hands—whether they are dialing, checking their messages, or just fondling the buttons. Just like cigarettes, the phone sits in a person's breast pocket or on a restaurant table, ready to bring quickly to his or her mouth. Often, it is in a fliptop case that pops open as easily as a cigarette pack.

3   It pollutes. Instead of filling the air with smoke, cell-phone users fill it with words. For those nearby, the cell is just as annoying as the cigarette because instead of secondhand smoke, they get secondhand conversation. It is voice pollution. One phone can pollute a room more quickly than a cigarette, especially on a bus, or in a checkout line, when others hear someone hollering about his or her cousin's prostate operation or planning the night's dinner menu.

4   "Honey! The veal chops were expensive so I got lamb chops instead. Whaddya think we should serve with them? Do we need potatoes?"

5   Many people feel they must yell to be heard, and there is usually only one way to shut them up. Join into their conversation and say, "You know, I don't really feel like lamb chops tonight—how about turkey and wild rice?"

6   Cell-phone users do not blow smoke rings from the next restaurant table, like smokers. But cell-phone rings can be just as annoying, whether they play the "William Tell Overture" or yodeling sounds or Christmas tunes like "Sleigh Bells Ringing." Phone users are even more oblivious to their own noise than smokers are to their wisps of smoke.

7   Furthermore, there is an anti-cell lobby. Cell-phone users are the target of a growing intolerance that is almost as zealous as the anti-smoking movement's. Go to a movie, play, or concert and no one bothers to tell you not to smoke anymore. They know your seatmates will take care of that. Instead, movie ads and other warnings are all about shutting off your cell, the new public enemy No. 1. Anti-cell rage is so extreme that if you forget to shut off your phone in a movie, there is only one safe strategy to avoid a lynching when your phone goes off. Look around for the culprit accusingly, like everyone else in the place, and bluff your way out until your phone stops ringing.

8   Lately, "No Cell Phone" signs are getting even bigger than "No Smoking" signs. I was in San Francisco recently, where half the shops were plastered with warnings like "Don't even think about it. Cell-phone users will be escorted out and made to feel extremely embarrassed." On the train from Washington to New York, there is now a special "quiet" car where cell phones are banned. How long before the whole train is divided into cell and noncell sections, in a new version of smoking **apartheid?** If they ever find the slightest link between cell phones and any illness, you can expect to see cell-free hotel rooms, cell-free rest rooms, and a growing number of cell-free cities.

apartheid: former political system in South Africa that separated the privileged whites from people of other races

9   Cell phones may be addictive. Just like cigarettes, the cell phone spreads by targeting the young. The Big Phone companies keep offering teenagers dirt-cheap plans, trying to hook them for life. The cell has become the cool teen status symbol, as powerful as the cigarette, though less lethal. How long before we see class actions against the big phone companies for deliberately addicting our kids to the nicotine of words? How long will it be before the first cell-phone pollution settlement?

10   I suspect cell-phone makers will eventually be forced to come up with special filters, like cigarettes. All phones will be sold with a soundproof helmet or at least a mask-and-muffler to protect others from the noise. Get ready for the cell-phone snorkel.

VOCABULARY AND COMPREHENSION

1.   What is the meaning of *zealous* in paragraph 7? Guess the meaning using context clues.

_____

2.   What is Freed's main point?

_____

_____

3.   List five examples the author uses to support his main point.

_____

_____

_____

_____

_____

4.   What is the author's tone (his attitude toward the subject)?
a. Serious   c. Lighthearted
b. Cynical   d. Detached

5.   What can you infer, or guess, about the author?

_____

_____

GRAMMAR LINK

6.   In paragraph 4, the author writes "Whaddya." What does this word mean? Why does the author include an invented word in his text?

_____

_____

7.   Why does the author use dialogue in paragraphs 4 and 5?

_____

_____

DISCUSSION AND WRITING

8.   Choose two addictive items and compare them, just as Freed did in this essay. Do not compare cell phones and cigarettes.

9.   Should cell phones be banned or restricted? Explain your answer. If you think cell phones should be restricted, what types of restrictions should be placed on them?

READING 8

Sports and Life: Lessons to Be Learned
Jeff Kemp

Jeff Kemp was a National Football League quarterback for the Los Angeles Rams, the San Francisco 49ers, the Seattle Seahawks, and the Philadelphia Eagles. Kemp describes a lesson that he learned during his football years. As you read this narrative essay, notice how the author also uses elements of illustration, description, and cause and effect writing.

1   Sports are elevated life. They are noble and ignoble, beautiful and ugly. They reveal the best and worst of human nature in an action-packed arena dominated by intense emotion. When sports commentators repeat the old cliché about "the thrill of victory and the agony of defeat," we all know exactly what they are talking about. As players or spectators, we have experienced both. Yet, underneath the adrenaline rush is something even more powerful: our value system. Sports, in other words, reveal what we treasure most.

2   In 1988, I was playing for the Seattle Seahawks against my old team, the 49ers, when I learned firsthand that there are two competing value systems. I wasn't bitter that my old team had traded me, but I wanted to beat them all the same. Quarterback Dave Krieg had been injured, and I was to start. I had a great week of practice and felt totally prepared. I entered the Kingdome in Seattle **brimming** with excitement. I envisioned leading my team to victory and establishing myself as the Seahawks' starter.

brimming: filled; overflowing

3   Coming out of the pre-game meal, one of the offensive coaches put his arm around me and strongly affirmed his faith in me: "I want you to know how happy I am that you are the Seahawk quarterback. I've been waiting for this day." I felt honored, valued, and esteemed. This was going to be a great day!

4   Well, we ran the ball on our first two plays, and we did not gain much. On third down and eight, I threw to Hall of Famer wide receiver Steve Largent, who split two defenders. The pass hit him right in the hands, yet he dropped the ball. Next to Jerry Rice, Largent is, statistically speaking, the greatest receiver in history. He also is one of my best friends. All I could do at that moment was chuckle and moan, "Steve, what's the matter? You never drop the ball. Why are you doing this to me?"

5   After that, he did not make any mistakes, but I did. In fact, I played the worst game of my life. At the end of the first half, the 49ers were ahead 28–0. Every person in the Kingdome, with the exception of my wife (and there isn't even a witness to vouch for her), was booing me. Have you ever heard nearly 60,000 people booing you? It's quite an experience.

6   As I came off the field at halftime, I knew that I might be benched, but I wasn't defeated. Ever since I was a small boy, my father had been drumming into my head British Prime Minister Winston Churchill's brave words to the students at Harrow School in the dark days of 1941: "Never give in, never give in, never, never, never, never—in nothing, great or small, large or petty—never give in except to convictions of honor and good sense."

7   I waded through the players to find the coach who had been so supportive before the game. I wanted to discuss some offensive strategies that might turn things around in the second half. As I approached him and began,

"Coach . . ." he turned his back on me without a word. Then he called to another quarterback, put his arm around him, and began to discuss plays that player would run in the second half.

8   Now, I understood that I was being taken out of the game. That made sense. I was hoping it would not happen, but I understood. However, that coach did not say one word to me for the rest of the game even though we stood next to each other on the sidelines. Nor did he say anything on Monday when we watched the game films. For about a month, there was complete rejection. He simply couldn't deal with the fact that I had not lived up to his hopes and that I had not helped the team to succeed. He rejected me relationally because my performance had fallen short.

9   I discovered during this painful episode a faulty value system that is conditional and performance-based. It rejects relationships and dishonors the diverse yet equal value of every person. My coach, as well as other coaches and even team owners, was not only exerting but also feeling the pressure of this value system that has been adopted by so many in business and the culture at large.

10   My career slowly, steadily had been rising, and now, all of a sudden, it seemed it was on a speedy downward course. The fifth-stringer had made it to first string only to be benched, booed by the crowd, and shunned by his own coach. It looked like my last chance to succeed had come and gone.

11   Eventually, though, I found renewed hope and confidence through a **transcendent** value system, which is quite different. It is an unconditional, relational, and character-based value system. It leads us to treat others as we wish to be treated. Of course, performance and competition are important, as are rewards and incentives, but none of these things enhances or **demeans** the value of an individual.

transcendent: inspirational

demeans: degrades; lowers

VOCABULARY AND COMPREHENSION

1. In paragraph 6, the author says, "As I came off the field at halftime, I knew that I might be benched." What does he mean by *benched?*

    _____

    _____

2. In paragraph 6, why does the author quote Winston Churchill?

    _____

    _____

    _____

3. Explain how the coach's attitude toward Kemp changes during the Seattle Seahawks game.

    _____

    _____

    _____

4. Why does Kemp reject the value system of his coach?

    _____

    _____

    _____

5. Kemp tells a story about a specific event in his life. Retell the story in two or three sentences.

_____

_____

_____

_____

GRAMMAR LINK

6. Look at the quotation in paragraph 3. Why is there a colon before the quotation? Explain the punctuation rule.

_____

_____

7. Underline an example of a simple sentence, a compound sentence, and a complex sentence. Why does the author use different types of sentences?

_____

_____

DISCUSSION AND WRITING

8. Kemp describes an experience that changed his outlook on life. What life-changing experiences have you had? Choose one, and describe what happened.
9. What lessons can people learn when they play team sports?

READING 9
What's Your Humor Style?
Louise Dobson

> Louise Dobson has written for _Psychology Today_. As you read this text, look for patterns of classification and illustration.

1 In today's personality stakes, nothing is more highly valued than a sense of humor. We seek it out in others and are proud to claim it in ourselves, perhaps even more than good looks or intelligence. If someone has a great sense of humor, we reason, it means that he or she is happy, socially confident, and has a healthy perspective on life.

2 This attitude would have surprised the ancient Greeks, who believed humor to be essentially aggressive. And in fact, our admiration for the comedically gifted is relatively new, and not very well founded, says Rod Martin, a psychologist at the University of Western Ontario who studies the way people use humor. Being funny isn't necessarily an indicator of good social skills and well-being, his research has shown; it may just as likely be a sign of personality flaws.

3 He has found that humor is a double-edged sword. It can forge better relationships and help us cope with life, or it can be corrosive, eating away at self-esteem and antagonizing others. "It's a form of communication, like speech, and we all use it differently," says Martin. We use bonding humor to

enhance our social connections—but we also may wield it as a way of excluding or rejecting an outsider. Likewise, put-down humor can at times be an adaptive, healthy response: employees suffering under a vindictive boss will often make the office more bearable by secretly ridiculing their tyrant.

4   Though humor is essentially social, how people use it says a lot about their sense of self. Those who use self-defeating humor, making fun of themselves for the enjoyment of others, tend to maintain that hostility toward themselves even when alone. Similarly, those who are able to view the world with amused tolerance are often equally forgiving of their own shortcomings.

Put-down Humor

5   This aggressive type of humor is used to criticize and manipulate others through teasing, sarcasm, and ridicule. When it's aimed against politicians, it's hilarious and mostly harmless. But in the real world, it has a sharper impact. Put-down humor, such as telling friends an embarrassing story about another friend, is a socially acceptable way to deploy aggression and make others look bad so the storyteller looks good.

6   When challenged on their teasing, put-down jokers often turn to the "just kidding" defense, allowing the aggressors to avoid responsibility even as the barb bites. Martin has found no evidence that those who rely on this type of humor are any less well adjusted. But it does take a toll on personal relationships.

Bonding Humor

7   People who use bonding humor are fun to have around; they say amusing things, tell jokes, engage in witty banter, and generally lighten the mood. These are the people who give humor a good name. They're perceived as warm, down-to-earth, and kind, good at reducing the tension in uncomfortable situations, and able to laugh at their own faults.

8   Talk show host and comedian Ellen DeGeneres embraces her audience by sharing good-natured, relatable humor. Her basic message is that we're alike, we find the same things funny, and we're all in this together.

9   Nonetheless, bonding humor can have a dark side. After all, a feeling of inclusion can be made sweeter by knowing that someone else is on the outs. J.F.K. and his brothers would often invite a hated acquaintance to vacation with them; they'd be polite to his face, but behind his back, the brothers would unite in deriding the hapless guest.

Hate-me Humor

10   In this style of humor, the funny person is the butt of the joke for the amusement of others. Often deployed by people eager to ingratiate themselves, it's the familiar clown or "fat guy" playfulness that we loved in John Belushi and Chris Farley—both of whom suffered for their success. A small dose of it is charming, but a little goes a long way: routinely offering oneself up to be humiliated erodes self-respect, fostering depression and anxiety. It also can backfire by making other people feel uncomfortable, finds Nicholas Kuiper of the University of Western Ontario. He proposes that it may remind others of their own tendency toward self-criticism.

11   Farley, who died at age 33 from an overdose, had a streak of self-loathing. "Chris chose the immediate pleasure he got in pleasing others over the long-term cost to himself," his brother wrote after his death. The

bottom line: Excelling at this style of humor may lead to party invitations but can ultimately exact a high price.

Laughing at Life Humor

12   When we admire someone who "doesn't take himself too seriously," this is the temperament we're talking about. More than just a way of relating to other people, it's a prism that colors the world in rosier shades. Someone with this outlook deploys humor to cope with challenges, taking a step back and laughing at the absurdities of everyday life. *The Onion* is a repository of this benign good humor. The columnist Dave Barry has perfected it with quips like this: "Fishing is boring, unless you catch an actual fish, and then it is disgusting."

The Onion: a satirical online newspaper

13   Studies that link a sense of humor to good health are probably measuring this phenomenon; when people have a wry perspective, it's hard to remain anxious or hostile for long. Martin calls it "self-enhancing humor," because they don't need other people to entertain them—if something peculiar or annoying happens, they're perfectly capable of laughing at it on their own.

VOCABULARY AND COMPREHENSION

1. In paragraph 10, what is the meaning of *erodes*?
    a. improves   b. adds to   c. slowly destroys
2. In your own words, state the writer's main point.

    _____

    _____

3. What is the difference between put-down humor and hate-me humor?

    _____

    _____

    _____

4. Which type of humor is the most positive? Support your answer with evidence from the text.

    _____

    _____

    _____

5. How has contemporary society's attitude toward humor changed from ancient times?

    _____

    _____

6. The author uses different types of support to develop her ideas. For each type of support listed, find an example from the text.

    expert opinion: _____

    example: _____

GRAMMAR LINK

7. There is a sentence in paragraph 2 that uses a semi-colon. Explain why the writer uses a semi-colon in this sentence.

    _____

8.   Why does the writer use reflexive pronouns in paragraphs 4 (*themselves*) and 10 (*oneself*)?

_____

_____

DISCUSSION AND WRITING

9.   Think of another emotion such anger or sadness. Then divide that emotion into categories, and list types of that emotion. Give examples to support each type.

10.   What type of humor do you have? Describe your sense of humor.

READING 10

The Hijab
Naheed Mustafa

Naheed Mustafa, a North America–born Muslim woman, has taken to wearing the traditional hijab scarf. While studying in a Canadian university, she wrote about her reasons for wearing the hijab. As you read this definition essay, notice how the author also uses argument.

1   I often wonder whether people see me as a radical fundamentalist Muslim terrorist packing an AK-47 assault rifle inside my jean jacket. Or maybe they see me as the poster girl for oppressed womanhood everywhere. I am not sure which it is. I get the whole **gamut** of strange looks, stares, and covert glances. You see, I wear the hijab, a scarf that covers my head, neck, and throat. I do this because I am a Muslim woman who believes her body is her own private concern.

gamut: the whole range

2   Young Muslim women are reclaiming the hijab, reinterpreting it in light of its original purpose—to give back to women ultimate control of their own bodies. The Qur'an teaches us that men and women are equal, and that individuals should not be judged according to gender, beauty, wealth, or privilege. The only thing that makes one person better than another is her or his character.

3   Nonetheless, people have a difficult time relating to me. After all, I'm young, Canadian born and raised, and university-educated. Why would I do this to myself, they ask. Strangers speak to me in loud, slow English and often appear to be playing charades. They politely inquire how I like living in Canada and whether or not the cold bothers me. If I am in the right mood, it can be very amusing. But, why would I, a woman with all the advantages of a North American upbringing, suddenly, at twenty-one, want to cover myself so that only my face and hands show?

4   Women are taught from early childhood that their worth is proportional to their attractiveness. Women feel compelled to pursue abstract notions of beauty, half realizing that such a pursuit is futile. When they reject this form of oppression, they face ridicule and contempt. Whether it is women who refuse to wear makeup, to shave their legs, or to expose their bodies, others have trouble dealing with them.

5   In the Western world, the hijab has come to symbolize either forced silence or radical, unconscionable militancy. Actually, it is neither. It is simply a woman's assertion that judgment of her physical person is to play no role

whatsoever in social interaction. Wearing the hijab has given me freedom from constant attention to my physical self. Because my appearance is not subjected to public scrutiny, my beauty, or perhaps lack of it, has been removed from the realm of what can legitimately be discussed. No one knows whether my hair looks as if I just stepped out of a salon, whether or not I can pinch an inch, or even if I have unsightly stretch marks. And because no one knows, no one cares.

6 Feeling that one has to meet the impossible male standards of beauty is tiring and often humiliating. I should know; I spent my entire teenage years trying to do it. I was a borderline bulimic and spent a lot of money I did not have on potions and lotions in hopes of becoming the next Cindy Crawford. The definition of beauty is ever-changing; waifish is good, waifish is bad, athletic is good—sorry, athletic is bad.

7 Women are not going to achieve equality with the right to bare their breasts in public, as some people would like to have you believe. That would only make us **party to** our own objectification. True equality will be had only when women don't need to display themselves to get attention and won't need to defend their decision to keep their bodies to themselves.

party to: a part of

Vocabulary and Comprehension

1. Find a word in paragraph 4 that means *pressured*.

   _____

2. What do you know about the author?

   _____

3. Why does Mustafa choose to wear the hijab?

   _____

   _____

   _____

4. According to Mustafa, what does the hijab symbolize to non-Muslim North Americans?

   _____

   _____

5. How does Mustafa define *hijab*? Give both the literal and symbolic meanings.

   _____

   _____

Grammar Link

6. In paragraph 4, the first sentence uses the passive voice. Rewrite the sentence using the active voice.

   _____

   _____

7. In the last sentence of paragraph 5, highlight the verbs that follow *no one*. Why does each verb end in *s*?

   _____

   _____

DISCUSSION AND WRITING

8. In paragraph 4, the author claims, "Women are taught from early childhood that their worth is proportional to their attractiveness." Do you agree or disagree with this statement? Explain your answer.

9. In the introductory paragraph, the author says she thinks that people judge her because she wears the hijab. What are some stereotypes that people might have about your city, state, nation, or culture? Describe those stereotypes, and give examples showing that the stereotypes are or are not based on reality.

10. Think of a term that could describe your nationality or your generation. Define the term, and give examples.

 **The Writer's Room**   **Images of Entertainment, Culture, and Beliefs**

Writing Activity 1: Photo Writing

1. Describe a music concert or performance that you have seen. Use imagery that appeals to the senses.

2. Do you think music lessons should be compulsory in school? Explain why or why not.

3. Does a song bring back specific memories for you? Describe the song and the memories that it evokes.

Writing Activity 2: Film Writing

1. Watch a film clip from a silent movie, and then create possible dialogue for the clip.

2. Watch *Dreamgirls*. Choose one of the characters, and describe the process the character goes through to achieve his or her goals.

3. View a film biography about a real-life person. For example, watch *American Gangster*, *Ray*, *Walk the Line*, or any film of your choice. Write about the causes or effects of the character's actions.

Theme: **The Earth and Its Creatures**

READING 11

What It Feels Like to Walk on the Moon
Buzz Aldrin

On July 20, 1969, *Apollo 11* landed on the moon. Astronauts Neil Armstrong, Michael Collins, and Edwin E. Aldrin, Jr. (also known as Buzz Aldrin) spent two and a half hours walking on the moon's surface. In the next essay, Aldrin describes that experience. As you read, notice how the author mainly uses description but also elements of process writing.

1   The surface of the moon is like fine talcum powder. It is very loose at the top. At a deeper level, a half inch or so, it becomes much more compact, almost as if it were cemented together. It seems that way because there are no air molecules between the molecules of dust.

2   When I put my foot down in the powder, the boot print preserved itself exquisitely. When I would take a step, a little semicircle of dust would spray out before me. It was odd because the dust did not behave at all the way it behaves here on Earth. On Earth, dust is sometimes puffy or sandy. On the moon, the powdery dust travels through no air at all, so the dust is kicked up, and then it all falls at the same time in a perfect semicircle.

3   I am trying the best I can to put it into words, but being on the moon is just different—different from anything I have ever seen. To use the word *alien* would mislead people. *Surreal* is probably as good a word as I have. When I looked out the window of the lunar lander as we touched down, the sun was out, the sky was velvety black, the engine was shut down, and everything was silent. That was surreal.

4   When I was on the moon, there was very little audio around, only the sounds of my suit—the hum of pumps circulating fluid. But I didn't hear any amplified breathing inside my mask; that is a Hollywood **contrivance**. The name of the game on the moon was staying cool and not exerting too much so that I would never be out of breath.

contrivance: deceitful invention

5   If you remember the television images we sent back, you know that I was attempting to demonstrate different walking motions, going back and forth in

inertia: inability to move with ease; sluggish movement

front of the camera. I tried what you might call a kangaroo hop, and then I demonstrated how I needed a few steps to change direction because of the **inertia** that was up there. I found that the best way to move around at a fairly good clip was not by using a jogging motion—one foot, then the other—but rather by moving more the way a horse gallops: one-two, one-two, two steps in rapid succession, followed by a lope, followed by two more rapid steps.

6   And then there is the picture where I was standing next to the flag. I was leaning forward a good bit because of the center of gravity of the backpack that I was wearing. On the moon, it was sometimes hard to tell when I might be on the verge of losing my balance. As I leaned a little bit to one side or the other, I came in danger of falling. But it was easy to right myself by pushing down on the surface with my feet. The lunar surface is so easy, so natural, and so readily adapted to by any human being. The low gravity makes it very convenient to get around. It is really a very nice environment.

metaphysically: refers to abstract, philosophical thinking

wafted: floated

7   While we were on the moon, there was no time to savor the moment. It seemed as though what we were doing was so significant that to pause for a moment and reflect **metaphysically** was really contrary to our mission. We were not trained to smell the roses. We were not hired to utter philosophical truisms on the spur of the moment. We had a job to do.

8   I do remember that one realization **wafted** through my mind when I was up there. I noted that here were two guys farther away from anything than two guys had ever been before. That is what I thought about. And yet, at the same time, I was very conscious that everything was being closely scrutinized a quarter of a million miles away.

9   Everything and anything we did would be recorded, remembered, and studied for ages. It felt a little like being the young kid in the third or fourth grade who is all of a sudden asked to go up on stage in front of the whole school and recite the Gettysburg Address. And as he tries to remember the words, he has got gun-barrel vision. He does not see what is going on around him; he is focused on that particular task, conscious only of his performance. It was like that but even more so. The eyes of the world were on us, and if we made a mistake, we would regret it for quite a while.

levity: lightness; humor

extemporaneousness: improvised or unplanned action

10   I guess, if I look back on things, there was one little moment of **levity,** a bit of unusual **extemporaneousness.** When the countdown came to lift off from the moon, when it got to twenty seconds, Houston said, "Tranquility Base, you're cleared for liftoff." And I said in response, "Roger, we're number one on the runway." Now comedy is the absurd put into a natural position. There was no runway up there. And there certainly wasn't anyone else waiting in line to lift off. I was conscious of that, being first.

VOCABULARY AND COMPREHENSION

1.   Find a word in paragraph 7 that means "to say."

_____

2.   In the introduction, Aldrin uses an analogy, or comparison of two things, to make the reader understand the situation. What is this analogy, and how effective is it?

_____

_____

_____

3. In paragraph 3, Adrin describes the moonscape as *surreal*. What does he mean? You might try dividing *surreal* into the prefix and the main word.

4. What is the main point of paragraphs 5 and 6?

5. What does Aldrin mean when he writes in paragraph 7 that astronauts "were not trained to smell the roses"?

6. What did Aldrin hear when he was on the moon?

7. Underline five descriptive phrases that best describe what it feels like to walk on the moon.

GRAMMAR LINK

8. In the first sentence of paragraph 9, underline four main verbs and circle two helping verbs. Then explain which verbs in the sentence are active and which are passive.

9. Why does the author use a semicolon in the second sentence of paragraph 4?

DISCUSSION AND WRITING

10. Go for a walk in a new place. Use your senses and give details about what you see, hear, smell, and touch.
11. In the future, it may be possible for ordinary citizens to travel to outer space. Would you like to go on a space flight? Why or why not?
12. Buzz Aldrin does not introduce his topic. Instead, he immediately describes his sensations when he walked on the moon. Write an introduction for this essay.

READING 12
The Zoo Life
Yann Martel

Yann Martel, the son of diplomats, was born in Spain but has lived in various countries throughout the world. In 2002, he won the prestigious Man Booker Prize for his novel *The Life of Pi*, from which this excerpt is taken. As you read the selection, notice how the author mainly uses comparison and contrast writing as well as elements of argument.

1   If you went to a home, kicked down the front door, chased the people who lived there out into the street, and said, "Go! You are free! Free as a bird! Go! Go!"—do you think they would shout and dance for joy? They wouldn't. The people you've just evicted would sputter, "With what right do you throw us out? This is our home. We own it. We have lived here for years. We're calling the police, you scoundrel."

2   Don't we say, "There's no place like home"? That's certainly what animals feel. Animals are territorial. That is the key to their minds. Only a familiar territory will allow them to fulfill the two relentless imperatives of the wild: the avoidance of enemies and the getting of food and water. A biologically sound zoo enclosure—whether cage, pit, moated island, corral, terrarium, **aviary,** or aquarium—is just another territory, peculiar only in its size and in its proximity to human territory. That it is so much smaller than what it would be in nature stands to reason.

aviary: enclosure for birds

3   Territories in the wild are large not as a matter of taste but of necessity. In a zoo, we do for animals what we have done for ourselves with houses: we bring together in a small space what in the wild is spread out. Whereas before for us the cave was here, the river over there, the hunting grounds a mile that way, the lookout next to it, the berries somewhere else—all of them **infested** with lions, snakes, ants, leeches, and poison ivy—now the river flows through taps at hand's reach, and we can wash next to where we sleep, we can eat where we have cooked, and we can surround the whole with a protective wall and keep it clean and warm.

infested: invaded by

4   A house is a compressed territory where our basic needs can be fulfilled close by and safely. A sound zoo enclosure is the equivalent for an animal (with the noteworthy absence of a fireplace or the like, present in every human habitation). Finding within it all the places it needs—a lookout, a place for resting, for eating and drinking, for bathing, for grooming, etc. and finding that there is no need to go hunting, food appearing seven days a week, an animal will take possession of its zoo space in the same way it would lay claim to a new space in the wild, exploring it and marking it out in the normal ways of its species, with sprays of urine perhaps. Once this moving-in ritual is done and the animal has settled, it will not feel like a nervous tenant, and even less like a prisoner, but rather like a landholder, and it will behave in the same way within its enclosure as it would in its territory in the wild, including defending it tooth and nail should it be invaded.

5   Such an enclosure is neither better nor worse for an animal than its condition in the wild; so long as it fulfills the animal's needs, a territory, natural or constructed, simply *is*, without judgment, a given, like the spots on a leopard. One might even argue that if an animal could choose with intelligence, it would opt for living in a zoo, since the major difference between a zoo and the wild is the absence of parasites and enemies and the abundance of food in the first, and their respective abundance and scarcity in the second. Think about it yourself. Would you rather be put up at the Ritz with free room service and unlimited access to a doctor or be homeless without a soul to care for you? But animals are incapable of such **discernment.** Within the limits of their nature, they make do with what they have.

discernment: judgment

6   A good zoo is a place of carefully worked-out coincidence: exactly where an animal says to us, "Stay out!" with its urine or other secretion, we say to it,

"Stay in!" with our barriers. Under such conditions of diplomatic peace, all animals are content, and we can relax and have a look at each other.

VOCABULARY AND COMPREHENSION

1. In paragraph 5, what is the meaning of *scarcity*?

   a. shortage   b. insufficient c. large amount

2. What is Martel's main argument?

   _____

   _____

   _____

3. Martel compares a house and an animal's enclosure. What are the similarities?

   _____

   _____

   _____

4. Reread paragraph 1. The author suggests that people would not want to be kicked out of their homes. He then goes on to suggest that a zoo enclosure is an animal's home. Do you think this is a fair comparison? Explain your answer.

   _____

   _____

   _____

   _____

5. In paragraph 5, the author asks, "Would you rather be put up at the Ritz with free room service and unlimited access to a doctor or be homeless without a soul to care for you?" How would you answer the question? Explain why.

   _____

   _____

   _____

   _____

GRAMMAR LINK

6. The next-to-last sentence in paragraph 2, beginning with "A biologically sound," has many commas. What rule could you write about the use of commas with a series of items?

   _____

   _____

7. The first sentence in paragraph 6 contains the word *carefully*. Why do you have to spell *carefully* with two *l*'s?

   _____

   _____

DISCUSSION AND WRITING

8. The author mentions that animals mark their territories in some way, perhaps with a spray of urine. What are ways that humans mark or identify their territory?

9. Compare and contrast a zoo enclosure and life in the wild. What are some similarities and differences?

10. Develop arguments that oppose Martel's main points.

READING 13

Shark Bait

Dave Barry

Dave Barry is a Pulitzer Prize-winning humor columnist. He has written many hilarious columns for the *Miami Herald*. In this text, Barry narrates events that took place on a fishing expedition.

1   It began as a fun nautical outing, ten of us in a motorboat off the coast of Miami. The weather was sunny, and we saw no signs of danger, other than the risk of sliding overboard because every exposed surface on the boat was covered with a layer of snack-related grease. We had enough cholesterol on board to put the entire U.S. Olympic team into cardiac arrest. This is because all ten of us were guys.

2   I hate to engage in gender stereotyping, but when women plan the menu for a recreational outing, they usually come up with a nutritionally balanced menu featuring all the major food groups, including the Sliced Carrots Group, the Pieces of Fruit Cut into Cubes Group, the Utensils Group, and the Plate Group, whereas guys tend to focus on the Carbonated Malt Beverages Group and the Fatal Snacks Group. On this particular trip, our food supply consisted of about fourteen bags of potato chips and one fast-food fried-chicken Giant Economy Tub O' Fat. Nobody brought, for example, napkins, the theory being that you could just wipe your hands on your stomach. Then you could burp. This is what guys on all-guy boats are doing while women are thinking about their relationships.

3   The reason the grease got smeared everywhere was that four of the guys on the boat were ten-year-olds, who, because of the way their still-developing digestive systems work, cannot chew without punching. This results in a lot of dropped and thrown food. On this boat, you regularly encountered semi gnawed pieces of chicken skittering across the deck toward you like small but hostile alien creatures from the Kentucky Fried Planet. Periodically, a man would yell "CUT THAT OUT!" at the boys, then burp to indicate the depth of his concern. Discipline is vital on a boat.

4   We motored through random-looking ocean until we found exactly what we were looking for: a patch of random-looking ocean. There we dropped anchor and dove for Florida lobsters, which protect themselves by using their tails to scoot backward really fast. They've been fooling predators with this move for millions of years, but the guys on our boat, being advanced life forms, including a dentist, figured it out in under three hours.

5   I myself did not participate because I believe that lobsters are the result of a terrible genetic accident involving nuclear radiation and cockroaches. I mostly sat around, watching guys lunge out of the water, heave lobsters into the boat, burp, and plunge back in. Meanwhile, the lobsters were scrabbling

around in the chicken grease, frantically trying to shoot backward through the forest of legs belonging to ten-year-old boys squirting each other with gobs of the No. 197,000,000,000 Sun Block that their moms had sent along. It was a total Guy Day, very relaxing, until the arrival of the barracuda.

6   This occurred just after we'd all gotten out of the water. One of the men, Larry, was fishing, and he hooked a barracuda right where we had been swimming. This was unsettling. The books all say that barracuda rarely eat people, but very few barracuda can read, and they have *far* more teeth than would be necessary for a strictly seafood diet. Their mouths look like the entire $39.95 set of Ginsu knives, including the handy Arm Slicer.

7   We gathered around to watch Larry fight the barracuda. His plan was to catch it, weigh it, and release it with a warning. After ten minutes, he almost had it to the boat, and we were all pretty excited for him, when all of a sudden . . .

8   *Ba-DUMP . . . Ba-DUMP . . .* Those of you who read music recognize this as the soundtrack from the motion picture *Jaws.* Sure enough, cruising right behind Larry's barracuda, thinking sushi, was: a shark. And not just *any* shark. It was a hammerhead shark, perennial winner of the coveted Oscar for Ugliest Fish. It has a weird, T-shaped head with a big eyeball on each tip, so that it can see around both sides of a telephone pole. This ability is of course useless for a fish, but nobody would dare try to explain this to a hammerhead.

9   The hammerhead, its fin breaking the surface, zigzagged closer to Larry's barracuda, then surged forward.

10   "Oh ****!" went Larry, reeling furiously.

11   *CHOMP* went the hammerhead, and suddenly Larry's barracuda was in a new weight division.

12   *CHOMP* went the hammerhead again, and now Larry was competing in an entirely new category, Fish Consisting of Only a Head.

13   The boys were staring at the remainder of the barracuda, deeply impressed.

14   "This is your leg," said the dentist. "This is your leg in *Jaws.* Any questions?"

15   The boys, for the first time all day, were quiet.

VOCABULARY AND COMPREHENSION

1.   This text is written using what type of narrator?
     a. first-person   b. third-person
2.   Summarize the story answering *who, what, where, when, why,* and *how* questions.

_____

_____

_____

_____

3.   How many men were on the boat? _____

     How many boys were on the boat? _____
4.   Barry uses imagery to describe the events of the day. Give examples from the text of the following types of imagery.

sight: _____

_____

_____

sound: _____

_____

_____

5. A simile is a comparison using *like* or *as*. Underline a simile in paragraph 3.
6. Why does Barry include dialogue in this text?

_____

GRAMMAR LINK

7. In paragraph 6, the writer uses the word *this* two times. Explain what *this* refers to each time.

_____

_____

_____

8. In paragraphs 10 and 14, Barry inserts direct quotations. Explain the rule for end punctuation when quoting someone.

_____

_____

DISCUSSION AND WRITING

9. Using humor, describe something silly, amusing, or dangerous that you and your friends have done.
10. Compare tasteful and distasteful humor. Give specific examples to support your point.

Images of the Earth and Its Creatures

Writing Activity 1: Photo Writing

1. What animal scares you the most? Explain why.

2. How do animals contribute to humans' lives? Think about products or services that animals provide for humans. List specific examples.

3. What can humans learn by watching animals? List specific examples.

Writing Activity 2: Film Writing

1. Watch a classic film about a fear of animals. For example, watch Spielberg's *Jaws*, Hitchcock's *The Birds*, or Cronenberg's *The Fly*. Classify the types of animal fears that people have. You might also choose one of the movies and describe the most frightening scene. Include details that appeal to the senses.

2. View the film *Into the Wild*. Narrate the journey of the main character as he retreats from civilization and journeys into the wild.

3. Watch a film about aliens or about travel. For example, view any of the *Star Trek* or *Star Wars* movies. Choose a hero from one of the movies, and define the characteristics of a film hero.

Theme: **Politics and the Business World**

READING 14

How to Handle Conflict
P. Gregory Smith

> P. Gregory Smith writes for *Career World*. In the next essay, he describes some steps a person can take to avoid conflict. As you read this process essay, notice how the author also uses elements of argument writing.

1   "Hey, college boy," Mr. Jefferson smirked as Ramon walked into the supermarket, "a lady just dropped a bottle of grape juice in aisle six. Do you think you could lower yourself enough to mop it up?" Ramon was seething inside as he grabbed the mop and headed off to clean up the spill. Ever since he told some of his co-workers that he had applied to the state university, Mr. Jefferson, the night manager, had teased and taunted him. As Ramon returned to the front of the store, he remembered the presentation his guidance counselor, Mrs. Chang, gave last week on something called assertiveness. It is a way of standing up for one's rights without creating conflict. As Ramon walked toward Mr. Jefferson, the main points of the presentation started to come back to him.

2   Find the right time and place. Mr. Jefferson was talking with a customer when Ramon reached the front of the supermarket. Ramon waited until Mr.

Jefferson was finished and then asked, "Can I talk with you in your office when you have a moment?" By waiting for the right time, Ramon was likely to have Mr. Jefferson's attention. Also, by asking to speak with him in private, Ramon reduced the chances that Mr. Jefferson would feel that he had to impress others, protect his reputation, or save face.

stance: manner; position

3   Maintain good posture, eye contact, and a relaxed **stance.** Before Ramon said the first word, he reminded himself of a few important things. If he wanted to stand up for himself, he would need to stand up straight! He knew that it was important to make eye contact. Ramon also knew the importance of relaxing his hands and keeping a comfortable distance from Mr. Jefferson. He did not want to appear hostile or threatening. Even though he was angry, Ramon reminded himself that he must speak calmly, clearly, and slowly in order to get his point across. If he let his anger creep in, he would probably get an angry or defensive response from Mr. Jefferson. Even worse, if he hid his feelings behind a quiet tone or rapid speech, then Mr. Jefferson would probably doubt his seriousness.

4   Use *I* statements. Mr. Jefferson closed the office door, folded his arms, and looked at Ramon questioningly. Ramon took a deep breath and began, "Mr. Jefferson, I really feel embarrassed when you call me 'college boy.' I like it a lot better when people call me Ramon. I don't mind doing my fair share of the dirty jobs around here," Ramon continued, "but I feel like I'm getting a lot more mop time than anyone else." By using a statement that began with *I*, Ramon was able to state his feelings honestly, without accusing Mr. Jefferson. *I* statements usually can't be considered false or cause an argument because they're simple statements of feelings.

5   Then introduce cooperative statements. Ramon said, "We used to get along fine until everybody started talking about me going to college next year. I haven't changed, and I'd like to go back to the way things were." Cooperative statements—or statements that connect you with the other person—create common ground for further discussion. They also serve as a subtle reminder that you share experiences and values with the other person.

6   "Remember that standing up for your personal rights, or being assertive, is very important," explains Betty Kelman of the Seattle University School of Nursing. "Standing up for your rights involves self-respect—respect for your rights and the other person's rights. Respecting yourself is the ability to make your own decisions involving relationships, how you spend your time, and whom you spend it with." Kelman also explains what assertiveness is not. "Standing up for yourself does not mean that you express yourself in an aggressive, angry, or mean way." She sums it up this way: "Think of standing up for yourself as being in a win-win situation. You win, and they win."

VOCABULARY AND COMPREHENSION

1.   What are *cooperative statements* (paragraph 5)?

_____

_____

2.   What introduction style does the essay have?
   a. Anecdote   c. Historical
   b. General   d. Contrasting position

3.   What is Smith's main point?

   _____

   _____

4.   List the steps in the process that Smith describes.

   _____

   _____

   _____

   _____

5.   How does the quotation from Betty Kelman (paragraph 6) support the author's point of view?

   _____

   _____

   _____

GRAMMAR LINK

6.   Underline the verbs in the first sentences of paragraphs 2 through 5. Who or what is the subject in each sentence?

   _____

7.   In paragraph 5, the author says, "I haven't changed, and I'd like to go back to the way things were." Write out the long form of each contraction.

   _____

   _____

DISCUSSION AND WRITING

8.   Can you think of a time when you should have been more assertive? Describe what happened.
9.   Explain the steps that you take when you are faced with a major problem. What do you usually do?

READING 15
How to Remember Names
Roger Seip

> Roger Seip is the President of Freedom Speakers and Trainers, a company that specializes in memory training. In this process essay, he describes how to remember people's names. As you read, notice how the author uses elements of argument and cause and effect writing.

1   If you live in fear of forgetting people's names, sometimes within mere seconds of being introduced to them, you are not alone. Surveys show that 83 percent of the population worries about an inability to recall names. While common, this frustrating phenomenon can be relatively easy to overcome. The most important key to really effective learning of any kind is to understand that there are three learning styles: visual, auditory, and kinesthetic

(physically interactive). The more you can apply all three of these styles to a task, the more quickly and solidly you will learn anything. Practice each of the following steps to improve your name recollection in every sales and social situation.

2   When you are first introduced to someone, look closely at his or her face and try to find something unique about it. Whether you find a distinctive quality or not is irrelevant; by really looking for a memorable characteristic in a new face, you are incorporating the visual learning style. And a word of advice: if you do find something that really stands out about someone's face, don't say anything!

3   The next step utilizes both auditory and kinesthetic learning styles. When you meet someone, slow down for five seconds, and concentrate on listening to him or her. Focus on the person, and repeat his or her name back in a conversational manner, such as "Susan. Nice to meet you, Susan." Also make sure to give a good firm handshake, which establishes a physical connection.

4   Creating a mental picture of someone's name incorporates the visual sense again. Many people have names that already are pictures: consider Robin, Jay, Matt, or Dawn, to name just a few. Some names will require you to play with them a bit to create a picture. Ken, for example, may not bring an immediate image to your mind, but a "can" is very close. Or you might envision a Ken doll. The point is not to create the best, most creative mental image ever, so don't get caught up in your head during this step of the process, thinking, "Oh, that's not a very good picture. What is a better one?" The worst thing you can do when learning is to stress yourself out and overthink the process. If an image does not come to you right away, skip it and do it later. You will undo all of your good efforts if you are staring dumbly at the person, insisting, "Hey. Hold still for a minute while I try to turn your name into a picture!"

5   Once you have identified a mental image that you associate with a person's name, the next step is to "glue" that image to the person's face or upper body. This bridges that gap many people experience between being able to recall faces but not the names that belong to those faces. If you met a new prospect named Rosalind, for example, you might have broken her name down into the memorable image of "rose on land." Now you must create a mental picture that will stick with you as long as you need it and pop into your head every time you meet her; this should be something fun, even a little odd, that will bring "rose on land" to mind when you see her face. You might imagine her buried up to her neck in earth, with roses scattered around her, for example. Because you created the image, it will come up next time you see her and enable you to recall her name.

6   At the end of the conversation, integrate auditory learning by repeating the prospect's name one more time, but don't ever overuse someone's name in an effort to place it more firmly in your mind. For example, in formal situations, use the person's name only at the beginning of the conversation, and then again at the end. If you feel that you can do so naturally, you might insert someone's name once or twice in a natural fashion during the course of the conversation, too.

7   Writing is a form of kinesthetic learning—you are getting a part of your body involved in the learning process—so if you are really serious about

wanting to remember people's names for the long term, keep a name journal or a log of important people you meet, and review it periodically.

8 People can't remember names for one main reason: they are just not paying attention. This process forces you to think. If, for example, you struggle with the step of creating a mental picture, the other steps—looking at the person closely, shaking his or her hand confidently, and repeating the name a few times—are easy to do, will solidify the name in your memory, and will ultimately convey a positive image of you to others.

VOCABULARY AND COMPREHENSION

1. In the first paragraph, the author mentions three learning styles. Using your own words, define each style:

    a. visual _____

    b. auditory _____

    c. kinesthetic _____

2. Who is the audience for this essay?

    _____

3. Underline the thesis statement.

4. Underline the topic sentences in paragraphs 2–6.

5. In the essay, which activities integrate kinesthetic learning?

    _____

    _____

GRAMMAR LINK

6. In paragraph 1, highlight the first five commas. Then write three rules about comma usage.

    _____

    _____

    _____

7. In paragraph 3, the author writes *his or her*. What is the antecedent for those pronouns? In other words, whom do the pronouns refer to?

    _____

DISCUSSION AND WRITING

8. Describe a process that people can follow to remember details such as birthdays, exam deadlines, appointments, telephone numbers, or computer passwords.

9. Think about a time when you forgot a person's name. What strategy did you use to deal with the situation?

10. Describe the first time you met your best friend, spouse, or colleague. Why did you decide to keep that person in your life?

READING 16

Meet the Zippies

Thomas L. Friedman

> Thomas Friedman is a Pulitzer Prize–winning journalist for *The New York Times*. His most recent book is *The World Is Flat: A Brief History of the Twenty-First Century*, in which he analyzes the great changes in the world economy due to China's and India's rising economic clout. As you read, notice how the writer uses elements of definition, cause and effect, and argument.

1   We grew up with the hippies in the 1960s. Thanks to the high-tech revolution, many of us became yuppies in the 1980s. And now, fasten your seat belt because you may soon lose your job to a "zippie" in the 2000s.

2   "The Zippies Are Here," declared the Indian weekly magazine *Outlook*. Zippies are this huge cohort of Indian youth who are the first to come of age since India shifted away from socialism and dived headfirst into global trade, embraced the information revolution, and turned itself into the world's service center. *Outlook* calls India's zippies "Liberalization's Children," and defines a zippie as "a young city or suburban resident, between fifteen and twenty-five years of age, with a zip in the stride. Belongs to generation Z. Can be male or female, studying or working. Oozes attitude, ambition, and aspiration. Cool, confident, and creative. Seeks challenges, loves risks, and shuns fears." Indian zippies carry no guilt about making money or spending it. They are, says one Indian analyst quoted by *Outlook*, destination driven, not destiny driven; outward, not inward, looking; upwardly mobile, not stuck-in-their-station-in-life.

3   With 54 percent of India under the age of twenty-five—that's 555 million people—six out of ten Indian households have at least one zippie, *Outlook* says. And a growing slice of them (most Indians are still poor village-dwellers) will be able to do your white-collar job as well as you for a fraction of the pay.

4   I just arrived here in Bangalore, India's Silicon Valley, to meet the zippies on the receiving end of U.S. jobs. Judging from the construction going on every block here, the multiple applicants for every new tech job, the crowded pub scene, and the families of four you see zipping around on a single motor scooter, Bangalore is one hot town.

5   Taking all this in, two things strike me about this outsourcing issue. First, economists are surely right: the biggest factor in eliminating old jobs and churning out new ones is technological change—the phone mail system that eliminated many secretaries. Second, when the zippies soak up certain U.S. or European jobs, they will become consumers, the global pie will grow, and ultimately we will all be better off. As long as America maintains its ability to do cutting-edge innovation, the long run should be fine. Saving money by outsourcing basic jobs to zippies so Americans can invest in more high-end innovation makes sense.

6   But here's what I also feel: this particular short run could be politically explosive. The potential speed and scale of this outsourcing phenomenon make its potential impact enormous and unpredictable. As we enter a world where the price of digitizing information—converting it into little

packets of ones and zeros and then transmitting it over high-speed data networks—falls to near zero, it means the vaunted "death of distance" is really here. And it means that many jobs you can now do from your house—whether data processing, reading an X-ray, or basic accounting or lawyering—can now also be done from a zippie's house in India or China.

7   And as education levels in these overseas homes rise to U.S. levels, the barriers to shipping white-collar jobs abroad fall, and the incentives for businesses to outsource rise. At a minimum, some very educated Americans used to high salaries—people who vote and know how to write op-ed pieces—will either lose their jobs or have to accept lower pay or become part-timers without health insurance.

8   "The fundamental question we have to ask as a society is, what do we do about it?" notes Robert Reich, the former labor secretary and now Brandeis University professor. "For starters, we're going to have to get serious about some of the things we just gab about—job training, life-long learning, and wage insurance. And perhaps we need to welcome more unionization in the personal services area—retail, hotel, restaurant, and hospital jobs that cannot be moved overseas—in order to stabilize wages and health care benefits." Maybe, as a transition measure, adds Mr. Reich, companies shouldn't be allowed to deduct the full cost of outsourcing, creating a small tax that could be used to help people adjust.

9   Either way, managing this phenomenon will require a public policy response—something more serious than the Bush mantra of let the market sort it out, or the demagoguery of the Democratic candidates, who seem to want to make outsourcing equal to treason and punishable by hanging. It's time to get real.

VOCABULARY AND COMPREHENSION

1.   In your own words, describe the zippies.

    _____

    _____

    _____

2.   Friedman uses the expression "death of distance" in paragraph 6. Explain what he means by this phrase.

    _____

    _____

    _____

3.   Why has outsourcing become an important political issue for Americans?

    _____

    _____

4.   According to Friedman, what are some immediate consequences of outsourcing?

    _____

    _____

5. Why does Friedman think that outsourcing will have a positive effect on the American economy in the long term? See paragraph 5.

_____

_____

_____

6. What is the writer's main point in paragraphs 6 and 7?

_____

_____

_____

7. What can the American government do to offset some of the harsh consequences of outsourcing?

_____

_____

_____

GRAMMAR LINK

8. Circle four contractions in the text. Then write out the long form of each contraction.

_____

_____

9. In paragraph 2, why is _Outlook_ italicized?

_____

_____

DISCUSSION AND WRITING

10. Define one of the following terms: _office politics, glass ceiling, the corner office, wheeler-dealer, officespeak, watercooler discussions,_ or _mouse potato_. Give examples to support your definition.
11. Poll five students. Ask them why they have chosen to go to college. Write about your poll results, and mention the names and approximate ages of the people you have polled.

READING 17

The Rewards of Dirty Work

Linda L. Lindsey and Stephen Beach

Linda L. Lindsey teaches sociology at Maryville University of St. Louis, and Stephen Beach teaches at Kentucky Wesleyan College. In the next essay, they list some surprising rewards of dirty work. As you read, notice how the authors mainly use the illustration writing pattern but also use elements of description and argument.

1   As sociologist Everett Hughes once pointed out, in order for some members of society to be clean and pure, someone else must take care of

unclean, often taboo work, such as handling dead bodies and filth. In India and Japan, such jobs were, and to some extent still are, relegated to the Dalits (or Untouchables) and the Eta, respectively. Both groups were regarded as ritually impure. Our society does not have formal taboos against dirty work, but some jobs are rated near the bottom of the scale of occupational prestige and are viewed as not quite respectable and certainly not something to brag about. Garbage collection is a good example. Why would anyone choose to become a garbage collector? Stewart Perry asked this question to sanitation workers for the Sunset Scavenger Business in San Francisco. For a job that requires little training or education, the pay is relatively good. But pay was not what drew men to the job.

2   One attraction of becoming a garbage collector was variety. The job involves many different activities. Collecting garbage also means being outdoors and moving around. On another level, variety means the unexpected. For the sanitation workers, every day brought something different: witnessing a robbery, calling in a fire alarm and getting residents out of the building before the fire truck arrived, and responding to FBI requests to save all the rubbish from a house under surveillance.

3   Also, the garbage itself was full of surprises. Almost every day the men found something of interest, whether a good book, a child's toy, or a fixable radio. Almost inevitably, garbage men became collectors. In the course of his research, Perry himself acquired a rare seventeenth-century book of sermons and a sheepskin rug.

4   Garbage men got to know intimately the neighborhoods in which they worked. Watching children grow up, couples marry or separate, or one house or block deteriorating while another was being renovated had the appeal of an ongoing story, not unlike a soap opera on TV. They witnessed not just public performances, but also what Erving Goffman called the "backstage" of life. The respectable facades in affluent neighborhoods cannot hide the alcoholism a garbage man detects from cans full of empty liquor bottles or the sexual longings symbolized by bundles of pornographic magazines.

5   Another attraction of garbage collection was a sense of camaraderie among workers. The friendships people make on the job are a major source of satisfaction in any occupation. Many Sunset workers came from the same ethnic background (Italian) and in some cases from the same neighborhood. All of the men hoped that their own sons would go to college and make something better of themselves. But at least thirty were following in their fathers' footsteps. These intergenerational family ties and friendships made the company a familiar and welcome place and a stronghold of tradition for members of ethnic communities that were beginning to break apart.

6   The garbage collectors liked working at their own pace, scheduling their own breaks, deciding when to do their paperwork—in short, being their own bosses. Collecting garbage may be "dirty work" in many peoples' eyes, but these men were proud of what they did for a living.

VOCABULARY AND COMPREHENSION

1.   What is a *taboo?* See paragraph 1 for clues.

_____

_____

2. How is Western society different from other societies regarding garbage collecting or other dirty work?

_____

_____

_____

_____

3. How do Western societies judge the profession of garbage collecting?

_____

_____

_____

4. The authors give a positive spin on garbage collecting. List the main points.

_____

_____

_____

_____

_____

_____

5. How do garbage collectors see the "backstage" of life?

_____

_____

_____

GRAMMAR LINK

6. Underline five irregular past tense verbs in paragraphs 3 and 4. Then write the present and past forms of each verb.

_____

7. In paragraph 5, who does the word *themselves* refer to?

_____

DISCUSSION AND WRITING

8. List some jobs that might be considered dirty. What do the jobs have in common?
9. What are some stereotypes that we have about other professions? These professions could be prestigious or nonprestigious. Give some examples.
10. Think of another job that lacks prestige. Explain why that job has value and is rewarding.

The Writer's Room

Images of Politics and the Business World

Writing Activity 1: Photo Writing

1. Define a term that comes to mind when you look at the photo. Some ideas might be *great speaker*, *charisma*, *public eye*, *politically savvy*, *voter discontent*, *voter apathy*, or *political hack*.

2. What steps can public officials take to earn voter trust?

3. Who is your favorite political leader? Explain why.

Writing Activity 2: Film Writing

1. View a political film such as *The Last King of Scotland*, *Primary Colors*, *Bobby*, or *Charlie Wilson's War*. Describe a scene which depicts a conflict. What happens.

2. View *Beauty Shop* and examine the character, Gina, played by Queen Latifa. Explain why Gina decides to open her own business.

3. Watch a *Mighty Heart*. Explain the steps Mariane Pearl goes through as she deals with her husband's disappearance and death.

Appendix 1

Grammar Glossary

Term	Meaning	Examples
Active voice	• Form of the verb when the subject does the action	Maria will mail the letter.
Adjective	• Adds information about the noun	quiet, clear, decent
Adverb	• Adds information about the verb; expresses time, place, or frequency	quietly, clearly, decently, easily; sometimes, often, usually, never
Base form of verb	• The main form of a verb that is found in a dictionary	go, rent, discuss, meet, rely
Clause	• An independent clause has a subject and verb and expresses a complete idea.	The athlete was thrilled.
	• A dependent clause has a subject and verb but cannot stand alone. It "depends" on another clause to be complete.	because she won a gold medal
Conditional sentence	• Explains possible, imaginary, or impossible situations; each type of conditional sentence has a condition clause and a result clause.	Possible future: If I win, I will fly to Morocco. Unlikely present: If I won, I would fly to Morocco. Impossible past: If I had won, I would have flown to Morocco.
Conjunctive adverb	• Shows a relationship between two ideas	also, consequently, finally, however, furthermore, moreover, therefore, thus
Conjunction	• Coordinating conjunction: connects two ideas of equal importance	but, or, yet, so, for, and, nor
	• Subordinating conjunction: connects two ideas when one idea is subordinate (or inferior) to the other idea	after, although, because, before, unless, until, when
Determiner	• Identifies or determines whether a noun is specific or general	a, an, the; this, that, these, those; any, all, each, every, many, some, one, two
Indirect speech	• Reports what someone said without using the person's exact words	Mr. Simpson said that he would never find a better job.
Infinitive	• *To* plus the base form of the verb	He wants to think about it.
Interjection	• A word expressing an emotion; interjections usually appear in quotations	ouch, yikes, wow, yeah, oh
Irregular verb	• A verb that does not have an *-ed* ending in at least one of its past forms	broke, ate, had, swam
Linking verb	• Describes a state of being; joins the subject with a descriptive word	is, am, are, was, were, act, appear, look, seem
Modal	• A type of helping verb that indicates willingness, possibility, advice, and so on	may help, can go, should deliver
Noun	• A person, place, or thing	Singular: man, dog, person Plural: men, dogs, people
Passive voice	• Form of the verb when the subject does not perform the action (formed with *be* + the past participle)	The letter will be mailed shortly.
Preposition	• Shows a relationship between words (source, direction, location, etc.)	at, to, for, from, behind, above
Pronoun	• Replaces one or more nouns	he, she, it, us, ours, themselves

Term	Meaning	Examples
Regular verb	• A verb that has a standard -*d* or -*ed* ending in the past tense	walked, looked, checked, carried, moved
Sentence types	• A simple sentence has one independent clause that expresses a complete idea.	Some food is unhealthy.
	• A compound sentence has two or more independent clauses joined together.	Some restaurants serve junk food, and others serve healthy meals.
	• A complex sentence has at least one dependent and one independent clause joined together.	Although the food is not healthy, it is very tasty.
	• A compound-complex sentence has at least two independent clauses joined with at least one dependent clause.	Although the food is not healthy, it is very tasty, and I enjoy eating it.
Transitional word or expression	• Linking words or phrases that show the reader the connections between ideas	in addition, however, furthermore, in fact, moreover, for example
Verb	• Expresses an action or state of being	go, run, have, wear, believe

PRACTICE 1

Label each word with one of the following terms.

adjective	conjunction	noun	pronoun
adverb	interjection	preposition	verb

EXAMPLE:

Carried _____verb_____

1. but _____
2. them _____
3. below _____
4. believe _____
5. famous _____
6. slowly _____
7. although _____
8. ouch _____

9. student _____
10. pretty _____
11. yikes _____
12. behind _____
13. laugh _____
14. we _____
15. never _____
16. people _____

Appendix 2
Verb Tenses

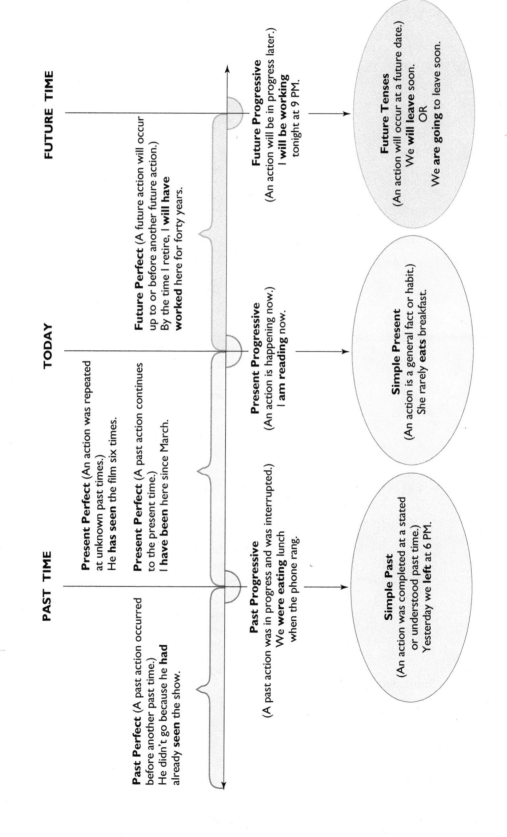

PAST TIME   **TODAY**   **FUTURE TIME**

Past Perfect (A past action occurred before another past time.)
He didn't go because he **had** already **seen** the show.

Present Perfect (An action was repeated at unknown past times.)
He **has seen** the film six times.

Present Perfect (A past action continues to the present time.)
I **have been** here since March.

Future Perfect (A future action will occur up to or before another future action.)
By the time I retire, I **will have worked** here for forty years.

Past Progressive (A past action was in progress and was interrupted.)
We **were eating** lunch when the phone rang.

Present Progressive (An action is happening now.)
I **am reading** now.

Future Progressive (An action will be in progress later.)
I **will be working** tonight at 9 PM.

Simple Past (An action was completed at a stated or understood past time.)
Yesterday we **left** at 6 PM.

Simple Present (An action is a general fact or habit.)
She rarely **eats** breakfast.

Future Tenses (An action will occur at a future date.)
We **will leave** soon.
OR
We **are going** to leave soon.

Appendix 3
Combining Ideas in Sentences

Making Compound Sentences

A.

| Complete idea | **, coordinator**
, but
, or
, yet
, so
, for
, and
, nor | complete idea. |

B.

| Complete idea | **;** | complete idea. |

C.

| Complete idea | **; transitional expression,**
; however,
; in fact,
; moreover,
; therefore,
; furthermore, | complete idea. |

Making Complex Sentences

D.

| Complete idea | **subordinator**
although
because
before
even though
unless
when | incomplete idea. |

E.

| **Subordinator**
Although
Because
Before
Even though
Unless
When | incomplete idea | **,** | complete idea. |

Apostrophe (')

Use an apostrophe for the following reasons.

- To join a subject and verb

    She's tired.

- To join an auxiliary with *not*

    You **shouldn't** smoke.

- To indicate possession

    Mike's camera is new.

Comma (,)

Use a comma in the following cases.

- To separate words in a series of more than two things

    Everyone needs food, water, and shelter.

- After an introductory word or phrase

    After the election, the candidate rested.

- Around interrupting phrases that give additional information about the subject

    Isabelle, an artist, makes astonishing paintings.

- In compound sentences before the coordinator

    The job is easy, but it does not pay well.

- Around relative clauses containing *which*

    The files, which are in my office, contain important information.

- In quotations, after an introductory phrase or before an end phrase

    Durrell said, "Personality is an illusion."

    "Personality is an illusion," Durrell said.

Note: Do not join two complete sentences with a comma.

Colon (:)

Use a colon in the following cases.

- After a complete sentence that introduces a list or after *the following*

    An essay has the following parts: an introduction, a body, and a conclusion.

■ After a complete sentence that introduces a quotation

Durrell's point was clear: "Personality is an illusion."

■ Before an explanation or example

Kaitlin realized what she really needed: time alone.

■ To separate the hours and minutes in expressions of time

The college bookstore opens at 8:30 a.m.

Semicolon (;)

Use a semicolon to join two independent and related clauses.

Many Brazilian tribes are isolated; they do not interact with the outside world.

Quotation Marks (" ")

Use quotation marks around direct speech. When a quotation is a complete sentence, do the following:

■ Capitalize the first word in the quotation.
■ Place the end punctuation mark inside the closing quotation marks.

In her essay, Dorothy Nixon said, "I am the television addict."

Integrated Quotation

If you integrate a quotation into your sentence, just add quotation marks.

Dorothy Nixon calls herself a "television addict."

"Inside" Quotation

If one quotation is inside another quotation, use single quotation marks (' ') around the inside quotation.

Maya Angelou describes the moment: "She turned on the light and said, 'Look at the baby.' "

Citing Page Numbers

Put the page number in parentheses. Place the final period *after* the parentheses.

In her novel, Maya Angelou says, "I didn't feel lonely or abandoned" (127).

Capitalization

Always capitalize the following:

■ The pronoun *I* and the first word of every sentence

The doctor and I discussed the problem.

■ The names of days of the week, months, and specific holidays

Wednesday   April 14   Labor Day

- The names of specific places, such as buildings, streets, parks, public squares, lakes, rivers, cities, states, and countries

    Elm **S**treet   **M**ississippi **R**iver   **M**iami, **F**lorida

- The names of languages, nationalities, tribes, races, and religions

    Greek   **M**ohawk   **C**hristian

- The titles of specific individuals

    General **S**mith   **P**resident **B**ush   **M**rs. **S**loan

- The major words in titles of literary or artistic works

    War and Peace   *The Last Supper*   *The Departed*

- The names of historical events, eras, and movements

    Boer **W**ar   **D**adaism   the **D**epression

Punctuating Titles

Capitalize all of the major words in a title. Place quotation marks around the titles of short works (songs, essays, short stories, poems, newspaper articles, magazine articles, etc.).

> Chopin's most famous story was called "The Storm."

Underline or italicize the titles of longer works (television series, movies, plays, books, works of art, magazines, newspapers, etc.).

> I read the classic novel The Awakening.

> I read the classic novel *The Awakening*.

Appendix 5

Spelling, Grammar, and Vocabulary Logs

The goal of keeping spelling and grammar logs is to help you stop repeating errors. When you do new writing assignments, you can consult the lists and hopefully break some ingrained bad habits. The vocabulary log can provide you with interesting new terms that you can incorporate into your writing.

Spelling Log

Every time you misspell a word, record both the mistake and the correction in your spelling log. Then, before you hand in a writing assignment, consult your list of misspelled words. The goal is to stop repeating the same spelling errors.

EXAMPLE:

Incorrect	*Correct*
alot	*a lot*
responsable	*responsible*

Grammar Log

Each time a writing assignment is returned to you, identify one or two repeated errors and add them to your grammar log. Then, consult the grammar log before you hand in writing assignments to avoid making the same errors. For each type of grammar error, follow these steps.

- Identify the assignment, and write down the type of error.
- In your own words, write a rule about the error.
- Include an example from your writing assignment.

EXAMPLE: *Narration Paragraph (Sept. 28): Run-on*

Do not connect two complete sentences with a comma.

We hit a telephone ~~pole, the~~ airbags exploded.
(pole. The)

Vocabulary Log

As you read, you will learn new vocabulary words and expressions. Keep a record of the most interesting and useful vocabulary words and their meanings. Write a synonym or definition next to each new word.

EXAMPLE:

Term	*Meaning*
reminisce	*to recollect in an enjoyable way*

Spelling Log

Grammar Log

Vocabulary Log

Credits

TEXT:

Page 13: *College Culture*, Veena Thomas. Reprinted by permission of Veena Thomas; **p. 23**: Yudkin, Jeremy *Understanding Music*, 3rd edition © 2003 Reprinted by permission of Pearson Education, Inc., Upper Saddle River, NJ; **p. 25**: *The Night Crawler*, Louis Tursi. Reprinted by permission of Louis Tursi; **p. 45**: *Freedom For Adults Only*, Mike Males. Reprinted by permission of Youth Today; **p. 50**: *Dancing with Fear*, Bebe Moore Campbell. Used with permission; **p. 55**: Reprinted with permission: **p. 61**: Reprinted with permission of Yannick Roy-Viau; **p. 418**: *When the Paranoids Turn Out to Be Right*, Brent Staples. Reprinted with permission; **pp. 421–422**: Copyright © 1987 by Amy Tan. First appeared in *Seventeen Magazine*. Reprinted by permission of Sandra Dijkstra Literary Agency; **pp. 423–424**: From *I Know Why a Caged Bird Sings* by Maya Angelou, copyright © 1969 and renewed 1997 by Maya Angelou. Used by permission of Random House, Inc.; **pp. 425–428**: *The Cult of Emaciation*, Ben Barry, *The National Post*, May 17, 2007. Reprinted by permission of Ben Barry; **p. 429**: *Is Marriage and Outdated Institution?*, Kirsteen McLeod. Reprinted by permission of the International Database Association; **p. 430**: Reprinted with permission; **pp. 433–435**: *The Appalling Truth*, Dorothy Nixon. Reprinted with permission of Dorothy Nixon; **pp. 436–438**: *The New Addiction*, Josh Freed, *The Montreal Gazette*, Dec. 20, 2003. Reprinted with permission of Josh Freed; **pp. 439–440**: *Sports and Life: Lessons to be Learned*, *USA Today Magazine*, March 1999. Reprinted with permission of Jeff Kemp;

pp. 441–443: *What's Your Humor Style*, Louise Dobson, *Psychology Today*, July-August 2006. Reprinted with permission of Sussex Publishers, LLC; **pp. 444–445**: *My Body Is My Own Business*, Naheed Mustafa, *Globe and Mail*, June 29, 1993. Reprinted with permission of Naheed Mustafa; **pp. 447–448**: From *Esquire Presents: What It Feels Like*, edited by A.J. Jacobs, copyright © 2003 by Esquire Magazine. Used by permission of Three Rivers Press, a division of Random House, Inc.; **pp. 449–451**: From *Life of Pi* by Yann Martel (Harcourt 2001). Copyright © 2001. Yann Martel. With permission of the author; **pp. 452–453**: "Breaking The Ice," copyright © 1994 by Dave Barry, from *Dave Barry Is Not Making This Up* by Dave Barry. Used by permission of Crown Publishers, a division of Random House, Inc.; **pp. 455–456**: *How to Handle Conflict*, P. Gregory Smith, *Career World*, Dec. 2003. Special permission granted by Weekly Reader, published and copyrighted by Weekly Reader Corporation. All rights reserved; **pp. 457–459**: *How to Remember Names*, Roger Seip. Reprinted with permission; **pp. 460–461**: From The New York Times, February 22, 2004 © 2004 The New York Times All Rights Reserved. Used by permission and protected by the Copyright Laws of the United States. The printing, copying, redistribution, or retransmission of the Material without express written permission is prohibited; **pp. 462–463**: Lindsey, Linda Lane, and Beach, Stephen, *Essentials of Sociology*, 1st edtion © 2003. Reprinted by Pearson Education, Inc., Upper Saddle River, NJ.

PHOTOS:

Page 3: Photolibrary.com; **p. 12**: Peter Cade/Getty Images Inc.—Stone Allstock; **p. 30**: Photos.com; **p. 31**: John Ross/Robert Harding World Imagery; **p. 32**: Photos.com; **p. 32 (margin)**: Courtesy of www.istockphoto.com; **p. 34**: Photos.com; **p. 35**: Pixtal/Superstock Royalty Free; **p. 36**: Photos.com; **p. 44**: Pamela Moore/istockphoto.com; **p. 54**: Ben Blankenburg/ istockphoto.com; **p. 60**: Burke/ Triolo Productions/Jupiter Images–FoodPix—Creatas—Brand X—Banana Stock—Picture-Quest; **p. 66**: Photos.com; **p. 70**: Images.com; **p. 76**: istockphoto.com; **p. 82**: Hill Street Singing/Jupiter Images—Blend Images; **p. 87**: Julie Masson/istockphoto.com; **p. 93**: Lawrence Migdale/Photo Researchers, Inc.; **p. 94**: Photos.com; **p. 108**: istockphoto.com; **p. 122**: Donald Gargano/istockphoto.com; **p. 130**: Lise Gagne/istockphoto.com; **p. 137**: E. Pablo Kosmicki/AP Wide World Photos; **p. 162**: J Prescott/ BigStockPhoto.com; **p. 170**: SuperStock, Inc.; **p. 181**: Lee Pettet/istockphoto.com; **p. 191**: Corbis/Bettmann; **p. 199**: EyeWire Collection/Getty Images—Photodisc; **p. 201**: *Ta Matete: The Market*, Gauguin, Paul, 1848–1903, French, Kunstmuseum Basel © SuperStock, Inc; **p. 211**: Photos.com; **p. 214**: istockphoto.com; **p. 227**: Tomasz Resiak/istockphoto.com; **p. 238**: Photos.com; **p. 241**: Jupiter Images—FoodPix—Creatas—Brand X—Banana Stock—PictureQuest; **p. 243**: Thaddeus Robertson/ istockphoto.com; **p. 247**: Saniphoto/Shutterstock; **p. 251**: Haviv/VII Photo; **p. 256**: Echos/Jupiter Images; **p. 264**: Jim Wilson/The New York Times: **p. 272**: Jeff Widener/AP Wide World Photos; **p. 276**: AP Wide World Photos; **p. 289**: Photos.com; **p. 304**: Jupiter Images—PictureArts Corporation; **p. 312**: NASA/Johnson Space Center; **p. 316**: Walace Marly/Hulton Archive/Getty Image; **p. 319**: istockphoto.com; **p. 333**: Photos.com; **p. 344**: Photos.com; **p. 357**: Photos.com; **p. 361**: Erik Isakson/Jupiter Images Royalty Free; **p. 370**: Jochen Tack/Peter Arnold, Inc.; **p. 383**: AFP Photo/Liu Jin/ Agence France Presse/Getty Images; **p. 392**: Kutay Tanir/ Photos.com; **p. 394**: Kutay Tanir/istockphoto.com; **p. 406**: Getty Images—Stockbyte; **p. 417**: istockphoto.com; **p. 446**: Photodisc/Getty Images; **p. 454**: Chuck Babbitt/istockphoto.com; **p. 465**: Comstock Images/Jupiter Images—Comstock Images.

Index

A

a, an
  as determiners, 120–21
  singular noun after, 116
Abstract nouns, 119
Academic writing
  contractions, avoiding, 384
  if clause in, 218
  slang, avoiding, 285
accept/except, 360
Action verbs, 156
Active voice, 193–94, 467
Addresses, 379
  Web, 402
Adjectives, 316–21, 467
  with same form as adverbs, 322
  comparative form, 325–30
  defined, 317
  -ed and *-ing* endings, 320
  -ful or *-less* endings, 320
  good/bad, 324–25
  order of, 318
  parallel, 307, 310
  past participles as, 192–93
  placement of, 317–18
  possessive, 138
  problems with, 319–21
  punctuating, 319
  singular form, 320
  superlative form, 325–30
Adverbs, 321–32, 467
  adjectives with same form as, 322
  beginning sentences with, 279
  comparative form, 325
  conjunctive, 467
  defined, 321
  forms of, 321–22
  frequency, 322–23
  introductory word, 372
  -ly ending, 321–22
  negative, 177
  parallel, 307, 310
  placement of, 322–23
  problems with, 323–24

  superlative, 325
  well and *badly*, 324–25
affect/effect, 79, 360
Affirmative forms
  past progressive, 205
  present progressive, 202
Agreement
  pronoun-antecedent, 131–33
  subject-verb, 164, 227–42
all, plural noun after, 117
a lot, 352
and
  compound antecedents joined by, 131
  as coordinating conjunction, 252
  multiple subjects joined by, 234
  parallel structure with, 308
  pronouns joined by, 141
Anecdote, 91
  in introduction, 104
Annotations, making, 418
another, 352
  singular noun after, 116
Antecedent, 131
  compound, 131
  pronoun-antecedent agreement, 131–33
  vague pronouns referring to, 135
Antonyms, 419
any, spelling two-part words with, 352
Apostrophe, 383–93, 471
  in contractions, 384–87
  defined, 384
  errors, 390
  in expressions of time, 389–91
  possession and, 387–89
  possessive pronouns and, 139–40
Appositives, commas with, 373
Argument paragraphs, 88–93
  circular reasoning, avoiding, 91
  plan/outline, 91
  supporting details, 90–91
  topic sentence, 89–90
Articles
  as determiners, 120
  in titles, 402

as, comparisons with, 141
Assignment, understanding, 4
at versus to, 124
Audience, 4, 97
    instructor as, 5

B

Background information in introduction, 104
Base form of verb, 467
    after *did*, 174
    past participle of, 183–84
    simple present tense, 163
been/being, 360
be verb
    adjectives and, 317
    common errors with, 175
    contractions with, 385
    frequency adverbs after forms of, 322
    helping verb, 159
    passive voice formed with, 193–97
    past tense (*was/were*), 173
    present tense forms, 165
    in progressive form, 202
    before subject in questions, 232
    subject-verb agreement, 229
Body of paragraph, 94, 95
Body sentences, 13. *See also* Supporting details
both . . . and, parallel structure using, 310
Brainstorming, 7
    to generate ideas, 20
    to generate supporting details, 101
    to narrow topic, 14, 97
Business letters, 379–80
    addresses, 379
    commas in, 379–80
    complimentary closings, 380
    dates, 379
    editing practice, 412–14
    salutations, 380
but
    as coordinating conjunction, 252
    parallel structure with, 308
by . . . phrase in passive sentences, 194
by/buy, 360

C

Capitalization, 400–402, 472–73
    of computer terms, 401

of days of week, months, holidays, 400, 472
of first word of quotation, 395
of first word of sentence, 400
of historical events/eras/movements, 401, 473
of institutions/companies, 400
of names of
    languages/nationalities/tribes/races/religions,
        400, 473
of place names, 400, 473
of pronoun *I*, 400, 472
of titles, 402–3
of titles of courses/programs, 400
of titles of literary/artistic works, 401, 473
of titles of people, 400, 473
Case, pronoun, 137–39
    objective, 138
    possessive, 138
    subjective, 138
Category, definition by, 68
Cause and effect paragraphs, 77–82
    plan/outline, 80
    supporting details, 80–81
    topics, 81–82
    topic sentence, 79–80
Checklists
    for adjectives and adverbs, 332
    for apostrophes, 393
    for argument paragraphs, 93
    for cause and effect paragraphs, 82
    for classification paragraphs, 87
    for commas, 382
    for commonly confused words, 368
    for comparison and contrast paragraphs, 77
    for complex sentences, 276
    for compound sentences, 263
    for definition paragraphs, 71
    for descriptive paragraphs, 61
    for essays, 109
    for illustration paragraphs, 49
    for modifiers, 343
    for narrative paragraphs, 54
    for nouns, determiners, prepositions, 129
    for parallel structure, 315
    for past participles, 199–200
    for present and past tenses, 179–80
    for process paragraphs, 66
    for progressive verbs, 210
    for pronouns, 148–49
    for quotations marks and capitalization, 404–405
    revising and editing, 43

for run-ons, 305
for sentence fragments, 298
for sentence variety and exact language, 288
for spelling rules, 357–58
for subjects and verbs, 161
for subject-verb agreement, 242
for tense consistency, 249
for verb forms, 226
Chronological order. *See* Time/chronological order
Circular reasoning, 35, 91
Classification chart, 86
Classification paragraphs, 82–87
plan/outline, 85–86
supporting details, 85
topic sentence, 84–85
Classification principle, 83
Clauses, 467
dependent, 265, 376
essential *versus* nonessential, 377
if, 218
independent, 265
nonrestrictive, 377–78
paired, 308
relative, modifiers beginning with, 336
restrictive *versus* nonrestrictive, 377
who (*whom, whoever, whomever, whose*), 143, 270–71
Clichés, 283–84
Closing of letter, complimentary, 380
Clustering, 8–9
to generate ideas, 20
to generate supporting details, 101
to narrow topic, 14, 97
Cognates, 419
Coherence, revising for, 36–38, 107
Collective nouns, 236–37
Colons, 471–72
after introductory sentence, 398
Commands, 153
Commas, 370–82, 471
between adjectives, 319
with appositives, 373
in business letters, 379–80
in clauses beginning with relative pronouns, 270
in complex sentences, 376–78
in compound sentences, 375–76
before coordinating conjunction, 252
coordinators and, 375
defined, 371
after dependent clauses, 376–77

around interrupting words and phrases, 373–75
after introductory words and phrases, 372–73
with nonrestrictive clauses, 377–78
around quotations, 395–96
in quotation with interrupting phrase, 396
in a series, 371–72
with subordinator, 267
after transitional expression, 258
which clause set off by, 377, 378
Comma splice, 300
Commonly confused words, 359–69
accept/except, 360
affect/effect, 360
been/being, 360
by/buy, 360
complement/compliment, 360
conscience/conscious, 361
considered/considerate, 361
everyday/every day, 361
find/fine, 361
fun/funny, 361
its/it's, 361
knew/new, 362
know/no, 362
lose/loose/loss, 362
past/passed, 363
peace/piece, 363
personal/personnel, 363
principal/principle, 363
quiet/quite/quit, 364
right/write, 366
set/sit, 364
taught/thought, 364
than/then/that, 364
their/there/they're, 364
through/threw/thorough, 365
to/too/two, 365
where/were/we're, 366
who's/whose, 366
you're/your, 366
Common nouns, 113
Comparative forms, 325–30
the in, 329
-er ending, 325–26
irregular, 326
more, 326
problems with, 329
Comparison and contrast, 71
comparisons with *than* or *as*, 141
parallel structure in comparisons, 310

Comparison and contrast paragraphs, 71–77
 plan/outline, 74
 supporting details, 74
 topic sentence, 73
complement/compliment, 360
Complete subject, 151
Complex sentences, 264–76, 467
 combining simple sentences to make, 278, 470
 commas in, 376–78
 defined, 265
 using embedded questions, 273–74
 punctuating, 267
 using relative pronouns, 270–73
 subordinating conjunctions in, 265–70
Complimentary closings, in business letters, 380
Compound antecedents, 131
Compound-complex sentences, 265, 467
Compound nouns, 114
 possessive forms of, 388
Compound sentences, 251–63, 467
 combining simple sentences to make, 278, 470
 commas in, 375–76
 using coordinating conjunctions, 252–56
 "finger" technique and, 252
 making, 470
 recognizing, 252
 using semicolons, 256–58
 simple *versus*, 252
 using transitional expressions, 258–61
Compound subjects, 152–53
Compound verbs, 156
Computers
 capitalizing terms, 401
 spelling checker, 40, 354
Concluding paragraph, 105
Concluding sentence of paragraph, 13, 95
Conclusion of essay, 94, 95, 105–106
 problems, avoiding, 105
Conditional sentences, 217, 467
Conditional verb forms, 217–21
 avoiding mixing, 219
Conjunctions. *See* Coordinating conjunctions;
 Subordinating conjunctions
Conjunctive adverb, 467
conscience/conscious, 361
considered/considerate, 361
Consonants, 345
 doubling final, 350–51
Constructive criticism, from peers, 40
Context clues, using, 419

Contractions
 apostrophes in, 384–87
 common, 384
 defined, 384
 negative verb forms, 167, 213, 384
 possessive adjectives *versus*, 139–40
 with proper nouns, 385
 with two meanings, 387
Contrast. *See* Comparison and contrast
Controlling idea, 15. *See also* Thesis statement;
 Topics; Topic sentences
Coordinating conjunctions
 chart of, 253
 commas before, 252
 in compound sentences, 252–56
 coordinating sentences with, 252–56
 meanings of, 253
 in titles, 402
Coordinators, commas and, 375
could, 213, 245
 past tense, 214
could of (nonstandard form), 215
Count nouns, 118–20
 determiners before, 121

D
Dangling modifiers, 338–41
 correcting, 340
Dates
 in letters, 379
 numerals of decade of century, writing, 389
Definition, 66
 by category, 68
 by negation, 68
 by synonyms, 68
Definition paragraphs, 66–71
 plan/outline, 69
 supporting details, 69
 topics, 70
 topic sentence, 68
Demonstrative pronouns, as determiners, 120
Dependent-clause fragments, 293–96
 correcting, 293
Dependent-clause modifiers, 336–37
Dependent clauses, 265
 commas after, 376–77
Description, 44
Descriptive paragraphs, 44, 55–61
 plan/outline, 58–59

supporting details, 57–58
topic sentence, 56–57
Details. *See* Supporting details
Determiners, 120–23, 467
Developing stage of writing process, 12–30
    first draft of paragraph, 28–29
    narrowing topic, 14–15
    plan/outline of paragraph ideas, 27–28
    supporting details, 20–27
    topic sentence, 13, 15–20
Development, of supporting details, 74
    point-by-point, 74
    topic-by-topic, 74
Dictionary, using, 355, 420
Direct quotations, 395
Dominant impression, creating, 56
Double negatives
    avoiding, 176
    correcting, 176
Doubling consonants, in spelling, 350–51
    one-syllable words, 350
    two- or more syllable words, 350
do verb
    base form of verb after *did*, 174
    helping verb, 159
    negative past forms, 174
    negative present forms, 167
    past tense, 171
    present tense forms, 229
    question form, 166–67
    subject-verb agreement, 229
Drafts. *See* Final draft; First draft
during versus for, 125

E

each
    plural noun after, 117
    singular noun after, 116
Editing, 31
    checklist, 43
    for errors, 39–41, 107
    essay, 107
    peer feedback, 40–41
    symbols, 409
Editing practices, 406–15
    essay, 414–15
    formal letters, 410–14
    paragraph, 406–409
    workplace memo, 409

effect/affect, 79, 360
Effects. *See* Cause and effect paragraphs
either . . . or, parallel structure using, 310
Embedded questions, 273–74
Emphatic order, 23–25
    in process paragraph, 61
End phrase after quotation, 397
English, nonstandard *versus* standard American, 216
Entertaining writing, 5
Errors
    in apostrophes, 390
    with *be* verb, 175
    editing for, 39–41, 107
    fragments, 290–92
    with *have* verb, 175
    of progressive tense, 204
    with reflexive pronouns, 146
ESL teaching tips (AIE)
    for versus during, 125
    the, 120
    a, an, 120
    adjectives, 318, 320
    adverb placement, 322
    apostrophes, 384, 390
    argument paragraphs, 88, 91
    business letters, 379, 380
    cannot, spelling of, 213
    capitalization, 400
    circular reasoning, 35
    clichés, 284
    cognates, 419
    commonly confused words, 364
    contractions, 384, 385
    coordinating conjunctions, 253
    determiners, 120, 121
    double negatives, 177
    double subjects, 135
    exploring strategies, 5
    fragments, 293
    -ful words, 347
    fun/funny, 361
    gerunds, 221
    grammar, 112
    group work, 37, 126, 258
    helping verbs, 232
    his/her, 140
    infinitives, 158
    -ing form, 207
    interrupters, 159
    main verb, errors with, 216

ESL teaching tips (AIE) (*cont.*)
   modals, 212
   more, 329
   negative forms, 167, 168, 174
   noncount nouns, 119
   paragraph form, 14
   past participles, 183
   past tense, 162, 174, 175
   plural nouns, 114, 116, 117
   prepositions, 123, 124, 126, 154
   present participles, 203
   present perfect tense, 186
   present perfect *versus* simple past, 186
   present tense, 162
   progressive tenses, 202, 203
   pronouns, 138
   question forms, 168
   reading strategies, 419
   reflexive pronouns, 146
   relative pronouns, 143
   repeated subject, 152
   salutations, 380
   simple *versus* progressive tense, 163
   spelling, 345, 350
   subjects, 151
   subject-verb agreement, 169, 228, 229, 230, 462
   subordinating conjunctions, 266, 269
   tense consistency, 245
   there/here, 232
   third-person singular form, 164
   time markers, 188
   topic sentences, 16
   verb tense, 163, 231
   vivid vocabulary, 57
Essay links, 12
   classification paragraphs, 82
   coherence, 36
   concluding paragraph, 29
   exploring steps, 3
   organizational methods, 22
   revising and editing, 32
   style, 38
   supporting details, 20
   thesis statement, 34
   thesis statements, 16
Essays, 94–109
   body, 94, 95
   conclusions, 94, 95, 105–106
   defined, 94, 95
   editing, 107

   editing practice, 414–15
   final draft, 108
   first draft, 107
   introduction, 94, 95, 103–105
   length, 94
   narrowing topic of, 97
   plan/outline, 102–103
   pronoun shifts in, avoiding, 136–37
   revising, 107
   structure of, 96
   supporting details, 101–102
   thesis statement, 98–100
   title, 402
   topics, 108
every
   single noun after, 116
   spelling two-part words with, 352
everyday/every day, 361
Evidence. *See* Supporting details
Exact language, 277–88
Examples
   in cause and effect paragraph, 80
   to avoid circular reasoning, 91
   in illustration paragraphs, 47–48
   supporting details, 47–48
except/accept, 360
Explanatory fragments, 291–92
Exploring stage of writing process, 3–11
Exploring strategies (prewriting strategies), 5–9
   to generate ideas, 20
   to narrow topic, 14

F
Facts, 90, 91
farther/further, 326
Faulty parallel structure, 308–14
Feedback, peer, 40–41
few, 121
Final draft
   of essay, 108
   of paragraph, 42
find/fine, 361
"Finger" technique, 252
First draft
   of essay, 107
   of paragraph, 28–29
First-person narration, 50
Focused prewriting, 5
for, as coordinating conjunction, 252

for/four, 360
for versus during, 125
Fragments, sentence, 289–98
   defined, 290
   dependent-clause fragments, 293–96
   explanatory, 291–92
   phrase fragments, 290–91
   understanding, 290
Freewriting, 5–6
   to generate ideas, 20
   to generate supporting details, 101
   to narrow topic, 14
Frequency adverbs, 322–23
-ful ending, 347
fun/funny, 361
further/farther, 326
Fused sentence, 300
Future conditional, 217
Future perfect tense, 469
Future progressive tense, 207, 469
Future tense, 469
   active and passive voice, 193
   subject-verb agreement and, 231

G

Gender of possessive adjective, 140
General prewriting, 5
Gerunds, 221–24
   common verbs and expressions followed by,
     222
   prepositions plus, 222
   progressive tense compared to, 221
   as subjects, 151–52
   using, 221, 223
gonna, gotta (nonstandard forms), 216
good/bad, 324–25
Grammar checkers, computer, 40, 354
Grammar glossary, 467–68
Grammar links
   active *versus* passive voice, 449
   adjectives, 422
   antecedents, 459
   apostrophes, 428
   commas, 267, 451, 459
   compound sentences, 36
   concluding sentence, 445
   contractions, 457, 462
   dialogue, 438
   direct quotations, 454

   editing, 107
   fragments, 428
   invented words, 438
   irregular past tense verbs, 464
   italicizing, 462
   passive voice, 445
   possessive pronouns, 139
   present perfect tense, 231
   present tense, 228, 436
   quotations, 425, 441
   reflexive pronouns, 444
   relative clauses, 271
   semicolon usage, 443, 449
   sentences, 441
   spelling, 169, 358, 451
   subject, 457
   subject-verb agreement, 164
   themselves, 464
   this, 454
   transitional words and expressions, 432
   underlining, 436
   verb tenses, 428
   vivid language, 425
   which clauses, 143
Grammar log, 39, 474, 475

H

have verb
   common errors with, 175
   contractions with, 385
   helping verb, 159
   past tense, 172
   present perfect tense, 186–90
   present tense forms, 165
   subject-verb agreement, 229
Helping verbs, 158–59
   embedded questions in, 273
   frequency adverbs after, 322
   modals, 159, 212–16, 467
   in negative forms, 167
   past participle with, 182
   in progressive form, 202, 203, 205
   in questions, 232–33
here, sentences beginning with, 153, 232
Highlighting reading, 418
his or *her,* choosing, 140
hisself (nonstandard form), 146
Historical background in introduction, 104
Hyphenated compound nouns, 114

I

I, capitalizing, 400, 472

if clause, 218

Illustration, 44, 45

Illustration paragraphs, 44, 45–49
    plan/outline, 47–48
    supporting details, 47–48
    topic sentence, 46–47

Impression, expressing dominant, 56

Incomplete verbs, 290

Indefinite pronouns, 133–35
    as determiners, 120
    one-word, spelling, 352
    plural, 134, 235
    singular, 133, 134, 235
    subject-verb agreement, 235–36

Independent clauses, 265
    parallel structure of joined, 308

Indirect quotations, 395

Indirect speech, 467

Infinitives, 158, 222–23, 467
    fragment beginning with, 158
    parallel, 308, 311
    using, 222–23

Informational writing, 5

-ing verbs, 203

-ing words
    as gerunds, 151–52
    present participles, 203

Integrated quotation, 472

Interjection, 467

Interrupting words and phrases
    commas around, 373–75
    identifying, 237
    in quotation, commas around, 396
    subject-verb agreement, 237–38
    between verbs, 159
    who, which, that clauses, 239–40

Introduction to essay, 94, 95, 103–105

Introductory paragraph, 103–104
    styles, 103–105
    thesis statement placement in, 104

Introductory phrases, 372
    commas to set off, 372
    introducing quotation, commas around, 395–96

Introductory sentence, 398–99

Introductory words, 372
    commas after, 372

Irregular comparative forms, 326

Irregular plural nouns, 113

Irregular superlative forms, 326

Irregular verbs, 467
    be (was/were), 173
    past participles, 183–86
    past tense, 171–72
    present tense, 165

it, as vague pronoun, 135

Italicizing titles, 402

its/it's, 361

J

Journal, 10

K

knew/new, 362

know/no, 362

L

Language
    clichés, 283–84
    exact, 277–88
    slang *versus* standard English, 285–86
    vivid, 281–83

Letters
    addresses, 379
    business, 379–80
    complimentary closings, 380
    dates, 379
    editing practice, 410–14
    formal, editing, 410–14
    salutations, 380

Linking verbs, 157, 467
    adjectives after, 317

little, 120

Look-alike words. *See* Commonly confused words

lose/loose/loss, 362

M

Main verb, 158
    gerunds following, 221–23
    infinitives following, 221–23
    following modal, 216

many, 121
    plural noun after, 116

Memo, workplace, 409

Misplaced modifiers, 334–38
    common, 334
    correcting, 337

Misspelled words, commonly, 353–54
Modals, 159, 212–16, 467
   active and passive voice, 193–94
   common forms, 212
   consistency of, 212
   negative forms, 213
   past forms, 213
   present forms, 213
   subject-verb agreement, 231
Modes, paragraph, 44–45. *See also specific types of paragraphs*
Modifiers, 333–43
   creating vivid language with, 281–83
   dangling, 338–41
   defined, 334
   dependent-clause, 336–37
   misplaced, 334–38
   past participle, 335–36
   prepositional phrase, 334
   present participle, 335
more, 326, 329
most, 326
much, 120

N

Names
   capitalizing, 402
   historical events/eras/movements, 401, 473
   languages/nationalities/tribes/races/religions, 400, 473
   places, 400, 473
Narration, 44
   first-person, 50
   tense consistency in, 246–47
   third-person, 50
Narrative paragraphs, 44, 50–54
   first-person narration, 50
   plan/outline, 52–53
   supporting details, 52
   topics, 54
   topic sentence, 51
Narrowing topic, 14–15, 97–98
Negation, definition by, 68
Negatives, double, 176
Negative verb forms
   contractions, 167, 213, 384
   correcting, 168
   double negatives, 176
   modals, 213
   past progressive, 205

   past tense, 174
   present progressive, 202
   present tense, 167
   simple past tense, 174
neither . . . nor, parallel structure using, 310
new/knew, 362
no/know, 362
Noncount nouns, 118–20
   common, 119
   determiners before, 120
Nonprogressive verbs, 207
Nonrestrictive clauses, commas with, 377–78
Nonstandard English, 216
   gonna, gotta, wanna, 216–17
   should of, could of, would of, 215
   verb forms, 216–17
nor
   as coordinating conjunction, 252
   multiple subjects joined by, 234
   neither . . . nor, 310
nor . . . but, parallel structure using, 310
Notes, taking, 418
Nouns, 113–20, 467. *See also* Pronouns
   abstract, 119
   collective, 236–37
   common, 113
   compound, 114
   count, 118–20
   determiners and, 120–23, 467
   irregular, 113
   modifying for specificity, 281
   noncount, 118–20
   object of preposition, 154
   plural, 113–18
   possessive, 387–89
   proper, 113, 385
   regular, 113
   -s/-es ending, 113
   singular, 113–18, 320
Numbers
   as determiners, 120
   numerals of decade of century, writing, 389
   pronoun consistency in, 137–38
   writing, 379

O

Objective case, 138
Objects
   defined, 138
   in prepositional phrase, 154

of the expressions
    indefinite pronouns with, 134
    in interrupting phrases, 237
    plural nouns following, 117
one, singular noun after, 116
Opinions, 90
Opposing position in introduction, 104
Opposition, answers to, 91
or
    compound antecedents joined by, 131
    as coordinating conjunction, 252
    multiple subjects joined by, 234
    parallel structure with, 308
    pronouns joined by, 141
Order
    emphatic, 23–25
    space, 25–27
    time, 22–23
    word, 273
Organization of supporting details, 22–27
Outline
    for argument paragraphs, 91
    for cause and effect paragraphs, 80
    for classification paragraphs, 85–86
    for comparison and contrast paragraphs, 74
    for definition paragraphs, 69
    for descriptive paragraph, 58–59
    essay, 102–103
    for illustration paragraph, 47–48
    for narrative paragraphs, 52–53
    paragraph, 27–28
    for process paragraphs, 64
    as reading strategy, 420

P
Page numbers, citing, 472
Paired clauses, 308
Paragraph plan, 27–28
Paragraphs, 13. *See also specific types of paragraphs*
    argument, 88–93
    body, 94, 95
    cause and effect, 77–82
    classification, 82–87
    coherence of, 36–38, 107
    comparison and contrast, 71–77
    concluding sentence, 13, 29
    controlling idea, 15
    defined, 95
    definition, 66–71
    descriptive, 44, 55–61

development, 12–30
editing, 31
editing practice, 406–409
emphatic order, 23–25
final draft, 42
first draft, 28–29
form, 14
illustration, 44, 45–49
introductory, 103
narrative, 44, 50–54
patterns (modes), 44–45 (*See also specific types of paragraphs*)
plan/outline, 27–28
process, 44, 61–66
pronoun shifts, avoiding, 137
revising/editing, 31–39
space order, 25–27
supporting details, 20–27
time order, 22–23
topic, 14–15
topic sentence, 13, 15–20
unity, 21, 32–33
Parallel structure, 306–15
    in comparisons, 310
    faulty, 308–14
    identifying, 307, 308, 309
    in paired clauses, 308–309
    in series of words or phrases, 308
    in two-part constructions, 310
Parentheses, page or paragraph number of quotation in, 472
Passive voice, 193–97, 467
    by . . . phrase in, 194
    overuse of, 194
    use of, 196
    verb *be* suggested but not written, 196
Past conditional, 218
    problems with, 220
Past participles, 181–200
    as adjective, 192–93
    defined, 182
    of irregular verbs, 183–86
    modifiers, 335–36
    passive voice and, 193–97
    past perfect tense, 190–92
    present perfect tense, 186–90
    of regular verbs, 182–83
past/passed, 170, 363
Past perfect tense, 190–92, 469
    in past condition *if* clause, 218
    subject-verb agreement in, 231

Past progressive tense, 204–205, 469
   affirmative forms, 205
   negative forms, 205
   question forms, 205
Past tense
   agreement, 230–32
   be verb, 173
   frequency adverbs before, 322
   irregular verbs, 171–72
   modals, 215
   narration in, 246
   negative forms, 174
   question forms, 174–75
   regular, 169–71
   simple, 169–76
   subject-verb agreement, 230–31
peace/piece, 363
Peer feedback, 40–41
   form, 41
Perception verbs, 207
Perfect tense
   past, 190–92
   present, 186–90
   present perfect progressive, 202, 207
Person, pronoun consistency in, 137
personal/personnel, 363
persons versus people, 114
Persuasive writing, 5. *See also* Argument
   paragraphs
Phrase fragments, 290–91
   correcting, 290
Phrases. *See also* Prepositional phrases; Transitional
   words and expressions
   defined, 154
   interrupting, 159, 237, 239–40, 373–75, 396
   introductory, 372, 396
piece/peace, 363
Plan. *See* Outline
Plural nouns, 113–18
   forms, 113–14
   irregular, 113
   key words for, 116
   possessive forms of, 387–88
Plural subject, 151
Plural verbs. *See* Subject-verb agreement
Point-by-point development, 74
Portfolio, writing, 10
Possession
   apostrophes and, 387–89
   defined, 387
   verbs, 207

Possessive case, 138
   adjectives, 138
   pronouns, 138, 139–43
Possessive nouns, 387–89
   's to show ownership, 387–89
Prediction, ending conclusion with, 105
Preference verbs, 207
Prefixes, 347–48
Prepositional phrases, 141
   beginning sentences with, 279
   defined, 154
   identifying, 154–56
   as interrupting phrase, 373
   as introductory phrase, 372
   modifiers, 334
   object in, 154
   parallel, 307
   pronouns in, 141
Prepositions, 123–28, 467
   common, 154
   commonly confused, 360
   common prepositional expressions, 126
   plus gerunds, 222
   of place, 123–25
   of time, 123–25
   in titles, 402
Present conditional, 217
Present participle
   modifiers, 335
   in progressive tenses, 202, 207
   spelling of, 203
Present perfect progressive, 207–208
Present perfect tense, 186–90, 469
   active and passive voice, 193–94
   subject-verb agreement, 231
Present progressive tense, 202–204, 469
   active and passive voice, 193–94
   simple present tense compared to, 203–204
Present tense
   agreement, 228–30
   be verb, 165
   frequency adverbs before, 322
   have verb, 165
   modals, 213
   narration in, 246
   negative forms, 167
   present progressive tense compared to, 203–204
   question forms, 166–67
   simple, 163–64
Previewing, 417–18
Prewriting strategies (exploring strategies), 5–9

principal/principle, 363
Process, 61
   steps *versus* examples of, 64
Process paragraphs, 44, 61–66
   plan/outline, 64
   supporting details, 63–64
   topic sentence, 62–63
Progressive tense, 201–10
   common errors, 204
   future, 207
   gerunds *versus*, 221
   past, 204–205
   present, 202–204
   present perfect, 207–208
Pronoun-antecedent agreement, 131–33
   consistency in number, 137–38
   consistency in person, 136
   indefinite pronouns, 133–35
   vague pronouns, 135–36
Pronouns, 130–49, 467
   with *and* or *or*, 141
   case, 137–39, 141
   in comparisons with *than* or *as*, 141
   complete the thought strategy, 141, 142
   defined, 131
   demonstrative, 120
   ending with *-self/-selves*, 146
   I, capitalizing, 400, 472
   indefinite, 120, 133–35, 235–36
   objective case, 138
   object of preposition, 154
   possessive, 138, 139–43
   in prepositional phrases, 141
   pronoun-antecedent agreement, 131–33
   reflexive, 145–48
   relative, 143–45, 270–73
   shifts, 136–37
   subject, 151
   subjective case, 138
   vague, 135–36
Proofreading, 31. *See also* Editing
   essay, 107
Proper nouns, 113
   contractions with, 385
Punctuation, 471–73. *See also* Capitalization
   between adjectives, 319
   apostrophe, 383–93, 471
   colon, 471–72
   commas, 370–82, 471
   of complex sentences, 267, 376–78

   of compound sentences, 256–58, 375–76
   hyphen, 114
   after opening words/phrases, 280
   quotation marks, 394–99
   of quotations, 395–99
   with relative pronouns, 271
   run-ons and, 301
   semicolons, 472
   sentences with relative pronouns, 271
   of series, 371
   of titles, 402, 473
   before and after transitional expressions, 258
Purpose for writing, 5, 97

Q
Questioning (strategy), 9
Questions
   correcting, 168
   embedded, 273–74
   helping verbs in, 159, 232–33
Question verb forms
   past progressive, 205
   past tense, 174–75
   present progressive, 202
   present tense, 166
quiet/quite/quit, 364
Quotation marks, 394–99, 472
   with end phrase, 397
   with interrupting phrase, 396–97
   with introductory phrases, 395–96
   with introductory sentence, 398–99
   around title of short works, 402, 472
Quotations
   citing page or paragraph numbers, 472
   commas in or ending, 395, 397
   direct, 395
   ending conclusion with, 105
   indirect, 395
   inside another quotation, 472
   integrated, 472
   introducing and integrating, 472

R
Reading links
   for argument paragraphs, 93
   beliefs, 250
   business world, 405
   cause and effect writing, 82

for classification paragraphs, 87
comparison and contrast readings, 76
definition essay, 70
descriptive paragraphs, 60
entertainment and culture, 226
illustration readings, 49
narrative essays, 54
politics, 288
process paragraphs, 65
relationships, 343
science, 315
social sciences, 149
zoology, 369
Reading selections
"Against Marriage" (Murray), 430–32
"Birth" (Angelou), 423–25
"Fish Cheeks" (Tan), 421–22
"For Marriage" (Macleod), 429
"How to Handle Conflict" (Smith), 455–57
"How to Remember Names" (Seip), 457–59
"Meet the Zippies" (Friedman), 460–62
"Shark Bait" (Barry), 452–54
"Sports and Life: Lessons to Be Learned"
  (Kemp), 439–41
"The Appalling Truth" (Nixon), 433–36
"The Cult of Emaciation" (Barry), 425–29
"The Hijab" (Mustafa), 444–46
"The New Addiction" (Freed), 436–38
"The Rewards of Dirty Work" (Lindsey and
  Beach), 462–64
"The Zoo Life" (Martel), 449–52
"What It Feels Like to Walk on the Moon"
  (Aldren), 447–49
"What's Your Humor Style?" (Dobson), 441–44
Reading strategies, 417–21
highlighting and making annotations, 418
outlining, 420
previewing, 417–18
summarizing, 420
unfamiliar words, understanding, 419
written response, 420–21
Reflexive pronouns, 145–48
common errors with, 146
Regular verbs, 467
past participles of, 182–83
past tense, 169–71
Relative clause, modifiers beginning with, 336
Relative pronouns, 143–45
in complex sentences, 270–73
defined, 270

dependent-clause modifiers beginning with, 336
dependent clauses beginning with, 293
punctuating sentences with, 271
Repeated subject, 135
Restrictive clauses, 377
Revising, 31–39. *See also* Editing
for adequate support, 34–36, 107
checklist, 43
for coherence, 36–38, 107
essay, 107
for style, 38–39
for unity, 32–33, 107
right/write, 366
Root words, looking up, 420
Run-ons, 299–305
correcting, 301
identifying, 300
punctuation, 301
understanding, 300

S
Salutations, in business letters, 380
-self/-selves, 145–48
Semicolons, 472
in compound sentences, 256–58
joining related ideas, 257
before transitional expression, 258
Senses, description appealing to, 55
Sensory details, listing, 57
Sentences
body, 13
capitalization in, 400
combining, 256–61
complex, 264–76, 467
compound, 251–63, 467
compound-complex, 265, 467
concluding, 13, 29, 95
conditional, 217
coordinating conjunctions in, 252–56
defined, 95, 151
fragments, 289–98
fused, 300
introductory, 398–99
length, 278
opening words of, 278–81
parallel structure in, 307–13
punctuating, 271
run-on, 299–305
simple, 467

Sentences (*cont.*)
 simple *versus* compound, 252
 style, 38
 subject of, 151–54
 transitional words with, 37
 types, 467
 variety, 277–88
 verb in, 156–60
Series
 commas in a, 371–72
 punctuating, 371
 of words or phrases, in parallel structure, 308
set/sit, 364
several, plural noun after, 116
should, past tense of, 214
should of (nonstandard form), 215
Simple past tense, 169–76, 469
 active and passive voice, 193–94, 467
 agreement, 230–31
 irregular verbs, 171–72
 negative forms, 174
 past perfect tense compared to, 190
 past progressive, 204–205
 present perfect tense compared to, 186–88
 question forms, 174–75
 regular, 169–71
Simple present tense, 163–64, 469
 active and passive voice, 193–94, 467
 agreement, 164
 forms of, 163
 irregular verbs, 165
 negative forms, 167
 present progressive tense compared to, 203–204
 question forms, 166–67
 subject-verb agreement, 228–29
Simple sentences, 252, 467
 combining, 256–61
 comparing compound and, 252
Simple subject, 151
Singular nouns, 113–18
 key words for, 116
 possessive forms of, 387–88
Singular subject, 151
sit/set, 364
Slang *versus* standard English, 285–86
so, as coordinating conjunction, 252
some
 plural noun after, 116
 spelling two-part words with, 352–53
Sound-alike words. *See* Commonly confused words

Space order, 25–27
Spelling, 344–58
 changing *y* to *i*, 351
 commonly misspelled words, 353–54
 doubling final consonant, 350–51
 dropping final -*e*, 349
 -*ful* words, 347
 ie and *ei*, 345–47
 improving, 345, 355
 look-alike and sound-alike words, 359–69
 adding prefixes, 347–48
 of present participles, 203
 of regular verbs, 169
 rules, 344–58
 adding -*s/-es*, 348
 strategies, 355
 adding suffixes, 347–52
 two-part words, 352–53
Spelling checker, computer, 40, 354
Spelling log, 39, 474, 475
Standard American English, 285–86
State verbs, 207
Statistics, 91
Storytelling. *See* Narration
Style, introduction, 103–105
Style, revising for
 paragraphs, 31–39
 sentence, 38–39
Subjective case, 138
Subject pronouns, 151
Subjects of sentence, 151–54
 collective nouns as, 236–37
 complete, 151
 compound, 152–53
 contraction joining verb and, 385
 defined, 138, 151
 gerunds as, 151–52
 indefinite pronouns, 235–36
 multiple, 234
 plural, 151
 pronouns as, 151
 repeated, 135
 in sentence fragment, 290
 simple sentence, 252
 simple subject, 151
 simple *versus* complete, 151
 singular, 151
 special problems, 153
 after subordinator, 269
 unstated, 153

verb before, 232–33

who or *what* to determine, 153

Subject-verb agreement, 227–42

basic rules, 228–32

collective nouns, 236–37

indefinite pronouns, 235–36

interrupting words and phrases, 237–38

multiple subjects, 234

present perfect tense, 231

simple past tense agreement, 230–31

simple present tense, 164

simple present tense agreement, 228–29

verb before subject, 232–33

Subordinating conjunctions, 265–70

comma usage with, 267

common, 265

in complex sentences, 265–70

dependent-clause modifiers beginning with, 336

dependent clauses beginning with, 293

subject after, 269

using, 265–67

Suffixes, 347–52

doubling final consonant, 350–51

adding -*s*/-*es*, 348

to words ending in -*e*, 349

to words ending in -*y*, 351

Suggestion, ending conclusion with, 105

Summarizing, as reading strategy, 420

Superlative forms, 325–30

-*est* ending, 325–26

irregular, 326

most, 326

problems with, 329

Supporting details, 20–27

for argument paragraphs, 90–91

for cause and effect paragraphs, 80

choosing best, 21–22

for comparison and contrast paragraphs, 74

for definition paragraphs, 69

for descriptive paragraphs, 57–58

developing, 74

for essay, 101–102

generating, 20–21, 101

identifying best, 22

for illustration paragraphs, 47–48

for narrative paragraphs, 52

organizing, 22–27

for process paragraphs, 63–64

revising for adequate, 34–36, 107

Synonyms, 419

definition by, 68

T

taught/thought, 364

Teaching tips (AIE)

adjectives, 316, 329

adverb placement, 322

adverbs, 316, 321, 329

apostrophes, 383, 391

appositives, 373

argument paragraphs, 88, 91, 92

audience, 4

brainstorming, 21, 444

business letters, 380

capitalization, 403

categories, sorting, 87

cause and effect paragraphs, 78, 79, 80

cause and effect writing, 447

checklists, 29

classification paragraphs, 83, 84, 86

class work, 16

clichés, 283

clustering, 9

commas, 370, 371, 380

commas in clauses, 378

commonly confused words, 359, 360, 367

comparison and contrast, 72, 73

comparison and contrast paragraphs, 75

comparisons, 141

complex sentences, 264, 265, 275

compound sentences, 251, 255, 261

concluding sentence, 29

conditional forms, 218

conditional sentences, 220

constructive criticism, 40

coordinating conjunctions, 252

definition, 68

definition paragraphs, 67

definition writing, 455

descriptive paragraphs, 56, 59

dictation exercise, 405

editing practice, 406

embedded questions, 273

emphatic order, 25

error, types of, 39

essays, 429

essential *versus* nonessential information, 271

exact language, 286

Teaching tips (AIE) (*cont.*)
  exploring strategies, 4, 5
  film prompts, 433
  first draft, 28
  fragments, 289, 290, 296
  fused sentences *versus* comma splice, 300
  grammar, 112
  grammar logs, 474
  group work, 103, 312
  illustration paragraph, 45, 46, 47, 48
  illustration paragraphs/essays, 436
  indefinite pronouns, 133, 235
  -ing form, 151
  introductory phrases, 395
  introductory sentences, 398
  modifiers, 333, 341, 342
  narrative paragraphs, 51, 53
  narrowed topics, 14
  negative forms, 167
  nonprogressive forms, 207
  nouns, determiners, prepositions, 112, 128
  pair activity, 341
  pair reading, 429
  pair work, 17, 32, 34, 99, 105, 190, 195, 217, 246,
      259, 260, 275, 278, 282, 285, 337, 339, 340,
      342, 353, 365, 367, 459
  paragraph plan, 64, 69
  paragraph structure, 13
  parallel structure, 306, 307, 313
  past modals, 215
  past participles, 181, 197
  past tense, 184
  plural nouns, 115
  possessive pronouns, 139
  prepositional phrases, 280
  present tense, 162
  process paragraphs, 61, 62, 64
  process writing, 465
  progressive tenses, 201, 202, 204, 208
  pronouns, 130, 133, 141, 147, 149
  pronouns, complete the thought strategy with,
      142
  punctuating titles, 402
  question forms, 166
  questioning strategy, 9
  quotation marks, 394
  quotations, 447
  reading selections, 421
  run-ons, 299, 300, 301, 303
  sentence variety, 277
  singular and plural subjects, 153
  slang, 285
  spelling, 344–58, 345, 355
  spelling bee activity, 369
  spelling logs, 474
  subjects, 150, 154
  subject-verb agreement, 227, 240
  subordinating conjunctions, 266
  supporting details, 21, 28, 64, 69, 74, 75, 80, 86, 92
  team paragraph, 449
  team work, 290
  tense chart, 469
  tense consistency, 243, 247
  thesis statement, 98
  topics, 4, 16, 97
  topic sentences, 15, 17, 27, 88, 89
  transitional expressions, 37
  verb forms, 211
  verbs, 160, 224, 226
  verb tenses, 178, 190
  vivid language, 282
  vivid verbs, 425
  vocabulary logs, 474
  whoseversuswho's, 143
  writing process, 423, 425, 432, 436, 438, 441,
      444, 446, 449, 452, 454, 457, 459, 462, 464
Technology links
  cutting and pasting, 22
  spelling and grammar checkers, 40
  topic sentences, 20
Tense, verb, 163–79, 469
  active *versus* passive voice, 193–94
  conditional, 217–21
  consistency, 243–50
  future progressive, 207
  modals, 159, 212–16, 467
  narration, 246–47
  parallel, 307, 308
  past (*See* Past tense)
  past participles, 182–86
  past perfect tense, 190–92
  past progressive, 204–205
  present (*See* Present tense)
  present perfect, 186–90
  present perfect progressive, 207–208
  progressive, 201–10
  simple past, 169–76
  simple present, 163–64
Tense shift, 244–46
than, comparisons with, 141

than/then/that, 364
that
    indirect quotations beginning with, 395
    as relative pronoun, 143
    as vague pronoun, 135
that, those, 121–22
that clauses
    commas to set off, 377, 378
    dependent-clause modifiers beginning with, 336
    punctuating, 271
    subject-verb agreement, 239
the
    in comparative form, 329
    as determiner, 120–21
    overuse of, 120
theirselves (nonstandard form), 146
their/there/they're, 364
there, sentences beginning with, 153, 232
there/here, 153
Thesis statement, 98–100
    characteristics of good, 98
    defined, 95
    placement of, 104
    specific details in, 99
    writing effective, 98–99
they, as vague pronoun, 135
Third-person narration, 50
Third-person singular form
    negative and question forms, 166–68
    of simple present tense, 163, 228
this, these, 121–22
thought/taught, 364
through/threw/thorough, 365
Time/chronological order, 22–23
    descriptive paragraph, 58
    narrative paragraph, 52
    process in, 61
    process paragraph, 61
Time expressions, apostrophes in, 389–91
Time markers, 188
Titles
    articles in, 402
    capitalizing, 402–403
    of courses and programs, 400
    essay, 402
    of individuals, 400
    of institutions/departments/companies/schools, 400
    of literary or artistic works, 401
    prepositions in, 402

    punctuating, 402, 473
    underlining and italicizing, 402
to be. See be verb
to do. See do verb
to have. See have verb
Topic-by-topic development, 74
Topics, 4
    clustering ideas related to, 8–9
    essay, 97–98
    exploring, 4
    exploring/prewriting strategies, 5–9
    generating ideas about, 5–7, 9
    illustration paragraph, 49
    journal writing, 10
    narrowing, 14–15, 97–98
Topic sentences, 13, 15–20
    for argument paragraphs, 89–90
    for cause and effect paragraphs, 79–80
    characteristics, 15
    for classification paragraphs, 84–85
    for comparison and contrast paragraphs, 73
    debatable, 90
    for definition paragraphs, 68
    for descriptive paragraphs, 56–57
    in illustration paragraphs, 46–47
    interesting, 17
    for narrative paragraphs, 51
    placement, 18
    for process paragraphs, 62–63
    writing effective, 16–20
to/too/two, 365
to versus at, 124
Transitional words and expressions, 22, 467
    for coherence, 36–37
    common, 37
    with complete sentences, 37
    in compound sentences, 258–61
    in emphatic-order paragraphs, 24
    in space-order paragraphs, 25
    in time-order paragraphs, 22
Transitions, 22
Two-part constructions, parallel structure for, 310

U
Underlining titles, 402
Unity
    in paragraph, 21
    revising for, 32–33, 107
used to, 223

498 INDEX

V

Vague pronouns, 135–36
Verbs, 467
    action, 156
    adjectives acting like, 192–93
    complete, 206–207
    compound, 156
    conditional forms, 217–21
    contraction joining subject and, 385
    -d or -ed endings, 169
    gerunds, 221–24
    helping, 158–59
    identifying, 156–60
    incomplete, 290
    infinitives, 158, 221–24
    interrupting words between, 159
    linking, 157
    modals, 159, 212–16
    modifying for specificity, 281
    negative forms, 167–69
    nonprogressive, 207
    nonstandard forms, 216–17
    past participles, 181–200
    past perfect tense, 190–92
    past progressive tense, 204–205
    present perfect tense, 186–90
    progressive tenses, 201–10
    question form, 159
    regular, 467
    simple past tense, 169–76
    simple present tense, 163–64
    spelling of regular, 169
    before subject, 232–33
    tenses, 469
Vivid language, 281–83
Vocabulary. *See also* Words
    descriptive, 57
    specific and detailed, 281–83
    unfamiliar words, understanding, 419
Vocabulary log, 474, 476
Voice
    active, 193–94
    passive, 193–97
Vowels, 345

W

wanna (nonstandard form), 216
Web addresses, 402
well/badly, 324–25

were/where/we're, 366
where/were/we're, 366
which clause
    comma to set off, 271
    dependent-clause modifiers beginning with, 336
    subject-verb agreement, 239
which clauses, 143
    commas to set off, 377, 378
who clauses
    commas to set off, 271, 377, 378
    subject-verb agreement, 239
who or *whom*, choosing, 143
whose/who's, 143
who's/whose, 366
whoversuswhom, 144
who (whom, whoever, whomever, whose) clauses, 143, 270–71
    dependent-clause modifiers beginning with, 336
will, contractions with, 385
Word order
    adjectives, 318
    in embedded questions, 273
Words
    commonly confused, 359–69
    commonly misspelled, 353–54
    interrupting, 237–40, 373–75
    introductory, 372
    look-alike and sound-alike (*See* Commonly confused words)
    opening, 280
    vague, 135–36
    vivid, 281–83
Workplace memo, editing practice, 409
would, 213, 245
    contractions with, 385
    past tense, 214
write/right, 366
Writers' Circle activities
    for commonly confused words, 369
    for modifiers, 343
    for parallel structure, 315
    pronouns, 149
    for quotations marks and capitalization, 405
    slang, 288
    tense consistency, 249–50
    verb forms, 226
Writer's Desk exercises
    argument paragraphs, 92
    brainstorming, 7
    cause and effect paragraphs, 81

clustering, 8–9
comparison and contrast paragraphs, 75
conclusions, 106
definition paragraphs, 70
descriptive paragraphs, 59
essay plan, 103
exploring, 46, 51, 56, 62, 67, 72, 78–79, 84, 89
final draft, 42, 108
first draft, 107
freewriting, 6
illustration paragraphs, 48
images and impressions, 58
introductions, 106
narrative paragraphs, 53
narrowing topics, 14–15, 97–98
organizing ideas, 27
paragraph plan, 28
process paragraphs, 65
revising and editing essay, 107
revising and editing paragraph, 40
supporting details, 21, 22, 48, 53, 59, 64–65, 69,
    75, 80–81, 86, 92, 102
thesis statement, 100
topic sentences, 19–20, 47, 52, 57, 63, 68, 79–80,
    85, 90
Writer's Room activities
essay topics, 108
images of Earth and its creatures, 454–55
images of entertainment, 446–47
images of human history, habits, and
    relationships, 432–33
images of politics and business world, 465
paragraph topics, 42–43
topics, 10–11, 29–30, 129, 148, 161, 179, 199,
    209, 225, 241, 249, 262, 276, 287, 298, 304,
    315, 331, 342, 357, 368, 382, 392, 404
topics for argument paragraphs, 92–93
topics for cause and effect paragraphs, 81–82

topics for classification paragraphs, 87
topics for comparison and contrast paragraphs, 77
topics for definition paragraphs, 70
topics for descriptive paragraphs, 60–61
topics for illustration paragraphs, 49
topics for narrative paragraphs, 54
topics for process paragraphs, 65–66
Writing from reading, 420–21
outlining reading, 420
summarizing reading, 420
written response, 420–21
Writing links
for argument paragraphs, 93
for cause and effect paragraphs, 81
for classification paragraphs, 87
for comparison and contrast paragraphs, 76
definition paragraphs, 70
descriptive paragraphs, 58, 60
essays, 102, 107
illustration writing topics, 49
narrative paragraphs, 52, 54
process paragraphs, 65
Writing portfolio, 10
Writing process, 2–11
audience, 4
developing stage in, 12–30
exploring stage of, 3–11
exploring strategies, 5–9
journal, 10
portfolio, 10
purpose, 5
topic, 4

Y

yet, as coordinating conjunction, 252
you, as unstated subject, 153
you're/your, 354, 366

Notes

Notes

Notes